THE WOULD-BE WRITER

The Would-be Writer

THIRD EDITION

Clinton S. Burhans, Jr.
MICHIGAN STATE UNIVERSITY

Xerox College Publishing
LEXINGTON, MASSACHUSETTS
TORONTO

For Gina with love, forever and a day.

Preface

It is most gratifying to be doing a third edition of a text one believes in strongly; for one thing, there arises no compulsion to change it substantially. Consequently, I have made what I believe are useful improvements but no major changes in this edition of *The Would-be Writer*. Like the first two, it makes no pretense at being either a rhetoric, a logic, a glossary, a handbook, or a reader. Neither is it an attempt to be all of these at once. It is simply and only a basic course in writing, a book designed to help students in writing courses begin at the beginning — that is, to approach writing first as writing before they go on to study ways to do it more effectively.

The Would-be Writer rests, therefore, on three premises. First, I agree with F. L. Lucas in the essay reprinted in Chapter Two that writing cannot be taught but that it is possible to help students improve their writing habits and develop whatever writing abilities they possess. In other words, I do not believe that writing is basically a mechanical process or that any essentially mechanical approach to teaching it will produce either uniform or lasting improvement.

Second, I consider training in grammar, mechanics, logic, rhetoric, and exposition to be invaluable for any student of writing; but long and varied experience has convinced me that they are seldom very useful unless the student already possesses at least a rudimentary ability to put words together in meaningful and interesting patterns. The complaint that students are not being taught to write either effectively or correctly is an old and an increasing one; and much of the reason for it, I believe, is that too often we try to teach technical and advanced ways of thinking and writing before the student has developed a useable grasp of the basic writing process. *The Would-be Writer* is designed to help him achieve this fundamental ability and thereby to make his subsequent training in more advanced thinking and writing more meaningful and useful to him.

Third, I am convinced that writing courses should be something more than just service courses, skills courses, how-to-do-it courses. Surely writing and composition should be part of the family of liberal arts, of the disciplines which humanize and liberalize man. To find oneself in language, to express oneself in words — surely, these ought to be liberating experiences as well as technical proficiencies. *The Would-be Writer* is therefore student-centered rather than content- or materials-centered; it intends to help the beginning writer explore his own humanity and the particular context of reality it functions in by discovering the language of his own unique being and experience. As I have suggested above, however, I do not consider this approach an alternative to more conventional approaches to writing and composition courses; rather, I view it as an essential foundation for them. For the would-be writer, indeed, the student-centered approach may well be not just the best but the only way to secure the kind of involvement in writing necessary for both humanistic development and lasting technical improvement.

In effect, then, I make no extravagant claims for this book, either for its premises, its methods, or its materials. It contains no secret or magical way to teach writing guaranteed to produce results; I doubt, indeed, that many teachers believe any such method exists. The particular aims of *The Would-be Writer* are limited and consistent with its basic premises, but within these premises and aims, it has worked satisfactorily and often excitingly both for myself and other teachers and also for most of the students who have used it.

First, the book aims at freeing the student from what too often seem to be conditioned responses to writing assignments. It has become conventional in most writing courses to require regular essays of one kind or another; and many students regard such assignments only as necessary routine, as unavoidable obstacles en route to a grade. This kind of student response helps to explain the studies showing that students in courses requiring regular essays make no more progress than students in courses not requiring such assignments. Where there is progress, then, it would seem to stem not from the regularity but from the kind of writing the student does.

Second, by freeing the student from stock responses to writing assignments, *The Would-be Writer* aims to make more available to him the results of his earlier training in writing. Most people are at least exposed to some kind of such training from grade school on, and one mystery has always been why they don't benefit more from it. One reason, as I have suggested, may be that too often writing has been taught as something else before it has been taught as writing; another reason is surely that the more a student responds to a writing assignment as dull routine, the less he is likely to make full use of any earlier training he has had.

Third, the book is designed to give a student instruction and practice in thinking into a subject in ways that will help him discover what aspects of it his experience and knowledge best fit him to write about.

And fourth, the book aims at helping the student develop his ability to use the same techniques to make his writing more vivid and interesting and also at improving his command of basic structure and development in writing.

To fulfill these premises and aims, *The Would-be Writer* is now divided into four parts instead of the previous three, a new division intended to clarify the book's evolutionary program and make it easier to follow and to strengthen the book's pre-writing section. Part One, *Pre-writing*, considers basic problems in writing and in style and involves the student in an expanded series of exercises designed to stimulate patterns of thought preliminary to writing. Free association, categorical lists, and existential sentences are interesting and fruitful devices for helping a would-be writer think his way into a subject by discovering the unique language of his own self and experience.

Part Two, *Writing*, moves from pre-writing exercises to specific problems and techniques in clear and interesting writing. Chapters on concrete language, figures of speech, analogy, exemplification, allusion, paragraphing, and basic structure provide explanation, illustrative passages, and practical exercises and refer the student to a variety of models to analyze the ways in which these methods and techniques produce successful writing. Here, too, in the chapters on structure, the student proceeds from the earlier short exercises to applying the techniques he has learned from them in fully developed essays.

Part Three, *Re-writing*, seeks to convince the would-be writer of the absolute need for and the creative aspects of careful and thorough revision and contains chapters on usage and on common errors in mechanics and style. A marking chart is included in the back of the book for the teacher's use in referring students to the pertinent sections of these chapters to revise weaknesses and errors in his exercises and essays.

Part Four, *A Collection of Essays*, like Part One, is much expanded. Where the earlier editions of the book contained only fourteen or fifteen professional and student essays for models, this edition offers forty. Moreover, I have made a special effort to include essays reflecting not only the effective use of the methods and techniques treated in the text but also subjects of particular interest and concern to teachers and students today. I have also included several fine essays by great nineteenth and early-twentieth-century writers. Thus, while most of the selections are keyed to chapters in the text, they combine to form, beyond this function, a collection of essays comparable in range and general utility to the best of the traditional composition readers.

With its expanded materials and improved format, then, this new edition of *The Would-be Writer* offers the most useable features of the three separate texts usually required in traditional composition courses: a rhetoric, a handbook, and a reader. And, where only a fraction of the materials in such books is usually needed in such courses, everything in *The Would-be Writer* is meant to be used by the student to evolve his own style and to improve his technical proficiency.

Even more than the earlier versions of *The Would-be Writer*, this third edition offers both teacher and student an interesting variety of approaches to the eternal problems of writing and composition courses. First, students generally seem to enjoy this kind of experience in writing; many become genuinely excited by it. Second, most students clearly profit from it. They improve markedly in their ability to use the techniques the book gives them for thinking about a subject and then for expressing it in clear and vivid language. Moreover, their essays improve — sometimes dramatically — in structure and development. And surprisingly, because the teacher spends little or no time on grammar or mechanics except for his comments on exercises and essays, most students make substantial progress towards eliminating many of their basic mechanical weaknesses. This supports my earlier contention that the methods and materials in *The Would-be Writer*, by involving the student personally and creatively in the writing process, make his earlier training more available and useable to him.

For the teacher, too, the book provides real advantages. First, because it gives the student most of what he needs to know at this level and because it contains a variety of materials and exercises, the teacher has relatively little preparation to make for his classes and even less lecturing to do in them. In class, he can make sure that his students understand the expository material in each chapter either by short lectures or by discussing it with them. He is then free to discuss the essays and the exemplifying passages at the end of the chapters and to work directly in class with student writing, good and bad. Second, *The Would-be Writer* reduces the teacher's usual marking burdens. For about two-thirds of the course, he must mark only short exercises; and when he does face regular essays, they are usually better done and therefore easier and quicker to mark.

If this all sounds somewhat Utopian, it isn't. What I have claimed for the book holds true only within its basic premises and aims. Still, I am convinced that these are valid; and I know that *The Would-be Writer* has worked well for me and just as well for other teachers who have used it. Moreover, the second edition, along with another similar approach to composition, was tested against a traditional course in a Federal Project English experiment at Michigan State University in 1966–67. Entitled *Extended Testing of a Unified Experimental Course in Composition in a Variety of Materials and Formats* (Cooperative Research Project No. 7-1149), the experiment evaluated a randomized sampling from 2,400 essays written during three consecutive terms of a three-track division of Michigan State's English 213 composition course. The evaluation data were coded and analyzed by a CDC 3600 computer and established *The Would-be Writer* as clearly superior to the traditional methods and materials in the categories of ideas, organization, wording, and flavor. It is most satisfying to add such test results to the book's several years of practical success in many classrooms; and I have drawn heavily on both in improving this third edition.

As always, there are more people I want to thank for helping me than I have room to thank them. The many who contributed so much to the first two editions and whom I have named therein will always hold a large and special measure of my gratitude. Dr. Alan Hollingsworth, Chairman of Michigan State University's English Department, has fueled me with constant and enthusiastic encouragement. Christopher Jennison, my editor at Ginn, has given me the patience and understanding of a good friend and the invaluable advice of a sharp mind. And Gina, my wife — this book is hers, as I am.

Clinton S. Burhans, Jr.

Acknowledgments

JAMES AGEE, "Knoxville: Summer, 1915," from *A Death in the Family*. Copyright © 1957 by James Agee Trust. First published in *The Partisan Review*. Reprinted by permission of the publisher, Grosset & Dunlap, Inc.

KENNETH ALLSOP, "Music by Muzak," *Encounter* (February, 1967). Reprinted by permission of the author and *Encounter* magazine.

CARLOS BAKER, "The Function of the Critic," *The New York Times* (July 17, 1960). © 1960 by The New York Times Company. Reprinted by permission.

HANSON W. BALDWIN, from "R. M. S. *Titanic* — 1912," *Harper's Magazine*. Reprinted by permission of Collins-Knowlton-Wing, Inc. Copyright 1933 by Harper & Row, Publishers Incorporated; copyright renewed 1961.

JOHN BARTH, "Muse, Spare Me," *Book Week* (New York World Journal Tribune: September 26, 1965). Reprinted with permission of *Book Week, Chicago Sun-Times*.

RICHARD BISSELL, from *The Monongahela*. Copyright 1952 by Richard Bissell. Reprinted by permission of Holt, Rinehart and Winston, Inc.

JIMMY BRESLIN, "The Sign in Jimmy Breslin's Front Yard," from *The World of Jimmy Breslin*. Copyright © 1963, 1964, 1965, 1966, 1967 by Jimmy Breslin. Reprinted by permission of The Viking Press, Inc.

CHARLES S. BROOKS, "On the Difference Between Wit and Humor," *Chimney-Pot Papers*. Copyright © 1919 by Yale University Press. Reprinted by permission of Yale University Press.

J. BRONOWSKI, "The Creative Mind in Science and Art," from *Science and Human Values*. Copyright © 1956, 1965 by J. Bronowski. Reprinted by permission of Julian Messner, division of Simon & Schuster, Inc.

JOHN MASON BROWN, from "Pleasant Agony," *Still Seeing Things* (Part One: June 25, 1949; Part Two: July 9, 1949). Copyright 1949 The Saturday Review Associates, Inc. Reprinted by permission of *Saturday Review*, Catherine Meredith Brown and Manufacturers Hanover Trust, Executors of the Estate of John Mason Brown.

ROBERT BRUSTEIN, from "The Cult of Unthink." Copyright © 1958 by American Heritage Publishing Co., Inc. Reprinted by permission from the September 1958 issue *Horizon* magazine.

RACHEL L. CARSON, "The Long Snowfall," from *The Sea Around Us.* Copyright © 1950, 1951, 1961 by Rachel L. Carson. Reprinted by permission of Oxford University Press, Inc.

BRUCE CATTON, from "The Great American Game." Copyright © 1959 by American Heritage Publishing Co., Inc. Reprinted by permission from the April 1959 issue of *American Heritage* magazine.

JOHN CIARDI, "The Unfading Beauty: A Well-Filled Mind," from *Glamour* magazine. Copyright © 1959 by The Conde Nast Publications, Inc. Reprinted by permission.

ELDRIDGE CLEAVER, from *Soul on Ice.* Copyright © 1968 by Eldridge Cleaver. Used with permission of McGraw-Hill Book Company.

MALCOLM COWLEY, "Papa and the Parricides," *Esquire* (June, 1967). © 1967 by Esquire, Inc. Reprinted by permission of *Esquire* magazine.

EDITORS, "Home is the Soldier," *Newsweek* magazine. Copyright Newsweek, Inc., June 5, 1967. Reprinted by permission of Newsweek, Inc.

LOREN EISELEY, from "Paw Marks and Buried Towns," *The American Scholar* (Spring, 1958). Also "The Judgment of the Birds," from *The Immense Journey.* Copyright © 1956 by Loren Eiseley. Reprinted by permission of Random House, Inc. Originally appeared in *The American Scholar.*

JEROME ELLISON, from "American Disgrace: College Cheating," *The Saturday Evening Post* (January 9, 1960). Reprinted by permission of Jerome Ellison.

WILLIAM FAULKNER, from *Light in August.* Copyright 1950 by Random House, Inc. Reprinted by permission of Random House, Inc.

GEORGE FEINSTEIN, "Letter from a Triple-Threat Grammarian," *College English* (April, 1960). Reprinted with the permission of the National Council of Teachers of English.

ERICH FROMM, from "Is Love an Art?" *The Art of Loving.* Copyright © 1956 by Erich Fromm. Reprinted by permission of Harper & Row, Publishers, Inc.

PAUL GALLICO, from *An American Hero.* Copyright 1941, 1942 by Paul Gallico. Reprinted by permission of Harold Ober Associates Incorporated.

GEOFFREY GORER, "Success and the Dollar," reprinted from *The American People,* rev. ed., by permission of W. W. Norton & Company, Inc., and the Cresset Press, Ltd. Copyright 1948 by Geoffrey Gorer. Revised edition copyright © 1964 by Geoffrey Gorer.

J. B. S. HALDANE, "On Being the Right Size" from *Possible Worlds.* Copyright 1928 by Harper & Row, Publishers, Inc., renewed, 1956 by J. B. S. Haldane. Reprinted by permission of Harper & Row, Publishers, Inc., Mrs. Helen Spurway Haldane and Chatto and Windus.

DONALD HALL, from "The Blueberry Picking," *String Too Short To Be Saved.* Copyright © 1961 by Donald Hall. Originally appeared in *The New Yorker.* Reprinted by permission of The Viking Press, Inc.

EDITH HAMILTON, from "The Idea of Tragedy," *The Greek Way.* Reprinted by permission of W. W. Norton & Company, Inc. Copyright 1930, 1943 by W. W. Norton & Company, Inc. Copyright renewed 1958 by Edith Hamilton.

ERNEST HEMINGWAY, from *For Whom the Bell Tolls.* Reprinted by permission of Charles Scribner's Sons. Copyright 1940 Ernest Hemingway; renewal copyright © 1968 Mary Hemingway.

ROBERT HENDERSON, from "The Enamelled Wishbone," *The Enamelled Wishbone.* Copyright 1961, 1963 by Robert Henderson. Reprinted by permission of The Macmillan Company.

PAUL HORGAN, from "Pages From a Rio Grande Notebook," from *The Heroic Triad*. Copyright © 1955, 1970 by Paul Horgan. Reprinted by permission of Holt, Rinehart and Winston, Inc.

BILLIE HOLIDAY with WILLIAM DUFTY, from *My Lady Sings the Blues*. Copyright 1965. Reprinted by permission of Doubleday and Company.

FRED HOLYE, "The Expanding Universe," from *The Nature of the Universe*, rev. ed. Copyright 1950, 1960 by Fred Hoyle. Reprinted by permission of Harper & Row, Publishers, Inc., and Curtis Brown Ltd.

JOHN KEATS, from "The Call of the Open Road," from *The Insolent Chariot*. Copyright © 1958 by John Keats. Reprinted by permission of J. B. Lippincott Company.

JAMES SIMON KUNEN, "Introduction," from *The Strawberry Statement*. Copyright © 1968, 1969 by James Simon Kunen. Reprinted by permission of Random House, Inc.

F. L. LUCAS, "On the Fascination of Style," *Holiday*. Reprinted by permission of Mrs. F. L. Lucas.

NORMAN MAILER, "Chicago, August 24–29," from *Miami and the Siege of Chicago*. Copyright © 1968 by Norman Mailer. Reprinted by permission of The World Publishing Company.

MALCOLM X, "Nightmare," from *The Autobiography of Malcolm X*. Copyright © 1964 by Alex Haley and Malcolm X; copyright © 1965 by Alex Haley and Betty Shabazz. Reprinted by permission of Grove Press, Inc.

H. L. MENCKEN, from *A Mencken Chrestomathy*. Copyright 1927, 1949 by Alfred A. Knopf, Inc. Reprinted by permission of Alfred A. Knopf, Inc.

HENRY MILLER, from "The Creative Life." Reprinted by permission of Mr. Miller.

JOSEPH MITCHELL, from *Old Mr. Flood*. Reprinted by permission of Hawthorn Books, Inc.

JOSEPH MORGENSTERN, "Stay? No Stay?" from *Newsweek* magazine. Copyright Newsweek, Inc., July 28, 1969. Reprinted by permission of Newsweek, Inc.

FREDERIC MORTON, from "The Art of Courtship," *Holiday* (March, 1957). Copyright © 1957 by The Curtis Publishing Company. Reprinted by permission of Harold Ober Associates Incorporated.

EDWARD R. MURROW, from "Speech to Radio and TV News Directors' Association," *The Reporter* (November 13, 1958). Copyright 1958 by The Reporter Magazine Company. Reprinted by permission of *The Reporter* and Mrs. Edward R. Murrow.

LONG JOHN NEBEL, from "The Pitchman," *Harper's Magazine* (May, 1961). Reprinted by permission of Mr. Nebel.

ERIC NICOL, "The White Knight," from *A Herd of Yaks*. 1962. Reprinted by permission of The Ryerson Press, Toronto.

CHARLTON OGBURN, JR., "Catastrophe by the Numbers," *American Heritage* magazine (December, 1969). Copyright © 1969 by American Heritage Publishing Co., Inc. Reprinted by permission from the December 1969 issue of *American Heritage* magazine.

GEORGE ORWELL, "Some Thoughts on the Common Toad," from *Shooting an Elephant and Other Essays*. Copyright 1945, 1946, 1949, 1950 by Sonia Brownwell Orwell. Reprinted by permission of Harcourt Brace Jovanovich, Inc., Brandt & Brandt, Miss Sonia Brownwell and Secker & Warburg.

DONALD CULROSS PEATTIE, from "Chlorophyll: The Sun Trap," *Flowering Earth*. Copyright 1939 by Donald Culross Peattie. Reprinted by permission of Noel R. Peattie and his agent, James Brown Associates, Inc. Also from *Green Laurels*. Reprinted by permission of Simon & Shuster, Inc.

LIONEL RUBY, from *The Art of Making Sense*. Copyright © 1954, 1968 by Lionel Ruby. Reprinted by permission of J. B. Lippincott Company.

BERTRAND RUSSELL, from "Functions of a Teacher," *Unpopular Essays*. Copyright © 1950 by Bertrand Russell. Reprinted by permission of Simon & Schuster, Inc., and George Allen & Urwin Ltd.

WILLIAM SERRIN, "The Incredible World of Barney Stutesman," from *The Detroit Free Press* magazine section (May 28, 1967). Reprinted by permission of The Detroit Free Press.

ERIC SEVAREID, from "The Dark Side of the Moon," *The Reporter* (April 17, 1958). Copyright 1958. Reprinted by permission of Harold Matson Company, Inc.

JEAN SHEPHERD, "I Hear America Singing; or 'Leaves of Grass' Revisited, Like," *Mademoiselle* (August, 1964). Reprinted by permission of Mademoiselle Magazine.

WALLACE STEGNER, from "One Way to Spell Man," *Saturday Review* (May 24, 1958). Reprinted by permission of Brandt & Brandt.

WALTER TELLER, "The World and We that Dwell Therein." Reprinted by permission of Walter Teller.

WADE THOMPSON, from "My Crusade Against Football," *The Nation* (April 11, 1959). Reprinted by permission of *The Nation* and Wade Thompson.

JAMES THURBER, "University Days." Copyright © 1933, 1961 by James Thurber. From *My Life and Hard Times*, published by Harper & Row, Inc. Originally printed in *The New Yorker*. Reprinted by permission of Mrs. Helen Thurber.

MARK TWAIN, from ("My Uncle John Quarles' Farm") *Mark Twain's Autobiography, Vol. I.* Copyright 1924 by Clara Gabrilowitsch; renewed 1952 by Clara Clemens Samossoud. Reprinted by permission of Harper & Row, Publishers, Inc.

LIONEL TRILLING, from *Of This Time, Of That Place.* Copyright 1943 by Lionel Trilling. Originally appeared in *Partisan Review* (January–February 1943, 10:1). Reprinted by permission of The Viking Press, Inc.

JOHN UPDIKE, "Concerning the Three Great Secret Things," from "The Dogwood Tree: A Boyhood," from *Five Boyhoods*, Martin Levin, ed. Published by Doubleday & Co.; copyright © 1962 by Martin Levin. Reprinted by permission of Martin Levin.

E. B. WHITE, from "Walden" (June 1939), *One Man's Meat*. Copyright 1939 by E. B. White. Reprinted by permission of Harper & Row, Publishers, Inc. Also, from "A Slight Sound at Evening" (Allen Cove, Summer, 1954), *The Points of My Compass* by E. B. White. Copyright 1954 by E. B. White. Originally appeared in *Yale Review*, under the title "Walden — 1954." Reprinted by permission of Harper & Row, Publishers, Inc.

EDMUND WILSON, from "The Old Stone House," *The American Earthquake*. Copyright 1958 by Edmund Wilson. Reprinted by permission of Mr. Wilson.

TOM WOLFE, "O Rotten Gotham — Sliding Down Into the Behavioral Sink," from *The Pump-House Gang*. Copyright © 1968 by Tom Wolfe, copyright © 1966 by the World Journal Tribune Corporation, copyright © 1964, 1965, 1966 by the New York Herald Tribune Inc. Reprinted by permission of Farrar, Straus & Giroux, Inc.

Contents

1st assignment

Part 3   Re-Writing   *123*

Part 4   A Collection of Essays   *165*

Part 1

Pre-Writing

1

The Way of the Writer

Ready or not, here you go — off on another obstacle course in writing. You don't need me to tell you writing is tough work; if it weren't, you probably wouldn't be reading this. But it's more than just labor, a lot more. Nearly everyone who writes, for whatever reason, occasionally escapes the sludge of one weary word after another and soars into the strange headiness of writing well. Something almost magical happens: for a moment, at least, you are saying exactly what you want to say exactly as you want to say it, and it rings like music in your inward ear. The great trick is to strike up this band more often and on call.

You could sit around waiting for inspiration to spur you; most people do, usually with uninspired and uninspiring results. Like luck, you generally have to make your own inspiration, and that's mostly what this book is about. It doesn't pretend to take the work out of writing; it contains no mystical formulas guaranteed to make you a great writer overnight. It argues that good writing begins in the excitement of self-discovery, in the kindling exploration of what you really know and feel in your own individual way; and it offers you practice in several techniques not only for making this exploration but also for giving its results vivid and interesting expression. You'll have to work at these techniques, but because they take you into the fascinating territory of your self and objectify what's there for someone else to experience, they never become dull or routine. And the more able you become in their use, the more likely you are to fly than to trudge when you write.

This process of self-exploration and the techniques which exploit it are, of course, only the first step in writing. Beyond it lie the problems of structure and revision, each essential for effective writing. But without something worth shaping and revising, you might as well forget the whole business. This first step, then, the process of *discovery*, is crucial: here you discover what you want to say, the best materials available to you for saying it, and the most useful methods for communicating it to someone else.

Once you've located and gathered these raw materials, you are ready for the next step: *shaping* them in the most effective structure and development. This is where you stop exploring and begin expressing; here you write the first version, the rough draft, of your essay or whatever it is you are writing. This done, you put it aside for awhile to cool off before you begin the third step: the process of *revision*. This means going over what you've written to identify and eliminate any errors and weaknesses in mechanics; to squeeze out any water — get rid of any unnecessary, free-loading words and expressions; and to clarify structure and development. It means, in general, paring, sharpening, heightening, and polishing. You should — you must — revise what you've written before you submit it to anyone as a finished product; and if you get it back from an editor or a teacher, you should revise it still again.

Discovery, shaping, revision — these mark the way of the writer, and there just aren't any shortcuts or detours. The way is hard, but the country roundabout is exciting and often beautiful, and few who pass through it with their eyes wide open and their attention focused are disappointed. They come at least in sight of the goals of all good writing: *something to say, a sense of style,* and *a feeling for structure.* The first is, of course, the point of your writing, its fundamental reason for being. Whoever your potential reader may be, you are demanding his time, attention, and effort; and whatever else it may do, your writing should justify its demands by giving him some meaning worth his consideration. Finding such meaning and expressing it clearly and interestingly are largely matters of *style* and *structure,* for *style* means the *I-ness* at the center, the sense of a unique person with something to say evoked by his language, by its words, its rhythms, its images, its texture, and its tone; and *structure* is the shape he gives what he has to say, the way he arranges and develops its parts.

In effect, then, *something to say, style,* and *structure* are simply different aspects of the same process — the process of writing. As a would-be writer, it must be your primary goal to master as much as you can of this process and make it work for you. It won't be easy — things worth having seldom are — but its rewards can be rich and overwhelming. Listen to John Mason Brown, a critic for *Saturday Review,* who made his living by writing:

For several years now, mine has been the privilege, hence the pleasant agony, of filling a page each week, or almost every week, in the *Saturday Review of Literature*. I say pleasant agony because I know of no other words with which to describe what writing is to me.

I claim no singularity in this. There may be, there must be, writers to whom writing comes as effortlessly as breathing. There may even be (though I doubt it) writers whose happiness is complete while they are actually writing. But most of us who live by putting words together are not so fortunate. We are tortured while we write and would be tortured were we not allowed to do so. Although when we are done we feel "delivered," as Sainte-Beuve put it, this delirium of delivery is not accomplished without labor pains for which medicine has, as yet, provided no soothing drugs. If all attempts to coerce words into doing what we would have them do are at best plainful pleasures, the pains and pleasures of summoning the right words to meet a weekly deadline are of a special kind.

Brown is worth your regard: if he affirms the pleasures of the writing process, he also admits, with severe honesty, the price to be paid for them. "Writers," he says, "notwithstanding their hopes or ambitions, may or may not be artists. But there is no excuse for their not being artisans." Like you, then, even successful professional writers have to sweat the words onto the page in order to communicate clearly and well. And if you accept the same responsibility, whatever your purpose in writing, you, too, like them, can know the true joy of fine craft, of putting words together and shaping them into patterns which say exactly what you want to say in a way only you could say it.

2

The Person

at the

Center

As the previous chapter suggests, the way of the writer begins within the writer — in the infinite complexity of inheritance, experience, thought, feeling, and emotion which makes each person a unique self and in the language by which ultimately and only he can know and express that self. The way of the writer thus begins with the search for that language of self, and good writing reveals an *I-ness* at the center, the feeling of a distinctive creative and shaping intelligence, a personality at the writing throttle. The writing goes not automatically but because someone is driving it and taking us with it. In short, the best writing has style. To write well, then, you must find your own best vehicle of communication, your own unique style; and you must look for it first of all in your self, in the language given you by the experiences which developed that self.

Style is a vague concept: everyone knows generally what it means, but making it specific is like grabbing a handful of water. You get your hand wet, but you don't have much to hang on to. Furthermore, style is not a separate part of a simple mixture; it works within a complex tissue and cannot be fully understood apart from subject, structure, and technique.

Still, if the style of good writing springs from an *I-ness* at its center, then your efforts to develop your own style will be essentially self-discovery, the creative release of your individual and most characteristic thought and feeling. Ultimately, then, your concern with style will lead outward to the other aspects of good writing, but it begins in the exciting exploration of your self.

6

STYLE

In general, style refers to the qualities of form and function, of appearance and action, which make persons or things or activities distinctively different from others like them. When we admire the lines and trim of a new car or applaud the verve and movements of a dancer or laugh at the way a comedian delivers his jokes, we are likely at some point to praise their style. In writing, therefore, style means the particular features of language and structure which distinguish the writing of one person from that of another. Look closely, for example, at the following passages:

Lieutenant Berrendo, watching the trail, came riding up, his thin face serious and grave. His submachine gun lay across his saddle in the crook of his left arm. Robert Jordan lay behind the tree holding onto himself very carefully and delicately to keep his hands steady. He was waiting until the officer reached the sunlit place where the first trees of the pine forest joined the green slope of the meadow. He could feel his heart beating against the pine needle floor of the forest.

—Ernest Hemingway, *For Whom the Bell Tolls*

It is as though they had merely waited until he could find something to pant with, to be reaffirmed in triumph and desire with, this last left of honor and pride and life. He hears above his heart the thunder increase, myriad and drumming. Like a long sighing of wind in trees it begins, then they sweep into sight, borne now upon a cloud of phantom dust. They rush past, forward-leaning in the saddles, with brandished arms, beneath whipping ribbons from slanted and eager lances; with tumult and soundless yelling they sweep past like a tide whose crest is jagged with the wild heads of horses and the brandished arms of men like the crater of the world in explosion. They rush past, are gone; the dust swirls skyward sucking, fades away into the night which has fully come. Yet, leaning forward in the window, his bandaged head huge and without depth upon the twin blobs of his hands upon the ledge, it seems to him that he still hears them; the wild bugles and clashing sabres and the dying thunder of hooves.

—William Faulkner, *Light in August*

Hemingway and Faulkner are two of America's greatest prose stylists; here, in characteristically contrasting ways, each describes the moment of a man's death. Hemingway's shorter paragraph, uncomplicated sentences, simple rhythms, and literal details evoke an austere understatement and a rigid control perfectly tailored to express the self-discipline in which Robert Jordan holds his pain and fear. Similarly, Faulkner's longer paragraph, intricate sentences, soaring rhythms, and figurative language are equally suited to convey the Rev. Hightower's final exaltation in the vision which has all his life tormented him. Beyond these specific differences, moreover, and ultimately causing them, each of these passages reflects a different stylist, a different person at the center.

These paragraphs are fiction, of course, but non-fiction is equally the function of its writer's self and of his purposes in writing. Here, for example, are two passages written by students like yourself:

The town was on a highway that bridged two larger cities and was a popular gas and food stop for travelers to the cities. The merchants of the town depended on the highway business for a living and treated every car that stopped with care and courtesy so they might be remembered as a friendly town and a good place to stop. The stores were clean and orderly and had a quaint, country atmosphere the townspeople worked hard to promote and maintain.

—Daniel Rosochacki, *"Herbie"*

Dusk falls, and with it, the deepening dark settles over the usually silent countryside. But in one commonly peaceful straw-colored field laced with quiet asphalt paths, the flickering kaleidoscope of the carnival sizzles against the richening sky. The noise of the carnival draws and builds to a billowing blare of a thousand metal megaphones blasting their asynchronous throb into the moving air, the clatter of feet and the turnstiles with their flashing chromium posts counting the human noises into dollars and cents.

—Bert Levy, *"Carnival"*

Both paragraphs describe a place and a scene in the context of a characterizing mood. In common general words arranged in the quiet even rhythms of balanced and uncomplicated sentence structures, Rosochacki suggests the external quaintness and friendliness of a picture-postcard village, the stereotype of the American small town. Similarly, Levy describes a conventional carnival scene, using specific concrete words, alliteration, and figurative language to make the color and noise of the carnival stand out against the silent dark of the surrounding countryside. And as he moves from the countryside to the carnival, Levy uses longer and more complicated sentence structures, whose quickening and complex rhythms deepen the reader's sense of the scene's tumultuous activity. Each paragraph, like the Hemingway and Faulkner passages, not only reflects a different style but also suggests a different stylist behind it. At one level, then, style is technique; but at bottom, it is character.

As technique, style is the result of a writer's choices of language and structure in seeking to communicate a particular meaning — *how* he says *what* he wants to say. It is a matter of paragraph length and coherence, sentence structure and rhythm, imagery, and diction. But because these are matters of choice, the *how* a writer says, *is* what he says. Words, structures, rhythms, images convey no single, circumscribed, and universal meanings; they carry a multitude of meanings and suggestions and evoke a variety of emotional responses. Two and two add up to four everywhere, but democracy can mean almost anything to almost anyone, depending on his experience. The linguistic and structural choices a writer makes, then, not only express what he means but are part of what he means; change a word, a phrase, or an image, and even if his logic remains essentially unaltered, the overtones, implications, and feelings which inevitably accompany its expression in language must also change. In short, a change in style inevitably involves some change, however subtle or obvious, in meaning.

Given the nature of language, then, the technical choices which constitute a writer's style have their origins not in some pre-existing external system of values but in the writer himself, in his experience and knowledge. At this, its deepest level, style is personality, individuality, character; in Buffon's famous definition, "Style is the man." Actually, this is a slightly inaccurate translation of the eighteenth-century French naturalist's "Le style est l'homme même," but both reflect essentially the same truth: style mirrors the man who makes it. Style is character molding language to express a particular subject, the individuality of the writer becoming one with the nature of his subject. Looked at another way, style is not a polishing or decorating of what a writer has to say; it *is* what he has to say, expressed at the highest level of clarity and interest he is capable of reaching at that time with that subject.

It's important that you understand the nature of style and its problems. Otherwise, you will face the trouble and disappointment of looking for some easy way to improve your own style — some sure-fire method guaranteed to produce positive results at once or your money back. There isn't any that I know of, not in this book or anywhere else. Style is an art, not a craft; you acquire it not in some mechanical process but in the creative activity of discovering what you want to say about some subject and saying it in the clearest and fullest and most interesting way you can. And the time and energy you save from looking for a non-existent formula for style can be freely and profitably committed to the real sources of style: your involvement in what you're writing about.

To give your writing the *I-ness* of style, then, you must begin by looking into your self. Whether you have a subject to write on or are free to find your own subject, your first target is you. That self which looks back at you from your inner mirror is the product of your experience and of the feelings and thoughts it has stimulated; and whatever you write about, your first job is to explore your self, your experience and its related feelings and thoughts, to discover what you can honestly and substantially say about your subject. Before you worry about grammar, logic, exposition, rhetoric, or esthetics, you must first establish a direct and personal relationship between your self and your subject. Without this relationship, your writing will almost certainly be relatively dull and ineffective; it will, that is, lack style.

This essential exploration of your self need be no unguided safari in a dark jungle; many guides are available if you will take the trouble to hire them. Associative thought, sense imagery, metaphor, analogy, exemplification, anecdote, allusion — these can help you relate a subject to your own experience, emotions, and ideas or find a subject within them. Moreover, these techniques are also invaluable for expressing your subject vividly and powerfully and thereby capturing a reader's imagination and attention. The first half of this book is designed to give you practice in these techniques, both as ways of exploring your self and also as a means of expressing what you find there; but before we go on to consider them specifically, let's read and analyze what F. L. Lucas, the English scholar and critic, has to say about style:

ON THE FASCINATION OF STYLE / *F. L. Lucas*

When it was suggested to Walt Whitman that one of his works should be bound in vellum, he was outraged—"Pshaw!" he snorted, "—hangings, curtains, finger bowls, chinaware, Matthew Arnold!" And he might have been equally irritated by talk of style; for he boasted of "my barbaric yawp"—he would *not* be literary; his readers should touch not a book but a man. Yet Whitman took the pains to rewrite *Leaves of Grass* four times, and his style is unmistakable. Samuel Butler maintained that writers who bothered about their style became unreadable but he bothered about his own. "Style" has got a bad name by growing associated with precious and superior persons who, like Oscar Wilde, spend a morning putting in a comma, and the afternoon (so he said) taking it out again. But such abuse of "style" is misuse of English. For the word means merely "a way of expressing oneself, in language, manner, or appearance"; or, secondly, "a *good* way of so expressing oneself"—as when one says, "Her behavior never lacked style."

Now there is no crime in expressing oneself (though to try to impress oneself on others easily grows revolting or ridiculous). Indeed one cannot help expressing oneself, unless one passes one's life in a cupboard. Even the most rigid Communist, or Organization-man, is compelled by Nature to have a unique voice, unique fingerprints, unique handwriting. Even the signature of the letters on your breakfast table may reveal more than their writers guess. There are blustering signatures that swish across the page like cornstalks bowed before a tempest. There are cryptic signatures, like a scrabble of lightning across a cloud, suggesting that behind is a lofty divinity whom all must know, or an aloof divinity whom none is worthy to know (though, as this might be highly inconvenient, a docile typist sometimes interprets the mystery in a bracket underneath). There are impetuous squiggles implying that the author is a sort of strenuous Sputnik streaking round the globe every eighty minutes. There are florid signatures, all curlicues and danglements and flamboyance, like the youthful Disraeli (though these seem rather out of fashion). There are humble, humdrum signatures . And there are also, sometimes, signatures that are courteously clear, yet mindful of a certain simple grace and artistic economy—in short, of style.

Since, then, not one of us can put pen to paper, or even open his mouth, without giving something of himself away to shrewd observers, it seems mere common sense to give the matter a little thought. Yet it does not seem very common. Ladies may take infinite pains about having style in their clothes, but many of us remain curiously indifferent about having it in our words. How many women would dream of polishing not only their nails but also their tongues? They may play freely on that perilous little organ, but they cannot often be bothered to tune it. And how many men think of improving their talk as well as their golf handicap?

No doubt strong silent men, speaking only in gruff monosyllables, may despise "mere words." No doubt the world does suffer from an endemic plague of verbal dysentery. But that, precisely, is bad style. And consider the amazing power of mere words. Adolf Hitler was a bad artist, bad states-man, bad general, and bad man. But largely because he could tune his rant, with psychological nicety, to the exact wave length of his audiences and make millions quarrelsome-drunk all at the same time by his command of windy nonsense, skilled statesmen, soldiers, scientists were blown away like chaff, and he came near to rule the world. If Sir Winston Churchill had been a mere speechifier, we might have lost the war; yet his speeches did quite a lot to win it.

No man was less of a literary aesthete than Benjamin Franklin; yet this tallow-chandler's son, who changed world history, regarded as "a principal means of my advancement" that pungent style which he acquired partly by working in youth over old *Spectators*; but mainly by being Benjamin Franklin. The squinting demagogue, John Wilkes, as ugly as his many sins, had yet a tongue so winning that he asked only half an hour's start (to counteract his face) against any rival for a woman's favor. "Vote for you!" growled a surly elector in his constituency, "I'd sooner vote for the devil!" "But in case your friend should not stand . . . ?" Cleopatra, that ensnarer of world conquerors, owed less to the shape of her nose than to the charm of her tongue. Shake-speare himself has often poor plots and thin ideas; even his mastery of character has been questioned; what does remain unchallenged is his verbal magic. Men are often taken, like rabbits, by the ears. And though the tongue has no bones, it can sometimes break millions of them.

"But," the reader may grumble, "I am neither Hitler, Cleopatra, nor Shake-speare. What is all this to me?" Yet we all talk—often too much; we all have to write letters—often too many. We live not by bread alone but also by words. And not always with remarkable efficiency. Strikes, lawsuits, divorces, all sorts of public nuisance and private misery, often come just from the gag-gling incompetence with which we express ourselves. Americans and British get at cross-purposes because they use the same words with different meanings. Men have been hanged on a comma in a statute. And in the valley of Balaclava a mere verbal ambiguity, about *which* guns were to be captured, sent the whole Light Brigade to futile annihilation.

Words can be more powerful, and more treacherous, than we sometimes suspect; communication more difficult than we may think. We are all serving life sentences of solitary confinement within our own bodies; like prisoners, we have, as it were, to tap in awkward code to our fellow men in their neigh-boring cells. Further, when A and B converse, there take part in their dialogue not two characters, as they suppose, but six. For there is A's real self—call it

A1; there is also A's picture of himself—A2; there is also B's picture of A—A3. And there are three corresponding personalities of B. With six characters involved even in a simple tête-à-tête, no wonder we fall into muddles and misunderstandings.

Perhaps, then, there are five main reasons for trying to gain some mastery of language:

1) We have no other way of understanding, informing, misinforming, or persuading one another.

2) Even alone, we think mainly in words; if our language is muddy, so will our thinking be.

3) By our handling of words we are often revealed and judged. "Has he written anything?" said Napoleon of a candidate for an appointment. "Let me see his *style*."

4) Without a feeling for language one remains half-blind and deaf to literature.

5) Our mother tongue is bettered or worsened by the way each generation uses it. Languages evolved like species. They can degenerate; just as oysters and barnacles have lost their heads. Compare ancient Greek with modern. A heavy responsibility, though often forgotten.

Why and how did I become interested in style? The main answer, I suppose, is that I was born that way. Then I was, till ten, an only child running loose in a house packed with books, and in a world (thank goodness) still undistracted by radio and television. So at three I groaned to my mother, "Oh, I *wish* I could read," and at four I read. Now travel among books is the best travel of all, and the cheapest. (Not that I belittle ordinary travel—which I regard as one of the three main pleasures in life.) One learns to write by reading good books, as one learns to talk by hearing good talkers. And if I have learned anything of writing, it is largely from writers like Montaigne, Dorothy Osborne, Horace Walpole, Johnson, Goldsmith, Montesquieu, Voltaire, Flaubert and Anatole France. Again, I was reared on Greek and Latin, and one can learn much from translating Homer or the Greek Anthology, Horace or Tacitus, if one is thrilled by the originals and tries, however vainly to recapture some of the thrill in English.

But at Rugby I could *not* write English essays. I believe it stupid to torment boys to write on topics that they know and care nothing about. I used to rush to the school library and cram the subject, like a python swallowing rabbits; then, still replete as a postprandial python, I would tie myself in clumsy knots to embrace those accursed themes. Bacon was wise in saying that reading makes a full man; talking, a ready one; writing, an exact one. But writing from an empty head is futile anguish.

At Cambridge, my head having grown a little fuller, I suddenly found I *could* write—not with enjoyment (it is always tearing oneself in pieces)— but fairly fluently. Then came the War of 1914–18; and though soldiers have other things than pens to handle, they learn painfully to be clear and brief. Then the late Sir Desmond McCarthy invited me to review for the *New Statesman*; it was a useful apprenticeship, and he was delightful to work for. But I think it was well after a few years to stop; reviewers remain essential, but there are too many books one *cannot* praise, and only the pugnacious enjoy amassing enemies. By then I was an ink-addict—not because writing is much pleasure, but because not to write is pain; just as some smokers do not so much enjoy tobacco as suffer without it. The positive happiness of writing comes, I think, from work well done—decently, one hopes, and not without use—and from the letters of readers which help to reassure, or delude, one that so it is.

But one of my most vivid lessons came, I think, from service in a war department during the Second War. Then, if the matter one sent out was too wordy, the communication channels might choke; yet if it was not absolutely clear, the results might be serious. So I emerged, after six years of it, with more passion than ever for clarity and brevity, more loathing than ever for the obscure and the verbose.

For forty years at Cambridge I have tried to teach young men to write well, and have come to think it impossible. To write really well is a gift inborn; those who have it teach themselves; one can only try to help and hasten the process. After all, the uneducated sometimes express themselves far better than their "betters." In language, as in life, it is possible to be perfectly correct —and yet perfectly tedious, or odious. The illiterate last letter of the doomed Vanzetti was more moving than most professional orators; Eighteenth Century ladies, who should have been spanked for their spelling, could yet write far better letters than most professors of English; and the talk of Synge's Irish peasants seems to me vastly more vivid than the later style of Henry James. Yet Synge averred that his characters owed far less of their eloquence to what he invented for them than to what he had overheard in the cottages of Wicklow and Kerry:

"*Christy.* 'It's little you'll think if my love's a poacher's, or an earl's itself, when you'll feel my two hands stretched around you, and I squeezing kisses on your puckered lips, till I'd feel a kind of pity for the Lord God is all ages sitting lonesome in His golden chair.'

"*Pegeen.* 'That'll be right fun, Christy Mahon, and any girl would walk her heart out before she'd meet a young man was your like for eloquence, or talk at all.'"

Well she might! It's not like that they talk in universities—more's the pity.

But though one cannot teach people to write well, one can sometimes teach them to write rather better. One can give a certain number of hints, which often seem boringly obvious—only experience shows they are not.

One can say: Beware of pronouns—they are devils. Look at even Addison, describing the type of pedant who chatters of style without having any: "Upon enquiry I found my learned friend had dined that day with Mr. Swan, the famous punster; and desiring *him* to give me some account of Mr. Swan's conversation, *he* told me that *he* generally talked in the Paronomasia, that *he* sometimes gave in to the Plocé, but that in *his* humble opinion *he* shone most in the Antanaclasis." What a sluttish muddle of *he* and *him* and *his!* It all needs rewording. Far better repeat a noun, or a name, than puzzle the reader, even for a moment, with ambiguous pronouns. Thou shalt not puzzle thy reader.

Or one can say: Avoid jingles. The B.B.C. news bulletins seem compiled by earless persons, capable of crying round the globe: "The enemy is reported to have seized this important port, and reinforcements are hurrying up in support." Any fool, once told, can hear such things to be insupportable.

Or one can say: Be sparing with relative clauses. Don't string them to-gether like sausages, or jam them inside one another like Chinese boxes or the receptacles of Buddha's tooth. Or one can say: Don't flaunt jargon, like Addison's Mr. Swan, or the type of modern critic who gurgles more technical terms in a page than Johnson used in all his *Lives* or Sainte-Beuve in thirty volumes. But dozens of such snippety precepts, though they may sometimes save people from writing badly, will help them little toward writing well. Are there no general rules of a more positive kind, and of more positive use?

Perhaps. There *are* certain basic principles which seem to me observed by many authors I admire, which I think have served me and which may serve others. I am not talking of geniuses, who are a law to themselves (and do not always write a very good style, either); nor of poetry, which has different laws from prose; nor of poetic prose, like Sir Thomas Browne's or De Quincey's, which is often more akin to poetry; but of the plain prose of ordinary books and documents, letters and talk.

The writer should respect truth and himself; therefore honesty. He should respect his readers; therefore courtesy. These are two of the cornerstones of style. Confucius saw it, twenty-five centuries ago; "The Master said, The gentleman is courteous, but not pliable: common men are pliable, but not courteous."

First, honesty. In literature, as in life, one of the fundamentals is to find, and be, one's true self. One's true self may indeed be unpleasant (though one can try to better it); but a false self, sooner or later, becomes disgusting—just as a nice plain woman, painted to the eyebrows, can become horrid. In writing, in the long run, pretense does not work. As the police put it, anything you say may be used as evidence against you. If handwriting reveals character, writing reveals it still more. You cannot fool *all* your judges *all* the time.

Most style is not honest enough. Easy to say, but hard to practice. A writer may take to long words, as young men to beards—to impress. But long words, like long beards, are often the badge of charlatans. Or a writer may cultivate the obscure, to seem profound. But even carefully muddied puddles are soon fathomed. Or he may cultivate eccentricity, to seem original. But really original people do not have to think about being original—they can no more help it than they can help breathing. They do not need to dye their hair green. The fame of Meredith, Wilde or Bernard Shaw might now shine brighter, had they struggled less to be brilliant; whereas Johnson remains great, not merely because his gifts were formidable but also because, with all his prejudice and passion, he fought no less passionately to "clear his mind of cant."

Secondly, courtesy—respect for the reader. From this follow several other basic principles of style. Clarity is one. For it is boorish to make your reader rack his brains to understand. One should aim at being impossible to mis-understand—though men's capacity for misunderstanding approaches infinity. Hence Molière and Po Chu-i tried their work on their cooks; and Swift his on his men servants—"which, if they did not comprehend, he would alter and amend, until they understood it perfectly." Our bureaucrats and pundits, unfortunately, are less considerate.

Brevity is another basic principle. For it is boorish, also, to waste your reader's time. People who would not dream of stealing a penny of one's money turn not a hair at stealing hours of one's life. But that does not make them less exasperating. Therefore there is no excuse for the sort of writer who takes as long as a marching army corps to pass a given point. Besides, brevity is often more effective; the half can say more than the whole, and to imply things may strike far deeper than to state them at length. And because one is particularly apt to waste words on preambles before coming to the substance, there was sense in the Scots professor who always asked his pupils—"Did ye remember to tear up that fir-r-st page?"

Here are some instances that would only lose by lengthening:

It is useless to go to bed to save the light, if the result is twins.
(Chinese proverb.)

My barn is burnt down—
Nothing hides the moon. (Complete Japanese poem.)

Je me regrette. (Dying words of the gay Vicomtesse d'Houdetot.)

I have seen their backs before. (Wellington, when French marshals turned their backs on him at a reception.)

Continue until the tanks stop, then get out and walk. (Patton to the Twelfth Corps, halted for fuel supplies at St. Dizier 8/30/44.)

Or there is the most laconic diplomatic note on record: when Philip of Macedon wrote to the Spartans that, if he came within their borders, he would leave not one stone of their city, they wrote back the one word—"If."

Clarity comes before even brevity. But it is a fallacy that wordiness is necessarily clearer. Metternich when he thought something he had written was obscure would simply go through it crossing out everything irrelevant. What remained, he found, often became clear. Wellington, asked to recommend three names for the post of Commander-in-Chief, India, took a piece of paper and wrote three times—"Napier." Pages could not have been clearer —or as forcible. On the other hand the lectures, and the sentences, of Coleridge became at times bewildering because his mind was often "wiggle-waggle"; just as he could not even walk straight on a path.

But clarity and brevity, though a good beginning, are only a beginning. By themselves, they may remain bare and bleak. When Calvin Coolidge, asked by his wife what the preacher had preached on, replied "Sin," and, asked what the preacher had said, replied, "He was against it," he was brief enough. But one hardly envies Mrs. Coolidge.

An attractive style requires, of course, all kinds of further gifts—such as variety, good humor, good sense, vitality, imagination. Variety means avoiding monotony of rhythm, of language, of mood. One needs to vary one's sentence length (this present article has too many short sentences; but so vast a subject grows here as cramped as a djin in a bottle); to amplify one's vocabulary; to diversify one's tone. There are books that petrify one throughout, with the rigidly pompous solemnity of an owl perched on a leafless tree. But ceaseless facetiousness can be as bad; or perpetual irony. Even the smile of Voltaire can seem at times a fixed grin, a disagreeable wrinkle. Constant peevishness is far worse, as often in Swift; even on the stage too much irritable dialogue may irritate an audience, without its knowing why.

Still more are vitality, energy, imagination gifts that must be inborn before they can be cultivated. But under the head of imagination two common devices may be mentioned that have been the making of many a style—metaphor and simile. Why such magic power should reside in simply saying, or implying, that A is like B remains a little mysterious. But even our unconscious seems to love symbols; again, language often tends to lose itself in clouds of vaporous abstraction, and simile or metaphor can bring it back to concrete solidity; and, again, such imagery can gild the gray flats of prose with sudden sun-glints of poetry.

If a foreigner may for a moment be impertinent, I admire the native gift of Americans for imagery as much as I wince at their fondness for slang. (Slang seems to me a kind of linguistic fungus; as poisonous, and as short-lived, as toadstools.) When Matthew Arnold lectured in the United States, he was likened by one newspaper to "an elderly macaw pecking at a trellis of grapes"; he observed, very justly, "How lively journalistic fancy is among the Americans!" General Grant, again, unable to hear him, remarked: "Well, wife, we've paid to see the British lion, but as we can't hear him roar, we'd better go home." By simile and metaphor, these two quotations bring before us the slightly pompous, fastidious, inaudible Arnold as no direct description could have done.

Or consider how language comes alive in the Chinese saying that lending to the feckless is "like pelting a stray dog with dumplings," or in the Arab proverb: "They came to shoe the pasha's horse, and the beetle stretched forth his leg"; in the Greek phrase for a perilous cape—"stepmother of ships"; or the Hebrew adage that "as the climbing up a sandy way is to the feet of the aged, so is a wife full of words to a quiet man"; in Shakespeare's phrase for a little England lost in the world's vastness—"in a great Poole, a Swan's nest"; or Fuller's libel on tall men—"Ofttimes such who are built four stories high are observed to have little in their cockloft"; in Chateaubriand's "I go yawning my life"; or in Jules Renard's portrait of a cat, "well buttoned in her fur." Or, to take a modern instance, there is Churchill on dealings with Russia: "Trying to maintain good relations with a Communist is like wooing a crocodile. You do not know whether to tickle it under the chin or beat it over the head. When it opens its mouth, you cannot tell whether it is trying to smile or preparing to eat you up." What a miracle human speech can be, and how dull is most that one hears! Would one hold one's hearers, it is far less help, I suspect, to read manuals on style than to cultivate one's own imagination and imagery.

I will end with two remarks by two wise old women of the civilized eighteenth Century.

The first is from the blind Mme. du Deffand (the friend of Horace Walpole) to that Mlle. De Lespinasse with whom, alas, she was to quarrel so unwisely: "You must make up your mind, my queen, to live with me in the greatest truth and sincerity. You will be charming so long as you let yourself be natural, and remain without pretension and without artifice." The second is from Mme. de Charrière, the Zélide whom Boswell had once loved at Utrecht in vain, to a Swiss girl friend: "Lucinde, my clever Lucinde, while you wait for the Romeos to arrive, you have nothing better to do than become perfect. Have ideas that are clear, and expressions that are simple." ("Ayez des idées nettes et des expressions simples.") More than half the bad writing in the world, I believe, comes from neglecting those two very simple pieces of advice.

In many ways, no doubt, our world grows more and more complex; Sputniks cannot be simple; yet how many of our complexities remain futile, how many of our artificialities false. Simplicity too can be subtle—as the straight lines of a Greek temple, like the Parthenon at Athens, are delicately curved, in order to look straighter still.

Essentially, then, Lucas agrees with Brown in defining style; but Lucas provides a specific prescription for achieving an effective style. Be your honest self, says Lucas, and be so clearly and concisely; and yours will be a style worth reading. Skim back over Lucas's valuable essay, using the following questions as a guide.

1. How does Lucas define style? What kind of practices does he suggest are abuses of style? Why are they abuses, and why do they make a concern with style seem "precious"? What is the difference between *expressing* oneself and *impressing* oneself on others? In Lucas's view, what makes each individual's self-expression unique? What qualities of *conscious* style does Lucas point to in some signatures?

2. Is style in language easy to achieve? What does Lucas mean by "verbal dysentery"? Why is it "bad style"? How did effective style in language affect the development and course of World War II? Why are words and style so important in our daily life? What *five* reasons does Lucas give for developing style in language? What does Lucas consider the best way to learn to write?

3. Does Lucas find writing easy and enjoyable? Why? Does he think that people can be taught to write well? If not, why bother with writing courses like this one? What is Lucas's warning about the use of pronouns? About frequently repeated syllables? About relative clauses?

4. What are Lucas's basic principles for good writing? What does he mean by honesty in writing? Which is more important, clarity or honesty? How are they related? What qualities does Lucas consider necessary for an attractive style? What two imaginative devices does he stress? Why are they so effective?

PRACTICE

Read whichever of the selections by Agee, Breslin, Kunen, Cleaver, Holiday, and Malcolm X your teacher assigns; and for each selection you read, write a one- or two-sentence answer to the following questions.

1. If you could meet the writer, what kind of person would you expect him to be?
2. What can you point to in his writing to explain your image of him?
3. What is the main point or points of the selection — that is, what do you think the writer is trying to communicate to you?
4. What do you like the most or find the most effective in the selection?
5. What, if anything, do you dislike or find ineffective in the selection?

3

Journal-Keepers
of Thoughts
and Days

The basic and probably the best way to learn to write well is to combine serious reading and analysis of good writing with your own efforts to write — and to do both as frequently and as substantially as possible. The end of the preceding chapter directs you, as will subsequent chapters, to reading and analysis; now, you should begin trying your hand at sustained and significant writing. If *your* way to becoming a writer begins in you and in the search for your own unique language, the place to start is your life and what matters most in it to you. You ought to begin a journal.

Perhaps you already keep one, or once did; a great many people and most good writers do. A journal is just what the word suggests: from the Latin *diurnal,* meaning daily, a journal is an accounting of you, a daily confrontation in language between you and the world you are experiencing and knowing. It's much more than a diary, another kind of daily writing. A diary is a simple record of events and persons, a catalogue of where you went, what you did, and who was with you. That's the outside you, the one who walks around in clothes, the you that other people see. A journal lights up the inside you, the thoughts and feelings, the insights and questions that only you can know and tell. More than a mirror, a journal can take you through the looking-glass to explore the mysterious self behind it.

If you can accept the self-discipline of setting aside a few minutes every day or so to write in it, keeping a journal can have many values for you. It will be your own writing, by you and for you alone — no rules, no teacher looking over your shoulder, no corrections. Just you, walking around in words in the most fascinating place in the world — your self. With only those pressures you impose, you can use your journal to have fun with language, to experiment freely in seeking the words and structures which will express your outer and inner worlds in ways no one else could, in your unique language. You possess such language, and your journal can help you find it. In the process, it can become, as it has for so many people, a central experience in the growth of your self-knowledge and a priceless record of that growth. And a good journal can also become a treasury of material to draw on for other writing assignments.

In your journal, then, you stand at the center of the universe, radiating lines of relationship in every direction and reading the echoes they send back. Read what Walter Teller writes about others who have found challenge and fulfillment, meaning, and sometimes fame, in recording such echoes.

THE WORLD AND WE THAT DWELL THEREIN / *Walter Teller*

From time to time a book appears that the world places in the genre associated with Henry Thoreau. The world is not without judgment, the genre not without honor; yet this species of literature lacks a name. By and large it consists of books one feels better for having read. Classified under whatever rubric — essay, personal history, travel, regional, nature, American scene — I call such books journals of thoughts and days; the men and women who write them, journal-keepers.

Mark off the journal-keeper of thoughts and days from the journal-keeper only of days. The former aspires, at bottom, to wisdom writing. He is the observer-philosopher. The latter, the observer uncompounded, usually reports on experience in some characteristic trade. He may be a whaler, farmer, man of letters, explorer or flower hunter. That both kinds of journal-keepers are likely, at times, to focus on nature tends to blur an important distinction. The distinction lies in a passion for philosophizing, in the good use of the word. One kind of journal-keeper goes to nature for subject matter, the other to find an environment in which to try to make sense out of life. One seeks his reality in the happenings of the external world, the other in the mental constructions he makes of them. Kant speaks of "the starry order without and the moral order within."

John Burroughs, dead 40 years and due for a literary comeback, wrote, "Man can have but one interest in nature, namely to see himself, reflected or interpreted there." The English writer, Cecil Torr, said in "Small Talk at Wreyland," "I meant to keep to local matters but have gone much further than I meant." Burroughs did not confine his journalizing to nature, nor did Torr restrict himself to events.

Masked in whatever form, a journal of thoughts and days seldom results in a book the mass of men will throb to. Recall the reception accorded the archetype. "Walden," published in 1854, sold 2,000 copies during its author's lifetime, nor was it reprinted until after his death eight years later. On the other hand, those who care about this sort of thing — either the writing or the reading of it — care deeply, and all down the generations. If the journal of thoughts and days is a style never quite in fashion, neither does it go wholly out. Thus any example of the genre, done right, may prove exceedingly durable.

The good place is important to journal-keepers. Where do they go in search of it? Not to fallout shelters. "I went to the woods," Thoreau wrote, "because I wished to live deliberately, to front only the essential facts of life, and see if I could not learn what it had to teach, and not, when I came to die, discover that I had not lived." Taking to the woods, a certain removal, is a constant in these intentionally personal equations. The journal-keeper of thoughts and days requires a space he can mentally compass. The rising tide of men and cities and objects forces him into strategic retreat. No recluse he, however. What he demands is life with flavor and meaning. Though he withdraws from the flow, he does not hide himself. On the contrary, he tries to place himself where he does not feel lost, where he counts for something, above all in such circumstances that his life does not pass him by unnoticed.

It's the personal life he seeks, not the private muse. History is sad, but the journal-keepers I think of do not despair. "I am sure of this," Emerson wrote in his "Journals," "that by going much alone a man will get more of a noble courage in thought and word than from all the wisdom that is in books." Life is hard — I don't know how else to say it — yet these writers delight in life. In effect, they say it is also good. If old philosophies finally fail, the journal-keeper of thoughts and days rides on.

Walks on, I should say, in various moods, often with a light heart. Most were great walkers; hoofing it is one of the common elements. "There is no fundamental difference between walking in the city and in the country," Brooks Atkinson wrote in his day-to-day "Once Around the Sun." "Seeing is the chief virtue of walking everywhere." John Muir, Scots-born nature philosopher and early leader of the forest conservation movement, was, I would guess, the walkingest. He kept a journal while navigating on foot from Indiana to the Gulf of Mexico, also on subsequent excursions.

Henry Beston, born in Quincy, Mass., in 1888, a Harvard man, journalized on the beach. In a two-room cabin, he spent a Thoreau-like year on the outer dunes of Cape Cod. In "The Outermost House," his record of that time, he wrote, "Eager was I to know this coast and to share its mysterious and elemental life. . . . I had no fear of being alone. . . . Living in outer nature keeps the senses keen, and living alone stirs in them a certain watchfulness."

The 10 by 12 cabin of the Spray, the 37-foot, home-built sloop in which he single-handed circled the world, proved the good place for Joshua Slocum. The story of that voyage, "Sailing Alone Around the World," based on the log-book he kept, has been called the nautical equivalent of Thoreau's account of his life in the hut at Walden. Slabside, the very name, hints at the sort of sanctum John Burroughs chose in the hills on the west shore of the Hudson, 80 or so miles above New York. "A hair may show where a lion is hid," he wrote in "Signs and Seasons."

Lewis Gannett, a family man earning a livelihood in New York, in his own words no Thoreau, went to northwest Connecticut. "We boast of our sky-scrapers," he wrote in "Cream Hill: Discoveries of a Weekend Countryman," "but we are not at home in them. . . . Perhaps that is why so many of us who live our lives in cities feel that we shrink and shrivel . . . unless we sometimes get back to the country."

The Southwest for some years has been Joseph Wood Krutch's Walden — without the pond. Before he took up his abode there, he too found in New England the margin for living Thoreau thought essential. In "The Twelve Seasons," he wrote, "From another year which I hope will be based in the country . . . I promise myself many advantages. But none of them is more obvious or more inclusive than the privilege of being permitted to be con-tinuously aware that I am indeed alive — for that is a fact which the city makes most people forget. . . . Only those within whose consciousness the suns rise and set, the leaves burgeon and wither, can be said to be aware of what living is."

Louis J. Halle, professor and scholar of diplomacy, met those very require-ments while at work in the national capital. His book, "Spring in Washington," an international and ornithological mix, tells of man in nature, specifically in Rock Creek Park. "To snatch the passing moment and examine it for signs of eternity is the noblest of occupations," he wrote.

E. B. White first went to Maine as a child. When almost 40, he returned with wife and young son, went to live on a salt-water farm, stayed five years. Meditating through long Maine winters, writing of small events in the course of his farming, he turned out a series of monthly pieces. Gathered together they appeared as "One Man's Meat." In a foreword to that collection, he wrote: "Usually when a man quits writing in his journal it is either because things are happening to him that he doesn't want to commit to paper or because he has lost interest in life."

Maine continues to be his magnet. "What happens to me when I cross the Piscataqua?" he asked in a later notational book, "The Points of My Com-pass." And answered, "I do not ordinarily spy a partridge in a pear tree, or three French hens, but I do have the sensation of having received a gift from a true love."

A generation and more ago, Gamaliel Bradford, half sick and housebound, posted his journals — more than a million words — in suburban Wellesley Hills. Nan Fairbrother, a young London woman, wrote from an old-country house where she and her two small children found refuge during the war. People have saved themselves by keeping journals. Her book, "An English Year," is one I liked very much.

Every journal-keeper of thoughts and days says, to all intent and purpose, "this is where I am now." None intends to let life go by the board. Emerson called his journals his savings bank in which he deposited opinions and views to be drawn out as needed. John Burroughs recommended keeping a journal "to preserve the flavor of the passing moment." A journal, he said, "is a sort of deposit account wherein one saves up bits and pieces of his life that would otherwise be lost to him."

When it came to hard cash, most managed with little. Most knew the joys of lean living. Rather different was Gamaliel Bradford. "Spent a considerable part of the day over my ledger," he wrote. "I do love to work on my money. . . . It will never play so large a part in my journal as it does in Pepys, but as it is not the least interesting part of his, so it may not be of mine. There is this difference, however . . . that he is dealing with a property which he had made himself, whereas I have seized all mine from somebody else." Bradford makes himself sound like a pirate. More likely he was an enthusiast.

What sort of fellow is the journal-keeper? A person gifted or skilled in judging qualities. Brooks Atkinson wrote in "Once Around the Sun" that, in criticism, there should be a large dash of the amateur. "For the amateur," he said, "is a man of enthusiasm who has not settled down and is not habit bound." The same goes for keeping thoughts and days; it too is a branch of criticism — not in the formal way, but rather in the ripening one of passing judgment, or reserving it, on the merits of many things.

If the journal-keeper of thoughts and days needs some of the cosmic sense of the poet, he also requires the common sense of the carpenter or sailor. Consistency is not a law of life; adaptability is. Bradford notwithstanding — and this, perhaps, was a weakness — journal-keepers are likely to know the beauty of parsimony, of economy in the use of specific means to an end. Is Henry Thoreau's "Simplicity, simplicity, simplicity!" the instrument with which he dissected all questions? Certainly to this class of writer, simplicity is an organizing principle. The principle, moreover, is an esthetic one; no scientific reason for it exists. It amounts to a search for an artistic presentation of life, unobscured by complexity of detail; or to put it another way, the quest for the clean and beautiful line.

Like Henry himself, journal-keepers do not remain in the woods. If they often take off, they as often return, and sometimes with something of social as well as personal value — such as a book. Thoreau called pitching his wigwam on the pond shore an experiment. What he learned from it was this: "If one advances confidently in the direction of his dreams, and endeavors to live the life which he has imagined, he will meet with a success unexpected in common hours." In other words, he experienced moments of grace.

To one so inclined, keeping a journal of thoughts and days brings its own reward; a happiness in the word and in the struggle to gain knowledge from experience. "It is hard to accept that we are here for no purpose which we can even vaguely understand," Nan Fairbrother wrote near the end of "An English Year." "We must manage as best we can," she concluded, finally begging all questions, perhaps, but bravely and with warmth.

Teller refers frequently to Henry David Thoreau and *Walden,* and you are probably familiar with both. *Walden* is a true classic: it is read and loved throughout the world. Based on Thoreau's own journal, it is a model for journal-keepers everywhere; and it will be worth your time to take a few moments to read and contemplate some of Thoreau's comments on the art of journal-keeping.

It is wise to write on many subjects, to try many themes, that so you may find the right and inspiring one. Be greedy of occasions to express your thought. Improve the opportunity to draw analogies. There are innumerable avenues to a perception of the truth. Improve the suggestion of each object however humble, however slight and transient the provocation. What else is there to be improved? It is not in vain that the mind turns aside this way or that: follow its leading; apply it whither it inclines to go. Probe the universe in a myriad points. Be avaricious of these impulses. You must try a thousand themes before you find the right one, as nature makes a thousand acorns to get one oak. He is a wise man and experienced who has taken many views; to whom stones and plants and animals and a myriad objects have each suggested something, contributed something.

Write often, write upon a thousand themes, rather than long at a time, not trying to turn too many feeble somersets in the air, — and so come down upon your head at last. Antaeus-like, be not long absent from the ground. Those sentences are good and well discharged which are like so many little resiliencies from the spring floor of our life — a distinct fruit and kernel itself, springing from terra firma. Let there be as many distinct plants as the soil and the light can sustain. Take as many bounds in a day as possible. Sentences uttered with your back to the wall.

To set down such choice experiences that my own writings may inspire me and at last I may make wholes of parts. Certainly it is a distinct profession to rescue from oblivion and to fix the sentiments and thoughts which visit all men more or less generally, that the contemplation of the unfinished picture may suggest its harmonious completion. Associate reverently and as much as you can with your loftiest thoughts. Each thought that is welcomed and recorded is a nest egg, by the side of which more will be laid. Thoughts accidentally thrown together become a frame in which more may be developed and exhibited. Perhaps this is the main value of a habit of writing, of keeping a journal, — that so we remember our best hours and stimulate ourselves. My thoughts are my company. They have a certain individuality and separate existence, aye, personality. Having by chance recorded a few disconnected thoughts and then brought them into juxtaposition, they suggest a whole new field in which it was possible to labor and to think. Thought begat thought.

My Journal is that of me which would else spill over and run to waste, gleanings from the field which in action I reap. I must not live for it, but in it for the gods. They are my correspondent, to whom daily I send off this sheet postpaid. I am clerk in their counting-room, and at evening transfer the account from the day-book to ledger. It is as a leaf which hangs over my head in the path. I bend the twig and write my prayers on it; then letting it go, the bough springs up and shows the scrawl to heaven. As if it were not kept shut in my desk, but were as public a leaf as any in nature . . .

From all points of the compass, from the earth beneath and the heavens above, have come these inspirations and been entered duly in the order of their arrival in the journal. Thereafter, when the time arrived, they were winnowed into lectures, and again, in due time, from lectures into essays. And at last they stand, like the cubes of Pythagoras, firmly on either basis; like statues on their pedestals, but the statues rarely take hold of hands. There is only such connection and series as is attainable in the galleries.

There is no such thing as pure *objective* observation. Your observation, to be interesting, i.e., to be significant, must be *subjective*. The sum of what the writer of whatever class has to report is simply some human experience, whether he be poet or philosopher or man of science. The man of most science is the man most alive, whose life is the greatest event. Senses that take cognizance of outward things merely are of no avail. It matters not where or how far you travel — the farther commonly the worse — but how much alive you are. If it is possible to conceive of an event outside to humanity, it is not of the slightest significance, though it were the explosion of a planet. Every important worker will report what life there is in him. It makes no odds into what seeming deserts the poet is born. Though all his neighbors pronounce it a Sahara, it will be a paradise to him; for the desert which we see is the result of the barrenness of our experience.

.   .   .

This earth which is spread out like a map around me is but the lining of my inmost soul exposed.

For Thoreau, his journal meant the ultimate confrontation — with himself; and so your journal can be for you. In our nervous days, uncertain and anxious, full of turmoil and action-centered, the journal and the moments of quiet contemplation it requires may seem old-fashioned and irrelevant. Precisely for these reasons, however, the journal may well be more relevant and valuable than ever; the search for self-knowledge and directions is never more essential or difficult than in times of change and the weakening of traditional guides. And beyond these values, your journal will certainly help you find your own language and use it more effectively — and isn't that the name of this game?

PRACTICE

1. Be a journal-keeper, then, at least during this course. Save enough time at the end of each day or so to discover in writing about them the points at which you really *lived* that day instead of simply *existed*. This means a kind of writing infinitely beyond the marginal notations and gossipy chatter of a diary; your journal should be less concerned with activities and other people than it is with their significance for your development as a person, with their effects on your feelings and thoughts. Keep your journal freely, fully, and honestly and without worrying about mechanics or style or anything else but writing it. Your instructor may want to check it occasionally but only to make sure you are writing a journal and not a diary. Take your journal seriously, and you'll be surprised how much fun it will be — and how beneficial for your writing.

2. In the essay collection, read "Where I Lived and What I Lived For," a chapter from Thoreau's *Walden*. Thoreau wrote this American classic from the journal he kept while living from 1845 to 1847 on the shores of Walden Pond near Concord, Massachusetts, in a cabin he built there because, he says, "I wished to live deliberately, to front only the essential facts of life, and see if I could not learn what it had to teach . . ." Read

the essay carefully; then write a one- or two-sentence answer to the following questions:

    a. If you could meet Thoreau, what kind of person would you expect him to be?

    b. What can you point to in his writing — in his choice of words, his images, his sentences, his rhythms — to explain your view of him?

    c. What is the main point — or points — of the essay: that is, what is Thoreau trying to communicate to you?

    d. What do you like the most or find the most effective in the essay?

    e. What, if anything, do you dislike or find ineffective in the essay?

4

*Exploring
Your
Language—
Free
Association*

If style is the man, the sum of the manners, attitudes, and behavior by which each of us, consciously or unconsciously, intentionally or unintentionally, identifies himself to others, then the language you use and the way you use it are central parts of the face you wear for others to see. Whenever you speak or write, you do it with some kind of style, whether you care a hoot about style or not. This being true, F. L. Lucas is certainly right in saying that "it seems mere common sense to give the matter a little thought." The problem is two-fold: first, recognizing the need to make language a vehicle of choice rather than one of impulse or accident; and second, finding your own authentic language — that is, language which will communicate clearly and effectively not only exactly what you mean but also exactly the way you mean it.

To find your proper tongue, your own authentic language, you need to stop taking language for granted and think a little about where it comes from. It has a least two basic sources: one, *experience*. This language comprises the words you learn to attach as names to your direct and immediate sensory, emotional, and intellectual experiences. Words like *red, love,* and *reward* form the language by which you learn to articulate what happens to and within you. Second, *acculturation*. This, at least in the beginning, is second- and third-hand language, the words you learn not as names for your own experience but from their use by your parents, teachers, ministers, newspapers, magazines, radios, televisions, movies, and the like. Words like *religion, patriotism, democracy,* and *communism* comprise the language of what goes on around you with little direct reference to your own immediate experience. Because you live not only in yourself but also in your relationships to others, both kinds of language are inevitable and necessary; but the language of experience is more likely to express what you really feel and think and the language of acculturation to express what you are expected to feel and think.

Your first task, then, is to recognize and distinguish clearly the two kinds of language. In his early years as a writer, Ernest Hemingway recalls, "I found the greatest difficulty, aside from knowing truly what you really felt, rather than what you were supposed to feel, and had been taught to feel, was to put down what really happened in action; what the actual things were which produced the emotion that you experienced." This *you* also must do: find the authentic language of your own unique experience, the words best able to communicate what you really think and feel. Once found, this language can become the controlling element in a style fully your own; moreover, it can give you the terms to explore and articulate the real meaning and value to you of the language of acculturation. If, that is, words like *religion* and *democracy* have any real and specific meaning for you, that meaning can best be found and expressed in the language of your own experience. As a would-be writer, then, you need to begin by taking a walk through your linguistic possessions.

FREE ASSOCIATION

One way to explore your resources in both kinds of language and thereby to distinguish between them is to take the mental exercise of free association. Life has left more extensive and profound linguistic riches in you than you probably fully realize: on almost any subject, about almost any object, you can feel, think, and express yourself at deeper levels and in greater variety than you probably believe you can. Think, for example, of what goes on in your mind during even a simple everyday walk down the street. Simultaneously, you are recalling a host of things from both the distant and the recent past, responding to a myriad of immediate stimuli around you and thinking of current problems and experiences, and wondering about and planning for future interests and activities. And most of this incredible wealth of mental activity occurs in words flowing through your mind in endless streams, each word linked to other words associated with it. If you could record even a few-second segment of this mental flow and then isolate the separate streams of associated words, you could probably fill a book. And if some of its chapters would be trivial and insignificant, others might well be rich in observation and insight.

Such a fixing and recording of the mind is, of course, impossible; but free association is one means of cutting the impossible down to the limits of the possible. Instead of trying to record the total random activity of the mind during some period or separating a specific stream from that total activity, free association begins by limiting the mind to one central stream and then records as much as possible of that stream during a particular period. You focus your attention on one specific object and let your mind roam freely around it, watching where your mind goes and recording the reports it sends back by writing down as many as you can of the words, phrases, and clauses the object suggests to you. Usually, this process produces one of two results: either a random list of ideas linked only by their relationship to the object; or ideas so linked but also revealing patterns of meaning within this central one.

Let's look at some examples drawn from student writing, beginning with this free association by Charles Bikfalvy:

AN OLD RUBBER BAND

> Grade-school Halloween party
> Man talking of blindness
> It's fun to shoot them
> Paperboxes of all shapes and colors
> Mother worked at *Associates*
> Shooting flies with folded paper
> A sharp snap on the thigh
> Slingshot
> Woolworth's ten-cent store
> Glue, paper, paste, and pencils
> Red rubber band
> Flat tire
> Inner tube
> Sandpaper
> Leeches
> Photographing green herons in the pond
> Camera-carrying strap with long ends

Each of these thoughts is apparently associated in Bikfalvy's mind with the rubber band he is looking at, but most of them are separate ideas unrelated to the rest. By contrast, notice how the thoughts in this free association of Mario S. Oddo are not only suggested by the central object but also occur in patterns of meaning:

A COFFEE CUP

It's really pink, but that's not my fault
Why *coffee* cup? What about tea?

Made by blind man

Very round — perfect, smooth finish . . . a new antique . . . reminds me of old things, durable like friendship . . . What's that commercial? . . .

"When good friends get together, share Maxwell House(?)"

I don't drink coffee — coffee and ulcers no! coffee and double cream, yes!

Prehistoric man had nothing — or did he?! Had no problems . . . had no time for problems — just survival

We take for granted our good fortune

I take for granted my good fortune and bitch because it isn't better

Better? What's better?

Health and happiness, friends and family, food and shelter

Shelter from what?

Storms

But what about storms inside you?

Inner conflict — coffee won't help . . . it lifts you up and lets you down

What about tea? Mary Jane — that's no answer . . . tea "pot" — teapot — potted tea — teapot of "pot" for Mary Jane — that's marijuana

Dreams and floating   not drunk but dreaming, lightness of limbs

Brightness of mind   clearness of vision on a cold night that doesn't feel cold

Mary Jane — woman . . . not a good woman — doesn't stay with you

Why do I wanna stop thinking *now*?

Sunlight — clearness of vision in the bright sun — different kind of exhilaration — sober

Cigarette a mistress? Coffee a mistress? . . . Lemme tell ya'

Use your eyes   use your brain

What gives pleasure?

I can give no answer — but I'm not unhappy — no answer — that makes me unhappy!

Why does a blind man make coffee cups?

Why?

Oddo's mental process, like Bikfalvy's, centers on a particular object; but Oddo's, without conscious effort on his part, reveals order and pattern. His thought ends where it begins — with a reference to the blind man who made the cup. In between, he connects the cup with both coffee and tea, associates coffee with companionship, and observes that coffee is no place for the storms that rage within people. This leads him to consider the possibility of escaping such storms by using "tea" — marijuana; but he concludes that "tea" is deceptive because the escape it provides is so short-lived. In the end, he concludes that there is no escape and that man has eyes and a brain but no sure way to pleasure.

By concentrating on a pink cup, Oddo discovers a wealth of associations in his mind and an apparently natural tendency to order and pattern. Sometimes, indeed, without the writer intending or even realizing it, such free association can rise almost to the level of poetry, as in this by Connie Gardulski:

A DEAD RED ROSE

The Rose Bowl
What a fiasco that was!
The petals once looked soft and dewy
Now they are old and dry and crinkled
It looks like the color of dried blood — like blood on a pavement
Mrs. Kennedy carried a bouquet of red roses in Dallas
The blood spattered on her suit, like crimson rose petals
I remember the corsage I wore to my first prom
It was yellow roses, though
I wonder where the corsage went?
I wonder where the boy went?
A rose is a rose is a rose
Gertrude Stein said that
She was a critic of Ernest Hemingway
He drank a lot
Maybe whiskey like Four Roses!
A long-stemmed beauty rose
Is that what they call Miss America?
She always gets a bouquet of roses, too
Rose is the flower for June, when my birthday is
I love roses the best, especially red ones
They die very quickly, though
That's why I'd rather see them in gardens
All colors — rows and rows of them
We have them in our garden every summer
I wonder why I like flowers so much
There's a song called "Everything's Coming Up Roses" From *Gypsy*
And I like to smell the fragrance of roses
Except, of course, everybody always mentions that even
beautiful red roses have thorns
Robert Burns said his love was like a red, red rose
She's dead now, too
Like this rose

Here, again, everything is related directly or indirectly to the central object, the dead rose; but Miss Gardulski's thought moves in a pattern which links thoughts of the beauty of roses with images of loss, violence, and death. The result is a free association which evokes poetically Miss Gardulski's profound sense of the tragic impermanence of all beauty and life.

In addition to the depth and variety of thought and suggestion in these free associations, their language is significant. Each was written quickly, as fast as the ideas came into the writer's mind, without concern for vocabulary, mechanics, style, form, structure, or rhythm; yet each piece of writing has a distinctive style, reflecting a different person behind it, and the last two pieces have an intrinsic structure and development.

In all three, the language is clearly authentic, the language of the writer's own real experience, feeling, and thought; and if good writing requires more than just this, here is at least a valid place to begin.

For the would-be writer, then, free associations can be a surprisingly fruitful technique. *First,* it can reveal the astounding riches locked in the vaults of your mind and give you a key to unlock them. If you learn to do free association and then use it, you will soon rid yourself of the paralyzing complaint that "I can't think of a thing to write about." *Second,* more specifically, free association can be a practical technique for marshalling your resources even for such required writing as term papers and essay examinations. By thinking of an object or concept centrally related to your topic and jotting down quickly whatever your mind associates with it, you can discover both what aspects of the topic you are best qualified to discuss and also the materials you can use most effectively in discussing them. And *third,* free association can help you to identify your own authentic language, the language of your own experience, feeling, and thought; and properly controlled, this is the most effective language for almost any writing you may have to do.

PRACTICE

1. Select some object, a single object, something familiar you see every day without paying any particular attention to it; or some treasured object, something you've saved for sentimental reasons. Set a time limit, a short one; concentrate on the object, for the moment clearing your mind of everything not in some way connected with the thing you're looking at; and then, as fast as you can, write down whatever the object suggests to you. Don't worry about sentence structure, spelling, punctuation, order, or form; just get your thoughts on paper as they come to you. And keep your focus on the object you are concentrating on; don't let some association divert you into a train of thought that takes you farther and farther away from the central object and never brings you back. Your object is not a point of departure for you to leave behind but a center of interest for you to revolve around, collecting the associations which cluster on it.

2. If time permits, your instructor will bring in some object and ask the whole class to use it for a free association. Don't worry if it doesn't particularly interest you at first; concentrate on it, and do your best in whatever time period your instructor sets. You will probably be surprised not only at how much the object suggests to you but also at the variety and depth of response throughout the class.

5

Exploring Your Language — the Categorical List

As the preceding exercises suggest, free association works best for objects, for things, though it can also be helpful and interesting in exploring abstractions, in finding the language of your particular experience and understanding of feelings, emotions, and ideas. Language, of course, is both concrete and abstract as well as denotative and connotative, distinctions the would-be writer must master and apply; and we will work in some detail with these problems in subsequent chapters. At this point, however, we need a pre-writing process to examine abstractions as effectively as free association explores objects. Such a process can begin with a categorical list.

A categorical list is a method of dividing an abstraction into the particular experiences and associations which make it uniquely meaningful to each individual. Nearly all normal people will see pretty much the same thing when they look at something red and experience fairly similar sensations when they taste something sour; these are sensual reactions, and words expressing them therefore have relatively objective and common centers of reference. But words expressing ideas like democracy, emotions like anger, and relationships like family are relatively subjective; that is, nearly everyone who uses or hears such words will understand them quite differently from anyone else beyond a very broad and vague common reference. One way of getting at your individual understanding of such terms is to divide it into categories which can stimulate you to recall particular experiences, influences, and associations connected with that understanding.

A categorical list, then, begins with an abstraction to be identified and explored and divides the identification and exploration into easily managed specific areas — for example, sense impressions, familiar relationships, places and conditions, and cultural associations. Here is such a list:

COLOR
SMELL
TASTE
SOUND
TEXTURE
SHAPE
OBJECT
ANIMAL
FOOD
BEVERAGE
CLOTHING
PLACE OR SETTING
FLOWER
WEATHER
COUNTRY
BUILDING OR STRUCTURE
CAR OR OTHER VEHICLE
MUSIC
PAINTING OR SCULPTURE
LITERARY WORK

Let's assume that you have to write something about the abstraction joy and can't think of a thing to say. Go down the list; and for each category, write down quickly whatever in your mind is connected with joy, with feeling joyful. When you think of joy, what color do you see? Red? Yellow? What taste? Maple syrup? Bacon? What country? Scotland? Japan? When you have the list completed, with one or two items for most of the categories, you will have the raw materials for a personal and interesting account of joy as only you know it and in terms that only you could use to express it. Let's look at a couple of completed lists:

JOY

COLOR: orange
SMELL: burning leaves
TASTE: salt water
SOUND: silence
TEXTURE: sand
SHAPE: round

OBJECT: rag doll
ANIMAL: fawn
FOOD: popcorn
BEVERAGE: cherry brandy
CLOTHING: bikini
PLACE OR SETTING: sunrise, bath
FLOWER: dandelion
WEATHER: windy
COUNTRY: Greece
BUILDING OR STRUCTURE: treehouse
CAR OR OTHER VEHICLE: Jaguar
MUSIC: raindrops, wind
PAINTING OR SCULPTURE: sky
LITERARY WORK: funnies

Would your list agree with this one at any points? Can you imagine the person who wrote this list, a person who understands joy in these terms? Male or female? Young or old? Introvert or extrovert? Notice, by the way, that the last three items in the list are less effective and useful than the others because they are too general. They should name an actual song or other piece of music, a painting, a particular comic strip or other work of literature. Here's another more specific categorical list on the same abstraction:

COLOR: yellow
SMELL: lilacs
TASTE: grape tootsie-roll pop
SOUND: a child's laughter
TEXTURE: suede
SHAPE: star
OBJECT: wine glass
ANIMAL: cat
FOOD: steak (medium-well)
BEVERAGE: Bourbon
CLOTHING: party dress
PLACE OR SETTING: walking by an ocean
FLOWER: daisies
WEATHER: sunny spring day
COUNTRY: Germany
BUILDING OR STRUCTURE: Empire State Building
CAR OR OTHER VEHICLE: Jaguar
MUSIC: "The Sky"
PAINTING OR SCULPTURE: water-color of a flower by my brother
LITERARY WORK: *A Friend Is Someone Who Likes You*, by
                         Charles Schulz

Compare the two lists. Do they reflect two different people? Do you think each person could use the materials in his list as the basis for writing something highly individual and interesting on the subject of joy? Hopefully, the memories, thoughts, and feelings which ought to bubble up in the process of filling in these categories would provide each person with a specific and varied awareness of exactly what he means by joy and therefore a rich abundance of things to write about on that subject. Hopefully, too, the categorical list can provide the same service for you.

PRACTICE

1. Make two or three categorical lists using any one or more of the following abstractions:

LOVE	HATE	HOPE	AUTHORITY
FREEDOM	SUCCESS	DESPAIR	POWER
PEACE	FAILURE	HOME	ANGER

Be sure each item in your list is something specific and particularly meaningful to you; that is, after car, don't put simply Ford, put Mustang — after music, not just rock but the title of your favorite song. For each category, search your memory for what you've done or know that most fully suggests that category of the abstraction you're working with.

2. Pick the one or two lists which seem to you the most interesting; and use each one — both the specific materials in the list and all that the process of making it has brought to mind — as the basis for a two- or three-page essay exploring your understanding of the abstraction heading the list.

6

Finding
Your
Meaning—
the
Existential
Sentence

Free association and the categorical list are ways of turning on your mind in preparation for the "pleasant agony" of writing; not only do they help you find your unique relationship to objects and abstractions but they do so in materials which enable you to express both in concrete and specific terms. Such language is a gift for your reader; it communicates your meaning to him with relative quickness and ease and engages his interest by involving his imagination. Another way to achieve this kind of thinking and writing is the existential sentence.

This rather high-flown but pleasantly intriguing term describes an essentially associative process and sets up a grammatical formula for operating it. The process functions somewhat like the separate items in a categorical list: you begin with an abstraction and then probe your experience for the sources of its unique meaning to you, but you are not limited to the divisions of the categorical list. The result is a kind of equation: the verb *is* functions as an equals-sign, on its right an abstraction, and on the left something concrete and specific expressing its meaning for you. A well-known and still a good example comes from a deservedly popular comic strip: "Happiness is a warm puppy." Recognize it? It comes from *Peanuts*, by Charles Schulz, a strip in which existential sentences frequently appear. See how they work? The abstraction *happiness* equals or *is* the concrete object *puppy*. And notice that the object is not just *puppy* but specifically *warm puppy*, with all the qualities of comfort and content that *warm* implies. Try the equation simply as *puppy*, and see how much it loses.

The reason for calling these sentences existential is that their meaning rides on specific, concrete objects, on materials drawn from the world of actual existence, not on theories or hypotheses, generalities or abstractions. The temptation in expressing abstractions is to define or describe them in further abstractions, to write that "happiness is feeling good" or "is a general sense of well-being." The problem with such statements is not that they are wrong but that they are vague and imprecise and dull. Except on the highest level of philosophical discourse, abstractions are slovenly servants of other abstractions. Which communicates most clearly and interestingly to you: "happiness is feeling comfortable and content" or "happiness is a warm puppy?"

Still, existential sentences have their traps, too. Sloppy thinkers and unwary writers seldom look beyond the first obvious or ordinary or familiar materials that come to mind, and their writing tastes like flat beer. It may be better than no beer at all, but not much. The trouble with obvious or ordinary or familiar materials is their empty dullness; here are a few examples:

Security is my new car
Success is a ranch-style house in the suburbs
Joy is a mother's praise

Having cost the writer little or no real mental effort, such expressions exact no imaginative price from a reader. They are, then, essentially mindless; and most mindless of all is the familiar expression, the overused image, the cliché. Clichés are conditioned responses in language — expressions heard so often that we use them automatically in any situation like those in which we became familiar with them, expressions like "put our noses to the grindstone." "pulled himself up by his own bootstraps," and "climbed the ladder of fame." Paradoxically, clichés like these are the victims of their own success: when they were first phrased, they were shining and bright — fresh new coins to buy fresh, new insights. So meaningful and interesting were they, indeed, that everyone who heard or read them picked them up and used them; and soon they grew worn and dull. "Her teeth were like pearls" must once have been an exciting image for a lover's smile; today, it is a tired joke. Even a diamond could be worn away by constant polishing.

The sentence from *Peanuts* is a good example of a fresh expression becoming a cliché. It became widespread coinage when it appeared only a few years ago, and it still has some power to affect the imagination and emotions with immediate communication. But it is wearing out, becoming too familiar, turning into the kind of conditioned response one knows without thinking.

To be effective, then, existential sentences must express abstractions not only in specific and concrete terms but also in fresh ones. Here are some student examples which I like:

Joy is listening to the sky
Security is a tree toad in your pocket when your mother said you couldn't have a pet
Joy is the wind making love to my umbrella
Security is the flavor of the trading stamp that completes the book
Joy is sand tickling my toes

Compare these with the less effective sentences above. What makes the latter ones so much better? Existential sentences like these can be a valuable device for focussing on the sources of your individual meanings and for giving your writing the sparkle of freshness.

PRACTICE

Write *five* existential sentences for any *three* of the following abstractions:

JOY	SUCCESS	HOPE	LOVE	HOME
ANGER	PEACE	DESPAIR	HATE	ANXIETY
SECURITY	FREEDOM	FAILURE	REVOLUTION	FUN

Draw from some of the categories in the lists you made for the preceding chapter, make new lists, or just deal with the abstractions directly. Beware of the obvious, the ordinary, the cliché; as a practical rule, don't use the first two things that come to mind as you think about each existential sentence. Chances are they will be commonplace or overused expressions your mind has stored up for just such occasions. Dig deeply, goad your imagination, until you discover experiences and associations you feel sure are yours in ways they can never be anyone else's.

Part 2

Writing

7

The

Concrete

Imperative

Pre-writing devices like free association, categorical lists, and existential sentences can help a would-be writer find his own authentic materials and language, but to control that language and use it effectively he must go on to become more consciously aware of it. To begin with, this means a concern for the building blocks of language — words. Whether you are thinking your way into a subject or writing your way out of it, your only tools are words. These conventionalized patterns of sound — for that's what words are: sounds which we have given particular meanings — are the record of our experience, the printing which life has left on the page of self. The words we know and the ways we use them reveal much of what we are: the objects we know, the emotions we feel, the ideas we think — all that gives us conscious being. We might say that man is the animal with words, except that it is probably a greater truth to say that man is more than animal *because* he has words. A would-be writer, then, must develop a word sense, a love for words, a respect, even a reverence, for them, certainly a delight in them. And to begin with, both to discover what he's going to write and then to write it effectively, he probably ought to begin — you ought to begin — by understanding clearly and practically the differences between the two basic kinds of words: abstract and concrete. Your categorical lists and existential sentences were ways of making abstractions concrete and specific; now let's look in further detail at why this process is essential to most effective prose.

In reality, abstract and concrete indicate a distinction without a difference. On the one hand, all words are abstractions, patterns of sound which stand for the objects outside us and the thoughts and feelings inside us. Cow, after all, is not *a* cow but a three-letter word whose sound generalizes the characteristic features and functions of millions of individual large female mammals. Without the ability to create such sounds and to endow them with meanings, we could not conceptualize our experience or think about it; we could understand and deal only with the individual animals one by one as we met them. We could not, in other words, be human and by conceptualizing our environment and our experience bring them within our rational control.

On the other hand, the apparently solid objects to which concrete words point are themselves abstractions. What we see when we look at an object is not the object itself but a series of electrical impulses registering in our brains after being transmitted along our optic nerves in response to light rays reflected through our eyes from the object. The tactile process functions in much the same way, and if we depend only on our senses, we conclude that the forms and textures we see and touch are concrete. But our senses are severely limited; and with its vastly more sensitive and accurate instruments for analysis and measurement, modern science reveals that objects are in no way concrete, that they are combinations of almost infinite numbers of particles in constant motion at varying rates within and around each other.

Take this book, for example. As you hold it, you see a particular shape and feel a particular texture. It seems real. But you know that its pages could be broken down into the substances from which their paper was made and these into their constituent molecules and these into their atoms and these into sub-atomic particles and these into who knows what. The farther science goes in its pursuit of reality, the farther it gets from anything concrete. In effect, then, the book you perceive as a concrete object is an abstraction which your brain makes from the limited impressions of your senses, and the word "book" is a verbal abstraction from a sensuous abstraction from a reality which is itself apparently abstract.

So there you sit with a handful of nothing, but even if you know this to be true, that nothing goes right on filling your hand. In your relationship to it as a functioning human being, the book is pragmatically real; we may know reality is abstract, but we experience much of it as concrete. Recognizing, then, that all words are abstractions and that no object is actually concrete, we can still make a legitimate and useful distinction between words which stand for concepts and emotions and words which represent the objects of sense impressions.

As your pre-writing exercises emphasized, abstract words express ideas, feelings, and emotions — good and evil, for instance, and delight and love and hate; concrete words point to things and actions — to trees and houses, to running and swimming. Moreover, both kinds of words can be relatively general or specific. Experience, emotion, and fear are all abstract words, but each is more specific than the one which precedes it. So, too, bungalow, house, and building are concrete words, but in an order of increasing generality.

In your writing, you will inevitably have to use all these kinds of words. When you express an opinion or venture a judgment or summarize your experience, you will do it more often than not in abstract words, and well you may. A really good abstraction can ring its wisdom across the ages, fresh and bright and clear as on the day of its conception: "Vanity of vanities, saith the Preacher, vanity of vanities; all *is* vanity." Again: "We hold these truths to be self-evident, — that all men are created equal; that they are endowed by their Creator with certain inalienable rights; that among these are life, liberty, and the pursuit of happiness."

Too much abstraction and generalization, however, will make your writing vague and fuzzy. Both abstract and concrete words are individualizing symbols: the experiences they stand for are never exactly the same in different people. No two people ever experience love in the same way or see the same thing when they look at a particular tree. Still, emotion is entirely subjective and impossible to verify, while sense impressions originate in something external which provides a common reference point for at least superficial verification. In effect, therefore, abstract words are relatively inexact and easy to misunderstand or to misinterpret; concrete words are relatively precise and vivid.

Furthermore, abstraction means drawn from, formed from, particular instances; and the experiences to which abstract words refer derive ultimately from the kind of sensual experiences recorded in concrete words. All learning begins in the stimulation of our senses, and in these five ways alone do we first learn about the world we live in. Watch a baby with a new toy: he looks at it, touches it, tastes and smells it, shakes it to see what noise it makes, and stares at you when you tell him it is a b-a-l-l ball. When he is old enough, ball will be one of his first words, and he will recognize similar object as balls. In the same way, love comes to mean for him the total of all the pats, hugs, squeezes, kisses, and general fondling by which he becomes sensually aware of his family's affection for him. So he learns, as do we all; and if abstract and concrete words are different, they are nevertheless closely related.

Clearly, then, only highly specialized writing can be exclusively abstract or concrete; most writing, if it is to reflect your experience and knowledge accurately, must be a combination of both kinds of words. Moreover, since both are rooted ultimately in the experiences through which you learned or understand them, the best way to make abstractions exact and vivid is to express or illustrate them in concrete words and figures of speech which will reflect your individual understanding of the experiences symbolized by the abstractions. Such concrete words and expressions will also contribute substantially to the *I-ness* of your style, and the search for them can make the whole writing process more personal and exciting.

Read the following paragraphs, and underline the clearly concrete words, both general and specific. What percentage of each paragraph is concrete? How much do these concrete words and expressions contribute to making the passages clear and interesting?

A tough Scotch-Irishman I know, Mr. Hugh G. Flood, a retired house-wrecking contractor, aged ninety-three, often tells people that he is dead set and determined to live until the afternoon of July 27, 1965, when he will be a hundred and fifteen years old. "I don't ask much here below," he says. "I just want to hit a hundred and fifteen. That'll hold me." Mr. Flood is small and wizened. His eyes are watchful and icy-blue, and his face is red, bony, and clean-shaven. He is old-fashioned in appearance. As a rule, he wears a high, stiff collar, a candy-striped shirt, a serge suit, and a derby. A silver watch-chain hangs across his vest. He keeps a flower in his lapel. When I am in the Fulton Fish Market neighborhood, I always drop into the Hartford House, a drowsy waterfront hotel at 309 Pearl Street, where he has a room, to see if he is still alive.

—Joseph Mitchell, *"Old Mr. Flood"*

Your fellow-townsmen were stirring abroad — not many afoot, most of them in their cars; and the sound which they made in Concord at evening was a rustling and a whispering. The sound lacks steadfastness and is wholly unlike that of a train. A train, as you know who lived so near the Fitchburg line, whistles once or twice sadly and is gone, trailing a memory in smoke, soothing to ear and mind. Automobiles, skirting a village green, are like flies that have gained the inner ear — they buzz, cease, pause, start, shift, stop, halt, brake, and the whole effect is a nervous polytone curiously disturbing.

As I wandered along, the toc toc of ping pong balls drifted from an attic window. In front of the Reuben Brown house a Buick was drawn up. At the wheel, motionless, his hat upon his head, a man sat, listening to Amos and Andy on the radio (it is a drama of many scenes and without an end). The deep voice of Andrew Brown, emerging from the car, although it originated more than two hundred miles away, was unstrained by distance. When you used to sit on the shore of your pond on Sunday morning, listening to the church bells of Acton and Concord, you were aware of the excellent filter of the intervening atmosphere. Science has attended to that, and sound now maintains its intensity without regard for distance. Properly sponsored, it goes on forever.

A fire engine, out for a trial spin, roared past Emerson's house, hot with readiness for public duty. Over the barn roofs the martins dipped and chittered. A swarthy daughter of an asparagus grower, in culottes, shirt, and bandanna, pedalled past on her bicycle. It was indeed a delicious evening, and I returned to the inn (I believe it was your house once) to rock with the old ladies on the concrete veranda.

—E. B. White, *"Walden"*

As I go north for the first time in years, in the slow, the constantly stopping, milk train — which carries passengers only in the back part of the hind car and has an old stove to heat it in winter — I look out through the dirt-yellowed double pane and remember how once, as a child, I used to feel thwarted in summer till I had got the windows open and there was nothing between me and the widening pastures, the great boulders, the black and white cattle, the rivers, stony and thin, the lone elms like featherdusters, the high air which sharpens all outlines, makes all colors so breathtakingly vivid, in the clear light of late afternoon.

The little stations again: Barnevald, Stittville, Steuben — a tribute to the Prussian general who helped drill our troops for the Revolution. The woman behind me in the train talks to the conductor with a German accent. They came over here for land and freedom.

Boonville: that pale boxlike building, smooth gray, with three floors of slots that look in on darkness and a roof like a flat overlapping lid — cold dark clear air, fresh water. Like nothing else but upstate New York. Rivers that run quick among stones, or, deeper, stained dark with dead leaves. I used to love to follow them — should still. A fresh breath of water off the Black River, where the blue closed gentians grow. These forests, those boulder-strewn pastures, those fabulous distant falls!

—Edmund Wilson, *"The Old Stone House"*

PRACTICE

1. In the essay collection, read whichever of the essays by Orwell, Twain, Serrin, Updike, Chesterton, and Mailer your teacher assigns. For each selection you read, write a one- or two-sentence answer to each of the following questions:

   a. If you could meet the writer, what kind of person would you expect him to be, and why?
   b. What is the main point or points he is trying to communicate in the essay?
   c. How much use does he make of concrete language, and what does it contribute to the essay's ability to communicate his ideas?
   d. What do you like the most or find the most effective in the essay?
   e. What do you like the least or find the least effective in the essay?

2. Rewrite *five* of the following passages, replacing generalities and abstractions with specific details and concrete words. For example, in place of a sentence like "It was a weird vehicle," write something on this order: "The red-and-cream Volkswagen with the top sawed off and one door missing clumped by on four flat tires." Be as *specific* and as *detailed* as you can; use *action* verbs in place of to-be verbs wherever possible; in short, be *concrete*.

   a. The room was attractively furnished.

b. She wore an odd-looking coat.

c. He's a real nut!

d. Intellectual endeavors stimulate a higher kind of response in most individuals than do physical tasks of a menial nature.

e. The American ideal is demonstrated in a variety of ways. For example, a fair proportion of those having attained a certain degree of chronological maturity exercise their invaluable privilege of participating in the selection of those who will direct the affairs of the locale in which they are constituents and the nation of which they are citizens. Such activity is evidence of individual democratic involvement in government, which is part of the "American way of life."

f. Gina's parents have always treated her very strictly.

g. The building was drab and uninteresting.

h. Jack is a trustworthy guy.

i. He is unpredictable.

j. Spring is in the air.

3. Write an objective description of the object you used for free association — or, if you did more than one association, choose one of the objects to describe. Center your attention on the thing itself, not on your feelings about it or your relationship to it. For illustration, here is Mario Oddo's description of the coffee cup on which he wrote his free association.

DESCRIPTION OF A COFFEE CUP

My landlady's cup was made by the skillful hands of a blind lady. Light pink, it is wider than it is tall and has a handle with room for one finger. From the side with the handle pointed to the right, it is two and one-half inches high, three inches across at the mouth, four inches at the widest point excluding the handle, four and three-quarter inches including the handle, and three inches across at the base. The handle is one-quarter inch thick and is attached to two places on the side of the cup. It connects one-quarter of an inch below the top edge and extends outward in a loop with an inner radius of three-quarters of an inch. It connects again seven-eighths of an inch above the base and has an extension slightly more than one-quarter of an inch below the lower connection.

Viewed from the top, the cup looks like a drawing of three concentric circles with a large apostrophe sticking through the outer one. The handle is one-half an inch wide at the top and tapers to one-quarter of an inch where it is attached to the cup. The largest circle is the widest part of the cup; the middle circle is the opening, or mouth; and the smallest circle is the base.

Examined closely, the cup is not a smooth pink but a combination of shades of red. Even a few small dabs of green and blue can be seen under a strong light. The darkest shade of red flows from the lower handle connection to the base; the lightest shade of red is on the base of the cup, where it is almost an off-white with just the smallest trace of pink.

The finish of the cup is smooth. Other than the handle, there are no projections except faint ripples on the inner base. When struck gently by a metal-cased ballpoint pen, the cup emits a clear, high tone that rings for just less than two seconds. When struck with the heavy handle of a metal kitchen knife, the cup makes a higher, grating sound that lasts for only a fraction of a second and breaks into . . . thirty-seven jagged pieces and an eviction notice!

Admittedly, this is not very interesting or exciting writing; and you won't enjoy it as much as you probably did the subjective free association. But this is informal and clear exposition and a necessary balance for personal and inner-directed subjective writing. You need to be able to communicate what is outside you as well as what is inside; indeed, on most writing occasions, you will need to do both at once. On this assignment, then, be as objective as possible: keep the object in your writing, and yourself out.

4. Take your free association and your object description, and combine them. Select what seem to you to be the best parts of each, put them together, and add whatever else this process suggests to you. Visualize your task in this way: imagine that you are writing for a particular person, some relative or acquaintance, and that you have to communicate your object to him in the round — that is, in both the personal and the objective dimensions. Let's see what Mario Oddo does in combining his free association and object description.

ONLY A COFFEE CUP

Coffee cups are pretty much alike — they all have handles, a flat bottom, and a wide mouth. Usually, their diameter is about the same as their height. Most coffee cups are made of thick, white porcelain. They are strictly functional, like a no-nonsense butler attending efficiently and unsmilingly to his master. Having no unique personality, they create as little interest in the persons using them as a private in parade formation inspires in the inspecting general. The butler, the private, and the cup are seen as merely necessary nonentities to the persons using them.

My cup is different — it's a lady cup, just right for a man like me. She's a pretty little thing with graceful curves and a smooth, blushing pink complexion. Her blush is not the embarrassed kind that means she wants to run away, but the kind that means she looks forward to my company with unconcealed pleasure. Her attraction does not lie in an artificial daintiness, but in her constant, pleasant companionship when I am drinking. She seems not to be angry with me if I pour liquor into her, but she seems to enjoy it best when warm beverages like coffee and tea are put in her mouth. I love to hear her high, tinkling laugh fill the room when I tickle her sides with my spoon.

Her mother was not a machine that made her just like her brothers and sisters, but a blind lady who carefully taught her the importance of serving gracefully. Her mother's skillful fingers molded her into a thing of beauty and strength, as well as a useful, functional object.

Oddo has used his free association and his object description as raw materials, choosing from them only what he needed to combine and expand effectively — that is, to write so that his reader would not only *understand* the subject clearly but also be *interested* in it.

Let's look at one more example of this three-step process.

TROLL — FREE ASSOCIATION

what a ridiculously ugly face — but he looks so happy

his hair is like a German Shepherd's fur only longer — singed on the ends — do you smoke?

why does he wear a skirt if he's a boy — trolls aren't girls

has a tan — maybe he doesn't belong in clothes, but he has bows in his hair — maybe his kind of people are neuter

what's so lucky about an ugly troll? You're so ugly you're cute — you seem to be inviting me to tell you my problems — then I'd feel better — maybe that's why you bring good luck

your hair is an awful mess — you're not cuddly

what are you smiling at?

what's he smiling at? does he see someone he knows?

maybe he's listening — he wouldn't smile at me, I don't like him — I don't believe he brings good luck — he doesn't like that

talk about a glassy stare — what are you looking at, troll?

why do you have only four fingers and toes?

where do your people live, under bridges? You all belong together, that's for sure — silly looking people with deformed little bodies and fuzzy hair

what are you really good for?

TROLL — OBJECT DESCRIPTION

White hair with black ends — fuzzy

Green bows in hair, white shirt, yellow skirt with suspenders and black buttons

Glassy orange eyes, many wrinkles on face — ugly

Big nose and goofy smile

Ears stick out of football-shaped head

Four fingers, four toes, chunky, square build, short legs, pot belly, tan skin

Leaning forward with outstretched arms ("kiss me!")

OCSIRAGUE

Troll is a perfect adjective for this creature. He has white cotton-candy hair with singed ends and fixed orange eyes that look like marbles. In the center of his face is a lumpy pug nose. The wrinkles on his face seem to radiate from his eyes like the ripples in a still pool as two stones are dropped in it. He is squarely built with a chunky body made up of short, fat arms and legs and a round, projecting tummy. He has only eight fingers and toes that make him look clumsy. It's fortunate he doesn't wear shoes; he'd have trouble tying them. He wears clothes, but his tanned skin leaves one to wonder if he belongs in them. The sex is hard to determine. He has green ribbons in his hair and wears a lemon-colored skirt, but black buttons attach suspenders. Maybe he's neuter. I prefer to think of him as male; what member of the fairer sex could have a face like that?

Every troll has a name and this one is no exception. His friends call him Ocsirague. Ocsirague is named for his uncle who lived with the king of Norway, although the family is originally from Italy. Ocsirague is not one of the stereotyped trolls, who live in castles or under bridges and have nasty dispositions and terrorize everyone they meet. Ocsirague and his family are a backward group. This particular family, with its members numbering in the thousands, couldn't find a bridge that would accommodate them all, and there were no castles available. Their residence became a dead tree stump with underground passageways. Dead tree stumps don't offer much contact with the outside world, so opportunities to terrorize the yeomen were at a minimum. It was brought to the attention of the International Association of Ancient Trolls (IAAT) that Ocsirague's family didn't operate according to the bylaws of the organization. By arrangement of the IAAT, lightning struck their tree-stump home. And as a consequence of not living up to the troll image, the entire family was frozen in the same position with outstretched arms and glassy stares. In protest, the family became symbols of good luck. This all happened 752 years ago, and since then Ocsirague merely stands smiling, in spite of his situation. He, of course, will never change; he is just a quiet observer.

Ocsirague's stance suggests his basic intention, as he leans forward in anticipation with outstretched arms. His ears are funnels as his hair wildly engulfs his head, and his expression seems to say, "Tell me your thoughts, your secrets, your problems, tell me!" Who can resist such an invitation from a tongue-tied troll who isn't capable of uttering a word? This is why Ocsirague is thought to bring good luck; he plays a game with us. He listens, and maybe laughs to himself but we don't care because we'll never know. Ocsirague is a scrapbook of love affairs, an index of secret thoughts and an ageless calendar of complaints; he is a journal of a million entries. In spite of his features, he's not so bad to have around.

This is the work of Lynda Bradstreet, and it reflects the values of controlled concrete expression. See if you can do as well.

8

Reaching
for
Resemblances

If our knowledge of the world we live in begins in our individual sensuous experience of it, we nevertheless live in essentially the same world and experience it with similar senses. In this interaction and interrelationship of our world and our senses, each of us responds and thereby develops differently; there are no human carbon copies. Still, these subjective and individualizing differences are neither total nor unique; rather, they are variations on a central theme. Every ballplayer plays the game differently in some respects than every other player, yet they all play baseball. In this sense, then, there is in human experience nothing truly new, nothing unique, but only different forms in which old and basically unchanging experience confronts us at different times and in different places. Everything we experience is therefore similar in some ways to other things; everything we know is related in some ways to something else. The recognition of these similarities and interrelationships is invaluable for the would-be writer, both as a means of exploring his own knowledge and also as ways of expressing it clearly and vividly.

Aristotle argues that the ability to perceive likeness in dissimilarity is a mark of intelligence; and certainly, when it is active and alert, the human mind seems naturally to seek connections between things, ideas, and emotions; to comprehend experience through resemblances and relationships. By recognizing this basic comparison process and putting it consciously to work, you, as a would-be writer, can explore your own experience and knowledge to find concrete or simple or familiar things or qualities or relationships to express or explain more abstract or complex or unfamiliar ones. You can seek such illustrative and clarifying resemblances in many ways — by direct comparisons, by figurative language, by analogy. Each is an effective way for a would-be writer to think his way into a subject, to find a personal relationship to it in the individualizing materials of his own experience and knowledge.

Moreover, these techniques, particularly figurative language and analogy, can become dynamic and exciting elements in a would-be writer's style. They can give your writing greater clarity, especially with subjects involving complex ideas or emotions or attitudes. Figurative language and analogy are also economy measures: they make it possible to say much and to suggest more in relatively few words. And because these are concrete techniques, they appeal vividly and forcefully to a reader's imagination and thereby involve him immediately and personally in the subject. Finally, figurative language and analogy, because they derive from the writer's own experience and knowledge, are individualizing techniques; they contribute dramatically to the *I-ness* at the heart of style. But they are radically different techniques, whether for thinking or for writing; and you need to consider them very carefully. To use them effectively, you must understand each clearly, both in itself and also in its differences from the other.

FIGURATIVE LANGUAGE

Figurative language is not a sweetener added to style like syrup to waffles: it is a way of knowing, a form of meaning. Most language, indeed, is essentially figurative; only in specialized uses, as in mathematics and science, is it entirely literal. Two plus two equals four; sodium plus chlorine equals salt. In statements like these, the words have a single, unshifting, and sharply defined meaning. Human experience, however, is seldom, if ever, single or sharply defined; and it cannot be expressed accurately in literal statements. Writing or talking about our actions, feelings, and thoughts, we simply cannot say exactly what we mean in literal terms; and so we turn inescapably to figurative language — the language of words with meanings expanded beyond the literal.

This expansion of meaning, this wrenching of words from their original literal contexts, begins in a comparison process which culminates in a transfer of meaning. Take, for example, the statement, "He flew across the street." You know at once, of course, that I mean the man ran across the street with unusual speed. Moreover, you most likely visualize him running so that his feet seem hardly to touch the ground. This simple, ordinary statement occasions no surprise, then; but take it literally for a moment, and see what happens. Clearly, in this context, the verb "flew" has assumed new and non-literal meanings. Once, probably, someone compared a man or an animal running to the speed and grace of a bird in flight; and in the course of time (there's another figurative expression), the specific comparison disappeared, leaving the meaning it evoked attached directly to the word.

Most of our language is composed of such essentially figurative words and expressions, and every day we necessarily add new ones and expand old ones. By a process of comparison and contrast, of perceiving and focusing on likeness in dissimilarity, *figurative language defines one thing in terms of similar features or qualities of something else.* More exactly, it uses something concrete to clarify or emphasize an abstraction or something unfamiliar or something which needs a fresh perspective, thereby constantly enriching language with vivid *figures of speech* and new meanings. The process should be familiar to you; essentially, it is what you were doing in your categorical lists and existential sentences. The point here is to build on that experience by expanding your knowledge of the figurative process and your ability to put it to practical use in your writing.

Figurative language is traditionally divided into different categories like simile, metaphor, metonymy, synecdoche, and personification; but these differ only technically. Essentially, they all function by the same figurative process: *something is defined or explained in terms of features or qualities of something else, something concrete.* Among these figurative techniques, the most common and probably the most useful for a would-be writer are the simile and the metaphor. In similes, the figurative process is explicit; that is, the transference of meaning from one word to another is signaled by *like, as,* or *as if:* "the sun looks *like* an orange"; "the plane touched down gently, *as* a bird lands"; "the jet took off *as if* it had exploded." Because it functions explicitly, a good simile has a vivid immediacy and a kinetic force. It makes a direct comparison and sets the mind in horizontal motion back and forth between the elements of the simile to discover their specific points of resemblance. Each perception of similarity brings the pleasant surprise of unexpected recognition, and the better the simile, the sharper and more frequent the surprises. The best similes, then, are both imaginatively exciting and also intellectually convincing, a double impact as in Joseph Conrad's "the ship, a fragment detached from the earth, went on lonely and swift like a small planet."

Similes like this are *closed* similes: they define or explain their subject in a direct comparison to something similar, and they also contain the particular points of likeness on which this similarity rests. By contrast, "the sun is like an orange" is an *open* simile; it establishes a general similarity but leaves it up to the reader to find his own specific points of resemblance — guided, of course, by the context in which the simile functions. Both kinds of simile are valuable ways to think your way into a subject to find your individual relationship to it and also effective techniques for giving your writing greater clarity and interest and for stamping it with your individuality.

In metaphors, the transference of meaning from one word to another occurs without signals; something is described not as being *like* something else, but as *being* something else. In effect, then, a metaphor is a way of getting at truth by telling lies. It declares serenely that something is what in reason it cannot be — and gets away with it. A metaphor, in short, is a perfectly clear photograph of something impossible.

"The sun *is* an orange"; "the plane *was* a great bird, landing gently"; "a metaphor *is* a perfectly clear photograph of something impossible": these are metaphors, and it is a mistake to view them, as they are sometimes defined, as similes without the *like* or *as*. Because the comparison is implicit, it doesn't function as a comparison at all. Instead of moving between two ideas and recognizing their similarities, the mind is forced to fuse them into a single image, to think of one as actually possessing specific features or qualities of the other. As it lands, the plane doesn't *look* in some ways like a bird; it spreads its wings wide, puts out its rubber-tired feet, and swoops to the runway in a quick, unbroken union. For a sudden moment in the imagination, metaphor has fused these two objects at particular points of resemblance, and the plane has become a bird. A metaphor, then, is a process not only of comparison, but also of fusion, a fusion which explodes in the imagination with the light and heat of unsuspected equivalences suddenly perceived:

> Consistency is a paste jewel that only cheap men cherish.
> —William Allen White, *Emporia Gazette, 1922*
> An iron curtain has descended across the Continent.
> —Winston S. Churchill, *Address at Westminster College,*
> *Fulton, Missouri, March 5, 1946*

Figures of speech, particularly similes and metaphors, can give your thinking direction and identity and your writing lucidity, vividness, delight, and individuality; but they are not techniques to be learned like formulae and then mechanically applied. They are the product of a mental attitude — the constant willingness to winnow experience for its resemblances and equivalences. Moreover, figurative language has its dangers. You can fall in love with it and overuse it. Dazzled by too many gems, the reader may overlook their settings.

Figures of speech can also rest on too weak a foundation or strain too hard for their effects. The points of similarity which make the figurative process possible must be essential and close. If they are tangential or involve any serious conflict, they become imaginatively untenable and sometimes absurd. "The plane landed gently, like a bird" is far from original, but it is a better simile than "the plane landed gently, like a falling leaf." The plane and the bird resemble one another *closely* at three *essential* points: they look alike, each can fly, and each is under conscious control. But the plane and the leaf are alike only at two relatively *tangential* points: each moves through the air, and each touches the earth gently; and they conflict at three essential points: they do not look alike, the leaf cannot fly, and it is not consciously controlled. Consequently, the leaf simile is imaginatively sloppy; moreover, it introduces the unintended possibility that the pilot lost control of the plane and that it fluttered to earth only by good fortune. Such weak resemblances can also be strained to crude and even vulgar extremes: "he's as conservative as a three-hole privy" has a shock value, but not the kind you are likely to want very often in your writing.

Another and more common danger is mixed metaphor. A series of related metaphors or a metaphor opening out in all its details can be tremendously effective, but two or more widely different or conflicting metaphors describing the same idea are usually disastrous. I once heard a speaker, talking about the need for American unity against the threat of communism, declare forcefully that "the war with Red ideals has reached a crossroad where we must sink or swim." He then went on, believe it or not, to argue that "we, like our forefathers, must tighten our belts and stick our chins out to meet the challenge" and that "America is a place with many mansions that can only live in harmony and progress if everyone pulls together."

These dangers and their attendant errors all stem from a common failure: the failure of imagination, of visualization. As a result, they defeat the purposes of figurative language; instead of clarifying and emphasizing your knowledge and meaning, ineffective figures of speech obscure them. Such failure, however, is a weakness not of figurative language but of the writer who misuses it, who fails to visualize clearly and carefully. As you think about your subject, then, try to compare its main points to something concrete and similar in your own experience or knowledge. Pursue the points of similarity as far as you can; then concentrate on the comparisons you can *see* most clearly and in most detail. These will be the parts of your subject you know best and can write about most effectively, for figures of speech reflect both objective similarities which you individually perceive and also your subjective attitudes in perceiving them. Use figurative language, then, to explore what you know about a subject and as a technique to express your meaning concretely and personally; it "is a great excellence in style, when it is used with propriety," Samuel Johnson declares, "for it gives you two ideas for one; conveys the meaning more luminously, and generally with a perception of delight."

Read the following paragraphs; underline the similes, and bracket the metaphors. How much, in your opinion, do these figurative expressions add to the clarity and interest of the passages?

The storm is gone, and here in the country a mild sun has bit by bit argued the cold and snow away. There is the upheaval of a final thaw in the March lawns that are the color of old straw, and in the ponderous black velvet loam, this Illinois sod without a pea-sized pebble in it. Across the roll and dip of the great plain I saw, as I went walking with my blackthorn, the distant woods as blueblack, rainy-looking islands upon the immense watery prairie, and near at hand the young yellow of the willow whips, first brilliance of the year. Now this was a scene a midlander could love, but I went thinking, thinking, wagging that human tail my cane, how all that I saw came to me thus only because of a specified convexity in the cornea of my eye.

My sense of proportion, to say nothing of esthetics, is really superbly egotistic. Matter, to regard it more exactly than humanly, is full of holes. The solidest thing is as a net; the space between the electronic particles is like unto the spaces between the sun and the planets. The trouble with our human concepts is that we are so pitifully small when it comes to the great, and so unbearably gross when it comes to the small. We occupy a position in the scale of things that is somewhat on the trivial side of total mediocrity. Little wonder if our ideas are mediocre too.

—Donald Culross Peattie, *Green Laurels*

I am frightened by the imbalance, the constant striving to reach the largest possible audience for everything; by the absence of a sustained study of the state of the nation. Heywood Broun once said, "No body politics is healthy until it begins to itch." I would like television to produce some itching pills rather than this endless outpouring of tranquilizers. It can be done. Maybe it won't be, but it could. Let us not shoot the wrong piano player. Do not be deluded into believing that the titular heads of the networks control what appears on their networks. They all have better taste. All are responsible to stockholders, and in my experience all are honorable men. But they must schedule what they can sell in the public market. And this brings us to the nub of the question.

—Edward R. Murrow, *Speech to Radio and TV News Directors*

There must come a time, in every generation, when those who are older secretly get off the train of progress, willing to walk back to where they came from, if they can find the way. We're afraid we're getting off now. Cheer, if you wish, the first general or Ph.D. who splatters something on the kindly face of the moon. We shall grieve for him, for ourself, for the young lovers and poets and dreamers to come, because the ancient moon will never be the same again. Therefore, we suspect, the heart of man will never be the same.

We find it very easy to wait for the first photographs of the other side of the moon, for we have not yet seen the other side of Lake Louise or the Blue Ridge peak that shows through the cabin window.

We find ourself quite undisturbed about the front-page talk of "controlling the earth from the moon," because we do not believe it. If neither men nor gadgets nor both combined can control the earth from the earth, we fail to see how they will do so from the moon.

It is exciting talk, indeed, the talk of man's advance toward space. But one little step in man's advance toward man—that, we think, would be truly exciting. Let those who wish try to discover the composition of a lunar crater; we would settle for discovering the true mind of a Russian commissar or the inner heart of a delinquent child.

There is, after all, another side—a dark side—to the human spirit, too. Men have hardly begun to explore these regions; and it is going to be a very great pity if we advance upon the bright side of the moon with the dark side of ourselves, if the cargo in the first rockets to reach there consists of fear and chauvinism and suspicion. Surely we ought to have our credentials in order, our hands very clean, and perhaps a prayer for forgiveness on our lips as we prepare to open the ancient vault of the shining moon.

—Eric Sevareid, *"The Dark Side of the Moon"*

PRACTICE

1. In the essay collection, read whichever of the essays by Carson, Baker, Brooks, and Allsop your teacher assigns. For each selection you read, write a one- or two-sentence answer to each of the following questions:

    a. If you could meet the writer, what kind of person would you expect him to be?

    b. What is the main point or points he is trying to communicate in the essay?

    c. How much use does he make of similes and metaphors, and what do they contribute to the essay's ability to communicate his ideas?

    d. What do you like the most or find the most effective in the essay?

    e. What do you like the least or find the least effective in the essay?

2. Write one simile and one metaphor for three of the following subjects. Don't use comparisons you've heard or read before; try for something fresh and different. Depend on your own unique experience and knowledge for materials to compare your subject to; and in seeking particular points of similarity to stress, let your imagination run free.

    a. The ugliest building on the campus — select a specific building, and name it

    b. Your girl friend's or boy friend's smile

    c. The latest dance

    d. Your own personality

    e. Television

    f. Baseball, football, or basketball fans

    g. Your favorite pet

    h. A teacher you particularly like or dislike

   i. Your roommate

   j. Your car

3. On two or three of the following subjects, write a paragraph in which you use similes and metaphors (not necessarily both in each paragraph) to communicate your ideas and observations.

   a. An embarrassing experience
   b. A celebrity at a party
   c. A job interview
   d. Your views on a current national or international political issue
   e. A favorite athlete in action
   f. A politician you despise
   g. A teacher whose methods you find ineffective
   h. A friend you feel sorry for
   i. Some aspect of our polluted environment
   j. Your favorite car

9

Recognition
of
Relationships

Analogy is often defined as an extended simile or metaphor, but this definition is vague and misleading. It suggests that analogy is simply a simile or a metaphor stretched out at greater length or developed in more detail; and, indeed, this fuzzy distinction does seem to hold up in many instances. But it falls down in just as many and probably more, and a careful look at both figurative language and analogy reveals that something different happens in each, that each communicates a different kind of meaning. The terms themselves point to this subtle but real difference: figurative language, figures of speech, emphasizes figures, images — that is, pictures in the imagination. Analogy — *ana*, according to and *logos*, ratio, relation — stresses relationship or principle. In other words, figurative language defines one thing in terms of something similar by concentrating on *particular sensuous details* perceived in the imagination; analogy goes beyond such details to concentrate on the *common principle* or *relationship* or *process* which links or animates them.

Still another way to understand the difference between figurative language and analogy is to discover the inadequacy of the usual — and generally unquestioned — definition of a simile: a comparison using *like* or *as*. The trouble is that you can have two different kinds of comparison using *like* or *as* — and they can't both be similes. When Einstein observes that splitting atoms is *like* shooting birds in the dark in a place where there are few birds, he communicates a different kind of meaning than Conrad's "the ship, a fragment detached from the earth, went on lonely and swift *like* a small planet." Conrad is not trying to say that the ship is related to the ocean of water in the same way that a planet is related to the ocean of space, that the same forces hold both objects in place and propel them; he is simply selecting the particular observable details of a planet's isolation in vast space and its relentless speed in orbit to define and emphasize the ship's position and movement. Conversely, Einstein is not trying to define atoms as bird-like or atom-smashers in terms of hunters stalking their prey; he is pointing out the almost incredible difficulty of splitting atoms by comparing this abstruse scientific problem to the familiar activity of hunting, but hunting altered in situation and action to present it as extraordinarily difficult. In other words, he is using details from hunting birds not to say something about the details of splitting atoms but rather to stress the *principle* of difficulty common to both activities. A comparison using *like* or *as*, then, can be either a simile or an analogy, depending on the kind of meaning it communicates. If the comparison centers on particular points of similarity sensuously perceived in the imagination, it is, like Conrad's, essentially figurative and a simile; but if it goes beyond such similar details to common principles or relationships informing them, it is, like Einstein's, an analogy.

Let's look at another example of how analogy works. In arguing that anthropologists should study man not in books or in laboratories or among primitive tribes but in their own hearts and in the doings of their own people, G. K. Chesterton declares that "when a man has discovered why men in Bond Street wear black hats he will at the same moment have discovered why men in Timbuctoo wear red feathers." Chesterton is not saying that men in Bond street are *like* or *are* men in Timbuctoo simply because both wear something on their heads; the specific resemblance to which he points is much too superficial for a good simile or metaphor. But he is suggesting that a common principle leads each group of men to wear what they do — that different men in different cultures wear different headgear for similar ceremonial reasons. He is, in other words, supporting his general argument with a specific analogy.

Here, too, is the principal use and value of analogy: illustration and corroboration. To illustrate an idea or to support an argument, you find another similar at several points and then generalize on the similarities. Whenever, for example, someone thinks Russian or Communist Chinese policies are being insufficiently blocked by the West, he is likely to make an analogy between that situation and the Munich Pact of 1938. At that time, he will argue, Great Britain and France tried to prevent war by appeasing Hitler but succeeded only in convincing him of their weakness, thereby making World War II inevitable. If, therefore, we fail to resist firmly any communist expansion, even at the risk of war, we will be guilty of similar appeasement and make another war inevitable anyway. In a sense, Western policy towards the communist nations since the late 1940's has been largely a working out of the Munich analogy. Similarly, the Japanese attack on Pearl Harbor in 1941 is the analogy behind much of contemporary America's almost endless vigilance and infinite preparation against another surprise attack.

Analogy, therefore, is a powerful and enormously influential technique. Like strained or mixed metaphor, however, it too can be dangerous. If it is based on inessential or insufficient similarities or on superficial principles and relationships, the illustration or corroboration it provides will be specious or shallow. You cannot, for example, say anything very meaningful about gasoline with an analogy involving water. Again, the analogy often drawn between the effects of debt on a family and on a nation is convincing only to the degree that it ignores the vast and fundamental differences between a family and a nation.

Such analogies are common in politics and advertising and in everyday conversation. It's easy for the unwary to be taken in by them, and it's just as easy for a careless writer to use them himself. Nevertheless, analogy can be an invaluable way to think about any subject you have to write on. By forcing you to think about it in terms of similarities and equivalents in your own knowledge and experience, analogy works like metaphor to involve you creatively in the subject and to identify the elements of it you are best fitted to write about. Furthermore, in writing about your subject, you can use analogy not only to illustrate or to support specific points, as in Chesterton's analogy, but also as the organizing technique for your treatment of the whole subject. Suppose, for instance, you want to describe the process by which a bill becomes a law in the American Congress. You could use the biological processes of labor and parturition as analogies for the principal stages in the bill's passage into law; or you could organize and develop the whole essay as a single unifying analogy detailing the bill's evolution from conception to christening.

Analogies, then, can be long or short, simple or involved, depending on your particular purposes in using them. They can be simple statements, like Chesterton's ceremonial analogy, in which the common principle or relationship is clearly implied or is made clear by the context in which it functions. Or they can be long and detailed, like this of Thoreau's from the "Conclusion" of *Walden*:

The life in us is like the water in the river. It may rise this year higher than man has ever known it, and flood the parched uplands; even this may be the eventful year, which will drown out all our muskrats. It was not always dry land where we dwell. I see far inland the banks which the stream anciently washed, before science began to record its freshets. Every one has heard the story which has gone the rounds of New England, of a strong and beautiful bug which came out of the dry leaf of an old table of appletree wood, which had stood in a farmer's kitchen for sixty years, first in Connecticut, and afterward in Massachusetts, — from an egg deposited in the living tree many years earlier still, as appeared by counting the annual layers beyond it; which was heard gnawing out for several weeks, hatched perchance by the heat of an urn. Who does not feel his faith in a resurrection and immortality strengthened by hearing of this? Who knows what beautiful and winged life, whose egg has been buried for ages under many concentric layers of woodenness in the dead dry life of society, deposited at first in the alburnum of the green and living tree, which has been gradually converted into the semblance of its well-seasoned tomb, — heard perchance gnawing out now for years by the astonished family of man, as they sat round the festive board, — may unexpectedly come forth from amidst society's most trivial and handselled furniture, to enjoy its perfect summer life at last!

Analogy, then, is a vivid and powerful technique, and it is useful both in thinking about a subject and also in writing on it. Before you write, think about your subject analogically, both in total and in its parts, until you find analogies whose comparisons are both essential and convincing. Then use the best ones in writing about your subject. Like metaphor, analogy can extend the range and significance of your thought and give you the materials to express it with clarity and interest.

In the following essay, Jacob Bronowski argues that metaphor and analogy are the central forms of thought by which both science and art find order in chaos. Read the essay carefully, and relate its main points to this and the preceding chapter's discussion of figurative language and analogy.

THE CREATIVE MIND IN SCIENCE
AND ART / *Jacob Bronowski*

No scientific theory is a collection of facts. It will not even do to call a theory true or false in the simple sense in which every fact is either so or not so. The Epicureans held that matter is made of atoms two thousand years ago and we are now tempted to say that their theory was true. But if we do so, we confuse their notion of matter with our own. John Dalton in 1808 first saw the structure of matter as we do today, and what he took from the ancients was not their theory but something richer, their image: the atom. Much of what was in Dalton's mind was as vague as the Greek notion, and quite as mistaken. But he suddenly gave life to the new facts of chemistry and the ancient theory together, by fusing them to give what neither had: a coherent picture of how matter is linked and built up from different kinds of atoms. The act of fusion is the creative act.

All science is the search for unity in hidden likenesses. The search may be on a grand scale, as in the modern theories which try to link the fields of gravitation and electro-magnetism. But we do not need to be browbeaten by the scale of science. There are discoveries to be made by snatching a small likeness from the air too, if it is bold enough. In 1932 the Japanese physicist Yukawa wrote a paper which can still give heart to a young scientist. He took as his starting point the known fact that waves of light can sometimes behave as if they were separate pellets. From this he reasoned that the forces which hold the nucleus of an atom together might sometimes also be observed as if they were solid pellets. A schoolboy can see how thin Yukawa's analogy is, and his teacher would be severe with it. Yet Yukawa without a blush calculated the mass of the pellet he expected to see, and waited. He was right; his meson was found, and a range of other mesons, neither the existence nor the nature of which had been suspected before. The likeness had borne fruit.

The scientist looks for order in the appearances of nature by exploring such likenesses. For order does not display itself of itself; if it can be said to be there at all, it is not there for the mere looking. There is no way of pointing a finger or a camera at it; order must be discovered and, in a deep sense, it must be created. What we see, as we see it, is mere disorder.

This point has been put trenchantly in a fable by Professor Karl Popper. Suppose that someone wished to give his whole life to science. Suppose that he therefore sat down, pencil in hand, and for the next twenty, thirty, forty years recorded in notebook after notebook everything that he could observe. He may be supposed to leave out nothing: today's humidity, the racing results, the level of cosmic radiation and the stock market prices and the look of Mars, all would be there. He would have compiled the most careful record of nature that has ever been made; and, dying in the calm certainty of a life well spent, he would of course leave his notebooks to the Royal Society. Would the Royal Society thank him for the treasure of a lifetime of observation? It would not. It would refuse to open his notebooks at all, because it would know without looking that they contain only a jumble of disorderly and meaningless items.

Science finds order and meaning in our experience, and sets about this in quite a different way. It sets about it as Newton did in the story which he himself told in his old age, and of which the schoolbooks give only a caricature. In the year 1665, when Newton was twenty-two, the plague broke out in southern England, and the University of Cambridge was closed. Newton therefore spent the next eighteen months at home, removed from traditional learning, at a time when he was impatient for knowledge and, in his own phrase: "I was in the prime of my age for invention." In this eager, boyish mood, sitting one day in the garden of his widowed mother, he saw an apple fall. So far the books have the story right; we think we even know the kind of apple; tradition has it that it was a Flower of Kent. But now they miss the crux of the story. For what struck the young Newton at the sight was not the thought that the apple must be drawn to the earth by gravity; that conception was older than Newton. What struck him was the conjecture that the same force of gravity, which reaches to the top of the tree, might go on reaching out beyond the earth and its air, endlessly into space. Gravity might reach the moon: this was Newton's new thought; and it might be gravity which holds the moon in her orbit. There and then he calculated what force from the earth would hold the moon, and compared it with the known force of gravity at tree height. The forces agreed; Newton says laconically: "I found they answer pretty nearly." Yet they agreed only nearly: the likeness and the approximation go together, for no likeness is exact. In Newton's sentence modern science is full grown.

It grows from a comparison. It has seized a likeness between two unlike appearances; for the apple in the summer garden and the grave moon overhead are surely as unlike in their movements as two things can be. Newton traced in them two expressions of a single concept, gravitation: and the concept (and the unity) are in that sense his free creation. The progress of science is the discovery at each step of a new order which gives unity to what had long seemed unlike. Faraday did this when he closed the link between electricity and magnetism. Clerk Maxwell did it when he linked both with light. Einstein linked time and space, mass with energy, and the path of light past the sun with the flight of a bullet; and spent his dying years in trying to add to these likenesses another, which would find a single imaginative order between the equations of Clerk Maxwell and his own geometry of gravitation.

When Coleridge tried to define beauty, he returned always to one deep thought: beauty, he said, is "unity in variety." Science is nothing else than the search to discover unity in the wild variety of nature — or more exactly, in the variety of our experience. Poetry, painting, the arts are the same search, in Coleridge's phrase, for unity in variety. Each in its own way looks for likenesses under the variety of human experience. What is a poetic image but the seizing and the exploration of a hidden likeness, in holding together two parts of a comparison which are to give depth each to the other? When Romeo finds Juliet in the tomb, and thinks her dead, he uses in his heartbreaking speech the words:

Death that hath suckt the honey of thy breath.

The critic can only haltingly take to pieces the single shock which this image carries. The young Shakespeare admired Marlowe, and Marlowe's Faustus had said of the ghostly kiss of Helen of Troy that it sucked forth his soul. But that is a pale image; what Shakespeare has done is to fire it with the single word honey. Death is a bee at the lips of Juliet, and the bee is an insect that stings; the sting of death was a commonplace phrase when Shakespeare wrote. The sting is there, under the image; Shakespeare has packed it into the word honey; but the very word rides powerfully over its own undertones. Death is a bee that stings other people, but it comes to Juliet as if she were a flower; this is the moving thought under the instant image. The creative mind speaks in such thoughts. . . .

The discoveries of science, the works of art are explorations — more, are explosions — of a hidden likeness. The discoverer or the artist presents in them two aspects of nature and fuses them into one. This is the act of creation, in which an original thought is born, and it is the same act in original science and original art. But it is not therefore the monopoly of the man who wrote the poem or who made the discovery. On the contrary, I believe this view of the creative act to be right because it alone gives a meaning to the act of appreciation. The poem or the discovery exists in two moments of vision: the moment of appreciation as much as that of creation; for the appreciator must see the movement, wake to the echo which was started in the creation of the work. In the moment of appreciation we live again the moment when the creator saw and held the hidden likeness. When a simile takes us aback and persuades us together, when we find a juxtaposition in a picture both odd and intriguing, when a theory is at once fresh and convincing, we do not merely nod over someone else's work. We re-enact the creative act, and we ourselves make the discovery again. At bottom, there is no unifying likeness there until we too have seized it, we too have made it for ourselves.

How slipshod by comparison is the notion that either art or science sets out to copy nature. If the task of the painter were to copy for men what they see, the critic could make only a single judgment: either that the copy is right or that it is wrong. And if science were a copy of fact, then every theory would be either right or wrong, and would be so forever. There would be nothing left for us to say but this is so or is not so. No one who has read a page by a good critic or a speculative scientist can ever again think that this barren choice of yes or no is all that the mind offers.

Reality is not an exhibit for man's inspection, labeled: "Do not touch." There are no appearances to be photographed, no experiences to be copied, in which we do not take part. We re-make nature by the act of discovery, in the poem or in the theorem. And the great poem and the deep theorem are new to every reader, and yet are his own experiences, because he himself re-creates them. They are the marks of unity in variety; and in the instant when the mind seizes this for itself, in art or in science, the heart misses a beat.

Bronowski illustrates clearly and eloquently the shaping values of both figurative language and analogy as central thought processes. There remains, however, a particular problem, one I mentioned in the beginning of the chapter — the difficulty that sometimes arises of distinguishing between similes, metaphors, and analogies. Not many people, of course, whether thinking or writing, worry to begin with about using such expressions. They simply want to understand or to communicate clearly and thus come naturally to the search for comparisons which leads to figures and analogies. It is necessary to be able to distinguish between them, then, not in order to contrive them on demand like putting raisins in rice pudding but in order to decide which to use when your thinking moves in comparative directions and to recognize and appreciate them more fully in your reading.

Of the three, the easiest to identify is the metaphor. Its fusion process, in which something is defined or described directly in terms of something else, creates a form clearly different from the simile and the analogy. In these, the comparison process works without the metaphor's point-by-point fusion; and if the comparison proceeds without the equals-sign of *like, as,* or *as if,* it is an analogy. The real problem, then, is distinguishing between non-metaphorical comparisons using *like, as,* or *as if.* Here, too, the difficulty is usually more apparent than real: if the comparison transfers specific features or qualities from some concrete image to whatever is being defined or described, it is a simile; if the comparison transfers general principles or relationships from a pattern of imagery or ideas to whatever is being defined or described, it is an analogy. To distinguish between these expressions, then, look first for metaphor. If a given expression is not a metaphor but obviously a comparison, look for *like, as,* or *as if;* without them, the expression is probably an analogy. If one of these terms is used, check on what meaning is primarily transferred: specific features or qualities make the expression a simile; general principles or relationships make it an analogy.

Read the following paragraphs, and underline any analogies. Could the ideas in these passages be communicated as clearly and concisely without the analogies?

From the girl's viewpoint, sex is closer to business. (This isn't shocking; business is the most respectable thing around.) Consciously or not, she regards her body as a parcel of real estate which will command a better price on a long-term basis. A short lease will buy fewer rights per date dollar. Practice varies with the individual, but I've compiled a roughly representative rate chart: The casual dater is accorded a goodnight kiss, a mere romantic token; the steady may neck (a generic term for kisses and caresses qualifying for the motion-picture seal); the fiancé holds petting privileges (petting is necking with territorial concessions); the husband, finally, as the holder of a life contract, is under no restraints.

— Frederic Morton, *"The Art of Courtship"*

It should be emphasized that incomes are normally judged from a relative and not from an absolute standpoint. Grades are relative within the class: to get all A's in the first grade is as meritorious as to get all A's in the twelfth, but absolutely this does not mean that the work of the first grader is equal in value to the work of the twelfth grader; so, in the same way, the young doctor or typist is not measured against John D. Rockefeller, Jr., or Doris Duke (or whoever today has the highest income in the United States) but against other doctors starting in practice at the same time, other typists who have been in the office about the same time. Competition is still primarily among near equals.

The analogy with school life can be carried further. Just as in school, success in one grade qualifies one for entry into the tougher competition of the next grade, and so on indefinitely, so success in one area of adult life qualifies one for competition in the next "income bracket" or professional group. Success is always relative, never absolute. There are practically no positions in American life where it will be generally conceded that a person has achieved final success and need make no further effort. There is always a higher grade.

— Geoffrey Gorer, *"Success and the Dollar"*

When a ship founders it settles slowly; the spars, the masts, the rigging float away. On the ocean floor of death the bleeding hull bedecks itself with jewels; remorselessly the anatomic life begins. What was ship becomes the nameless indestructible.

Like ships, men founder time and again. Only memory saves them from complete dispersion. Poets drop their stitches in the loom, straws for drowning men to grasp as they sink into extinction. Ghosts climb back on watery stairs, make imaginary ascents, vertiginous drops, memorize numbers, dates, events, in passing from gas to liquid and back again. There is no brain capable of registering the changing changes. Nothing happens in the brain, except the gradual rust and detrition of the cells. But in the mind, worlds unclassified, undenominated, unassimilated, form, break, unite, dissolve and harmonize ceaselessly. In the mind-world ideas are the indestructible elements which form the jewelled constellations of the interior life. We move within their orbits, freely if we follow their intricate patterns, enslaved or possessed if we try to subjugate them. Everything external is but a reflection projected by the mind machine.

—Henry Miller, *"The Creative Life"*

PRACTICE

1. In the essay collection, read whichever of the essays by Fromm, Haldane, Shepherd, and White your teacher assigns. For each selection you read, write a one- or two-question answer to each of the following questions:

   a. If you could meet the writer, what kind of person would you expect him to be?
   b. What is the main point or points he is trying to communicate in the essay?
   c. How much does he use analogy, and how important are the analogies in communicating his ideas clearly, concisely, and interestingly.
   d. What do you like the most or find the most effective in the essay?
   e. What do you like the least or find the least effective in the essay?

2. Choose *three* of the following subjects; and for each, write an analogy explaining your views on it.

   a. The current economic situation
   b. Conditions on your campus
   c. A current national political issue on which you have strong opinions
   d. A current international issue or situation
   e. Student–teacher relationships on your campus
   f. Man's pollution of his environment
   g. Space travel and exploration
   h. Current fashions in dress
   i. The role of the individual in a technological society
   j. Contemporary popular music

3. Thoreau points out that "the roots of *letters* are *things*. Natural objects and phenomena are the original symbols or types which express our thoughts and feelings . . ." To explore the roots of your own experience and knowledge and to gain practice in writing concretely, figuratively, and analogically, write a series of one- or two-page sense impressions. Do each sense separately; that is, as far as possible, describe something you've seen *or* heard *or* tasted, not a combination of several

senses. As much as you can, try to find words which will do more than just explain your sensuous experience: find the specific and concrete words, the figures of speech and the analogies, which will evoke that experience directly in a reader's imagination. In short, make your reader not only *understand* your subject but also *share* it with you. Read the following sense impressions, written by students, and then see what you can do.

SIGHT / *Dorinda Gray*

In the spring, the world is "mud-luscious and puddle-wonderful." I like to look at puddles spread about. It is as if someone sets out shallow pans to catch the raindrops that fall through the leaks in heaven. Sometimes the puddles are round—like big pizza pans. Sometimes, they're square cooky sheets. Spilling out of the pans and making little lakes, the water turns a penny-brown as if coined in 1924 and run through many hands. Of course, if I had to rinse off buildings and birds and trees and buses, I wouldn't look beauty-parlor fresh, either. Raindrops are busy workmen; they leave the world spring-fresh and deserve their slumber in lazy puddles. But the most fun is to wake them up in ripples of laughter as two boots nudge their sides or tickle their middle. One must be careful, though, for if the step is too heavy and painful, they will pick up the nearest thing at hand—a splash—and throw it at you.

SOUND / *Susan Hepler*

It is two o'clock in the morning. The howling wind is hurling gravel against the window like a mad drummer beating a wild staccato tattoo on a snare drum. The one yellow fluorescent light hums and buzzes a deep bass note and a few notes above that drones the electric clock. Someone suppresses a frantic squealing giggle as the soft click of hard-soled slippers passes by the door. The radiator hisses and heaves great wheezes of hot air into the room and then retires to recoup its losses, making hollow clangs like a blacksmith hammering cold steel in a long tunnel. The electric blanket whistles and clicks intermittently as I turn over on my squeaky-springed bed. Far down the hall a door booms shut and the sharp "ka-tich" of the lock echoes down the dark, empty corridor. And, as I drop off to sleep, I can hear the faint moan of truck horns—harbor sounds to my imagination set free by sleep.

TASTE / *Horace Albaugh*

The taste of a girl's lips . . . the sweet, perfumish flavor of creamy lipstick . . . or the slightly bitter taste of lips that have cradled a cigaret and bear traces of nicotine . . . or the wet, salty taste of lips that have been kissed by the spray of sea water . . . or lips that are sour from lemonade or sour-sweet from pickle . . . or the sterile tastelessness of dry lips that are closed and hide also the taste of the mouth . . . or the harshly clean taste of lips that have caught a smear of toothpaste . . .

And there is the taste of lips that are drab and waxy from Chap-Stick . . . or heavy with the earthy, scented taste of Clearasil which has been carelessly applied to a lip-line blemish.

And there is the sharp taste of lips that have caressed the mouth of a bottle of straight gin . . . and the sweeter taste of lips wet from rum . . . and lips with the solid, slightly acid flavor of black coffee . . . lips sweet and sugary from fudge.

Lips with the thick, salty taste of tears.

And, rarest of all, are the unpainted lips, uncorrupted by food-tastes and drink-tastes: the natural, flesh-sweet flavor.

10

Evidence

and

Extension

It should be fairly clear to you now that concrete words, figures of speech, and analogy can be profitable and exciting ways to work with almost any subject you have to write on — to find your individual relationship to it and then to express it in your individual style. Two slightly different but related techniques with similar functions and goals are exemplification and allusion. Concrete words focus on literal and objective details; figurative language makes a comparison to or a fusion with particular concrete similarities; analogy suggests common principles or relationships within either similar or different details; and exemplification and allusion illustrate a point by expressing it in different terms. Both exemplifications and allusion are essentially ways of giving evidence for or illustrations of an argument or discussion; and like the other techniques, they are invaluable basic tools for thinking and writing. If you think about a subject in terms of examples and allusions from your own experience and knowledge, you will discover in the process which aspects of it you are most qualified both objectively and subjectively to discuss; and if you use such examples and allusions in your writing, you will thereby add to its individuality, give it greater clarity and interest, and widen its intellectual and imaginative scope.

EXEMPLIFICATION

An example is explanation by representation — that is, it explains an idea in terms of particular and specific details which reflect it as their unifying meaning. In effect, then, examples are a kind of evidence, particular instances standing for general ideas. An example can be a simple series of details introduced explicitly by expressions like *for example* or *for instance*, as in the following passage by Meryl Smith, a student writer:

The plot, as well as the characterization in "The Fly," is developed to serve Katherine Mansfield's purpose in creating the story. The incidents comprising it are planned and follow each other logically with causal relationships. For example, Woodifield has something to tell the boss but cannot remember what. However, when the boss produces the whiskey Woodifield is detained and thus lingers long enough to remember. Had he not been detained he would have left without remembering to tell the boss of the report of his son's grave and the story could not have continued. Also, at the time when the boss was desperately trying to renew his grief for his son, he happened to notice a fly in his inkpot. Had he not noticed this, he would not have been distracted and the story could not have continued as it did. Thus, the actions of "The Fly" were carefully selected and arranged by the author to fulfill her purpose.

On the other hand, examples can be complicated and implicit:

There are two kinds of men, those who live for appearances and comfort and those who live in a world of raw realities slugging their way to the graveyard proud, and sinking their teeth in life like it was Kansas City sirloin medium rare. The members of the group who go for Sunday afternoon drives with the kids and bowl on Thursdays can't for the life of them understand *how* the others ever busted loose. They know *why* well enough, but of course they won't even admit that much, the most of them. They talk as though they're perfectly satisfied with the squirrel-cage routine of life at the office and the Elks and, by God, pretty soon they *are* satisfied. Meanwhile cousin Slim, who "was always kinda harum-scarum," or brother Bill, who "was pretty erratic as a kid," is slogging the seven seas in rusty old tramp steamers, laying pipe line across the Persian sands, building bridges, booming oil in Manitoba, or, close to home, railroading or steamboating or pulling the transports across the plains, and sucking in a hundred dollars' worth of fresh air a minute. I guess it boils down to those who thrive on taking chances and those who turn pale at the thought.

In this passage from *River in My Blood*, Richard Bissell obviously favors and romanticizes the second of the two categories into which he divides men — "those who thrive on taking chances." He makes this clear in the introductory definition of his categories in the first sentence and again in the summary definition in the last sentence. In between he uses exemplifying details which not only illustrate the contrast between the two kinds of men but also subtly support it. The activities describing the first kind of men are those of "the members of the group," of the impersonal "they." The other kind, however, are represented by individuals, by the personal "cousin Slim" and "brother Bill." After visualizing

Bissell's examples, it's hard not to sneer with him at the stay-at-homes "who turn pale at the thought" of taking chances.

Examples, then, can be simple and direct or complicated and subtle. Moreover, they can be actual or hypothetical — that is, you can draw them from real life or make them up in your imagination. Sometimes you may want to use a single highly detailed example to illustrate or to support an idea; other times, you may want to use several less extensive examples. Whatever kind of method you use, however, be sure of two things: *first*, be relevant and sufficient. Make certain that your examples are clearly and essentially relevant to the ideas they are supposed to illustrate or support and that you have enough details to make them convincing. Remember that an idea you are exemplifying is basically an inductive leap — that is, it's a generalization from specific evidence. Your examples must therefore provide particular details which justify the generalizations they explain. *Second*, be concrete. Fill your examples with sensuous details: name persons and places, be specific about observations and actions. The more sensuously you can embody an idea, the more clearly you know it, and the more vividly your reader will understand it.

ALLUSION

Still another way to think before you write and then to extend the range and interest of your writing is allusion. This means supplementing your own ideas and experience with references to the similar thought and experiences of others particularly as expressed in literature and in history. Allusion makes the whole range of human knowledge and expression a bank account for you to draw on at will — it is a way of borrowing from others and getting the interest yourself.

Direct allusion is an explicit reference or a direct quotation. Describing the "pleasant agony" of writing, John Mason Brown uses both techniques effectively:

There is a passage in *The Goncourt Journals* which has haunted me since I read it. Envy has kept it green for me, and wonder (or is it disbelief?) has kept it alive. I have in mind Gautier's boast that he never thought about what he was going to write. "I take up my pen," he explained, "and write. I am a man of letters and am presumed to know my job . . . I throw my sentences into the air and I can be sure that they will come down on their feet, like cats. . . . Look here: here's my script: not a word blotted."

When I think of the one-legged kittens that land on my pages; when I remember the false starts, illegible scribblings, unfinished sentences, discarded drafts, changed constructions, and altered words which mark my beginnings, my continuings, and my endings, I blush with shame and, like the voyagers in Dante's realm, abandon all hope.

Clearly, the quotation from Gautier and the reference to Dante broaden the scope of Brown's point and heighten its impact on the reader.

Another and more subtle technique is indirect allusion — that is, implicit references or indirect quotations. I could refer implicitly to the Japanese assault on Pearl Harbor, for example, simply by mentioning sneak attacks — if I were writing for an American audience. And if I wrote that the early days of 1942 were times that tried our national soul, I would be indirectly quoting Tom Paine's "These are times that try men's souls" and thereby suggesting that our participation in World War II was essentially another episode in an unending struggle for freedom.

As you think about your subject, then, whatever it may be, see if you can recall from your reading and studying any expressions or information which illuminate it or any aspect of it. Moreover, don't depend on your memory alone; use source works like Bartlett's *Familiar Quotations*. Look up your subject in the index and check on any references which seem in any way to bear on it. Not only will you find allusions to use when you write but even more valuably, reading through a series of quotations related to your subject will stimulate your thinking about it and help you to decide what aspects of it to write on.

As you recall quotations and references or read them in Bartlett's, evaluate them for *three* criteria: one, *relevance* — are they directly related to your subject or to some aspect of it? Two, *signficance* — are their writers of suffecient stature or the events referred to of sufficient importance to contribute something meaningful to anything you might say about the subject? Three, *freshness* — are the quotations and references which interest you fresh and vital, not worn out and made trite by overuse? Searching for and finding such allusions is fun and exciting; and, as with concrete words, metaphor, analogy, and example, it serves you double: *first*, it gives you a way to think about and into any subject you have to write on and helps you identify and concentrate on the aspects of that subject you know best and can write about most effectively. *Second*, allusions give you specific materials which broaden the significance of your writing and sharpen its interest.

Use allusions, then, both in your thinking before you write and also in your writing. Don't overuse them, however; too many will make your writing seem forced and affected and even suggest that you are hiding behind them because you have nothing to say for yourself. Use them judiciously — that is, to illustrate or support your main points — and they will enrich your writing with wisdom and charm.

Read the following paragraphs; and in the margins, put a check beside each example and an X beside each allusion. How much do these examples and allusions add to the clarity and interest of the passages?

There is probably a real quarrel between the arts and technology — what could Vermeer make of a General Electric kitchen? — but surely there is none between art and science, nor between their respective intentions and methods. Science does not represent a system that will ultimately freeze art and the other witchcrafts out, but a method that supplements, and will always need supplementing by, the artist's ancient and unverifiable insights. There are questions that science not only cannot answer but doesn't know how to ask; there are kinds of truth with which it should not concern itself, and which, if it does concern itself with them, go dead in its hands. The world, as John Foxe remarked in *The Book of Martyrs,* is a vast nursery, and men are children engaged in trying to spell God with the wrong blocks. In that effort, necessarily doomed to failure, the arts are as important as the vowels are in the alphabet. We do not help by asking our children to spell God with nothing but the consonants of science.

—Wallace Stegner, *"One Way to Spell Man"*

The huge football factories might make more money than Brown, but one can never be certain. The rank dishonesty of, say, Big Ten institutions would turn any inquiry into a farce. It is not inconceivable, however, that even those institutions do not make much money at football. It must cost Michigan State at least 200,000 customers just to field a team, and this is not computing anything for the millions of hours of voluntary labor that go into the formation of that team.

But let us suppose that some money is being made by the football factories. How about the tiny colleges? How about the hundreds of institutions all over the country — floundering even now in hopeless quantites of red ink? How much do they spend feeding this monster, under the impression that football develops character, or the full personality, or Christ-like meekness?

If football could be discussed simply as a sport, we could raise other questions, too. Are college and universities the best qualified institutions to sponsor it? There are, after all, plenty of other institutions. And even if you abolish the D.A.R., the FBI, the Navy, the fraternities and all other codifiers of moronity, you could still find plenty of institutions — such as towns — which could sponsor a sport like football without producing this terrible confusion of values which exists in universities. Wouldn't it be wise to hand the job over to someone else?

—Wade Thompson, *"My Crusade Against Football"*

Primarily a team game, baseball is also the game for the individualist. The team play is essential, and when you watch closely you can see it, but the focus is usually on one man. A base runner streaks for second with the pitch, falls away while in full stride, and slides in in a cloud of dust, baseman stabbing at him with gloved hand, umpire bending to peer through the murk and call the play; an outfielder runs deep and far, arching ball coming down — apparently — just out of his reach, trajectories of fielder and baseball coming miraculously together at the last, gloved hand going out incredibly to pick the ball out of the air; a pitcher who has been getting his lumps looks about at filled bases, glowers at the batter, and then sends one in that is struck at and missed . . . always, some individual is trying for an astounding feat of athletic prowess and, now and then, actually accomplishing it.

Hence baseball celebrates the vicarious triumph. The spectator can identify himself completely with the player, and the epochal feat becomes, somehow, an achievement of his own. Babe Ruth, mocking the Chicago Cubs, pointing to the distant bleachers and then calmly hitting the ball into those bleachers, took a host of Walter Mittys with him when he jogged around the bases. (There is some dispute about this, to be sure; he was jawing with the Cubs, but purists say he did not actually call his shot. This makes no difference whatever.) It was the same when old Grover Cleveland Alexander, the all-but-washed-up veteran of many baseball wars, came into the seventh inning of a decisive World Series game, found the bases filled with Yankees, and struck out Tony Lazzeri, going on to win game and Series; and this was after a wearing night on the tiles, Alexander having supposed that his work was over until next spring. Many an aging fan shared in Old Alex's triumph.

—Bruce Catton, *"The Great American Game"*

Romance has become as large a component of the American dream as success. Road signs shout romance, transmitters croon it, juke-bokes yowl it. Romance bulges on Cinemascope screens, flickers from TV sets, gleams on magazine covers. Laboratories hum from coast to coast making cheeks more kissable, hands more touchable, legs more lookable. Factories whir to resculpt waistlines, bosomize bosoms, cleopatrize eyes. A whole galaxy of industries labors to lure him to her with perfumes, parasols, pendants; her to him with the checks on his shirt, the monogram on his belt, the shaving lotion on his jaws. Under all this pressure, how pitiful the American who cannot command the smile of a sexpot.

Romance, again like success, is a glamorous but relentless necessity in America. Through free enterprise the lowliest newsboy makes his million; through love the homely wallflower acquires Prince Charming. Nowhere else on earth are there so few barriers of wealth or class to prevent anyone from kissing the ear of anyone else. And since everyone has a chance, nobody has an excuse for not trying. In a recent movie Humphrey Bogart's screen wife asked him why he was so eager for big money. Bogart intoned the national ethos: "All I know is, if you haven't got it, they call you a bum." And they do. We don't recognize a class below the fairly well-to-do (peasants and proletarians are transatlantic beings), nor is there a self-respecting niche for the nonromantic. A spring night spent in a solitary stroll marks you a drip. The silence of your telephone is something you keep secret, like the rejection of your credit application. Our standard, in romance as in success, is not the median but the top. This is the home of the brave, the rich and the sexy — and none else. So belong, will ya?

—Frederic Morton, *"The Art of Courtship"*

On certain levels of the American race, indeed, there seems to be a positive libido for the ugly, as on other and less Christian levels there is a libido for the beautiful. It is impossible to put down the wallpaper that defaces the average American home of the lower middle class to mere inadvertence, or to the obscene humor of the manufacturers. Such ghastly designs, it must be obvious, give a genuine delight to a certain type of mind. They meet, in some unfathomable way, its obscure and unintelligible demands. They caress it as "The Palms" caresses it, or the art of the movie, or jazz. The taste for them is as enigmatical and yet as common as the taste for dogmatic theology and the poetry of Edgar A. Guest.

Thus I suspect (though confessedly without knowing) that the vast majority of the honest folk of Westmoreland county, and especially the 100% Americans among them, actually admire the houses they live in, and are proud of them. For the same money they could get vastly better ones, but they prefer what they have got. Certainly there was no pressure upon the Veterans of Foreign Wars to choose the dreadful edifice that bears their banner, for there are plenty of vacant buildings along the track-side, and some of them are appreciably better. They might, indeed, have built a better one of their own. But they chose that clapboard horror with their eyes open, and having chosen it, they let it mellow into its present shocking depravity. They like it as it is: beside it, the Parthenon would no doubt offend them. In precisely the same way the authors of the rattrap stadium that I have mentioned made a deliberate choice. After painfully designing and erecting it, they made it perfect in their own sight by putting a completely impossible pent-house, painted a staring yellow, on top of it. The effect is that of a fat woman with a black eye. It is that of a Presbyterian grinning. But they like it.

Here is something that the psychologists have so far neglected: the love of ugliness for its own sake, the lust to make the world intolerable. Its habitat is the United States. Out of the melting pot emerges a race which hates beauty as it hates truth. The etiology of this madness deserves a great deal more study than it has got. There must be causes behind it; it arises and flourishes in obedience to biological laws, and not as a mere act of God. What precisely, are the terms of those laws? And why do they run stronger in America than elsewhere? Let some honest *Privat Dozent* in pathological sociology apply himself to the problem.

—H. L. Mencken, *A Mencken Chrestomathy*

This leads us to the second and equally remarkable transformation that the last ten or fifteen years have brought. As recently as 1947 it was possible for Lecomte de Noüy, in his widely read book *Human Destiny*, to maintain that living things could not possibly arise from "dead" inorganic matter by the operation of purely natural forces. The complexity of even the simplest single-celled organism was so enormous that to expect atoms of carbon, hydrogen, oxygen, and the rest to form one by spontaneous aggregation was much less probable than that Eddington's famous army of simian typists should produce the entire works of Shakespeare at the first attempt. Life's appearance on Earth (or elsewhere) must therefore have been consciously directed and controlled by some organizing force, which it was tempting to identify as the hand of God.

—Arthur C. Clarke, *"Space and the Spirit of Man"*

PRACTICE

1. In the essay collection, read whichever of the essays by Barth, Ciardi, Thurber, and Wolfe your teacher assigns. For each essay you read, write a two- or three-page analysis, concentrating on (1) the essay's main point or points; (2) its author's use of exemplification and allusion;

and (3) what these techniques contribute to its clarity and interest. Don't be disturbed by what may seem a new and strange assignment; if you have been doing the one- or two-sentence answers to the questions on your reading, you have been doing a form of analysis for some time. Analysis means reducing something to its constituent elements — taking something apart to see what makes it work. This process is just as valuable for the would-be writer as it is for the young man who wants to learn about automobiles. He buys an old heap, takes it apart piece by piece, discovers how each part works in itself and with others, and then puts the whole mess back together again.

So it should be for the would-be writer: looking separately and closely at the language, ideas, logic, and structure of a piece of writing by a recognized writer can do much not only to make that writing more meaningful but also to improve your own by increasing your awareness of what goes on in effective writing. Essentially, such analysis is what you have been doing in answering the five questions about the other essays you have read. Here, all you need to do differently is to center your analysis on the three areas indicated above and write the results as a coherent essay instead of as short answers to specific questions. The process is the same; only the form in which you express it differs. Give analysis a real try: it can be immensely valuable to you in a variety of ways, and you may even find it challenging and interesting.

2. From your own experience and knowledge, write examples for two or three of the following topics:

   a. Calmness in an emergency
   b. Courage
   c. Religious faith
   d. Hypocrisy
   e. Vanity
   f. Loyalty to a friend
   g. Failure
   h. Success
   i. Intellectual excitement
   j. Self-sacrifice
   k. Disappointment

3. From your memory or from Bartlett's *Familiar Quotations*, write a quotation or a reference based on a quotation which you could use as an allusion in writing on two or three of the following topics. Don't just state your allusions; incorporate them in sentences or short paragraphs where they can function within a context of meaning to which they give point or extension. Unless the allusion or its source is well known, phrase it so that its identity is clear. Here are two student examples: Andrea Moore, "By Machiavellian tactics, he gained the position he coveted";

Kay Blomquist, "With Emerson, I'll hitch my wagon to a star — if I ever get the wheels fixed." Now see what you can do.

  a. The values of education
  b. The cost of something
  c. The pleasures of literature
  d. The pain of grief
  e. The goodness of people
  f. The values of solitude
  g. The protection of Providence
  h. The uncertainty of the weather
  i. The benefits of science
  j. The need for law and order

4. To keep sharp your ability to use the techniques in the preceding chapters — indeed to give it an even finer cutting edge — practice these techniques by doing a set of "goodies" every other class day or so as long as your instructor thinks you need the training. "Goodies" are one- or two-page exercises containing a simile, a metaphor, an analogy, an example, and an allusion. To help you with these "goodies," here is a set done by Susan Hepler, a student writer; in the main, they are unusually good, but they are a goal *you* can aim at and achieve — if you work at it.

  a. Simile: It seems that we always argue when, like shooting ten Indians for Custer, it doesn't much matter.
  b. Metaphor: It was raining and muddy; little rivulets ambled up to the river's edge and jumped in.
  c. Analogy: Some teachers could make magnificent rugs even if they had never had a lesson from Omar Khayyam. They pull their students up by their woolly heads through the stretched canvas frame of learning and mold them into beautifully flowered patterns. But, in their haste for balance, they forget what even the best of Persian rugmakers know — that only God can make a perfect rug. We might better concentrate on making good yarn before we worry about whole rugs, which have a way of getting walked on anyhow.
  d. Example: Anything worth doing involves uncertainty. In swimming, the hardest thing is letting go of the side of the pool to float free; in thinking, the hardest thing is to let go of a comfortable idea to float free in the stratosphere of doubt.
  e. Allusion: He was a stranger in our midst and he proceeded to make Uriah-Heeps all over us.

Before you begin writing your own, see if you can pick out the "goody" in which Miss Hepler makes a mistake and then identify the technique she is actually using. Then see how often you can come up to her general level; that is, take these "goodies" seriously. They will help to improve your style while you are concentrating on matters of structure, and they will help to remind you to use these techniques in the full essays you will soon be writing.

11

*Structure
and the
Paragraph*

The techniques you have been working with in the preceding chapters are essentially matters of style, ways of establishing you as the person at the center of your writing. This *I-ness* of effective style makes writing much more than mechanical composition; style begins before writing, in the creative thinking by which you find your own way within a subject and identify it with yourself in terms of what you know and want to say about it. Only then, with this *I-ness* at the center controlling it, does style become a matter of writing techniques, of choosing the right words and expressions to mean precisely what *you* want to say.

Moreover, *style* is only one of the legs on which good writing marches: the other is *structure*. The kind of creative thinking necessary for developing the *I-ness* of style can help you discover the aspects of a subject you are best qualified to discuss and give you the means to express them effectively, but you still have the problem of putting your materials together in some clear and meaningful order. Occasionally, these materials will suggest their own best order of development; but most of the time, it will be up to you to give them direction and shape, to arrange them in the most coherent pattern.

In short, good writing demands not only an interesting style but also the coherent development of thought. No matter how engaging or powerful your style may be, if a reader finds your thought difficult to follow, you will soon lose him — unless, for some reason or other, he *has* to read what you've written. And if this happens, you will probably come to regret the impression of yourself you will thereby have given him.

The problem of coherence is a question of order, of *structure;* and in writing they are nearly always imposed, not revealed. Walt Whitman liked to pose as an "organic" writer: I am only the passive medium, he liked to say, through which nature expresses herself. But even Whitman felt bound to improve on nature: he revised *Leaves of Grass* at least nine times! "Chaos is the law of nature," Henry Adams declares; "order is the dream of man"; and despite the paradox in the first clause — or perhaps because of it (chaos and law may not be as contradictory as they seem) — Adams's aphorism can be a useful warning for writers. Let nature take its course in your writing, and most of the time the result will be relative incoherence: better to dream of order and then make your dream come true.

A CLASSICAL STRUCTURE FOR PROSE

By classical here, I don't mean necessarily to evoke echoes of ancient Greece and Rome or to insist that you take Plato or Aristotle for your master — though, as a matter of fact, Aristotle's observation that everything in time and space has a beginning, a middle, and an end suggests the kind of structre I have in mind. By classical, I mean something traditional, something which has proven its value generation after generation, century after century, and thereby become standard. In this sense, at least one structure can certainly be called classical in prose: the structure of introduction, main body, and conclusion. No one has ever devised a consistently better one, and most of the best writers have commonly used it. You might just as well follow their example; if you want to write with order and coherence, you'll come to it in the end anyway, most of the time. Give it half a chance, and it can become as good a friend to you as it has to innumerable others.

PARAGRAPHING

Instead of wading recklessly into a struggle with the problem of structure in a full essay, it would be wiser — and easier — to approach the problem first in a similar but much smaller unit — the paragraph. A good paragraph, after all, is almost an essay in miniature; and if you can't understand and manage effective structure in your paragraphs, you'll have nothing but luck going for you in your essays.

Furthermore, when you write essays and themes, you probably work basically in paragraphs. After creative thinking and careful planning, you begin writing your rough draft. Since you're working with language, it would seem logical to begin with words, build them into sentences, and tie the sentences together in paragraphs. Paradoxically, however, you probably don't think like this at all — or, if you do and are writing badly, this may be one of the reasons. Within the structure of whatever you're writing, paragraphs are the major divisions and sub-divisions of your thought; and since the sentences which make a paragraph must therefore be closely related in relevance, logic, and style, you can hardly expect to write effective sentences without knowing the context which unites them into a paragraph. And, taking the argument one step further, unless you know precisely what you want to do with a sentence, you are unlikely to choose the right words or to build them into the most appropriate sentence structures.

In short, to write effectively, you need to know enough about paragraphing to think about it specifically and to do it proficiently: you must have a working knowledge of core ideas, topic sentences, point of view, tone, unity, coherence, emphasis, and transition. A good paragraph is not a ho-hum indentation, a whimsical break in the wall of your words; it is a reasoned and an ordering act. And on the quality of this act will rest much of your writing's effectiveness.

Moreover, working with paragraphing, even at this elementary level, will acquaint you with and give you practice in the kind of structure that will serve you best in longer and more complex writing. Think of a paragraph as a miniature essay: it should be unified around a central topic; developed coherently through a definite beginning, middle, and end; and hold the reader's interest. And finally, each paragraph must be linked by adequate transitions to those which precede and follow it. When you can write this kind of paragraph, you should be able to extend its structural principles to your essays and themes; and when you can write within this structure with a controlled personal style, you will no longer be a would-be writer: you will be a very good one.

THE CORE IDEA

This is what a paragraph is all about, its principal reason for being. When you indent to begin a new paragraph, you signal the reader, "I'm shifting here — either to a different aspect or emphasis of the idea I've been discussing or to a new idea." It is true that length and complexity dictate a third reason for paragraphing: modern taste dislikes long and complicated paragraphs. Even here, however, breaking an overlong paragraph into shorter units should be related to content; indeed, if a paragraph seems too long or too involved, it is probably because it contains too many ideas, each or some of which require separate treatment in new paragraphs.

The core idea, then, is the central significance you want the reader to get from your paragraph. He won't get your point, however, if you're not sufficiently aware of it to put it there. Know what you want each paragraph to say, then build it around this core idea. When you've finished, the core idea should be clear and should summarize the paragraph; if it fails on either count, your paragraphing is faulty and needs reworking.

The best way to be sure your core idea is clear is to write it down as the *topic sentence*. Sometimes, of course, the topic sentence is implied rather than directly stated; take this paragraph of mine, for instance:

> In the second part of the main body, Steiner again stresses these thematic interrelationships as preface to his primary concern with *The Spire*, Golding's most recent novel. He then summarizes the plot of *The Spire*, comments on its form and style, and discusses what seem to him to be the novel's main strengths and weaknesses. Finally, in the conclusion, he returns to the central idea of the introduction — the concept of a writer's work as a grand design evolving through successive volumes — and speculates on the directions which Golding's work may be taking.

The core idea is simple and obvious — the analysis of the second part of the main body and the conclusion of Steiner's essay; and since I do nothing else in the paragraph such as commenting on or adding to Steiner's points, it needs no explicit topic sentence. Usually, however, and always in relatively long or complex paragraphs, you ought to shine the light of a strong topic sentence on the material in your paragraph.

In addition to focusing on the main point of a paragraph, a good topic sentence does other things for you, too. At the beginning of a paragraph, it establishes your point of view — whether, for example, you are writing personally or objectively, as observer, commentator, or participant — and the tone — formal or informal, serious or humorous, straightforward or ironic. At the end, it can summarize, suggest further implications, or evoke a powerful sense of climax. In other words, the topic sentence can appear anywhere in a paragraph, depending on how you want to use its many functions. But however and wherever you use the topic sentence, its primary purpose is to state the core idea of the paragraph. Whether it be a main point or a sub-division, the core idea is the light of a flashlight, the heat of a match, the force of a blow. Everything in the paragraph — its structure, its details, its development — exists to express this central point.

AMPLIFICATION

Essentially, therefore, a paragraph is the amplification, the detailed development, of the core idea stated in the topic sentence.

Writing a good paragraph presents in effect the same problems raised by the main body of an essay — that is, a good paragraph must also have unity, coherence, and emphasis. As the main body should give unified development to the aspects of the topic expressed in the introduction, the details of a paragraph mst be clearly and essentially relevant to its core idea. Like the main body, too, these details in a paragraph must be organized and developed on principles which give them order and coherence. And a good paragraph, again like a good main body, must be interesting and convincing. In subsequent chapters on introduction, main body, and conclusion, you will work with these problems in the full essay; here, let's look at them in a paragraph from a book review by George Steiner:

> Clearly, this is a book of great beauty and distinction of style. But it is not, I think, a good novel. The fierce excitement which is its theme grows static and rhetorical. We *know* from the first page on that the spire will be built and that Jocelin shall perish in the charring of his will. The very glitter of the language becomes monotonous. I found myself skipping ahead, hoping for some twist of life or modulation of tone. One has the impression of one of those Indian *ragas*, subtle, formal, beautifully played and controlled, but getting nowhere.

The first sentence is obviously transitional; it links this paragraph to the immediately preceding discussion of Golding's style. The second sentence states the core idea in a direct topic sentence which also stresses Steiner's subjective point of view and evaluative tone. The next four sentences amplify the core idea in directly relevant and important details: two thematic and stylistic weaknesses in the novel. Moreover, the fourth and fifth sentences stir the reader's imagination with sharp metaphors. Finally, the last sentence is a definite summarizing conclusion, widening the scope of evaluation beyond Steiner's personal responses by an allusion to another literature. The result is a unified, coherent, and interesting paragraph.

Amplifying a core idea into an effective paragraph like Steiner's, then, imposes several responsibilities on a writer. First, *selecting and expressing details*. The core idea at the heart of a paragraph becomes meaningful to a reader only in terms of the details in which you clothe it. A good topic sentence will give him the main point you're trying to make, but it's in the details by which you support or illustrate it that he will specifically understand that point and your reasons for making it. And his interest in what you're trying to say will depend largely on how you express those details. Make certain, therefore, that the details you use in building a paragraph are directly relevant to its core idea and important aspects of it. Moreover, express these details as concretely and specifically as possible; you want the reader to understand your core idea, but you also want him to care about it, to be interested or to become more interested in it. Wherever you can, then, use metaphors, analogies, examples, allusions, personal experiences, statistics, anecdotes — anything likely to make waves in the reader's intellect or emotions or imagination. Unity and coherence are essential in your paragraphs, but they need not be had at the sacrifice of interest and delight: well-wrought dullness is only the duller for being well-wrought.

Second, *organization.* Choosing the most effective details to amplify your core idea also involves the problem of putting them in the most appropriate order, of arranging them in the most meaningful and coherent pattern. Like the main body again, most of your paragraphs should follow one or several of five basic principles of organization: *chronological, spatial, climactic, dramatic, and logical.* In a paragraph, however, the organizing principle or principles will be implicit in the core idea, which comprises both your topic in the paragraph and also your purpose in discussing it. If, for example, you are describing the appearance of a new sports car, the visual details you choose should be organized spatially; if you are explaining how to change a tire, the functional details should be arranged chronologically from first to last. But an implicit principle of organization won't become explicit by itself; indeed, without your help, it will probably be repudiated in disorder and incoherence. Your responsibility, then, is to know exactly what you want to say in a paragraph and why, and to organize your amplifying details accordingly.

Third, *development.* The distinction between organization and development is real but difficult to define. In general, organization means the structural relationship between the parts of a whole, and development means the process by which something grows or expands. In paragraphing, then, *organization* is the principle governing the order in which the details amplifying the core idea are arranged; *development* is the process by which these details are related to the topic sentence. Both are essential for coherent paragraphing.

Sometimes the topic sentence is implicit; occasionally, it functions best in the middle of the paragraph. Usually, however, a paragraph is most coherent if it begins or ends with the topic sentence. However you *organize* your amplifying details, then, whether chronologically, spatially, climactically, dramatically, or logically, you should *develop* most of your paragraphs either down from the topic sentence or up to it. A "down" paragraph moves from the topic sentence to specific details which support or illustrate it or lead to conclusions drawn from it. This is how Steiner develops the following paragraph:

At present, Golding's place is even higher in America than it is in England. He has replaced Camus and Salinger as the idol of the college bookstore. *Lord of the Flies* has been a password among the young. Theses are starting to grind the living flesh to fine, dead powder. He has touched a particular American nerve.

The first sentence is clearly the topic sentence, and the next three not only illustrate its main point but also lead to the conclusion in the last sentence.

An "up" paragraph moves from specific details to a topic sentence which generalizes or summarizes or concentrates what they imply. Let's look at another example from Steiner's essay:

I say this with diffidence. When dealing with someone of Golding's stature and integrity of purpose, judgment is provisional. I have been rereading *Free Fall* and the purgatorial intimations in *Pincher Martin*. Obviously, some kind of quest is being pursued, and the next novel may give weight to what seems facile and rhetorical in the passion of Dean Jocelin. This is precisely where the notion of an *oeuvre* intervenes. Golding's novels modify each other in mutual response. We are in mid-course, and it would take rashness to assert that one had unraveled the mastering design.

Here, the last sentence is the topic sentence, the central point of the paragraph. The first sentence is transitional, and the second explains in general why Steiner feels diffident about criticizing Golding. The next four specify why such criticism must be provisional, and lead to the specific conclusion in the topic sentence.

Both paragraphs are organized logically; the details of each are arranged in deductive order: a generalization followed by specific examples or reasons leading to a particular conclusion. The first paragraph is developed in the same direction — down from the topic sentence; the second, however, is developed in the opposite direction — up to the topic sentence. In each paragraph, then, *organization* and *development* work together to produce coherence and emphasis.

TRANSITION

Unified and coherent paragraphing also requires clear transition from one paragraph to another and within each paragraph. Transition comes from the Latin *transitio,* meaning the act of going across; and this is what you do whenever you move from one idea or point to another both within and also between your paragraphs. It's the kind of thing that becomes noticeable only when it is ignored or badly done; effective transition succeeds in silence. Good paragraphing thus requires you to make careful and skilful transitions: you must build strong but unobtrusive verbal bridges for your reader to cross on.

You have a variety of materials to build with — for example, repetition of preceding words or phrases, references to preceding points, and linking words and phrases like *here, thus, moreover, again, in effect,* and *on the other hand.* In still another of Steiner's paragraphs, the italicized words are transitional:

The allegory creaks with labored clichés. The spire is the mast of a storm-battered ship. It is a phallus. It ends, in the instant of Jocelin's death, by being the apple tree of man's knowledge and "free fall." Sexual temptation has red hair. Most of the figures are as graphic and flat as playing cards.

That is becoming the main problem of Golding's art. *Allegory* generates a surface strength. *But* it goes hollow unless there is behind it a genuinely complex argument and reading of experience. Golding's *allegoric* fiction renders an incisive but increasingly narrow view of human possibility. *Notably*, it excludes a full treatment of the relations between men and women. The only woman who has ever come alive for me in Golding is Taffy, and all we see of her in *Free Fall* is a few glimpses. *Here again*, Golding's novels fit the pattern of tense masculinity that prevails in Poe, Hawthorne, and Melville.

That refers to the core idea of the preceding paragraph, and *here again* to the earlier discussion of Golding's relationship to the American novel. *Allegory* and *allegoric* repeat a key word from the topic sentence of the preceding paragraph. *But* and *notably* signal a movement in thought from the sentences which precede them, *but* to a contrasting point, and *notably* to a central example. In short (how about this as a transitional phrase to indicate the approach of a summary?), effective transitions link this paragraph to earlier ones and give it a closely knit development which contributes significantly to its unity, coherence, and emphasis. Be sure you build such necessary bridges for your readers.

PARAGRAPHING CHECKLIST

Obviously, paragraphing is neither a simple task nor one you are likely to master without much conscious effort. But it's one of the open secrets of good writing, and if you want to write well for any purpose, you're going to have to face up to its challenges. You can begin by making certain that in its final form, each of your paragraphs passes the following checklist: first, *justification* — is there a reason for the paragraph, or did you just feel like indenting? Does it have a core idea expressing a new point or a sub-division of the preceding one? Second, *opening* — have you given the paragraph a definite and interesting beginning? Do you have a question, a statement, or an assertion as the topic sentence or introducing the details leading up to it? Third, *support and illustration* — have you chosen clearly and significantly relevant details to amplify the core idea? Do you have enough to make your point convincing or to illustrate it adequately? Have you expressed it emphatically by using techniques to involve the reader's imagination and emotions? Fourth, *organization* — have you arranged your details in a pattern reflecting a clear principle or principles of organization? Fifth, *development* — have you developed your amplifying details either down from or up to the topic sentence? If not, have you a good reason? Sixth, *transition* — have you provided smooth and adequate transition between and within your paragraphs?

Read the following essay, by a student writer; and analyze its paragraphs, using the paragraphing checklist.

DEATH — AND ONE AFTERNOON / *Susan Hughes*

One day a few summers ago, when I'd cut the grass and finished the ironing and was looking for a book to read, I picked up *For Whom the Bell Tolls*. At that time I didn't know its author from Socrates, but the title sounded interesting. The following Sunday I was devouring the last few chapters and congratulating myself on choosing that particular book when an announcement on the radio caught my attention. That Sunday was July 2, 1961, and Ernest Hemingway had just shot himself.

On July 3, the newspapers poured out the sorrow of a shocked literary world. In a strange way I, too, was feeling a loss. In *For Whom the Bell Tolls* I had discovered, in the person of Robert Jordan, a hero whose every thought came alive for me. The author of the work seemed to be saying so many things my own mind had tried to understand and express. I had often stopped reading for a few minutes and thought, "Some day I've just got to meet that man." But now Ernest Hemingway was dead.

I think I cried about it a little, but when you're sixteen you're supposed to be too old to cry. Adults keep lecturing that life must go on, and for once I agreed. Life is very cooperative that way, and I soon forgot my tears. I did not, however, forget Ernest Hemingway. The local librarian grew rather amused at the redhead who spent hours looking up articles on Hemingway in *Newsweek*, *Saturday Review* and *Life*. She remarked several times that more than one author had written books worth reading, but I wasn't interested in any other author. I ordered Leicester Hemingway's biography of his brother the day it was released. I began a notebook containing every conceivably interesting detail that I could unearth in the life of my hero. Like a prospector who has found his cave of gold, I could not trade this new interest for the vague promise that there are other, bigger caves over the next mountain.

My parents were both pleased and concerned about my new interest. I spent hours trying to tell them why I wanted to learn all about Hemingway to make up for the fact that now I could never meet him.

My mother must have understood, because she was almost as happy as I was when a local family invited us to a tea being given for Marcelline Hemingway Sanford to celebrate the success of her newly released *At the Hemingway's*. I was dreaming! Me — an insignificant teenager from a booming metropolis of 3800 people — and now I had an actual chance to meet an actual person who not only had known Hemingway, but was his actual sister. My sixteen-year-old heart was working overtime and my mouth hung limply open. I mentally relinquished Elvis, Fabian and even Ben Casey. What were they compared with Ernest Hemingway's sister?

I did my homework well in those fourteen days before the tea, reading and rereading Mrs. Sanford's book, rehearsing questions and remembering to stand straight and speak properly. But the doubts were crushing. What if there were so many people there that I couldn't even meet my celebrity? What if she wasn't at all like Hemingway? What if my cold got worse and I sneezed in the middle of a question? The days passed agonizingly until I finally stepped into our friends' living room and tried to ignore the butterflies that were exploring my stomach lining.

I sat wilting in a corner, while the butterflies spun cocoons and the cocoons settled down for a long winter and I tried to wash them away with cups of tea. Community leaders flitted by, exchanging profound comments on the Hemingway death wish and the basic elements of existentialism in his writing. Through the fog of intellectuality I could see Mrs. Sanford smiling, laughing, very Hemingway, autographing copies of her book. She had signed mine, and had asked me my name, but some local literary-club member had interrupted and left me crushed by the weight of my own insignificance.

I smiled and answered questions and voiced shallow opinions whenever necessary, but from the seclusion of my corner I spent most of the time silently envious of every uncaring, name-dropping adult in sight. I could hear Mrs. Sanford's every word, and I listened in awe whenever she mentioned some experience with Hemingway. It was still unbelievable that I was in the same room with a person who had known Hemingway, but the so-near-and-yet-so-far element gnawed at my already upset digestive tract.

With the cooperation of my mother, who began talking to Mrs. Sanford, my chance finally came. Somehow in the next ten minutes my mother and the community socialites and even the room disappeared and I was talking alone with Mrs. Sanford. She was surprised at my interest in her brother because, she said, Hemingway did not write for young people. There was that inevitable phrase, young people, and I could feel my heart sinking. But I forgot it soon and was once again lost in the unbelievable experience of hearing about my hero, hearing him gradually change from a literary god to a moving, talking person with thoughts and faults and peculiarities all his own. For forty-five minutes Hemingway came down from his pedestal and became a human being.

The afternoon ended finally. I went home and opened my eyes and started noticing the world again. I tried writing down all that Mrs. Sanford had said, but I gave it up. It was still too unbelievable that I had actually met her and talked with her, and words could not express the feelings of admiration and wonder and awe I had built up that afternoon.

The anticlimax of the following weeks was lessened slightly, because Mrs. Sanford and I corresponded. When the first note came from her, I couldn't believe that she had remembered me. My ego was lost in the clouds for days.

Our friends planned another tea for last winter, and Mrs. Sanford had asked that I be there. I was looking forward to it, but not in the same way as to the first one. I had learned much more about Hemingway and about my own reactions. I had come two years closer to shedding the seeming stigma of being young. But mostly, I had learned to regard Mrs. Sanford as less of an encyclopedia and more of a person in her own right, a person with a vibrant, intense desire to get all she could out of life and give back in return all she had learned. I longed to meet her again, to find out what had given both her and her brother their capacity to live so fully. I wanted to know, too, what had gone wrong, what had changed in Hemingway and why he had ended his living as suddenly and intensely as he began it. I wanted to know so many things.

I never found out, though, because before I could ask, Mrs. Sanford was dead, too. She was sick, and then recovering, and then suddenly dead. I knew then why Hemingway had said you hate death for the people it takes away.

I knew also that I couldn't ask my questions. I had to learn for myself why he had also said, in the book that began our acquaintance, "The world is a fine place, and worth fighting for."

Much of the effectiveness of Miss Hughes' essay stems from the controlled and careful structure and development of most of her paragraphs, and you can profit from her example. When you can write clear, interesting, and well-constructed paragraphs, you will be ready to write equally effective essays.

PASSAGES FOR STUDY

Here are several additional paragraphs for you to analyze. The first three passages are the work of contemporary professional writers; the last four are by students. Analyze these paragraphs, using the checklist; then apply it to your own paragraphs. If they pass, they should be unified, coherent, emphatic, and interesting. As a would-be writer, you don't want any other kind.

However, I don't expect love to be saved by congressional intervention. I feel it could be done voluntarily. And so I call for slower courting by man and maid; for sharing walks and sights and small emergencies — for all those nice, casual, relaxing things men think they can do only with other men; for little arguments repeated often enough to become intimate; for getting lost in the woods or playing cards or fixing snacks. In fine, for strolling through life's low-pressure areas together. If our lovers' emotion is true and posture-proof, it alone will generate more than enough excitement.

—Frederic Morton, *"The Art of Courtship"*

In short, the Abstract Expressionists do not seem hostile to reality around them so much as completely indifferent to it. As far as these painters are concerned, the outside world might just as well not exist. They seek in their own souls for mystical states which they can transfer to canvas as "flux," "nonrational truths," and "personal myths." The painter no longer feels a need to describe or to reflect upon his subject but rather, like Grace Hartigan, to "distill it until I have its essence." When we hear more talk about "essences," we are on familiar territory. The spilled ink, the spattered paint, and the dripped pigment are expressions of "spontaneity," much like Kerouac's automatic writing. Drawing almost disappears, while color, with its exclusively emotional attack, becomes predominant. The intelligence is suspended in favor of intuitions, feelings, impulses.

—Robert Brustein, *"The Cult of Unthink"*

For centuries, "road" was a word of magic. Armies, gypsies, beggars, tinkers, peasants, merchants, highwaymen, scholars, minstrels and runaway apprentice boys were once found upon the road. As recently as fifty years ago, you could still build your house beside the road and be a friend to man, because mankind passed your doors. Today, this is not so. The road belongs entirely to the automobile, and he who builds his house beside it can only watch the Fords go by, because there is no human life on the road itself. Indeed, so mechanical, so abstract, so inhuman have our roads become that American drivers never think of passing the people ahead; they think of passing the car ahead.

—John Keats, *"The Call of the Open Road"*

You can watch a cup of coffee slowly give off thin wisps of steam that spiral upwards and fade away about an inch above the coffee's surface. If you blow lightly at the steam, it vanishes like a handful of dandelion seeds before a gust of wind. If you tire of watching the steam, you can add cream to your coffee and watch the kaleidoscopic spiral patterns of black and the invading brown. Or, you can merely stir the coffee in time with the rhythm of your thoughts. Then, when the coffee finally cools, you can leisurely sip it: a well-managed cup of coffee can be a pleasant fifteen-minute study break.

—John Reed

Little girls think, perceive life, and have problems just as pressing and depressing as ours. Little girls are not all sugar and spice and everything nice; their minds are not made of cotton candy. The small child in the portrait on the wall stands with idle hoop in hand and stares at me with sad, knowing eyes. Her innocence is reflected in every fold of her frilly dress, but not in the folds of her heart. I look at her and wonder if little girls are ever little girls.

—Andrea Moore

Mary Lou is an attractive young lady. Her pretty features compose a delicate and well-shaped glass sculpture. Her body is a trifle thin, not a little-girlish thinness, but a mature and shapely litheness. Her face and body augment one another like a set of ivory figurines. She is pleasant to be with; a smile easily finds its way to her lips and eyes, and a womanly sensitivity towards others can lend extra warmth to her laughter.

However, Mary Lou doesn't often show that sensitivity. She seems afraid to reveal herself to others, as though she feared being hurt. She may be a puppy who's been beaten once by a man and now fears all men. Nor will she allow others to reveal themselves to her, as though she didn't want the burden of caring for another. Even physically, Mary Lou tries to hide her femininity. She prefers levis and sweatshirts to skirts and blouses; she acts like a tomboy sometimes, and scars that pretty body. Mary Lou won't enter the world she belongs in. Mary Lou is afraid to be a woman.

—Lee Runkle

Every man lives in his own special world, a world different from everyone else's. Each person is the center of his own universe and perceives all things in terms of their relationship to the central figure. This paragraph is at the nucleus of my personal universe, because it is part of me; it exists only on the periphery of your world, only words, or at best, an idea, to you. God may abide at the core of another man's cosmos; He is housed at the very edge of my consciousness and is only infrequently brought into play. Freedom to choose friends and leaders, the opportunity to pursue and apply knowledge, and security for my person and belongings dwell at the heart of my world. But different possibilities, like the right to be left alone or the chance to join some Great Cause, may be basic to other men.

The whole spectrum of philosophers, from psychologists to theologians, have claimed that all men need a Christ-figure, a hero — that all men need something greater than themselves to adhere to and to derive meaning from. It is also widely held that personal freedom is essential to the actualization of man's humanity; however, Erich Fromm sees modern man scurrying to *escape* freedom. And all humans obviously require bread when hungry, wine when thirsty, warmth in winter, and shade in summer; yet, many would rather be "dead than Red." So it seems that there are no simple solutions, no pat answers, to what is really a very crucial question — what needs *are* common to all men, what basic rights *are* inherited at birth and are *never* to be abridged?

—Richard Smith

PRACTICE

1. Write one "up" paragraph and one "down" paragraph on different topics of your own contriving. Follow the paragraphing checklist, and use the writing techniques you have been working with in the preceding chapters.

2. Develop another topic of your own choosing in *two* paragraphs, beginning with either an "up" or a "down" paragraph followed by a second one developed in the opposite direction. For examples of this exercise, see the study passages above by Lee Runkle and Richard Smith.

12

The

Fundamentals

of Structure:

Introduction

If you have done at all well with your paragraph exercises, you should be ready to extend your work on structure to the full essay. As you do, however, don't forget or simply ignore what you've been learning about style; do your best to apply the attitudes and techniques which you have read about and practiced in the preceding chapters. In particular, use concrete words, simile, metaphor, analogy, exemplification, and allusion both to think your way into a subject to find out what you really know about it and also to write your way out of it in clear, vivid, and interesting language. Most importantly, as you begin writing full essays, don't just scribble them off frantic moments before they are due: take the time to do a careful outline, to write a rough draft, to put it aside for a day or so, and then revise it into a satisfying and impressive essay. Why do less than your best?

INTRODUCTION

It shouldn't be hard to understand why the three-part structure of introduction, main body, and conclusion dominates good writing: not only is it relatively simple, not only does it follow a logical order, but also it gives you three different chances to communicate your ideas. In the introduction, you tell the reader, "this is what I'm going to talk about"; in the main body, you tell him, "this is specifically what I'm trying to say"; and in the conclusion, you point out, "this is what I've said, and these are its consequences." As usual, however, opportunity involves risk; and triple repetition can be anesthetically dull.

In the introduction, you have the advantage of freshness. This is where the reader first finds out what you want him to know about the topic reflected in your title and where he decides whether or not to read any further — or, if he has to read the whole thing, whether it's going to be a pleasure or a pain. You have two main tasks in the introduction, then: one, *to give the reader a clear understanding of your central meaning in the writing that follows;* and two, *to do it in a way that stimulates his interest or curiosity.*

You can achieve these ends in numerous ways, depending on your particular purposes and materials. One method, however, you should avoid like a headache:

> The following essay will be concerned with the benefits of education. It will deal with formal academic education in American public schools and suggest some of its benefits to society and to the individual.

I'll admit that this introduction conveys clearly and concisely the general meaning I want to communicate and its main points, but isn't it wretchedly boring? You can do better than this; if you want to hook your reader, you'll have to.

Among the many ways you can capture a reader's attention, several have proven especially effective. 1. *Questions.* If you begin by putting your central meaning or purpose in a question or two, your reader will try to answer them. If he can't, he'll want to read on to learn the answers; if he can, he'll want to find out if he's right. 2. *Pointed anecdotes.* One way to get at a reader through his imagination is to start with an account of some happening which embodies your main point. This happening can be drawn from your own experience or knowledge, or you can simply make one up; either way, the reader becomes imaginatively involved in your anecdote and will probably want to know more about its point. 3. *Reminiscence.* If you can force your reader to identify with you and with your interest in a subject, you've probably got him. A good way to do this is to take him on a relatively short tour of your personal memory lane, concentrating on past experiences which led to your particular concern with the subject. 4. *Contemporary parallels and symbols.* Nearly everyone is interested in the events and persons of his own time. You can exploit this interest by introducing your subject with references to well-known events and famous people that parallel or symbolize its main points. 5. *Authority.* Ours is an age of increasing specialization, and we therefore rely increasingly on the "expert." If you can begin by citing an expert or two — the more well-known, the better — to illustrate or support your subject, you reader will probably be impressed enough to read further. 6. *Statistics.* Almost the same point can be made about this technique. We live in a statistics-minded time and culture, and if your subject is one you can introduce by reference to surprising or impressive statistics, you will arouse the interest and curiosity of most readers.

These are only a representative few of the techniques and devices you can use to make your introductions interesting as well as clear. Use them, and any others you can think of. Your subject, what you want to say about it, and your purposes in writing will govern what particular methods you choose, but choose you must, if you want to engage your reader from the beginning. Let's see what some other writers have done to solve this problem in structure.

Not long ago a professor in a Midwestern university, concerned about evidence of cheating, set up an experiment to discover the extent of it. He gave a difficult assignment and announced there would be a quiz. On the morning of the test he mentioned that the correct answers were on his desk. Then by prearrangement he was called from the room.

Unknown to the others, two graduate students had been enrolled in the class to observe and report on what then might happen. It exceeded the teacher's worst imaginings. No sooner was he out the door than there was a stampede to the desk. With the exception of two dean's-list geniuses, every student present copied the answers and handed them in as his own.

Cheating in college is not, of course, restricted to the Midwest. Students at a large eastern university recently produced evidence that fraud was so extensive as to raise a doubt whether the institution's examinations and assigned original work had any validity at all. Given the topic "Cheating at This University" as a social-research assignment, they tied into the task with confessional zeal.

There was, it developed, an ingenious assortment of cribbing and signaling devices in everyday use. "Original" written work, sometimes slightly used or from other campuses, was available at four to ten dollars per paper; "tutors" would perform any kind of homework at moderate fees; complete laboratory notes could be obtained without ever having to spend an afternoon in the lab. Examination questions were frequently obtained in advance through theft, pilfering wastebaskets near the duplicating machines, or bribery of staff employees. One student expressed the consensus: "At this school, cheating is standard practice."

The situation would be more reassuring if such places were the exception. Actually, institutions where large-scale, organized cheating has *not* been known are a small minority. The book *Changing Values in College*, the work of a Hazen Foundation committee headed by Philip E. Jacob, of the University of Pennsylvania, who correlated the material in book form, is the most extensive survey of student attitudes undertaken recently. It has this to say: "The chinks in the moral armor of American students are most obvious in regard to cheating. . . . The practice is so widespread as to challenge the well-nigh universal claim of students that they value honesty as a moral virtue. Frequent cheating is admitted by 40 per cent or more (of the students) at a large number of colleges, often with no apology or sense of wrongdoing."

Fairly reliable survey evidence, Professor Jacob wrote to me recently, suggests that one student in three cheats "rather regularly." At the last meeting of the American Council on Education, Dr. Edward D. Eddy, Jr., vice president and provost of the University of New Hampshire, told a discussion group that cheating throughout the country "has become a part of the student culture — it's taken for granted."

It has seemed to me, both as a university faculty member and as a citizen, that the matter is of fundamental importance, not only in the educational world but to the country as a whole. Are we becoming a nation of cheaters? If so, whom are we cheating and what are the likely consequences?

—Jerome Ellison, *"American Disgrace: College Cheating"*

Ellison's title indicates clearly both his topic and also his attitude towards it, and his introduction does a masterful job of forcing the reader to share his concern. A lesser writer might have been content with the last two paragraphs for his introduction, but without the preceding material, they would be little more than pallid generalities. Instead, Ellison begins with an anecdote which vividly dramatizes his central problem. Next, with another anecdote, he shows that the problem is not confined to one university or to one locality. Finally, he leaves no room for doubt that this is a national problem by citing statistical evidence and by quoting the opinion of a recognized authority.

Against this anecdotal, evidential, and authoritative background, the last paragraph becomes an effective lead-in to the main body of the essay. It establishes Ellison's personal relationship to the problem and suggests that college cheating has significance beyond the classroom. Aware now of the scope of such cheating, the reader can hardly disagree, and the questions which mark out the main points of the following discussion echo his own speculations. With this introduction, then, Ellison has the reader exactly where he wants him — interested in the specific questions Ellison wants to discuss and receptive to his answers.

When a hitherto unknown actor named Marlon Brando eleven years ago assumed the role of Stanley Kowalski, the glowering, inarticulate hero of Tennessee Williams' *A Streetcar Named Desire,* few people realized the symbolic importance of that creation. For Brando was to personify an entire post-war generation of troubled spirits trying to find an identity. Today we find his Kowalski wherever we look, whether in our latest literature, our poetry, our painting, our movies, our popular music, or on our city streets. In one guise or another he is the hero of the Beat Generation.

—Robert Brustein, *"The Cult of Unthink"*

Here we have an obviously much shorter and less complex introduction than Ellison's, but don't therefore underestimate it. Brustein gets a lot of mileage from this relatively small vehicle. If it is short and concise, it is pointed and packed; and it has a tempo that carries the reader into the main body whether he much wants to go or not.

Brustein's intriguing title indicates the general point of his essay but leaves its specific focus unstated to arouse the reader's curiosity. In the beginning of the introduction, he further catches the reader's interest by suggesting a relationship between the unstated topic and the most famous role of a popular movie star and by defining the six areas in which he means to explore that relationship. Then, with the reader's interest fully engaged, Brustein reveals the particular subject of his essay.

Many years ago, when the first cement sidewalks were being built in our neighborhood, we children took the paw of our dog Mickey and impressed it into a kind of immortality even as he modestly floundered and objected. This past summer, after the lapse of many decades, I stood and looked at the slab, now crumbling at the edges from the feet of many passers.

No one knows where Mickey the friendly lies; no one knows how many times the dust that clothed that beautiful and loving spirit has moved with the thistledown across the yards where Mickey used to play. Here is his only legacy to the future — that dabbled paw mark whose secret is remembered briefly in the heart of an aging professor. The mark of Mickey's paw is dearer to me than many more impressive monuments — perhaps because, in a sense, we both wanted to be something other that what we were. Mickey, I know, wanted very much to be a genuine human being. If permitted, he would sit up to the table and put his paws together before his plate, like the rest of the children. If anyone mocked him at such a time by pretending to have paws and resting his chin on the table as Mickey had to do, Mickey would growl and lift his lip. He knew very well he was being mocked for not being a man.

This reminder that he was only a poor dog with paws annoyed Mickey. He knew basically a lot more than he ever had the opportunity to express. Though people refused to take Mickey's ambition seriously, the frustration never affected his temperament. Being of a philosophic cast of mind, he knew that children were less severe in their classifications. And if Mickey found the social restrictions too onerous to enable him quite to achieve recognition inside the house, outside he came very close to being a small boy. In fact, he was taken into a secret order we had founded whose clubhouse was an old piano box in the back yard. We children never let the fact that Mickey walked on four legs blind us to his other virtues.

Now the moral of all this is that Mickey tried hard to be a human being. And as I stood after the lapse of years and looked at the faint impression of his paw, it struck me that every ruined civilization is, in a sense, the mark of men trying to be human, trying to transcend themselves. Like Mickey, none of them have quite made it, but they have each left a figurative paw mark — the Shang bronzes, the dreaming stone faces on Easter Island, the Parthenon, the Sphinx, or perhaps only rusted stilettos, chain mail, or a dolmen on some sea-pounded headland. The archaeologist, it is said, is a student of the artifact. That harsh, unlovely word, as sharply angled as a fist ax or a brick, denudes us of human sympathy. In the eye of the public we loom, I suppose, as slightly befuddled graybeards scavenging in gravel heaps. We caw like crows over a bit of jade or a broken potsherd; we are eternally associated in the public mind with sharp-edged flints and broken statues. The utter uselessness of the past is somehow magnificently incorporated into our activities.

No one, I suppose, would believe that an archaeologist is a man who knows where last year's lace valentines have gone, or that from the surface of rubbish heaps the thin and ghostly essence of things human keeps rising through the centuries until the plaintive murmur of dead men and women may take precedence at times over the living voice. A man who has once looked with the archaeological eye will never see quite normally. He will be wounded by what other men call trifles. It is possible to refine the sense of time until an old shoe in the bunch grass or a pile of nineteenth-century beer bottles in an abandoned mining town toll in one's head like a hall clock. This is the price one pays for learning to read time from surfaces other than an illuminated dial. It is the melancholy secret of the artifact, the humanly touched thing.

This past year, although the successful Russian satellites swung everyone's attention to outer space, a surprising number of archaeological books dealing with the lost city civilizations were published. The rapidity of their appearance and the avidity with which they were received suggest that while the public's eye has been forced upward it has also, in the same act, been cast downward toward the earth. Perhaps no great civilization has ever before been more self-consciously aware of the possible doom that confronts it, or more curious about those brother thinkers and artists who carved the gods that lie now in temples visited only by rain, or who ventured through the Pillars of Hercules when all beyond was wild and unknown as outer space today. They built in their separate ways, then fell, and we, with one winged foot poised toward the stars, hear in a preternatural quiet the old voices out of the grass. Whatever the disease that ate the heart of these lost cultures it was not the affliction of ignorance — not, at least, the technical ignorance of the savage who cannot lay one stone successfully upon another. In every one of these fallen cities which our spades have revealed, there existed the clever artisan, the engineer devoted to the service of the particular human dream that flourished there.

—Loren Eiseley, *"Paw Marks and Buried Towns"*

An anthropologist, Eiseley writes with a poet's graces. Only such a man could see correspondences between a dog's paw mark in a crumbling sidewalk and the tumbled ruins of vanished civilizations or see in a boy's pet the symbol of what man's great cities essentially represent. Notice, however, that Eiseley's informal and personal introduction is constructed much like Ellison's: the final paragraph is the real lead-in to the main body of the essay, but it would be relatively lifeless without the context in which Eiseley places it.

He begins with an effective reminiscence; triggered by the simple observation of a paw mark in a sidewalk, he recalls a kind of childhood experience common to most of us, and then draws a moral from it. Unobtrusively, he suggests that the moral of his vanished pet is equally the moral of men and that men have also left similar marks upon the earth. Such marks, he claims, are the subjects of the archaeologist, and he describes the common image of the archaeologist. Against this stereotype, he contrasts the archaeologist as he knows him to be, and it is this picture we unreservedly accept. What else could we do after having read *this* archaeologist's memories of Mickey? In the final paragraph, he then points out that the year of man's entry into space was also a year in which he turned back avidly to his ancient past; and we not only understand and feel the implications Eiseley draws from this dichotomy but also want to follow his exploration of them.

Eiseley's introduction does simply and beautifully what an introduction *should* do: it tells the reader what the essay is about, suggests its broader implications, and fully engages the reader's interest. It is informal and personal writing, but it is based on the same principles as the more objective introductions of Ellison and Brustein: order and coherence imposed by the writer to inform and interest the reader. Whatever particular techniques you use, make these your governing principles and your goals. Anecdotes, statistics, authority, contemporary parallels and symbols, questions, personal experience — as the three introductions suggest, the techniques are many and varied; and the ones you choose will depend on your materials and purposes. But it is your responsibility to make the choices and to control their functions. If you want your reader to follow, you must lead.

PASSAGES FOR STUDY

Read the following introductions to determine their effectiveness in giving a reader a clear understanding of the topic to be developed in the essay and in arousing his interest in the topic. Then analyze the passages for the specific techniques which each writer uses to achieve these goals.

For over half my life I have been a pitchman — if you accept a broad, generic definition of the term. From "pumpkin dates" (small towns) to radio microphone and TV screen, I have spent some thirty years doing the "vocal sell." Nowadays the props have been improved and the jargon refined; but the pitchman's approach has not altered measurably.

—Long John Nebel, *"The Pitchman"*

All advertisements show automobiles in unusual circumstances. They depict smiling, handsome people in evening clothes arriving in glittering hardtops beneath the porte-cocheres of expensive tropical saloons. A polished convertible, top down, filled with laughing young people in yachting costumes, whispers along an idealized shoreline. A ruggedly healthy Mom, Pop, Sis and

Buzz smile the miles away as their strangely dustless station wagon whisks over the Rockies. Sometimes, automobiles strangely shine on pedestals; sometimes they slip through astral voids like comets. None of the advertisements show you and me in the automobile as most of us know it — that is, wedged in a fuming line of commuter traffic at 8:30 a.m., or locked in an even worse outbound line at 6 p.m.

A manufacturer, of course, would commit economic hara-kiri if he were to try to sell us a car on truthful grounds, for how could he ask anyone to pay $4,500 for a three-hundred-horsepower contraption on grounds that it would be used only two hours a day for 240 working days a year, and would at all other times — except briefly, on vacations — be parked in an expensive parking lot or sit depreciating at a curb? Would you buy such a car if it were truthfully put to you that the thing would cost you more than $9 an hour to use? No manufacturer in his right mind would plead with you to buy a luggage compartment only slightly smaller than Delaware in order that you could use part of this space just twice a year. Manufacturers know very well that the American automobile is not primarily a means of transportation and that it cannot be sold as such. Therefore, their advertisements invariably portray the automobile as A Flying Carpet — as a thing to sweep us off to ineffable lotus lands — and this, we discover, is the greatest lie of all. Yet, we cannot plead surprise, because — as a friend remarked — if we now suspect that our automobiles are overblown, overpriced monstrosities built by oafs for thieves to sell to mental defectives, it is only logical to expect that there is not much point in driving them, and that any place an automobile can go is probably not worth visiting. Nevertheless, the advertisements have a certain appeal, because the dream they represent once had substance. There was a time in man's memory when travel was exciting.

—John Keats, *"The Call of the Open Road"*

Come what may, I change my razor blade each Saturday morning, and as I did so on a hot one not long ago, I found myself worrying about the Civil War. The trouble had to do with continuity — connection. I buy my blades in metal clips of ten or twenty, and I prefer twenties, as a rule. You can look twice as far ahead with them; they promise more. A set that is new in the middle of summer will span a whole other season. It will take you past the end of the heat and almost into winter, and there is no telling what is going to happen while it lasts. Then when it is done, you can glance backward if you want to. I play this game a good deal, as a matter of fact. Equipment of some kind is always handy. It can be played with a new shirt or an old calendar. I like to feel the connections between here and there. I am for continuity first, last, and always. Then, what, I wondered (starting a new set of blades, peering ahead, and reflecting that they would help get me ready for Thanksgiving dinner) — what did I have against the celebration of the centennial of the Civil War? *There* was continuity with a vengeance.

—Robert Henderson, *"The Enamelled Wishbone"*

"What do you read, my lord?" Polonius asks, and Hamlet answers: "Words, words, words." Unfortunately, there are times when this is all our reading and conversation give us: just words. Words are of little importance on their own account, or for their own sake. Their importance derives from what they stand for: their meanings. The function of words is to act as signs or symbols of something outside themselves. Words may be likened to checks drawn on a bank, worth nothing as paper, but valuable insofar as they represent cash in the bank. Words are "cashed" when we are directed to the things and events they stand for. Thus the admonition of Justice Oliver Wendell Holmes: "Let us think things, not words."

"Semantics" is a new word which has come to designate the study of words (and symbols generally) in relation to their meanings. Words are signs or symbols, that is, things that stand for something other than themselves. Another way of describing semantics is to say that it is the study of "the meaning of meaning." This is a rather curious expression, when we stop to think about it, for when we ask what "meaning" means, we assume that we know what "means" means, for otherwise we could not ask what meaning "means." The meaning of meaning, in other words, depends on the meaning of meaning. The simpler definition, however, is quite adequate for our purposes, and we shall define "semantics" as the study of symbols, such as words, and their meanings.

—Lionel Ruby, "Words, Words, Words"

TOPICS FOR ESSAYS

1. Explain what you like or dislike most about your home town or neighborhood.

2. Write a review of a novel you've read recently; point out and discuss what you consider its strengths and/or weaknesses. Try to convince your reader either to read or to ignore the book.

3. Defend your favorite sport against someone who dislikes it.

4. Describe your favorite kind of music, and explain what you like about it.

5. Discuss your principal reasons for coming to college.

6. Write an account of the most exciting experience in your life.

7. Go to a supermarket, and unobtrusively watch one woman and one man shopping. Describe them and their methods of shopping, and try to explain any differences you observe.

8. Explain your position on a current national or international issue or situation.

9. Describe your roommate or best friend, and explain your relationship.

10. Make up your own topic, and write on it.

13

The
Fundamentals
of Structure:
Development

If a good introduction gives a reader your main point or points and interests him in them, the main body which follows it should develop your subject specifically and do it in ways which justify the reader's time and effort. To develop means to expand, to unfold gradually, to elaborate, to work out by degrees, to explain more clearly, to enlarge upon; it means explaining your love for a book not in broad, vague generalities but in the specific terms of its plot, its characters, and the qualities of its style. In short, your primary task in the main body is to keep the promises you made the reader in your introduction. This means that everything you write in the main body must be directly relevant to the general topic and centered specifically on the point or points you've led the reader to expect. Relevance, however, is not enough: keeping your promise to the reader also means a detailed development of the ideas in the introduction, and these details must be arranged in a pattern which the reader can follow clearly with a minimum of difficulty. Whatever the nature of your subject, then, your task in the main body is to develop relevant and interesting details with order and coherence.

Most writing serves one or more of four basic purposes: one, *description* — the appearance and quality of a person, a place, or an object; two, *narration* — an event or a sequence of events; three, *exposition* — an explanation of something; and four, *argument* — convincing a reader that something is true or false, right or wrong, good or bad. Your particular subject may require one or several of these different kinds of writing, and it may require them separately or in combination; but either way, whichever of these purposes you serve, you still have the problem of developing the details of your subject coherently — that is, in the step-by-step development which will communicate your meaning most clearly and effectively.

In solving this problem, you must decide on the order in which your main ideas and their sub-divisions will most clearly and interestingly express what you want to say. This means arranging them according to some unifying principle of organization, both in the essay as a whole and also in its parts. For a would-be writer, at least five such organizing principles are fundamental. One, *spatial.* If you are describing or explaining the physical appearance or qualities of something, you need to create a clear and detailed picture of it in the reader's imagination. This involves you in a double responsibility: first, *establish and maintain a clear point of view.* Whatever you are describing or explaining, you should arrange your details in relationship to the particular position from which you want the reader to see them. If, for example, you are describing a house, put together the details a reader would see from one position before you go on to details which he could see only from another place. If you describe the front, the living room, the roof, the garden, the back windows, the dining room, and then the front porch, he may see the individual details, but he will lose sight of the house which unifies them. Second, *establish and maintain a consistent movement within your scene.* As you shift from point to point, you should move according to some principle of direction — for example, from left to right or right to left, vertically or horizontally, from north to south, from outside to inside. And once you've established a direction of movement, you should maintain it, even if you combine it with another. If, for instance, you describe a room as it would appear to someone in the doorway looking from left to right around the room, you might stop at one point to describe something from the floor to the ceiling; but you wouldn't suddenly shift to something on the right side of the room and then return to the left side. This, too, would imaginatively confuse and probably irritate the reader.

Both aspects of spatial development are reflected in Mark Twain's description of a nineteenth-century Missouri river town:

Once a day a cheap, gaudy packet arrived upward from St. Louis, and another downward from Keokuk. Before these events, the day was glorious with expectancy; after them, the day was a dead and empty thing. Not only the boys, but the whole village, felt this. After all these years I can picture that old time to myself now, just as it was then: the white town drowsing in the sunshine of a summer's morning; the streets empty, or pretty nearly so; one or two clerks sitting in front of the Water Street stores, with their splint-bottomed chairs tilted back against the walls, chins on breasts, hats slouched over their faces, asleep — with shingle-shavings enough around to show what broke them down; a sow and a litter of pigs loafing along the sidewalk, doing a good business in watermelon rinds and seeds; two or three lonely little freight piles scattered about the levee; a pile of skids on the slope of the stone-paved wharf, and the fragrant town drunkard asleep in the shadow of them; two or three wood flats at the head of the wharf, but nobody to listen to the peaceful lapping of the wavelets against them; the great Mississippi, the majestic, the magnificent Mississippi, rolling its milewide tide along, shining in the sun; the dense forest away on the other side; the point above the town, and the point below, bounding the river-glimpse and turning it into a sort of sea, and withal a very still and brilliant and lonely one. Presently a film of dark smoke appears above one of those remote points; instantly a Negro drayman, famous for his quick eye and prodigious voice, lifts up the cry, "S-t-e-a-m-boat a-comin'!" and the scene changes; The town drunkard stirs, the clerks wake up, a furious clatter of drays follows, every house and store pours out a human contribution, and all in a twinkling the dead town is alive and moving.

—Mark Twain, *Life On The Mississippi*

Twain arranges his remembered details so that the reader looks down on the town as though from above, seeing first the whole town and then its nearly empty streets. Then Twain moves him step by step to the point of action foreshadowed in the first sentence — down the river-front street to the wharf, where he sets the stage for the steamboat to appear far off on the vast and empty river. This is spatial development at its best: vivid and evocative concrete details seen from a clear point of view, with consistent and dramatic movement within the scene.

Two, *chronological*. This offers fewer opportunities for confusion than spatial organization. In most human experience, whatever occurs in time happens in some sequence — that is, something happens after one thing and before something else. Moreover, any occurrence, taken by itself, seems to have a beginning, a middle, and an end. Sometimes you may want to concentrate on the beginning of such a sequence — perhaps to stress causative forces or events first appearing then; other times, you may want to focus on the end of a sequence to emphasize its drama or irony. Most of the time, however, you can best narrate or explain a series of events or a process by arranging your materials in chronological order. Start with details of the beginning, move through those of the middle, and finish with details of the end. Here, for example, is Hanson Boldwin's account of the sailing of the *Titanic*:

The *Titanic's* sailing from Southampton, though quiet, was not wholly un-eventful. As the liner moved slowly toward the end of her dock that April day, the surge of her passing sucked away from the quay the steamer *New York*, moored just to seaward of the *Titanic's* berth. There were sharp cracks as the manila mooring lines of the *New York* parted under the strain. The frayed ropes writhed and whistled through the air and snapped down among the waving crowd on the pier; the *New York* swung toward the *Titanic's* bow, was checked and dragged back to the dock barely in time to avert a collision. Seamen muttered, thought it an ominous start.

Past Spithead and the Isle of Wight the *Titanic* steamed. She called at Cherbourg at dusk and then laid her course for Queenstown. At 1:30 p.m. on Thursday, April 11, she stood out of Queenstown harbor, screaming gulls soaring in her wake, with 2,201 persons — men, women, and children — aboard. . . .

The *Titanic* took her departure on Fastnet Light and, heading into the night, laid her course for New York. She was due at Quarantine the following Wednesday morning.

Sunday dawned fair and clear. The *Titanic* steamed smoothly toward the west, faint streamers of brownish smoke trailing from the funnels. The purser held services in the saloon in the morning; on the steerage deck aft the immigrants were playing games and a Scotsman was puffing "The Campbells Are Coming" on his bagpipes in the midst of the uproar.

—Hanson Baldwin, "R. M. S. *Titanic*"

This, of course, is only the beginning — the setting out of the "unsinkable" *Titanic* on her first and last voyage. In the rest of the essay, Baldwin shifts from a day-by-day account to the notable hours and minutes during which the great ship steams with blind arrogance among the icebergs until she meets the one that kills her. His purpose is not only to tell what happened but also to show the blind faith and simple carelessness which made it happen. By organizing his essay in chronological sequence, Baldwin not only forces the reader to focus repeatedly on details which reflect the contrast between the assumptions about the *Titanic* and what happened to her and suggest the part these assumptions played in the disaster but also generates suspense where there is no uncertainty.

Three, *climactic*. The climax of anything is its culmination, its point of highest interest, importance, or intensity. Climactic organization, then, means arranging your material to lead up to a final point you want to give particular emphasis. In the following passage, the astronomer Fred Hoyle uses this principle of organization in explaining his concept of the nature of the universe:

So for we have been entirely concerned with the rich fruits of twentieth century observational astronomy and in particular with the results achieved by Hubble and his colleagues. We have seen that all space is strewn with galaxies, and we have seen that space itself is continually expanding. Further questions come crowding in: What causes the expansion? Does the expansion mean that as time goes on the observable Universe is becoming less and less occupied by matter? Is space finite or infinite? How old is the Universe? To settle these questions we shall now have to consider new trains of thought. These will lead us to strange conclusions.

First I will consider the older ideas — that is to say, the ideas of the nineteen-twenties and the nineteen-thirties — and then I will go on to offer my own opinion. Broadly speaking, the older ideas fall into two groups. One of them is distinguished by the assumption that the Universe started its life a finite time ago in a single huge explosion. On this supposition the present expansion is a relic of the violence of this explosion. This big bang idea seemed to me to be unsatisfactory even before detailed examination showed that it leads to serious difficulties. For when we look at our own Galaxy there is not the smallest sign that such an explosion ever occurred. This might not be such a cogent argument against the explosion school of thought if our Galaxy had turned out to be much younger than the whole Universe. But this is not so. On the contrary, in some of these theories the Universe comes out to be younger than our astrophysical estimates of the age of our own Galaxy. Another really serious difficulty arises when we try to reconcile the idea of an explosion with the requirement that the galaxies have condensed out of diffuse background material. The two concepts of explosion and condensation are obviously contradictory, and it is easy to show, if you postulate an explosion of sufficient violence to explain the expansion of the Universe, that condensations looking at all like the galaxies could never have been formed.

And so we come to the second group of theories that attempt to explain the expansion of the Universe. These all work by monkeying with the law of gravitation. The conventional idea that two particles attract each other is only accepted if their distance apart is not too great. At really large distances, so the argument goes, the two particles repel each other instead. On this basis it can be shown that if the density of the background material is sufficiently small, expansion must occur. But once again there is a difficulty in reconciling all this with the requirement that the background material must condense to form the galaxies. For once the law of gravitation has been modified in this way the tendency is for the background material to be torn apart rather than for it to condense into galaxies. Actually there is just one way in which a theory along these lines can be built so as to get round this difficulty. This is a theory worked out by Lemaître which was often discussed by Eddington in his popular books. But we now know that on this theory the galaxies would have to be vastly older than our astrophysical studies show them actually to be. So even this has to be rejected.

I should like now to approach more recent ideas by describing what would be the fate of our observable universe if any of these older theories had turned out to be correct. According to them every receding galaxy will eventually increase its distance from us until it passes beyond the limit of the observable universe — that is to say, they will move to a distance beyond the critical limit of about 2,000,000,000 light years that I have already mentioned. When this happens they will disappear — nothing that then occurs within them can ever be observed from our Galaxy. So if any of the older theories were right we should end in a seemingly empty universe, or at any rate in a universe that was empty apart perhaps from one or two very close galaxies that became attached to our Galaxy as satellites. Nor would this situation take very long to develop. Only about 10,000,000,000 years — that is to say, about a fifth of the lifetime of the Sun — would be needed to empty the sky of the 100,000,000 or so galaxies that we can now observe there.

My own view is very different. Although I think there is no doubt that every galaxy we observe to be receding from us will in about 10,000,000,000 years have passed entirely beyond the limit of vision of an observer in our

Galaxy, yet I think that such an observer would still be able to see about the same number of galaxies as we do now. By this I mean that new galaxies will have condensed out of the background material at just about the rate necessary to compensate for those that are being lost as a consequence of their passing beyond our observable universe. At first sight it might be thought that this could not go on indefinitely because the material forming the background would ultimately become exhausted. The reason why this is not so, is that new material appears to compensate for the background material that is constantly being condensed into galaxies. This is perhaps the most surprising of all the conceptions of the New Cosmology. For I find myself forced to assume that the nature of the Universe requires continuous creation — the perpetual bringing into being of new background material.

—Fred Hoyle, *"The Expanding Universe"*

Hoyle begins by asking what causes the observable expansion of the universe. Instead of giving his own answer, however, he first presents earlier theories and shows how they have been disproved. He goes on to suggest what we could expect to happen to the universe if the earlier theories had been right and to fill in the background for his own hypothesis by arguing that something else is more likely to occur. Only then — as the end, the culmination, the climax of this chain of reasoning — does he finally offer his own answer to the question. As a result, his hypothesis seems almost inevitable and therefore powerfully convincing. Since he wrote this essay, new astronomical evidence has led Hoyle to repudiate the position he argues here so plausibly; but the nature and effectiveness of his argument remain the same and demonstrate clearly the values of climactic development.

Fourth, *dramatic*. When you are writing about other people and what they have said, you can often give your writing a welcome change of pace and make it more interesting by letting the people speak for themselves. A conversation heard is usually more absorbing than one heard about. Dramatize, then: occasionally, instead of telling the reader what in effect someone said, introduce him, and let him speak in his own words. If you haven't previously characterized him, bring him to life in the reader's imagination with a sentence or two of his most sharply distinguishing characteristics, and put quotation marks around what he says. Notice how such dialogue adds variety and interest to the following passage:

This morning I took my second cup of coffee in the kitchen, and ate breakfast in the old chair beside the window, under the canary named Christopher. I was impatient to be started. I heard a strange noise outside, a high-pitched hoot from behind the sheep barn, where railroad tracks of the Boston and Maine cut through the soft dirt. It was the time for the morning Peanut, the train that went up to White River Junction in the evening and came back in the morning, but the whistle of the Peanut was the long, throaty lament of the steam engine. I stared at the gap in the ensilage corn through which I would be able to see the train flash. When it came it looked like a trolley car, short and self-propelled, and it hooted again its ridiculous horn. "I suppose that's one of these new Diesels," my grandmother said. "Somebody said they'd seen one this summer."

When I had finished my eggs, I walked up to the tie-up where my grandfather was doing the morning chores. The cows were moving out to pasture, and behind them my grandfather was clapping his hands and shouting. In the spring they would gallop out like young horses, but by this time of year they acted like cows again, and my grandfather was in a hurry to shut the gates behind them. I went into the tie-up to start cleaning it. With the edge of a hoe I lifted up the hinged floorboard over the manure pit, and splattered the cowflops onto their cousins below. My grandfather came in. "How did you like the new whistle?" he said.

"Not so much," I told him. "I like the old kind."

"I suppose there's a reason for it," he said. He picked up the other hoe and scraped along with me. "You should be resting," he said, "for what's ahead of you." He sang one of his tuneless songs, and seemed as excited as I was.

When we walked into the kitchen, my grandmother was packing pie and sandwiches into an enormous paper bag. "You'll need your strength," she said. "Now, Wesley, you eat a good breakfast." He ate his oatmeal and bread and coffee, sitting at one of the set-tubs which was covered with oilcloth. My grandmother finished packing the paper bag and disappeared into the shed. A moment later I heard her pumping at the deep well in the back, and I followed her out to relieve her. I pumped and we filled three milk bottles with cold well water, and she put cardboard tops on the bottles.

We left them inside the shed, and brought the paper bag out with us when my grandfather had finished eating. Two huge pails, shaped wider at the bottom than at the top, lay waiting for us. We put the food in one and the water in the other. Then my grandfather found a wooden yoke which went over the back of his neck, from which the two great pails hung down like enormous earrings. It was the apparatus he used when he made maple sugar in the winter, pouring the sap from the little buckets at each sugar maple into the big pails. I carried two sap buckets in which we would pick the berries, and we started off.

—Donald Hall, *"The Blueberry Picking"*

Hall could easily have summed up in a few words what he and his grandparents said; but if he had, a reader would be less quick to visualize the scene and its separate characters, and Hall's writing would have lost part of its imaginative force and much of its charm. If you don't think so, try rewriting the passage, replacing the dialogue with summary statements, and then compare your version with Hall's original. In your writing, too, dramatize occasionally: not every time you refer to others and to things they have said but whenever it can increase the effectiveness of your writing as it does Hall's in this essay.

Fifth, *logical.* This is the most common and for most would-be writers the most difficult principle of development. Logic is the science of reasoning — that is, logic means developing related ideas in sequences which will lead to valid conclusions. The two basic logical patterns are induction and deduction: *induction* means deriving general concepts or principles from particular observations or ideas; and *deduction* means deriv- particular applications or conclusions from general premises. Logic is a formal and a rigorous intellectual discipline, and once you have mastered the basic processes of writing, you should study logic; it can sharpen your thinking and put an edge on your writing. Even as a would-be writer, however, you must be at least generally aware of the need to develop your ideas in closely related sequences which will give a reader a clear understanding of what you mean. In other words, whether you are working with particular points within the main body or with the entire main body itself, you must develop your ideas so that each one comes clearly from the preceding idea and leads plainly to the one that follows it and so that together they reveal the general premise that links them inductively or deductively.

When you write inductively, then, you express implicitly or explicitly some general premise or idea and provide the specific evidence it rests on. You can begin with a statement of your premise or idea and then give the evidence for it, or, as in the following paragraph, you can begin with your specific material and lead up to the culminating generalization which it suggests.

There were others cast in similar molds. . . . Rube Waddell, the wholly legendary character who, when cold sober, which was not often, may have been the greatest pitcher of them all: the man who now and then, on a whim, would gesture the entire outfield off the premises and then retire the side without visible means of support; Walter Johnson, who once pitched fifty-odd consecutive scoreless innings, and who to the end of his days had nothing much in his repertoire except an unhittable fast ball; Tris Speaker, who played such a short center field that he often threw a batter out at first on what ought to have been a legitimate down-the-middle base hit; and lean Satchel Paige, who in his great days in the Negro leagues had a way of pointing to the shortstop and then throwing something which the batter must hit to short, and who then would go on around the infield in the same way, compelling the opposition to hit precisely where he wanted it to hit. The legends are, in some ways, the most enduring part of the game. Baseball has even more of them than the Civil War, and its fans prize them highly.

—Bruce Catton, *"The Great American Game"*

By linking together the distinguishing actions of Rube Waddell, Walter John, Tris Speaker, and Satchel Paige, Catton makes the summarizing generalizations in the last two sentences very nearly inevitable and undeniable.

When you write deductively, on the other hand, you usually begin with a relatively general statement — some premise or principle or idea — and then go on either to apply it to specific instances or, as in this paragraph by Edward R. Murrow, to derive particular conclusions from it.

It may be that the present system, with no modifications and no experiments, can survive. Perhaps the money-making machine has some kind of built-in perpetual motion, but I do not think so. To a very considerable extent the media of mass communications in a given country reflect the political, economic, and social climate in which they flourish. That is the reason ours differ from the British and French, or the Russian and Chinese. We are currently wealthy, fat, comfortable, and complacent. We have currently a built-in allergy to unpleasant or disturbing information. Our mass media reflect this. But unless we get up off our fat surpluses and recognize that television in the main is being used to distract, delude, amuse, and insulate us, then television and those who finance it, those who look at it and those who work at it, may see a totally different picture too late.

—Edward R. Murrow, *"Speech to Radio and TV News Directors"*

Murrow begins by suggesting that the rich and powerful civilization of America has no magical or intrinsic guarantee of survival. He then argues more specifically that the mass communications media of any civilization reflect the basic forces which animate it and that American television is encouraging its viewers to escape from reality, not to confront it. If this goes on unchecked, he argues, then American television may help to destroy both America and itself.

Whenever you are primarily concerned with explaining an idea or arguing a position, you will probably use both induction and deduction to develop your material logically — induction to establish your general idea or position, and deduction to apply it to particular instances or to draw specific conclusions from it. In logical development, then, your central problem is with the kind of generalizations you express and the particular use you make of them. Avoid like an infectious disease broad, sweeping generalizations unsupported by clear and sufficient specific evidence: don't state them or apply them to particular examples unless you first show convincingly where you got them.

The validity of induction depends on the amount and quality of evidence supporting the generalization it suggests. If, for example, you saw several automobile accidents involving drunken drivers, you might conclude that most car accidents are caused by drinking. Your induction would be invalid, however; you would have to find drunken drivers in a far greater percentage of all automobile accidents before you could safely make such a generalization. The validity of deduction depends on the soundness of the general premise from which it derives. If I argue that all men are immortal, that I am a man, and that therefore, I am immortal,

I may be comforted — but only until someone asks me how I *know* that all men — or indeed, any men — are immortal.

Broad generalizations are the soft pillows of lazy thinkers and irresponsible writers. They are both comforting and inspiring: comforting because they are so easy to make if you don't bother to base them on anything except your own vague feelings; and inspiring because they sound so impressive. Don't fall victim to their tempting lure. When you make a general statement, be certain your reader can clearly understand precisely where you got it and exactly how you are using it.

Whatever kind of writing you do, then — narration, description, exposition, argument, or any combination of these — your task in the main body is to give the reader what you offered him in the introduction and to do it as coherently and as interestingly as possible. This means developing the main body according to some organizing principle or principles — spatial, chronological, climactic, dramatic, logical — depending on your subject, your purposes, and your materials. In a short essay, one of these principles may be sufficent to develop your main point; but in longer pieces, you will probably need several or even all of them to develop your main ideas and their sub-divisions. There are other ways to put a main body together, but these principles are basic and tested; master them before you look around for others.

PASSAGES FOR STUDY

Analyze the following selections from main bodies for the organizing principles and specific techniques designed to make them coherent and interesting.

Animal life lives always in the red; the favorable balance is written on the other side of life's page, and it is written in chlorophyll. All else obeys the thermodynamic law that energy forever runs down hill, is lost and degraded. In economic language, this is the law of diminishing returns, and it is obeyed by the cooling stars as by man and all the animals. They float down its Lethe stream. Only chlorophyll fights up against the current. It is the stuff in life that rebels at death, that has never surrendered to entropy, final icy stagnation. It is the mere cobweb on which we are all suspended over the abyss.

And what then is this substance which is not itself alive but is made by life and makes life, and is never found apart from life?

I remember the first time I ever held it, in the historic dimness of the old Agassiz laboratories, pure, in my hands. My teacher was an owl-eyed master, with a chuckling sense of humor, who had been trained in the greatest laboratory in Germany, and he believed in doing the great things first. So on the first day of his course he set us to extracting chlorophyll, and I remember that his eyes blinked amusement behind his glasses, because when he told us all to go and collect green leaves and most went all the way to the Yard for grass,

I opened the window and stole from a vine upon the wall a handful of Harvard's sacred ivy.

We worked in pairs, and my fellow student was a great-grand-nephew or something of the sort of Elias Fries, the founder of the study of fungi. Together we boiled the ivy leaves, then thrust them in alcohol. After a while it was the leaves which were colorless while the alcohol had become green. We had to dilute this extract with water, and then we added benzol, because this will take the chlorophyll away from the alcohol, which, for its part, very conveniently retains the yellow pigments also found in leaves. This left us with a now yellowish alcohol and, floating on top of it, a thick green benzol; you could simply decant the latter carefully off into a test tube, and there you had chlorophyll extract, opaque, trembling, heavy, a little viscous and oily, and smelling, but much too rankly, like a lawn-mower's blades after a battle with rainy grass.

Then, in a darkened room where beams from a spectroscope escaped in painful darts of light as from the cracks in an old-fashioned magic lantern, we peered at our extracted chlorophyll through prisms. Just as in a crystal chandelier the sunlight is shattered to a rainbow, so in the spectroscope light is spread out in colored bands — a long narrow ribbon, sorting the white light by wave lengths into its elemental parts. And the widths, the presence or the absence, of each cross-band on the ribbon, tell the tale of a chemical element present in the spectrum, much as the bands on a soldier's insignia ribbon show service in Asia, in the tropics, on the border, in what wars. When the astronomer has fixed spectroscope instead of telescope upon a distant star, he reads off the color bands as easily as one soldier reads another's, and will tell you whether sodium or oxygen, helium or iron is present.

Just so our chlorophyll revealed its secrets. The violet and blue end of the spectrum was almost completely blacked out. And that meant that chlorophyll absorbed and used these high-frequency waves. So, too, the red and orange were largely obliterated, over at the right hand side of our tell-tale bar. It was the green that came through clearly. So we call plants green because they use that color least. It is what they reject as fast as it smites the upper cells; it is what they turn back, reflect, flash into our grateful retinas.

—Donald Culross Peattie, "Chlorophyll: The Sun Trap"

As matters stand today, many teachers are unable to do the best of which they are capable. For this there are a number of reasons, some more or less accidental, others very deep-seated. To begin with the former, most teachers are overworked and are compelled to prepare their pupils for examinations rather than to give them a liberalizing mental training. The people who are not accustomed to teaching — and this includes practically all educational authorities — have no idea of the expense of spirit that it involves. Clergymen are not expected to preach sermons for several hours every day, but the analogous effort is demanded of teachers. The result is that many of them become harassed and nervous, out of touch with recent work in the subjects that they teach, and unable to inspire their students with a sense of the intellectual delights to be obtained from new understanding and new knowledge.

This, however, is by no means the gravest matter. In most countries certain opinions are recognized as correct, and others as dangerous. Teachers whose opinions are not correct are expected to keep silent about them. If they mention their opinions it is propaganda, while the mentioning of correct opinions is considered to be merely sound instruction. The result is that the inquiring young too often have to go outside the classroom to discover what is being thought by the most vigorous minds of their own time. There is in America a subject called civics, in which, perhaps more than in any other, the teaching is expected to be misleading. The young are taught a sort of copybook account of how public affairs are supposed to be conducted and are carefully shielded from all knowledge as to how in fact they are conducted. When they grow up and discover the truth, the result is too often a complete cynicism in which all public ideals are lost; whereas if they had been taught the truth carefully and with proper comment at an early age they might have become men able to combat evils in which, as it is, they acquiesce with a shrug.

The idea that falsehood is edifying is one of the besetting sins of those who draw up educational schemes. I should not myself consider that a man could be a good teacher unless he had made a firm resolve never in the course of his teaching to conceal truth because it is what is called "unedifying." The kind of virtue that can be produced by guarded ignorance is frail and fails at the first touch of reality. There are, in this world, many men who deserve admiration, and it is good that the young should be taught to see the ways in which these men are admirable. But it is not good to teach them to admire rogues by concealing their roguery. It is thought that the knowledge of things as they are will lead to cynicism, and so it may do if the knowledge comes suddenly with a shock of surprise and horror. But if it comes gradually, duly intermixed with a knowledge of what is good, and in the course of a scientific study inspired by the wish to get at the truth, it will have no such effect. In any case, to tell lies to the young, who have not means of checking what they are told, is morally indefensible.

—Bertrand Russell, *"The Functions of a Teacher"*

I had myself called with the four-o'clock watch, mornings, for one cannot see too many summer sunrises on the Mississippi. They are enchanting. First, there is the eloquence of silence; for a deep hush broods everywhere. Next, there is the haunting sense of loneliness, isolation, remoteness from the worry and bustle of the world. The dawn creeps in stealthily; the solid walls of black forest soften to gray, and vast stretches of the river open up and reveal themselves; the water is glass-smooth, gives off spectral little wreaths of white mist, there is not the faintest breath of wind, nor stir of leaf; the tranquillity is profound and infinitely satisfying. Then a bird pipes up, another follows, and soon the pipings develop into a jubilant riot of music. You see none of the birds; you simply move through an atmosphere of song which seems to sing itself. When the light has become a little stronger, you have one of the fairest and softest pictures imaginable. You have the intense green of the massed and crowded foliage near by; you see it paling shade by shade in front of you; upon the next projecting cape, a mile off or more, the tint has lightened to the tender young green of spring; the cape beyond that one has almost lost color, and the furthest one, miles away under the horizon, sleeps upon the water a mere dim vapor, and hardly separable from the sky above it and about it. And all this stretch of river is a mirror, and you have the shadowy reflections of the leafage and the curving shores and the receding capes pictured in it. Well, that is all beautiful; soft and rich and beautiful; and when the sun gets well up, and distributes a pink flush here and a powder of gold yonder and a purple haze where it will yield the best effect, you grant that you have seen something that is worth remembering.

—Mark Twain, *Life On The Mississippi*

It is born of winter, this river, in the longest season of cold in the United States. The source mountains in the Colorado Rockies are hard and wild. The air is thin and at such altitude subject to swift, crystalline changes of condition which may bring blue darkness in midday, and yield snow during nine months of the year.

Past monstrous peaks of ragged lifeless rock, clouds tear and roll from wall to wall up in the sky. Wind cries there much of the time, and when the atmosphere is overcharged with electricity, the cut and flare of lightning, the trundle and bounce of thunder after its valley-sharpened crash seem to require new senses, capacities, to be wholly heard.

The river's course — here as in its whole career — widens and narrows by turns. Where it is narrow, the slopes are dark, the stream is shadowed all day but for a little while at noon, when straight fingers of sunlight reach down through the forest. The stream is clear and icy, going rapidly over polished brown speckled stones. They remind us of something. At a glance the diamond water going over its stony bed makes the image of the fish it carries — the same speckled colors, the same watery flicker, the same half-lights of reflection and golden flecks. In and out of leaf shadow, protected by the dazzle of moving water, the trout in plain sight is safe because he and his river are so close in likeness.

The Colorado Rio Grande towns — Monte Vista, Del Norte, Alamosa — are pleasant young communities whose life in each place parallels the railroad tracks for a mile or two. About twenty miles southeast of Alamosa the first sign of Spanish adobe culture appears in a little village — Los Sauses, with houses built of earth, under grand cottonwoods, on a gentle slope above the river, encircled by fine hills. This scene made of slow water, bounteous tree, earthen brick and irrigated field is like a symbolic image of much that is to follow as the river goes south. It is the kind of cell of family, primal want and basic sustenance made visible from which, down-river, grew clusters of kinsmen, and then of neighbors, and then of material dependents, and then of parishioners, and then of descendants, in turn, until a village became a town which became a city, all originally and even now dependent upon the Rio Grande for life.

Over the three communities of Taos — the pueblo, the middle commercial town, and the old Ranchos — there is a piercing sweet illimitable clarity of light and sky. Sounds carry. Meadow larks, mockingbirds, blackbirds have returned. Over the long plain breathes the wind, sharply sweet and already warmed, disturbing nothing but the senses. Space is so great, vision is so plain, air is so clear that human activities can be seen from afar. Small figures like humanity in Brueghel go about their tasks. Earthen buildings go up. Carts travel. Winter rubble is cleared off the fields and out of the *acequias*. Furrows are seeded. Out in the sagebrush of Taos plain, where the old road winds toward the canyon, tiny new-born lambs take fright and scamper before the gusty sand devils whipped up by the darting wind. Flocks move more slowly than cloud shadows. Shepherds sit on a modern culvert and watch what the road brings. The valor and pity of men and women in their renewed use of a corner of the earth is as much a part of spring as everything else.

Here — above Albuquerque — begins the lyric grace of the river in its richest passage of the pastoral life. Where life is fed by water, the landscape here recalls the opulence and grandeur and occasional vistas of order in the image of classical country painted by Nicolas Poussin, who left so many celebrations of grove and meadow, shady leaf and column of light, reflecting stream and stepped mountain and composed bodies. There is more than a reminder here, there is a real likeness. It is a likeness of grace and plenty in the midst of dramatic nature; nourishment in the desert; bounty summoned by the most ancient of agricultural rites out of the most inscrutable of antiquities; cool for the heated, slaking for the parched, food for the hungry, rest for the weary, ease for the eye blinded in the unimpeded sun.

Up to now, going south, when you looked across the river, you knew exactly how things were on the other side — just more U. S. A. But at El Paso with the new concept of a boundary between nations, things are no longer the same on the opposite bank. It is another country, with another people, and with other ways. Many manners and customs have remained common to both sides of the Rio Grande since the time a little over a century ago when the river was not a frontier — when in fact both its banks and all its course were Spanish or Mexican. But in the United States, subject to a more powerful energy in a more technical society, such survivals remain as exotic, quaint, or commercially glamorous; while in Mexico the same expressions are sincere and not self-conscious. From El Paso southeastward, every United States town has its Mexican counterpart across the river. Commerce, appetite and corruption draw them together. Language, national boundary and law keep them apart. The river is hardly an obstacle anywhere, for it can be waded for most of the year, whatever else its common uses may be.

Seventy miles below El Paso, mountains reach in on both sides of the Rio Grande and present to it another of its many obstacles; but the stream bed passes between them and continues upon its depleted way. The river is dying. The desert finally seems ready to triumph over it and drink out of sight the last crawling trickles of the flow that was born in the Colorado Rockies.

—Paul Horgan, "Pages from a Rio Grande Notebook"

On July 4, 1939, there took place at the Yankee Stadium the most tragic and touching scene ever enacted on a baseball diamond. Lou Gehrig Appreciation Day it was called — a spontaneous reaching out to a man who had been good and kind and decent, to thank him for having been so. That day the stands held 61,808 people.

The most touching demonstration of what the day meant was the coming from the ends of the country of Gehrig's former teammates, the powerful

Yankees of 1927. Babe Ruth was there. He and Lou hadn't got along very well the last years they'd played together. But all that was forgotten now, as the Babe chatted pleasantly with Gehrig, who was very near collapse from the emotions that turmoiled within him.

To Lou this great celebration meant good-by to everything he had known and loved. Around him were his lifelong friends. In a box Lou observed his loved ones — his mother and father, unaware of his doom, and his wife.

Gifts piled up before him. They were from the Yankees, from their great rivals — the Giants, from their baseball writers, even from the ushers in the stadium and the peanut boys. The warmth of feeling that had prompted their presentation melted the iron reserve in him, and he broke down.

It was so human and so heroic that Gehrig should have wept there in public, not for pity of himself, nor yet for the beauty and sweetness of the world he would soon leave, but because the boy who all his life had thought himself of no worth understood for the first time perhaps, how much people — family, personal friends, and fans — loved him. And on that day he was the lone receiving station for all the love that was being broadcast to him. To tune in on so much love so suddenly was almost more than he could stand.

There were speeches and the presentation of the gifts.

Wave after wave of cheers rolled down from the stands and broke over Gehrig as he stood at the microphone with head bowed, dashing away the tears that would not stay back. At last, with head lifted, he spoke his heart-breaking, never-to-be-forgotten farewell: "For the past two weeks you have been reading about a bad break I got. Yet today I consider myself the luckiest man on the face of the earth."

The clangy echo of the Yankee Stadium picked up that last brave sentence as it poured from the loud-speakers and hurled it forth: ". . . the luckiest man on the face of the earth . . . the luckiest man on the face of the earth . . . the luckiest man . . ."

—Paul Gallico, *"An American Hero"*

TOPICS FOR ESSAYS

1. Describe your summer job, and explain what you like or dislike most about it.

2. Explain and comment on the registration procedure at your college or university.

3. Write a detailed account of your experience with a natural phenomenon — a storm, a fire, a flood, an earthquake, etc.

4. Attack or defend the fraternity or sorority system — or the absence of one — at your college or university.

5. Describe your favorite hobby, and explain what you like most about it.

6. Go to an art gallery or a museum, and select an abstract painting to look at. Describe in detail *exactly* what you see, and then — but not before — explain what you feel and think about the painting.

7. Explain your views on the purpose and functions of a college or university and on the extent to which it should or should not become involved in political activism.

8. Suppose you had three days in which to do exactly what you would like to do, and then describe how you would spend these days.

9. Describe the main aspects of American life as you think they may be in 1984, and explain why you think they will be so.

10. Make up your own topic, and write on it.

14

The Fundamentals of Structure: Conclusion

As someone is sure to say at the climax of a war movie, this is it — your last crack at the reader. You should make it count. Don't just end your essay; don't stop or allow it to wither away or unravel; conclude it.

A good conclusion does one or both of two vital things: one, *it summarizes what you've been saying in the main body;* and two, *it speculates on the implications of your ideas or projects their potential consequences.* In one direction, an effective conclusion gives the reader a satisfying sense of completeness, of tying together the loose ends; in the other, it sends him away thinking about the implications and significance of your subject. Or it may do both; again, the choice is yours and depends on what you're writing and on what you're trying to do with it.

In writing a good conclusion, you face the same hazard as in the introduction: it's perilously easy to be trite or obvious. Don't say something laboriously simple like, "There, now, reader, you see — my main ideas were such and so." This gets the job done, but it does it with a depressing lack of imagination and grace. In the introduction, you need these qualities to capture the reader's attention and to keep it; in the conclusion, you need them not only to make certain he has gotten your point or points but also to make him glad he took the trouble. Don't just summarize, then; give your main points a sharper focus and make them easier to remember by rephrasing them in fresh and concentrated terms. And don't just tell the reader your subject has implications and significance beyond your statement of it; show him their direction and start him off towards them, or put them concretely and vividly before him.

Here are two conclusions which illustrate these principles:

If the Greeks had left no tragedies behind for us, the highest reach of their power would be unknown. The three poets who were able to sound the depths of human agony were able also to recognize and reveal it as tragedy. The mystery of evil, they said, curtains that of which "every man whose soul is not a clod hath visions." Pain could exalt and in tragedy for a moment men could have sight of a meaning beyond their grasp. "Yet had God not turned us in his hand and cast to earth our greatness," Euripides makes the old Trojan queen say in her extremity, "we would have passed away giving nothing to men. They would have found no theme for song in us nor made great poems from our sorrows."

Why is the death of the ordinary man a wretched, chilling thing which we turn from, while the death of the hero, always tragic, warms us with a sense of quickened life? Answer this question and the enigma of tragic pleasure is solved. "Never let me hear that brave blood has been shed in vain," said Sir Walter Scott; "it sends an imperious challenge down through all the generations." So the end of a tragedy challenges us. The great soul in pain and in death transforms pain and death. Through it we catch a glimpse of the Stoic Emperor's Dear City of God, of a deeper and more ultimate reality than that in which our lives are lived.

—Edith Hamilton, *"The Idea of Tragedy"*

These concise and moving paragraphs conclude a self-contained chapter from Miss Hamilton's book, *The Greek Way to Western Civilization.* The first restates her analysis of the Greek sense of tragedy and what it reveals of Greek life and character. The second relates the tragic sense to our own experience, thereby emphasizing the contribution of the great Greek tragedies to our awareness of the depths of human life. One measure of this conclusion's effectiveness is its combination of economy and apparent inclusiveness: in a few packed sentences, it suggests that nothing important has been left out, that it distills the essence of the chapter. And if you check, you will discover it does. Another measure of this conclusion is its engrossing interest: with quotations, questions, and allusions, Miss Hamilton involves the reader immediately and personally in the significance of her subject.

I said earlier that the ruins of every civilization are the marks of men trying to express themselves, to leave an impression upon the earth. We in the modern world have turned more stones, listened to more buried voices than any culture before us. There should be a kind of pity that comes with time, when one grows truly conscious and looks behind as well as forward, for nothing is more brutally savage than the man who is not aware he is a shadow. Nothing is more real than the real; and that is why it is well for men to hurt themselves with the past — it is one road to tolerance.

The long history of man, besides its ennobling features, contains also a disrupting malice which continues into the present. Since the rise of the first neolithic cultures, as these volumes well reveal, man has hanged, tortured, burned, and impaled his fellow men. He has done so while devoutly professing religions whose founders enjoined the very opposite upon their followers. It is as though we carried with us, from some dark tree in a vanished forest, an insatiable thirst for cruelty. Of all the wounds man's bodily organization has suffered in his achievement of a thinking brain, this wound is the most grievous of all, this shadow of madness, which has haunted every human advance since the dawn of history and which may well precipitate the final episode in the existence of his race.

Not many months ago I chanced to be lecturing at a university whose grounds adjoin a depressed area of slums. After the conclusion of the class hour I sauntered out into a courtyard filled with sunshine and some fragments of Greek statuary. As I passed by the inner gate I was confronted by a scene as old as time. Approaching me along the path upon which they had intruded by squirming through a hedge, was a ragged band of children led by a sharp-featured boy with a bow and an arrow pointed with tin, which he held drawn. Instinctively we both paused — I because I feared for my eyes. There was no more human recognition in the face of the leader than I might have received from a group of hunting man-apes on the African savanna. We measured each other as mutually powerful and unknown forces, best to be avoided. The band drew in unconsciously about its leader and veered aside, with that wide, momentary animal stare haunting me as they passed. For there marched a million years of human history before my eyes, and I was a stranger and afraid although, in my own lifetime, I had made that formidable passage from the caves and sewers of my childhood to this deceptively quiet campus across which these ghosts of long ago now persisted in passing. There was no humor in them, no real play. They slunk on, cruel as man's past, deadly, with the bow poised and the sharp, observant eyes alert to spy out any helpless thing.

I sighed with relief as they clambered over an embankment and disappeared. On a nearby bench with my books spread out before me I did not read. "Man will survive," I said to myself, touched with a slight horror. "God should pity the world. Man will survive." All that passionate energy which in my own life, after many stumblings, had lodged me in these great silent halls, suddenly seemed dissipated and lost. I was as empty and filled with light as a milkweed pod whose substance has evaporated into the silvery autumn air. I thought of the beautiful ruined courts of an Aztec city in which I once had stood. I drew my hand over the bust of Hermes that I knew with surety would find a second burial in the earth. More ghostly, more insubstantial than that hunting pack which roams the world and its dark thickets forever, I felt the dissolving power of the light which falls across lost columns and bleaching mosaics. Beauty man has, but in the very act of possession he is dissolved. I saw in my hand against the statue the projected shriveling of the skin. Each man repeats that history — endlessly and forever.

Nor has any civilization sustained beauty without returning it to the earth. But perhaps man will eventually achieve this victory, I thought doubtfully, standing a little longer in that timeless eternal light that flowed from the great sculpture. Perhaps he will, I thought again, and went on my way toward the darkness.

—Loren Eiseley, *"Paw Marks and Buried Towns"*

This, of course, is the conclusion of the essay whose introduction I discussed in Chapter Twelve; and it is a brilliant example of the kind of conclusion that both summarizes and also projects the reader into further dimensions of meaning and feeling. In the first paragraph, Eiseley not only restates in different terms the essay's central ideas — which you probably recognize from having read the introduction — but also goes further to suggest that the study of the past is more than nostalgia or simple curiosity, that it is necessary for man if he is to rise above savagery to civilization.

In the next paragraph, Eiseley argues that if such study reveals man's possible nobility, it also shows his apparently inherent malice and cruelty. This concept is a logical extension of the preceding paragraph, but it seems at first to be less than directly relevant to the main topic of the essay. A sensitive and careful reader will recall, however, two phrases from the introduction: "possible doom" and "the disease that ate the heart of these lost cultures"; and with this recollection, he feels the full force of Eiseley's fascination with the lost cities of the past and the lesson he reads in their ruins. Nowhere does Eiseley state directly that what man erects in beauty and nobility, he tears down in malice and cruelty; Eiseley would not foster the illusion that the lessons of the past are written so clearly or so obviously on its remains. Instead, he makes the reader feel his way towards this sense of man's "disease" and then evokes it subtly as the culminating significance of the essay.

The anecdote of the children hunting through the college courtyard emphasizes this significance and gives it a compelling and chilling immediacy. This is not the childhood with the gentle Mickey which Eiseley nostalgically recalls in the introduction; this is the childhood of the race, projecting the primitive forces by which man survives but by which he also destroys himself. Against this background, Eiseley points again to the mutability of man, to the intense fragility of all that is human and the poignancy of man's crumbling footprints on the earth.

Like his introduction, then, Eiseley's writing is beautifully controlled and profoundly evocative — here, of course, to achieve the ends of a good conclusion. He sums up the central ideas of the essay and extends their significance, and he does it by making the reader understand them clearly and feel them deeply. Your writing may be less personal than Eiseley's, but the principles and techniques which make both his and Edith Hamilton's conclusions effective will work well for you, too — if you give them the chance.

In discussing Eiseley's conclusion, I refer at several points to his introduction. This implies a relationship which may seem too obvious to need stating but which can be obscured by the separate consideration of the introduction, main body, and conclusion. These are the structural elements of most good writing, but they function within the unifying context of the total essay, not as separate parts of it bolted together. Structure in writing should be like the skeleton in a beautiful girl: she wouldn't be much to look at without it, but it doesn't stick out all over her.

PASSAGES FOR STUDY

These selections are the conclusions to the essays whose introductions you analyzed at the end of Chapter Twelve. Analyze these conclusions for their relationship to the introductions and for the ways in which they function as conclusions.

It would not matter where the Foresights drove to their vacation. The scenes everywhere are much the same, because where one automobile can go, all other automobiles *do* go, and wherever the automobile goes, the automobile's version of civilization surely follows. To be sure, there are still some vacation resorts not yet in a stage of full development, but there are none in a stage of *arrested* development.

Twenty years ago, the slogan, See America First, still had some point. Nowadays, the fact is that if you've seen one part of America, you've seen it all. The automobile did not put the adventure of travel within reach of the common man. Instead, *it first gave him the opportunity to make himself more and more common,* so that when he reached the point in his development where he could find leisure for travel, the lotus lands had disappeared *because he was already there.*

Still, it cannot be said that the common man knows this. We find him constantly trying to pretend otherwise. Who, for instance, do you think really is in that advertised hardtop that swirls to a stop beneath the porte-cochere of the expensive tropical saloon?

Queen Marie of Roumania?

No.

It is merely Roger and June Foresight, or perhaps even Tom and Mae Wretch, listlessly fetching up at one more deadfall — this one in Miami — there to try to escape for a few numbing hours from the fantastic boredom of aimless wandering in the automobile age. They seek surcease in the familiar national joys of tough steaks, cigarette smoke, watered drinks, insolent service, padded bills and a noisy band.

Man, they say, is really living it up these days.

—John Keats, *"The Call of the Open Road"*

In the old-time medicine show you started out by entertaining the crowd — perhaps with a monologue, a banjo player, a dancer, or even a whole cast of performers. Then the good doctor came on to explain the miraculous curative powers of his Old World Herb Tea which always contained fennel seed: "And I think most of you mothers out there remember when your doctor recommended fennel seed for the baby's colic. And then you all know the value of couch grass, particularly you men who . . ." And on he went down the list describing the wonderful ingredients of his product.

And what is the format today? The announcer presents the entertainers and you watch and enjoy. Then the medicine man appears and makes the pitch. He tells you about the acid in your stomach, your unhappy blood, or melancholy muscles — and then he offers you something that has special ingredients that work "almost like magic." He tells you this is a special offer ("I may not pass this way again") and he pushes the giant economy size. Basically this is the same medicine show that rolled around the country for many, many decades, in an exciting and colorful carriage, behind the great white horses, driven by "Dr. John Friendly" or "Professor Brown" or "Chief Granite Cloud."

And neighbors, if you think the last few pages have been interesting, well, then — just move in a little closer; just a little closer, please, and I'll reveal to you the wonders of . . .

—Long John Nebel, *"The Pitchman"*

I do have other lines of continuity to the war, naturally — odd little zigzag ones that appear from time to time — but none of them ever takes me the whole way to it, which is what the reënacters want to do. Antietam has borrowed the snow of a winter weekend when I read about Piper's cornfield and Poffenberger's wood and the Dunker church, sitting beside the picture window of a friend's split-level in Connecticut. I visited Lincoln's house in Springfield once, and perhaps it linked me to him and the war, but I wouldn't swear that it didn't take me first to lilacs in Walt Whitman's dooryard, and even to the spring night when I read about them, in college. (The girl I was going with at the time, a neat blonde, may still not know she is part of the Civil War.) So I have to say that I am connected to the war by a chain of uneven, unlikely links, and that they are what I cherish about it. They *are* it.

One more thing. Edward's wishbone. It gives him his own link with the house and its rooms, but it must have meant something else to the person who hung it there: an occasion. Well, one is attached to an occasion by the things one can recall about it, the small things — the smell of lilacs or violets that may have attended it, the way an elderly relative talked, the songs an old friend sang — and any minor talismans one can save. So I guess I feel as if the reënacters are for all the world like Edward, except that what he does is his affair and what they do is mine. They are enamelling my war, so to speak, my particular war, which they don't know anything about. They are keeping it green, all right, but they are trying to take it away with them, and I wish they would let it alone. I like it right in the house where it always was.

—Robert Henderson, *"The Enamelled Wishbone"*

But the important point for semantics is this: etymologies enlighten us concerning meanings, and sometimes give precision to words whose meanings are somewhat vague to us. The etymology of "definition," for example. This word comes from the Latin roots *de* (off) and *finis* (end, limit, boundary). A definition, then, *delimits* the meaning of a word. The study of etymologies will help us in using the right word to express a precise shade of meaning. But etymologies do not control the use of language. No matter how a word may have originated, it means today what people use it for. Custom is king in matters of language, and if human beings use words in new senses, it cannot be said that they are wrong in doing so, for words are noises arbitrarily associated with things. An assassin today means one who kills in a treacherous manner, not a person who smokes hashish. And etymologies may also be misleading. The word "etymology" itself; for example. The word is based on *etymon*, meaning "the true sense," plus *logos*, or "words," but there are no "true" or "false" senses of words. There are only customary or uncustomary senses. And so, though etymologies illuminate the meaning of many words — like "philanthropist," and "planet" — they do not establish the "real" meaning of the word. Words mean what people intend that they shall mean. We are the masters of the words, not the words of us.

Words are wonderful engines of communication, but we must know what they mean, and how to handle them. And we must guard against being "taken in" by them. As that wise old English philosopher Thomas Hobbes wrote: "Words are wise men's counters — they do but reckon with them, but they are the money of fools."

—Lionel Ruby, *"Words, Words, Words"*

PRACTICE

In the essay collection, read whichever of the essays by Cowley, Eiseley, Morganstern, *Newsweek*, Nicol, Ogburn, and Santayana your teacher assigns. For each essay you read, write a three- or four-page analysis in which you (1) summarize the author's main point or points; (2) discuss his use of concrete details, similes, metaphors, analogies, examples, and allusions; and (3) identify the main elements in the structure of the essay.

TOPICS FOR ESSAYS

1. Indicate a major source of environmental pollution in your area, and explain what you think should be done to stop it.

2. Select one of your earlier essays, and rewrite it. Concentrate on making your structure more effective, both in total and in its parts.

3. Describe an accident in which you were involved or in which you lost a close friend or relative.

4. Find or remember an old house, preferably one deserted and run-down, and describe what you imagine it might have looked like when it was new.

5. Explain what seem to you to be the main principles underlying and animating American foreign policy.

6. Discuss what seem to you to be the main qualities that explain the appeal of your favorite musical group.

7. Explain why you prefer your favorite make of car.

8. Write a review of a movie or a television program which you have seen recently, and point out what you consider its main strengths and/or weaknesses.

9. Attack and/or defend the proposition that "it's better to be Red than dead."

10. Make up your own topic, and write on it.

Part 3

Re-Writing

15

The
Need
for
Revision

Like the first steps, creative thinking and careful planning, this final stage in the writing process is too often slighted by the would-be writer. It would be delightful if one could think his way into a subject, discover what he knew and wanted to say about it, plan the order in which to say it most effectively, and then write it fully and unblemished in clear, vivid, and convincing prose. But regretfully, such one-shot perfection is only the tantalizing dream of good writing, not its reality. When you first finish a piece of writing, what you have is a rough draft — only raw material in need of molding and polishing before you offer it to anyone. If there is a secret to good writing, this is it: to recognize a rough draft for what it is, and then to do something about it.

For the would-be writer, therefore, the first step is prospecting: you look for a rich vein of ore and set up the framework for mining it. Step two is digging: you get the ore out and separate it from the rock. Step three, finally, is shaping: you give the ore a final form and make it shine. It's no good putting in time and effort on the first two if you don't finish the job with the third. If you scribble off something the night before it's due, you'll be turning in writing that's less than your best — and you'll probably get back a grade that's less than what you want.

When you write, then, give yourself the time you need to do all three steps and to do them well. Before you begin writing, think creatively, and plan carefully; then, write clear paragraphs and varied sentences with the best words you can find for your purposes; and finally, make it worth all the trouble by revising what you've written until you're satisfied that you can't do anything else to improve it. In this last step, center your work on two controlling questions: one, *is what I've written any good?*; and two, *is it reasonably correct?*

Correct writing is a matter of convention; good writing of character and personality. Often, if not usually, they coincide; but there is no necessary relationship between them. Correct writing follows the grammatical rules and conventions prevailing at a given time — the conventions of spelling, sentence form, paragraphing, and punctuation established as standard by generally accepted dictionaries and grammar texts. Correct writing begins *outside* the writer in his society and its expectations.

By contrast, good writing is primarily experience more than behavior, psychological more than logical; creative and personal more than conventional and social. It transfers the writer's experience to the reader and involves him in it — makes him feel and think about something in essentially the same ways and at the depths in which the writer has felt and thought about it. Good writing begins *inside* the writer, in his exploration of his experience and knowledge focused on a particular subject, and emerges as his effort to objectify it for someone else to understand and share. If the writer happens to know and to be trained in the conventions of grammar, his writing, if good, will probably also be correct; but if he doesn't know these conventions or care about them particularly, his writing will be good nevertheless if it conveys his subject clearly and interestingly and involves the reader in it.

If a writer has nothing much to say or hasn't the time or the real desire to interest and involve the reader, he can still be rigidly correct in what he writes. But writing that is *only* correct is bad writing indeed. In Lionel Trilling's fine story "Of This Time, Of That Place," a young English teacher makes this disturbing discovery:

Suddenly he bowed. It was such a bow, Howe fancied, as a stage-director might teach an actor playing a medieval student who takes leave of Abelard — stiff, solemn, with elbows close to the body and feet together. Then, quite as suddenly, he turned and left.

A queer fish, and as soon as Howe reached his office, he sifted through the batch of themes and drew out Tertan's. The boy had filled many sheets with his unformed headlong scrawl. "Who am I?" he had begun. "Here, in a mundane, not to say commercialized academe, is asked the question which from time long immemorably out of mind has accreted doubts and thoughts in the psyche of man to pester him as a nuisance. Whether in St. Augustine (or Austin as sometimes called) or Miss Bashkirtsieff or Frederic Amiel or Empedocles, or in less lights of the intellect than these, this posed question has been ineluctable."

Howe took out his pencil. He circled "academe" and wrote "vocab." in the margin. He underlined "time long immemorably out of mind" and wrote "Diction!" But this seemed inadequate for what was wrong. He put down his pencil and read ahead to discover the principle of error in the theme. "Today as ever, in spite of gloomy prophets of the dismal science (economics) the question is uninvalidated. Out of the starry depths of heaven hurtles this spear of query demanding to be caught on the shield of the mind ere it pierces the skull and the limbs be unstrung."

Baffled but quite caught, Howe read on. "Materialism, by which is meant the philosophic concept and not the moral idea, provides no aegis against the question which lies beyond the tangible (metaphysics). Existence without alloy is the question presented. Environment and heredity relegated aside, the rags and old clothes of practical life discarded, the name and the instrumentality of livelihood do not, as the prophets of the dismal science insist on in this connection, give solution to the interrogation which not from the professor merely but veritably from the cosmos is given. I think, therefore I am (cognito etc.) but who am I? Tertan I am, but what is Tertan? Of this time, of that place, of some parentage, what does it matter?"

Existence without alloy: the phrase established itself. Howe put aside Tertan's paper and at random picked up another. "I am Arthur J. Casebeer, Jr.," he read. "My father is Arthur J. Casebeer and my grandfather was Arthur J. Casebeer before him. My mother is Nina Wimble Casebeer. Both of them are college graduates and my father is in insurance. I was born in St. Louis eighteen years ago and we still make our residence there."

Arthur J. Casebeer, who knew who he was, was less interesting than Tertan, but more coherent. Howe picked up Tertan's paper again. It was clear that none of the routine marginal comments, no "sent. str." or "punct." or "vocab." could cope with this torrential rhetoric. He read ahead, contenting himself with underscoring the errors against the time when he should have the necessary "conference" with Tertan.

Correct writing can be dull as December, then, and good writing can be grammatically unconventional or even incorrect. And if you had to choose one or the other, you would in most instances choose the good over the correct. For most would-be writers, however, the choice is unnecessary. You can, if you will, be both a good and a reasonably correct writer. Invest yourself fully in the first two steps of the writing process, and they will return you the substantial interest of a more or less good and correct rough draft. Then reinvest equally in the third step — revising the rough draft — and retire on the income of a piece of writing that really works.

THE AIMS OF REVISION

As you go through your rough draft, aim ceaselessly at *relevance*, *clarity*, and *interest*. Check first for structure. Make sure you have an introduction or some kind of definite beginning to tell the reader the main point or points you want to communicate and to interest him in them. See if you lead into the main body with clear transition; then be certain that in the main body you develop the points in the introduction with sufficient and convincing detail arranged in a coherent order. Finally, be sure you have a strong conclusion — one that develops with smooth transition from the main body and makes a powerful or evocative restatement of what you want to say. In the next three chapters, you will be working in detail and at length with these basic structural elements.

While you improve your structure, check each part of it carefully and eliminate every idea, every expression, which you can't easily defend as significantly related to your topic and necessary for its development. At the same time, don't be too easily satisfied with anything you've written; assume that what is immediately clear to you may be obscure to a reader. Be certain you understand exactly whom you are writing for and why; then put yourself in his place, and ask yourself honestly if you would understand distinctly and easily what you've written — without, that is, the personal background that made it clear to you when you wrote it. Finally, still looking through the eyes of your potential reader, ask yourself whether you'd ever read what you've written unless you had to — and if you had to, whether or not you could stay awake while you read it. Have you, in other words, made any real effort to interest your potential reader?

More specifically, to be *relevant, clear,* and *interesting,* you must write with *precision, economy,* and *color.* Be precise in the words you use. If you don't already have a dictionary, get one; and while you're at it, get or borrow a copy of Roget's *Thesaurus.* Then, make it a habit to use them both in writing your rough draft and also in revising. Don't accept without care or question the first words that come to your mind; they may be exactly the right ones, but they may not be, too. Look critically at every noun, verb, adjective, and adverb: ask yourself whether in the context in which you have used them, they carry a definite and unmistakable meaning and whether that meaning is precisely what you want to say.

Be particularly wary about "big" words: would-be writers too often fall in love with long polysyllabic words because they sound learned and look impressive. But your primary criterion should be not sound or appearance but precision of meaning; when you use "big" words unnecessarily, your writing actually sounds pedantic, and you appear a compositional hypocrite. Such words have their place, of course: almost always, they are abstract and conceptual and are therefore invaluable for expressing complex ideas and relationships. Indeed, "big" words are often the simplest way to say something complicated: *antidisestablishmentarianism* refers to the essence of an English religious movement which would require several sentences to explain. At this point in your development as a writer, however, you are unlikely to need such words very often; use the shortest and simplest ones you can find to express what you want to say sharply and clearly. If you have the slightest doubt about a word, check the dictionary for meanings and then the *Thesaurus* for possible alternatives. Every time you find a precisely right word to replace a fuzzy or a wrong one, a light will thrill on somewhere inside you, and suddenly, all the frustration and searching will be more than worth it.

Closely related to *precision* is *economy:* the more you force yourself to look for and to choose the words which will express your meaning exactly, the less likely you are to use more words than you need. Conversely, therefore, the more you force yourself to express your meaning in the fewest possible words, the more likely they are to be the right ones. Never use ten words where five will do; and never use five where three will do. Take it as a general rule that you can cut 25% to 35% of the words from your rough draft and vastly improve the quality of your writing. Cut out every word which you can't defend as necessary or valuable in some specific way, and be on the watch for groups of words which can be replaced by one or two words. "There were two airplanes that were waiting to take off into the sky" really means "two planes were waiting to take off; "on a day-to-day basis" really means "daily": "they corresponded on a day-to-day basis" means "they wrote daily." Be economical with words, then; don't use any you can't honestly justify. Wordy writing, like watered stock, is worth far less than its face value.

If your writing is *precise* and *economical*, it will probably be *relevant* and *clear*, but it will not therefore be automatically *interesting*. For this, you need to write with *color* — to give your writing qualities likely to involve your reader's imagination and emotions as well as his reason and intellect. Christ, for example, taught his ethical and moral principles not in abstract generalities but in simple, vivid parables; and they are still imaginatively effective after almost 2,000 years. Make sure you have expressed your ideas in terms which will appeal to your reader's senses and experience: see if you have used specific and concrete words wherever possible instead of general and abstract ones. Don't, for instance, write about picturesque panoramas; point to the green sides and brown floor of the valley where red roofs and white walls shine bright as glass in the shimmering sunlight. You can't avoid generalizations and abstractions, nor should you want to; but you seldom have to leave them at that. As you know from the earlier chapters of this book, you can embody generalizations and abstractions in concrete equivalents, in images, similes, metaphors; support them with analogies; illustrate them with examples; and enrich them with allusions. Be sure you've used these techniques, then: with them, you can lead your reader beyond just understanding your ideas to experiencing them directly in his imagination; and the more you can make him do this, the more *interesting* as well as *relevant* and *clear* he will find your writing.

A CHECKLIST FOR REVISION

The aims of revision are not difficult to understand; the main problem in revision is getting at it. For at least two reasons, most would-be writers look for almost any excuse to avoid revising something they've written: first, *a sense of completion*. When you've finally finished a piece of writing, especially one you've taken seriously and really worked on, you feel emotionally, intellectually, and even physically drained. You want nothing so much as to put it away and forget it; you want achingly to be done with it. Second, *objectivity*. It's difficult enough ever to be objective about something you've written, but it's almost impossible when you've just finished it. The easiest thing to do, then, is to leave it alone, relax with a huge sigh, and go to a movie.

The trouble is that way back in your mind you *know* you've done only two-thirds of the job, and you have a sneaking suspicion that your reader is going to know it, too. So, you don't even enjoy the movie. And when your paper comes back decorated in technicolor red, you wish — oh, how you wish! — you'd taken the time to revise it.

You can save yourself all this anxiety and remorse simply by doing what you know you should do — by revising your rough draft. Moreover, the pleasure of the feeling of accomplishment and pride that comes with knowing you've done your best is more than worth the agony of revising. The real secret of revision is time: on any writing task, you should plan to get your rough draft done soon enough to put it away and forget it for at least a day and still have time to take it out again and revise it. Getting rid of it for a day will help not only to satisfy your sense of completion but also to give you enough distance from your writing to be able to look at it with at least some objectivity.

When you do return thus refreshed to your rough draft, read it through once or twice to get the feel of it; then, to the best of your ability, improve its quality and correctness according to the following checklist.

1. *Structure*

a. Exactly what audience are you writing to and why?

b. Do you have a title indicating *both* the subject *and* also your particular aspect of it? Is it a catchy title — will it capture the reader's attention?

c. Do you have a definite introduction, main body, and conclusion? Do you have clear transition between them? Are they interesting and coherent?

2. *Relevance and Interest*

a. Is your material directly and essentially relevant to the topic? Do you have enough details to develop it convincingly?

b. Have you used any unnecessary words or expressions? Have you unintentionally repeated yourself?

c. Is your language as specific and concrete as possible?

d. Have you used techniques to interest the reader and involve his imagination — similes, metaphors, analogies, examples, and allusions?

3. *Mechanics and Style* — most of your writing is probably reasonably correct, and much of it stylistically effective. Nothing is to be gained, then, by a general worry over mechanics and style. Instead, concentrate on those weaknesses which appear repeatedly in your writing. Read through the list of common errors in Chapter Seventeen, and make a note of any old enemies you recognize. Then, as you get papers back from your instructor, look up the errors he indicates; those you haven't already noted, correct and add to your list. Those you have listed, correct and put a check after on your list; and thereafter, be doubly careful not to make the same errors again.

While you are building up your own list of errors, use the one in this delightful letter by Prof. George W. Feinstein. Nearly all the errors he illustrates and others as well are discussed in some detail in Chapter Seventeen, "Common Errors in Mechanics and Style"; use the marking chart inside the back cover to find the numbers of the pages on which the discussion of particular errors appears.

LETTER FROM A TRIPLE-THREAT GRAMMARIAN

Dear sir; you never past me in grammer because you was prejudice but I got this here athaletic scholarship any way. Well, the other day I finely get to writing the rule's down so as I can always study it if they ever slip my mind.

1. Each pronoun agrees with their antecedent.
2. Just between you and I, case is important.
3. Verbs has to agree with their subjects.
4. Watch out for irregular verbs which has crope into your language.
5. Don't use no double negatives.
6. A writer mustn't shift your point of view.
7. When dangling, don't use participles.
8. Join clauses good, like a conjunction should.
9. Don't write a run-on sentence you got to punctuate it.
10. About sentence fragments.
11. In letters theme reports articles and stuff like that use commas to keep a string of items apart.
12. Don't use commas, which aren't necessary.
13. Its important to use apostrophe's right.
14. Don't abbrev.
15. Check to see if you are words out.
16. In my opinion I think that an author when he is writing shouldn't get into the habit of making use of too many unnecessary words that he does not really need in order to put his message across.
17. In the case of a business letter, check it in terms of jargon.
18. About repetition, the repetition of a word might be real effective repeti-

tion — take, for instance, Abraham Lincoln.
19. As far as incomplete constructions, they are wrong.
20. Last but not least, lay off clichés.

Your primary problem with such errors in mechanics and style is to break the bad habits which cause you to make them. Notice, for example, how many of these mistakes you recognize as wrong and laugh at when you see them in obvious illustrations — and then see if you don't go blithely off and make some of them in your own writing. At some point in the past, you began writing this way, and no one made you stop and write correctly — at least not often enough to form new and good habits. Use your list of errors, then, not only to make a particular piece of writing more correct as you write and revise it but also to break your old bad habit patterns and to begin forming new and better ones. The more often you spell a word or punctuate a sentence correctly, the more likely you are to do it correctly again the next time.

Take revision seriously; think of it not as something dull and burdensome that has to be done to your rough draft but as an integral and creative part of your total writing process. Remember that as a would-be writer, it's not only what you do but also how you redo that counts. The following chapters on usage and mechanics should help you with this essential process.

16

The

Question

of

Usage

The difficulty in discussing usage is that people often mean conflicting things by it. To some, it means what people actually do when they speak and write; to others, it means what they should do. Frequently, linguistic questions become moral issues, and tempers explode at the idea of reducing language to mob rule or at the notion that it should conform to an artificial standard of perfection. What people want — what you want — are guidelines; football would be murder without rules and referees, and how can you write well without their equivalent in language? The real problem, then, is this: who makes the rules and on what basis?

For centuries, people went blithely along using English any way they wanted to consistent with what their family and friends in their social class were doing and influenced at the higher levels by literary models and at all levels after 1611 by the King James Version of the *Bible*. If the result was chaotic variety, it was also lively and rich. In the late seventeenth and eighteenth centuries, the rise of modern science began, and at the same time, many leading thinkers and artists turned to the traditions and principles of Graeco–Roman life and art for contemporary standards. In the resulting passion for order and classification, scholars seeking to systematize English and to establish laws for good usage produced the first English grammars. True to the spirit of the age, these were based largely on Latin, which meant making a different and a dead and therefor unchanging language the absolute standard for another very much alive and inevitably changing one. The efforts of these early grammarians were undeniably laudable, but their method and its results raised some obvious problems.

Most people either didn't know or simply ignored the new rules, but scholars and schoolteachers continued to write and to use prescriptive grammars modeled on the first ones. Twentieth-century developments in science and philosophy made such grammars and their method increasingly irrelevant, and in 1933, Leonard Bloomfield's *Language* marked out new directions for linguistic studies. Bloomfield argued that languages are unique human phenomena to be described as they function, not legislated by reference to logical systems or ideal standards. "Good" or correct usage, he declared, is a matter for rhetorical, not grammatical, determination.

With this book, the conflict was joined between traditional prescriptive and modern descriptive linguistics. Since then, the most important and influential work has been that of the descriptive linguists, and their ideas have been given widespread popular extension by Bergen Evans on television and by the controversy over *Webster's Third New International Dictionary*. Against this descriptive work, traditionalists of every kind have united, less for linguistic reasons, perhaps, than because in an age of vanishing absolutes, modern linguistics is chipping away at still another.

Like most such conflicts, especially at the popular level, this one often generates more heat than light. At one extreme, unyielding traditionalists argue that there is a perfect English and that the descriptive linguists are out to destroy all standards; at the other, radical modernists declare that there are no standards, that "good" usage is entirely relative to what people are actually saying and writing. As usual, the truth is somewhere in the middle, a position occupied by most professional linguists today. Dependence on an artificial perfection leads to pedantic unreality and to quarrels over whose perfection is the right one; and reliance only on what people are doing makes no distinction between enduring values and temporary fashions. There are standards, of course, but they aren't absolute: they are relative to your purposes and to the audience you are speaking to or writing for.

Different audiences implies different levels of usage, and efforts are often made to establish a standard by classifying such levels. The list of these categories is apparently endless and grows with each new effort: formal, informal, colloquial, vulgate, standard, sub-standard, common, provincial, illiterate, literary, scientific, technical, slang, jargon, cant, and so on. Moreover, the levels of usage these terms identify usually have wide variations within them, and a word or expression that is formal in one context could be informal in another. You'll be better off, then, to forget the idea of levels and their classification and to look at the problem of usage as one of attitude.

The primary function of language is communication, and it begins in speech. In your writing, therefore, your attitude should be one of desire to communicate fully and of willingness to use the patterns and expressions of speech or to polish them depending on your subject and its audience. This means giving up the notion that there are any formulas to write by and regarding each piece of writing you have to do as a unique challenge. And it means responding to this challenge with the hard work of knowing your subject and your audience well enough to be able to use the language which will most effectively bring them together. If you know thoroughly what you want to say and if you choose language your particular audience will understand most clearly and respond to most positively, only an occasional unregenerate purist is likely to quarrel with your usage or with its standards.

DENOTATION AND CONNOTATION

One central problem in communicating through language is the fact that words convey meaning in more than one way. Nearly all our words are content words — nouns, verbs, adjectives, and adverbs — and all have two kinds of meaning. A word *denotes* what it stands for, and denotation is the idea, emotion, object, or quality which a word identifies. But a word also *connotes* what we feel about it, and connotation is the feelings attached to a word by our past experience with it. These meanings function simultaneously and inseparably, though not always with equal force; and in some situations and contexts, one may temporarily overshadow the other.

Denotatively, *home* means the place where we live; connotatively, it means what the total of our experiences there have made us feel about it. If you grew up as part of a happy family in a neighborhood full of friends, the word home will give you a warm and pleasant feeling. But if you grew up moving back and forth between the different apartments of divorced parents, it will probably make you feel both cynical and wistful. Let's take another example. Denotatively, *champagne* is a sparkling wine produced originally in a particular region of France. It has become customary to drink this wine on special occasions, and the word *champagne* has consequently taken on connotations of superior quality and even of luxury. These connotations make it possible to advertise a brand of beer as "the champagne of bottled beers." Denotatively, of course, this is nonsense — unless the brewer has invented a beer that tastes like sparkling wine; connotatively, however, it makes good and, I imagine, profitable sense.

Good writers take advantage of this double meaning of words. Get in the habit of looking for words which will convey your ideas in a combination of the clearest denotation and most effective connotations. Suppose you want to describe a long touchdown pass:

Unitas threw a fifty-yard touchdown pass to Mackey.

Unitas flipped the ball fifty yards to Mackey, who lugged it in for the score.
Unitas hit Mackey with a fifty-yard bullet for the score.
Unitas hurled a fifty-yard strike to Mackey for six points.
Unitas propelled the football half the length of the field to Mackey, who
received it and scored.

Denotatively, each of these sentences means essentially the same thing,
but connotatively, each is different. Only the context can determine
whether any of these is appropriate or which is the best, and that makes
it a question of your conscious choice. Put the double meaning of words
to work, then, and make both denotation and connotation serve your
purposes.

A serious error you'll probably make if you're not careful is using
words whose denotations convey your ideas but whose connotations
cause reactions you don't want. Both *sensuous* and *sensual* denote
experience through the senses, but if you write, "He has *sensuous* appetites," you imply that he has healthy desires for such experience; and if
you write, "He has *sensual* appetites," you imply that he is lewd and full
of sexual lust. Similarly, both *slender* and *skinny* denote leanness and
a slight frame; and *figure* and *body* can each denote physical form. But
a *slender figure* is not the same thing as a *skinny body*. If you imagine
it is, comment on your girl friend's or your boy friend's *skinny body* —
and then start looking for a new girl friend or boy friend.

Another consequence of the double meaning of words is the problem
of loaded language. Words can become so highly charged with feelings
and emotions that they can be used to arouse these feelings and emotions
without regard to what the words denote. *Communism* is a good example.
Denotatively, it means a political–social–economic doctrine and a historical phenomenon. In the middle of the twentieth century, however, few
Americans know or even think about what the word denotes. The only
real threats to our national existence are Soviet Russia and China, and
both are nominally communist states. It is easy, therefore, to identify
our fears of nuclear war and annihilation with the word *communism* and
thereafter to respond to it as though it were a live time-bomb about to go
off in our faces.

The danger of such loaded language should be obvious. Unrestrained
by any limiting denotation, such words can become damaging weapons
for anyone who wants to use the feelings and emotions they contain for
his own purposes. Notice, for instance, how often one politician attacks
another as "soft on communism." He seldom specifies exactly what he
means by "soft" nor does he show that the object of his attack accepts
communist doctrines or supports the expansionist policies of communist
states. He doesn't have to. The people he's addressing won't expect such
evidence. Many will assume that "where there's smoke, there's fire," and
wait for the attacked man to prove that he isn't "soft on communism."

With no evidence to disprove, he can defend himself only by shouting loudly and often that in fact he's been "hard on communism" for years. And in the minds of some people the suspicion will linger that there's something wrong with that man.

In short, neither the politicians nor the audience involved act like rational human beings. Loaded language can turn us into frightened animals and put us on the road back into the jungle. Watch out for it. Reject it as inaccurate or dishonest when others use it, and refuse to use it yourself. You should be among those who use language as a beacon in the dark, not with those who would bring the darkness back.

SOME TIPS ON GOOD USAGE

In the following short glossary, I've discussed the specific problems in usage — particularly in diction — which I've found most often during recent years in the work of would-be writers. These tips and the next chapter on common mechanical and stylistic errors may not by themselves make you a good writer, but they should dress you up and point you in that direction.

Ad. The short and easy way to write *advertisement,* but use the full word in formal writing. Few people would object to *plane* — from *airplane* — and someday words like *ad, auto, phone,* and *photo* will probably be equally acceptable. While you're waiting, use them informally, and don't put periods after them.

Affect, effect. You won't have any difficulty with these except when you use them as verbs, and then the trouble is that they not only sound alike but also have similar meanings. Still, the differences are real, and you must observe them. *To affect is to influence; to effect is to make something happen:* "the drug *affects* the circulation and thereby *effects* a cure."

Aggravate, irritate. This is the sort of thing that makes the purist cry. Until fairly recently, *to aggravate* meant to *make something worse,* and *to irritate* meant *to make impatient or angry.* Gradually, however, people began using *aggravate* when they meant *irritate,* and now this usage is widespread and turns up even in formal writing. It's too bad, really, because the two words preserved a useful distinction. But unless your instructor objects or you want to impress your date, you might as well go with the tide. It seems to be a very big tide.

Already, all ready. If you confuse these, you're just being careless. *Already* means that whatever you're talking about happened earlier: the book is *already* overdue. *All ready* means that everyone is prepared:

"they were *all ready* in the house"; or that something is completely finished or prepared: "my essay is *all ready* now."

Alright, all right.   These mean the same thing, and I don't know where *alright* came from. It's probably part of the simplifying process which has been one side of the development of English, but it doesn't seem to be catching on very fast, especially in formal writing. For the time being, forget it.

And etc.   Etc. is bad enough: it seldom says anything except that you've run out of things to say. But why compound the misery with *and? Et cetera* means *and so forth;* and etc. means AND *and so forth.*

As, because.   This is another distinction in the process of disappearing. Both can be subordinating conjunctions. *As* means *when* or *while:* "as he walked down the street, his hat blew off" and *because* indicates *causation:* "*because* he walked down the street, his hat blew off." Except in direct and strong causal relationships, however, *as* seems to be used increasingly in place of *because,* and even here the distinction seems to be breaking down. You should probably continue to observe it in formal writing, but I'll bet you won't be doing it much longer.

Being that, being as how.   Unless you want to sound like the *Beverly Hillbillies,* don't write such awkward and illiterate phrases. You mean *since* or *because* — they sound better and do the job in fewer words.

Beside, besides.   Beside means *alongside* or *by the side of:* "she sat *beside* me." It can also mean *not part of:* "that's *beside* the point." *Besides* means *furthermore* or *in addition to:* "I have to go to class; *besides,* I want to go."

Among, between.   Between implies two: "Tom and Jack divided the money *between* them"; and *among* implies more than two: the gang divided the money *among* them."

Consensus.   Don't write "*consensus* of opinion" unless you are also willing to write "symphony of music." And if you are, you shouldn't be. *Consensus* means *a general agreement or opinion;* if you say "*consensus* of opinion," you are saying "a general opinion of opinion." Why say the same thing twice?

Continual, continuous.   This useful distinction seems to be surviving unchallenged. *Continual* means *often repeated;* "he goes to the movies *continually.*" *Continuous* means *uninterrupted, unbroken:* "the movies are shown *continuously.*"

Could of.   You mean *could have.* The contraction "*I wish I could've* gone," sounds like *could of*, and some people start saying it that way. Don't you do it — especially in your writing.

Different from, different than. Most of the time, *different from* is the only acceptable choice. Where things differ, they differ *from*, not *than*, each other. Still, *different than* has a long and not ignoble history, and sometimes, it is a clear and economical form. If you are contrasting nouns or pronouns, always use *different from*: "motorcycles are *different from* motor scooters." But if a clause is the second element in your contrast, use *different than*: "she looked *different than* I expected." The alternative is this: "she looked *different from what* I expected"; but if you can convey the same meaning in two words, why use three?

Each and every. You're trying to sound impressive and only being wordy. Say *each;* or say *every.*

Emigrate, immigrate. People *emigrate* from one country in order to *immigrate* to another.

Except, accept. These verbs sound almost alike, but they have widely different meanings. *To except* means *to leave out, to exclude*: "the coach *excepted* Paul from the extra practice"; *to accept* means *to take something offered to you* or *to agree to something*: "I *accepted* the invitation," or "Japan *accepted* the terms of surrender." You probably won't use *to except* very often; your real problem is spelling *accept* correctly.

Except for the fact that. This is wordy and awkward nonsense. Don't write, "*Except for the fact that* he failed this course, he would still be in college"; write, "*If* he hadn't failed this course, he would still be in college."

Family, group, team. These and words like them are collective nouns; they can take either singular or plural verbs and pronouns depending on whether you think of them as a unit or as several people. "The *family* is well and happy" emphasizes the condition of the whole group; "The *family* are well and happy" points to the condition of each person in the group. In sentences with both a collective noun and also a pronoun referring to it, be consistent: don't write, "The *team* are playing *its* best." Write either "The *team* is playing *its* best" or "The *team* are playing *their* best."

Farther, further. They mean exactly the same thing, and you can use them interchangeably. Nearly everyone else does. A few people argue that *farther* should be used for distance and *further* for degree or quantity, but the argument has neither precedent nor reason.

Fine. Most people use it both as an adjective: "it's a *fine* day"; and also as an adverb: "it works *fine*." The trouble is that people use it too much and have worn it out as an adjective, and many people object to its use as an adverb in formal writing. Give it a rest for a while.

Funny.   This can mean either *humorous* or *queer,* but it is not yet fully accepted in formal writing to mean *queer.* Better write *odd,* or *strange,* or *eccentric.*

Good, well.   There is no logical difference between "He swims *good*" and "He swims *well,*" but most people will look at you oddly if you say "He swims *good.*" And if you use good adverbially in formal writing, you'll be penalized for it one way or another. Strike a blow for reason if you must, then, but be prepared to take the consequences.

In case.   This is a kind of verbal crabgrass — it spreads everywhere, and it's hard to get rid of. *In case, in the case of, in this case, in many cases, just in case* — it goes back at least to the sixteenth century. At that time, it was probably a fresh metaphor drawn from the law, but by now it's worn out and empty. "*In that case,* don't use it *in the case of* your writing, *just in case* it's one of the *many cases* your instructor dislikes."

In many instances.   Wordy. You mean *often* or *frequently.*

In my estimation, judgment, opinion.   Wordy and pompous. What's wrong with *I think* and *I believe?*

Inside of.   "*Inside* the car" is shorter and sounds better than "*Inside of* the car." If you are referring to time — "*inside* of a year" — either *within* or *in less than* sounds better in formal writing.

Irregardless.   It's pointless to tell you there's no such word — not when you've heard it used and I've just written it. But it is a needless and silly word. It's an illegitimate and illogical mixture of *irrespective* and *regardless,* two clear and established words. Use one or the other.

Its, it's.   An apostrophe usually means possession: "the *plane's* engine caught fire"; or contraction: "I'm going home." But pronouns form their possessive without an apostrophe: their–theirs; your–yours. Therefore, *its* is possessive: "the dog ran to *its* master"; and *it's* is a contraction: "*it's* my dog." The difference can be confusing, and I don't know any way to remember it except to get in the habit of thinking *it is* whenever you write *it's.*

Lie, lay.   It's easy to confuse these because their last two principal parts sound alike: *lie, lay, have lain; lay, laid, have laid;* and because the past form of *lie* is the same as the present of *lay. Lie* means *to recline; lay* means *to put down;* and the only way to keep from saying things you don't mean is memorization and careful usage. Watch out for confusions like this: "I think I'll *lay* down now" when you mean "I think I'll *lie* down now"; and "He *lay* the book away in a safe place" when you mean "He *laid* the book away in a safe place."

Like, as, as if.   In formal writing, most people expect *like* to take an object: "this cloth feels *like* silk"; and if you use *like* as a subordinating conjunction in place of *as* or *as if*, you'll make a bad impression. Don't write, "Fords look good, *like* an automobile should" for "Fords look good, *as* an automobile should"; or "My old car rides *like* it had new tires" for "My old car rides *as if* it had new tires."

Loan, lend.   Here's another distinction which seems to be losing its force. Generally, *loan* is a noun and *lend* a verb: "if you want a *loan*, the bank will *lend* you what you need." But in business dealings both are commonly used as verbs, and *loan* seems to be replacing *lend:* "the bank *loaned* the company a million dollars." In daily usage, too, you would probably say, "I *loaned* him my car" rather than "I *lent* him my car." In formal writing, however, the distinction still holds; and unless you are discussing business, you would be wise to follow it. Why borrow trouble?

Loose, lose.   This is another example of similar sounds leading to careless misspelling. *Loose* means *to release* or *to set free; lose* means *to suffer a loss.* If you are making this error, stop whenever you write either word, and check it.

Might of, should of, ought to of, must of.   The *of's* should be *haves.* See *could of.*

Nice.   A convenient word for lazy thinkers — and writers. Like *fine*, it conveys a vague approval, but it, too, has been used to death. Bury it, and say exactly what you approve. Don't write, "It's a *nice* day" or "She's a *nice* girl"; write, "It's a *warm* and *happy* day" and "She's a *kind* and *friendly* girl."

Off of.   Forget the *of.* See *inside of.*

One.   The use of *one* to hide behind in expressions like, "*One* thinks taxes are too high" seems to be diminishing. Hurray! Hurry it on its way, and write, "*I* think taxes are too high." And while you're at it, send the editorial *we* after the indefinite *one:* unless you represent a group, don't write, "*We* think taxes are too high."

One and the same.   More wordy nonsense. You mean *the same.*

Only.   For clarity, modifiers should be placed as close as possible to the word or words they modify. Logically, there is a difference between "He *only* lost his wallet" and "He lost *only his* wallet." In practice, however they mean the same thing — his wallet is gone; and most of the time, no one will criticize you for saying or writing "He *only* lost his wallet." It might bother some people in formal writing, though, so avoid this usage there.

Outside of.   You don't need the *of*; see *inside of*. And don't use *outside of* where you mean *except* or *besides*. "They all left *outside of* Gina" is an awkward — and a slightly silly — way to say "They all left *except* Gina." And "*Outside of* writing this paper, I have to read three books" is equally awkward for "*Besides* writing this paper, I have to read three books."

Passed, past.   *Passed* indicates an action; *past* refers to something earlier: "in the *past* two games, Unitas *passed* for five touchdowns." Don't let this similarity in sound confuse your spelling, either.

Principal, principle.   Or this one. *Principal* means *highest* or *main*; *principle* means *fundamental truths* or *beliefs, rules of conduct*: "the *principal* task of a church is to teach religious *principles*"; "the *principal* of our school is a man of high *principles.*

Rarely ever, seldom ever.   Both *rarely* and *seldom* mean *infrequently, hardly ever.* If you write *rarely ever*, therefore, you're saying *hardly ever ever.* Don't. Write, *rarely* or *seldom.*

Real, really.   Both mean *actually* or *truly* and are used like *very*, but in formal writing, use *really.*

Reason is because, reason why.   These are both redundant: they repeat the same idea without changing it or adding anything to it. The reason for something is its cause, its why; so *the reason is because* means *the cause is because,* and *the reason why* means *the why why.* Don't write, "*The reason* I'm leaving *is because* I'm tired" or "That's *the reason why* I'm leaving"; write, "*The reason* I'm leaving *is that* I'm tired" or "I'm leaving *because* I'm tired"; "That's *the reason* I'm leaving" or "That's *why* I'm leaving."

Seasons.   It's no longer customary to capitalize spring, summer, fall, autumn, or winter.

Seeing that.   Wordy and awkward. Use *since* or *because.*

Toward, towards.   Use whichever sounds better to you in a particular context. They mean the same thing.

Type.   Adding *type* after a noun is a device for making a quick comparison or classification. It's been much overused; moreover, there are better ways to do both. "He has a balloon-like face" makes a much stronger comparison than "He has a *balloon-type* face." And, "Westinghouse is building a nuclear reactor" is simpler and sounds better than

"Westinghouse is building a *nuclear-type* reactor." Don't use this trite-type device; it gives your writing a dull-type sound.

Unique, perfect.   Logically, a thing is either *unique* or not *unique; perfect* or not *perfect;* it can't have degrees of oneness or of perfection. If it is even the tiniest bit like anything else, it isn't *unique;* if it has the tiniest flaw, it isn't *perfect.* People aren't always logical, however, especially with language, and *unique* is often used to mean *extraordinary,* and *perfect* to mean *extremely good.* Thus, people can say, "That's a *very unique movie*" and "It's the *most perfect* day I ever say." In formal writing, however, logic still rules, and you will be wise to obey it. Write, "That's an *almost unique* movie" and "It's the *most nearly perfect* day I ever saw."

Who, which, that.   Use *who* to refer only to people, *which* to refer to anything else, and *that* to refer to either, depending on which sounds best in the context. Write, "The man *who* or *that* spoke to me," but not "The man *which* spoke to me"; and "The dog *that* bit me," but not "The dog *who* bit me."

Wise.   In recent years, it's become fashionable to add *wise* to a word when you want to stress it as the key word in a sentence. Advertising and business seem especially enamored of this device, but it has become widespread in common speech and even in much writing. *Saleswise, salarywise, gradewise, consumerwise, stylewise* crop up everywhere. It's easy to react against it and to sneer at it, and in the end, this may be the best reaction. But it is too soon yet to tell whether this device is merely a fad or whether it has any lasting value. "*Saleswise,* the campaign succeeded" is simpler and more emphatic than "*In terms of sales,* the campaign was a success" or "The campaign succeeded in *stimulating sales*" or "The *sales* campaign succeeded." Often, however, this use of *wise* seems awkward or forced, and it is undeniably being overused. In your writing, then, if you use it at all, use it only when you can defend it in terms of simplicity and emphasis.

Would have.   People sometimes use this form instead of *had* in expressing wishes and in if-clauses: "I wish I *would have bought* that book when I had the chance"; and "if I *would have bought* that book, I would have my assignment done by now." Use the standard *had;* it's simpler, and it sounds better: "I wish I *had bought* that book when I had the chance"; and "If I *had bought* that book, I would have my assignment done by now."

17

Common
Errors in
Mechanics
and Style

Agreement of Pronoun and Antecedent. A pronoun is a word that stands for a noun or another pronoun and is therefore a means of avoiding the dull and awkward repetition of the noun it replaces. This advantage becomes a liability, however, if the pronoun obscures or conflicts with the idea its antecedent — the noun or pronoun it stands for — conveys. Make certain, then, that when you use a pronoun in place of an earlier noun or pronoun, you use it to convey the same idea. Generally, this won't cause you much trouble, but in a few constructions, it may.

ONE: When the pronoun is relatively distant from its antecedent, be careful not to forget the nature of the antecedent. In "The farther a man marches on hot and humid days, the wearier they get," the pronoun should, of course, be *he.*

Two: With collective nouns like crew and family, be consistent in a subsequent pronoun. If you give the noun a singular meaning and a singular verb, give it a singular pronoun. Look up *team* in the preceding chapter's tips on usage.

THREE: Words like *any, anyone, every, everyone, each, someone, somebody,* and *everybody* usually take singular pronouns: "*everyone in* the room clapped *his* hands." But *every, everyone, everybody,* and *each* can have plural meaning; and then they require a plural pronoun: "*everybody* agreed that *they* should go."

144

Four: In an *either-or* or a *neither-nor* construction in which one of the terms is plural, a following pronoun should agree with the nearest term: "neither Jack nor his roommates finished *their* work"; or, "neither his roommates nor Jack finished *his* work." If both antecedents are singular, use a singular pronoun.

Agreement of Subject and Verb.   Singular subjects require singular verbs; plural subjects require plural verbs. The way to avoid errors here, then, is to know what word or group of words is the subject and whether it is singular or plural. If you know this clearly, you aren't likely to use the wrong verb form. Like pronoun agreement, this problem will probably bother you only in certain constructions.

One: Phrases separating the subject and verb can distract you from the subject and cause you to use the wrong verb form: "the old man with the many cats and dogs *live* in a shack by the river." *Man*, not *cats and dogs*, is the subject; and the verb should be *lives*. Watch your writing carefully for this error; it's an easy one to make.

Two: If one of the terms in an *either-or* or a *neither-nor* subject is plural, the verb should agree with the term closest to it: "either Jack or his friends *are* responsible"; or, "either his friends or Jack *is* responsible." If both terms are singular, the verb should be singular: "neither Jack nor his friend *is* responsible."

Three: In a sentence beginning with *there*, the subject follows the verb, but the verb must still agree with the subject, not with the singularity suggested by *there*: "there *are* still a hat and a coat on the chair."

Four: In *who-* and *that*-clauses, the verb should agree with the antecedent of *who* or *that*: "Lynn is the only one of the girls in both neighborhoods who *is* going to the party." Don't let the plural *girls* and *neighborhoods* distract you; Lynn is the antecedent of *who*, and you wouldn't say "Lynn *are* going."

Ambiguous Reference of Pronouns.   Just as a pronoun should *agree* clearly *with* its antecedent, so too it should *refer* clearly *to* a particular antecedent. Any doubt about which antecedent a pronoun refers to or any illogical reference will make your writing fuzzy. When you proofread your rough draft, check every pronoun carefully, and whenever you sense any possibility of vague or illogical reference, repeat the noun. Repetition is better than confusion. Watch particularly for the following possibilities.

One: *It, this, that, which, you,* and *they* can easily become vague or indefinite. *It, this, that,* and *which* can refer to a general idea as well as to a specific noun and be equally vague in either: "he bought a knife as well as a gun and gave *it* to his brother." Maybe you know which one he gave his brother, but you haven't made it clear to the reader. Repeat either *knife* or *gun*. Again, they couldn't decide between going to the movies and walking in the park, and finally agreed *it* was too much trouble." What was too much trouble? Going to the movies, walking, doing anything at all, or deciding what to do?

When *it*, *you*, and *they* are used without definite antecedents, they make your writing wordy and general: "in the weather report, *it* says tomorrow will be sunny." Get rid of the *it*: "the weather report says tomorrow will be sunny." Similarly, "*they* expect a large registration in Jackson" is much sharper without the indefinite *they*: "Jackson anticipates a large registration."

Two: The farther the pronoun is from its antecedent, the more obscure is the connection between them. Concerned with the intervening words, the reader loses sight of the antecedent or connects the pronoun with some word or idea closer to it. Whenever the antecedent is remote, then, repeat it; don't replace it with a pronoun: "when the lamp fell, *it* spilled the ink, messing up the desk, and knocked several books to the floor; he rushed over to pick *it* up." Avoid any confusion here by repeating *lamp* in place of the second *it*.

THREE: If a pronoun can refer to more than one antecedent, repeat the noun, or rewrite the sentence to make your meaning clear: "Jack told Fred that *he* ought to give *him* the book." Who is giving the book to whom? Write, "Jack told Fred that *Fred* ought to give *him* the book"; or, "Jack told Fred that *he* ought to give *Jack* the book"; or, "Jack said that Fred ought to give *him* the book."

FOUR: A pronoun must refer logically to its antecedent: "Jack writes magazine articles, and his brother wants to be *one*, too." Jack's brother wants to be a magazine article? "Jack writes magazine articles, and his brother wants to write *them*, too"; or, "Jack writes magazine articles, and his brother wants to be a *writer*, too." The best way to avoid this error — and the other pronoun errors as well — is to think of its antecedent whenever you write a pronoun.

Apostrophe. Apostrophes are used mainly to indicate possession or contraction.

ONE: Singular and plural nouns not ending in *s* and indefinite pronouns form their possessives by adding an apostrophe and an *s*: "the *man's* car," "the *men's* cars"; "*anybody's* guess." Singular nouns ending in *s* usually add an apostrophe and an *s*, but if this would sound awkward, they add only an apostrophe: "*Thomas's* house," but "*Nicholas'* house" rather than "*Nicholas's* house"; "the *kiss's* duration," but "the *stimulus'* effect" rather than the *"stimulus's* effect." Plural nouns ending in *s* add an apostrophe: "the *books'* covers," "the *Hayes'* home." Compound words and nouns indicating joint possession form their possessives on the last word: *"brother-in-law's* name," *"sisters-in-law's* names," "Jack and *Fred's* room." Nouns indicating separate possessions are each possessive: *"Jack's and Fred's* rooms."

Two: In contractions, apostrophes indicate the omitted letter or letters: *"that's* the phone," "nine *o'clock,"* *"aren't* you," *"it's* time."

THREE: *Whose, his, hers, ours, yours, theirs,* and *its* are possessive pronouns; don't add apostrophes to them. And don't confuse the contraction *it's* with the possessive *its;* see *it's* in the tips on usage.

Awkward. This means you've written something so rough, so crooked, or so clumsy that you can't improve it by repairing specific errors. It reads like walking through mud, and your meaning isn't as clear as it should be. The whole thing is a mess. Read it out loud a few times; usually, this will help you sense its awkwardness and give you some idea of what's wrong with it. Then tear it up and start over again. Remember: your primary purpose is to communicate CLEARLY and PLEASINGLY. If you don't do it in phrases, clauses, and sentences, how can you do it in paragraphs and essays?

Careless Complexity. You're using a pile driver to pound a nail. To be clear and pleasing, writing must be as simple and direct as its subject and purpose will allow. This doesn't mean that all writing has to use one- and two-syllable words in five- or ten-word sentences: simple and direct writing in a technical report is not the same as it is in a description of your room. Effective writing on each level and on all the levels in between is simple and direct in terms of the nature of its materials and the demands of its audience. Expressing relatively simple ideas in big words and complicated structures only obscures meaning instead of clarifying it, and the only impression such unnecessary and careless complexity makes on a reader is a bad one. Rewrite this passage, then, to make its language and syntax correspond more closely to your subject, material, and audience. Use a hammer to drive your nail.

Case. Case means the form of a noun or pronoun which indicates its function in a sentence and its meaning. With the loss of most of its inflections, English has lost most of its case distinctions. Nouns have only two: plain and possessive; and pronouns only three: nominative, possessive, and objective. Moreover, although the question of which case to use is still an occasional problem, even some of these are becoming increasingly less important.

ONE: As the object of a verb, a pronoun is normally in the objective case: "Jack called *her.*" Traditionally, however, formal English has required the nominative case of personal pronouns after the verb *to be:* "it's *I,*" "It's *we,*" "it was *she.*" This distinction is disappearing, though not without some vigorous rear-guard resistance. The leader in this change is "it's *me*" and "it's *us*"; I doubt if many people any longer say "it's *I*" or "it's *we*" without feeling, even on formal occasions, at least a little self-consciously "correct." The objective case here seems to be exerting pressure on the other personal pronouns, and before too long, all of them will probably be in the objective case after the forms of *to be,* even in formal usage. In this situation, it is difficult to say what you should do in your writing. The most reliable guide here, as usual, is your audience. If you think your reader expects the traditional form, use the nominative case; if not, use whichever you prefer.

Two: After a preposition, a pronoun is almost always in the objective case: "give it to *me.*" "three of *us* players couldn't get to the game." If you have two or more pronouns following the preposition, remember that the preposition controls the case of each: "he gave the books to *you* and *me,*" "Jack went to the game with *him* and *her.*" Before a gerund, however, use the possessive case of a noun or a pronoun: "there was no point in *his* leaving the party" (not, in *him* leaving the party); "Fred objected to *Jack's* taking the book" (not, to *Jack* taking the book).

THREE: When *than* or *as* introduces an implied clause, put a pronoun in the nominative case if it is the implied subject and in the objective case if it is the implied object: "Jack knows Fred better *than she*" (if *than* she knows *him* is implied), "Jack knows Fred better *than her*" (if *than* Jack knows *her* is implied); "I like Tom as much *as her*" (if as much *as* I like *her* is implied), "I like Tom as much *as she*" (if as much *as she* likes Tom is implied).

FOUR: *Who* and *whom, whoever* and *whomever* are distinctions that seem to be gradually wearing away, like "it's *I*" and "it's *we,*" though not as rapidly. Traditionally, *who* and *whoever* function as subjects of clauses, and *whom* and *whomever* as objects: "*who* is going?"; and "*whom* are you going with?" For a while yet, you'll be safer using the traditional distinction in formal writing.

Clichés. These are tried and true expressions, and if you use them to make your writing bigger and better and bright as a dollar, you'll probably end up sadder but wiser, because experience is the best teacher. Clichés — like those I just used — are tired, worn-out, stereotyped expressions. Once, when they were first used, they were fresh and emphatic; so fresh and emphatic, indeed, that everyone began using them. The greatest tribute to a cliché is that it *is* a cliché; pay it your respect not by using it further but by giving it a retirement party. Sometimes you can extend its usefulness by employing it for humor; read Oscar Wilde's *The Importance of Being Earnest* to see how this can be done. Line after line is a reverse cliché, and usually, in the context, delightful. Your best bet, however, is to avoid using clichés, and here your problem may be that you don't always recognize them. Your instructor tells you an expression you've used is a cliché, but you haven't heard it very often, and you conclude that he just doesn't like you. Whether he does or not, you've still used a cliché; the test of an expression or image is not whether you recognize it as trite but whether it has been overused. If someone with clearly wider experience than yours tells you that you've written a cliché, take his word for it. You can avoid writing such trite expressions in two ways: *one,* don't use any image not drawn from your own experience: don't write old hacks like "early birds get the worms" (do you really like worms?); try for something of your own, like "a day that begins at dawn brings more sunshine." *Two,* go over your rough draft with a fine-toothed comb, and cut out or rewrite every expression or image that you think sounds trite or that you think anyone else might find trite. And don't miss things like "fine-toothed comb"; it's not only a cliché, but with "cut out," it's a mixed metaphor.

Colon.   A colon provides the longest pause among the internal punctuation marks. It tells the reader to pay particular attention to what follows: a word, phrase, or clause you want to emphasize; an appositive, especially a long one; a summary; an amplification of the preceding idea; or a list of items. Use colons: they can be extremely valuable for clarifying and emphasizing your ideas and for varying your sentence rhythms.

Comma Misused.   There are two ways to misuse the comma: *one,* putting one in where it isn't needed or where it performs no valuable function; and *two,* leaving one out where it is needed. Using commas where you don't need them breaks up your thought into bits and pieces and makes your style choppy: "several of Lenore's friends, especially, Jack, and Fred, feel, that she shouldn't go to Mexico, by herself, either by train, or bus, or plane, because, they feel, it's too dangerous for a young, pretty, girl to travel, alone." That's an extreme example, but you get the idea. On the other hand, leaving commas out where they are needed usually leads to misreading — to the running together of ideas that should be separated: notice the difference between "two weeks before he had taken the pledge to the United Fund" and "two weeks before, he had taken the pledge to the United Fund." You have to read the first version at least twice to get its real meaning. You shouldn't confuse your reader or make him do unnecessary work to understand you.

The best way to avoid misusing commas is never to use one without a clear reason you are prepared to defend. The old rule "when in doubt, leave it out," is a fairly good one to follow. Sometimes, however, you must use commas; and a better rule to follow is this: "when in doubt, find out."

Comma Required.   A comma is the most frequently used — and misused — punctuation mark, but it's not a small device contrived just to give you big trouble. Nor is it something extraneous that you add to a sentence occasionally for one reason or another. A comma is an integral part of the form and meaning of a sentence. It provides a tiny pause to separate different ideas or different parts of one idea and to break up long constructions into shorter segments easier and more pleasing to read. A comma is a marvelous writing tool, and it isn't difficult to master. Apart from such conventional uses as in geographical locations: *Weedsport, New York;* in dates: *September 5, 1962;* and in numbers: *5,280;* a comma has only six principal uses.

ONE: After a word or an expression introducing the main clause and before a word or expression added to it, use a comma if there is any danger of misreading, of the introductory or following ideas becoming part of the main clause. If you write, "From above the city looks orderly and clean," the reader will first think you mean that something or someone is looking out above the city. But that won't make any sense when he gets to "orderly and clean," and he will have to go back and reread the sentence. Save him the trouble: write, "From above, the city looks orderly and clean." Similarly, "I decided to go anyway leaving her behind" is so confusing that even rereading doesn't help much. Look what a difference a comma makes: "I decided to go anyway, leaving her behind." Traditionally, a comma after introductory and before additional material has been mandatory; but modern usage, following the principle of discarding all unnecessary punctuation, makes this use of the comma a question of judgment. If these is no danger of misreading or of awkward length, why use it? You will need it nearly always before expressions added to the main clause; but much of the time, your introductory words will be short enough and their meaning sufficiently distinct from the idea in the main clause to make a comma superfluous: "at the bookstore he spent ten dollars." But watch long introductory expressions carefully: the longer they are, the more likely that they will get confused with the main clause or be difficult to read without a comma.

Two: When you use a word or an expression within a sentence for transition or emphasis, you should usually put commas around it: "that, however, is what I meant"; "that, I repeat, is what I meant." Think of the commas here as scissors: these expressions are useful but not essential, and you could cut them out without significantly altering the main idea. Sometimes, however, you may want to make such expressions part of the main idea: if you write, "His contribution I think was substantial," your opinion becomes a subtly important part of the idea, stressing the size of the contribution. "His contribution, I think, was substantial" could imply that others might not consider it so large or that you aren't sure how large it was. Here again, then, it is a question of what you want to do, of using commas to express your exact meaning. Remember one thing, though: if you do treat such expressions parenthetically, if you do view them as useful but non-essential, put commas on both sides of them. What good are scissors with only one blade?

THREE: Parenthetical clauses introduced by *who* or *which* are called non-restrictive modifiers, but don't let the term confuse you. If you understand the scissors analogy I just used in discussing short parenthetical expressions, you'll have no trouble with these parenthetical clauses. The principle is exactly the same; relative clauses not essential to the main idea have commas around them to indicate that they could be cut out without changing that idea: "Jack, *who* doesn't like football, gets free tickets"; "the airliner, *which* carries three stewardesses, took off." Use your scissors on each of these clauses, and the main idea remains unaltered. With such clauses, you have no choice; because they are not logically necessary to the main idea, you *must* invariably put commas around them.

The best way to remember this comma usage is: ALWAYS put commas around a clause beginning with *which* — or before it, if it comes at the end of the main clause; NEVER use a comma before a clause beginning with *that*; and look carefully at a clause beginning with *who* to see whether it is essential to the main idea, and put commas around it if it isn't. With *who*-clauses, then, the problem is a little more complicated: the question of whether to use commas can depend on your meaning: "The man *who* robbed the First National Bank was sentenced to five years in prison" makes the robbery as important or more important than the sentence; "The man, *who* robbed the First National Bank, was sentenced to five years in prison" makes the sentence more important.

FOUR: When you list a series of three or more items or ideas, you can separate them by *ands* or by commas replacing the *ands*: "I like apples and peaches and pears"; or "I like apples, peaches, pears." Usually, however, when commas replace the *ands*, the final item retains the *and*: "I like apples, peaches and pears." No comma is necessary, then, before the final *and*; but sometimes, misreading occurs without it: "he ran into the house, jumped into bed and fell asleep." Without the comma to separate them, "jumped" and "fell" seem to be parts of the same action. Even with the *and*, then, the comma is necessary here, as it is similarly in "I like Jack,

Fred likes Jack, and Mary likes Jack." As usual, therefore, your guiding principle should be to know what you are saying and then to say it clearly.

FIVE: Traditionally a comma has been required before the coordinating conjunction separating the clauses of a compound sentence. Modern usage discards this comma, too, unless the clauses are very long or there is danger of misreading them as one clause: "I sent Jack and Fred went along for the ride." At first glance, the reader would think I had sent Jack and Fred; the comma is therefore necessary before the *and*. The longer the clauses are, the more possible such misreading becomes. If you have any doubt whatever about the clarity of the idea in each main clause or of the relationship between them, use the comma before the conjunction that links them. Most of the time, however, you probably won't have such obvious ambiguity or such long clauses and you won't need the comma.

SIX: Any time you want to make the reader pause momentarily, either to make your thought clearer or your style more pleasing, use a comma. But if you aren't using it for one of the conventional reasons or for one of the above five reasons, be sure you know why you *are* using it, what contextual or stylistic effect you want it to produce. It's an available tool, the comma, and one mark of a good writer is his ability to use it effectively as part of his meaning. Know when to use a comma, then, and use it only when you must or when you gain something from it.

Comma Splice. This means that you've "spliced" — joined — independent clauses with a comma. In other words, you've written a compound sentence with a comma before the coordinating conjunction, but without the coordinating conjunction: "I read all day, there wasn't anything else to do." This construction appears frequently, sometimes even in the work of the best writers; but it is usually an error because it nearly always is the weakest possible way to express the ideas in the clauses. A comma splice increases the danger of misreading; at first glance, my example could suggest that there — in a particular place — I read all day. Furthermore, a comma splice fails either to give main clauses the separation a normal compound sentence provides or to indicate the linking relationship between them. You can see this double failure more clearly when more than two clauses are involved: "I read all day, there wasn't anything else to do, besides, the nurse advised me to read." See why you shouldn't join main clauses with commas?

You can use almost anything else but commas: use a dash, a semicolon, or a colon; make a complex sentence, stressing the relationship between the clauses with a subordinating conjunction; or make two sentences:

I read all day — there wasn't anything else to do.

I read all day; there wasn't anything else to do.
I read all day: there wasn't anything else to do.
Because there wasn't anything else to do, I read all day.
I read all day. There wasn't anything else to do.

Each of these is subtly different, stressing either the separate importance of each clause or the relationship between them; but any of these constructions is acceptable and infinitely preferable to a comma splice. The rare occasions when a comma splice can give you a positive value — "I see it one way, he sees it another." — aren't worth the bad habits you may get into, even writing this way infrequently. Stay out of trouble; don't join main clauses with a comma.

Contractions.   A contraction is a word or a group of words shortened by the omission of one or more letters indicated by an apostrophe. *It's* a useful device, but most people frown on it in formal writing. Don't use contractions, then, unless you are sure your reader won't react against them. As you've probably gathered long since, I like them, and I've got my typewriter crossed that you do, too.

Dangling Modifiers.   These are phrases or clauses that modify something they can't logically modify. Thus, they *dangle* from the sentence illogically and usually foolishly: "writing this book, the hours pass swiftly." The hours are writing the book? To revise the sentence, you have to make the real actor clear: "as I write this book, the hours pass swiftly"; or, "writing this book, I feel the hours pass swiftly." Again, if you write, "After getting up, the bed was made," you create a silly image — unless you have an unusual bed. Make it clear *who* made the bed: "after I got up, I made the bed"; or, "after getting up, I made the bed." Here's another example: "my car broke down while going to class." Tell your instructor not to give the car such large assignments — or revise the sentence.

Dangling modifiers are the result of sloppy thinking, and they give your reader the impression either that you don't care what he thinks or that you are hopelessly childish. You can keep dangling modifiers out of your writing in two ways; *one,* as you write, keep your mind on what you're doing, and make sure when you write a modifying phrase or clause that whatever it modifies is clearly and logically stated in the sentence. *Two,* when you proofread your rough draft — and you *are* going to do a rough draft, *aren't* you? — check every modifying phrase or clause to make sure that what it modifies is clearly and logically stated. You might as well give your reader a good impression.

Dash.   This is an extremely useful punctuation mark. Its main function is to indicate a break in thought: you can use it instead of parentheses if you want to make an aside informally: "he refused — I told you he would

— and went home." Or you can use it instead of a colon if you want a less formal effect: "he lost three things — his pen, his keys, and his cigarette lighter." You can also use the dash to show an almost complete break in thought: "she said — but I can't repeat what she said." Indeed, so useful is the dash that some people happily throw away most of the other punctuation marks. When this happens, their writing becomes awkward and choppy to read and peculiar to look at, and the dash loses its value. Use it wisely, then, but not too willfully.

Flowery Writing.   This is writing that tries to impress the reader with words instead of with ideas. If you are writing this way, you may be doing it unintentionally, but the effect is the same. You are using big words and long, complicated constructions where small words and short, simple constructions will convey your thought clearly and directly. Or you are trying to sound poetic with lofty language and florid expressions. Big words and complex structures have their place: they are usually necessary to express complicated ideas. And language whose effect is poetic can function in some esthetic prose as well as in poetry. In most of your writing, however, you won't need big words and complicated constructions, nor will you need to sound poetic. You will impress your reader most powerfully and most favorably, therefore, if you express your ideas in the simplest and most direct terms possible supported by imagery drawn from your own experience. Don't write, "This is a very lion of a book, unparalleled in its power to stimulate the reader's mind and heart and to send him away after perusing its rapid-fire pages with his blood pressure up and his breath coming in startling gasps." Write, "This is an exciting book."

Fused Sentences.   This is even worse than a comma splice; you can't ever do this. It means melting your main clauses together — writing them without either a coordinating conjunction or punctuation between them: "the car was being repaired it needed new rings." Nearly everything under Comma Splice applies here and with double emphasis. But there is simply no excuse for writing fused sentences, and if you are making this error, stop it.

Hyphen.   The hyphen has two principal uses: *one,* to indicate the division of a word at the end of a line; and *two,* to make compound words. If you have to divide a word, do it between syllables: *prin-cipal,* not *princ-ipal; mani-fest,* not *manif-est.* You must have more than one letter on each side of the hyphen; and if the word has double consonants, break it between them, unless it is a simple word ending in a double consonant with an added ending: *der-rick and fis-sion;* but *sell-ing,* not *sel-ling;* and *mass-ing,* not *mas-sing.*

Compound words generally are a question of spelling. Older ones like foot-ball have dropped the hyphen — *football* — and new ones are constantly being formed. Your main difficulty with compound words is probably with compound adjectives — linking two or more words together to function as a single adjective: "*run-proof* stocking," "*never-to-be-forgotten* experience," "*twentieth-century* literature." The only way to solve this problem is to make sure while you are writing and when you proofread your rough draft that whenever you use two or more words to modify another word, the modifying words are hyphenated.

Jargon.   This means language with vocabulary and idiom meaningful only to a relatively small and specialized group whose characteristic activities it expresses. To these people, it isn't jargon at all, but a direct, simple, and emphatic means of communication. We usually associate such language with technical and scientific groups, but it also includes any kind of shop talk not intelligible to a general audience. What, for example, do you make of this:

It's our 8 look-in with green left slow, which is like a bend-in deep. It's not much more than a back dividing to the left, but the same as a swing in the flat. We did it this time off our opposite, calling it from a 2-right.

These are the words of a quarterback describing a touchdown play, but only a football player — and perhaps an informed fan — could make any sense out of them. Some people feel superior in using jargon — it gives them a sense of belonging to something apart from the majority. Some even like to read jargon for the same reason — they feel as though they are being allowed access to the hallowed mysteries of a cult. In either instance, this is pure snobbery, and jargon has no place in formal writing for a general audience. If you are writing for a special group, then, use its language; but if you are writing for a general audience, use only the language such an audience is most likely to understand. Either way, the principle is the same: express your ideas in the language that will convey them most clearly and pleasingly to the audience you are addressing.

Misplaced Modifiers.   These are modifying words, phrases, or clauses placed in a sentence where their reference is obscure, illogical, or ambiguous. Words like *almost, even, only, nearly* are often logically misplaced: "I *almost think* I'm through" should logically be "I think I'm *almost* through"; and "I *nearly* read this book all day" should be "I read this book *nearly* all day." In ordinary usage, these modifying words seldom cause any confusion, wherever they appear, but in formal writing, you should put them as close as possible to the word or words they modify. Watch especially for words that can modify other words on either side of them: "His instructor advised him *regularly* to read" could be either "His instructor *regularly* advised him to read" or "His instructor advised him to read *regularly*." So, too, "Gambling *unquestionably* can be dangerous" is ambiguous. Put the modifier where it will make your exact meaning clear.

Misplaced phrases and clauses can also be confusing and sometimes silly: "He went to visit Jack *in the hospital with a broken leg*"; and, "He bought a hat *at the store that had a large feather on it.*" Rewrite such sentences to give their modifying phrases and clauses an immediately clear and logical reference: "He went *to the hospital* to visit Jack, *who was there with a broken leg*" and "*At the store,* he bought a *hat that had a large feather on it.*"

Mixed Construction.   This is what happens when you start out to write one thing and shift in the middle to something else: "Although writing was difficult for me in high school, college classes are smaller makes it more interesting even if the reading lists are longer"; and "Compared to other compact cars in terms of mileage, the Maverick is setting new sales records." Mixed constructions like these are usually the result of trying to write as fast as you think. You can't do it, not and write well. Good writing is the careful organization and shaping of thought, not just the record of it. Write more slowly and carefully, then, and if you still mix up your constructions, proofread that rough draft with particular care.

Omission.   You've something out. Watch you're doing.

Parallelism.   When you write a sentence expressing ideas of equal weight or equal parts of the same idea, you should indicate their logical equality by putting them in parallel — identical — grammatical constructions. If you express the first idea or division of an idea in a participle, an infinitive, a phrase, or a clause, use the same construction for the idea or ideas that follow. Write, "I like *to fly* and *to play* softball" or "I like *flying* and *playing* softball"; but not "I like to *fly* and *playing* softball." Again, you can write, "I like *mature, good-humored,* and *intelligent* girls" or "I like girls *who are mature, who have a good sense of humor,* and *who are intelligent*"; but not "I like girls who are *mature, good-humored,* and *to be intelligent.*" Be careful with constructions like *either — or, neither — nor, both — and,* and *not only — but also;* it seems to be easy to lose parallelism in such correlatives. Write, "Either *he is going* or *I am going,*" but not "He is either *going or I am going*"; and "He planned not only *to buy* a new car but also *to pay* the mortgage on the house," but not "He planned not only *on buying* a new car but also *that he would pay* the mortgage on the house." Parallelism is essential if your reader is to understand your ideas clearly without frequent rereading. Give him a break; he'll like you better for it.

Parentheses.   Like dashes or commas around a word or a group of words, parentheses indicate a break in thought, something added but not essential to the main context. Usually, they contain explanatory or illustrative

material: "His long career (he began teaching in 1920) is nearly over."
Put punctuation belonging to the parenthetical material inside the parentheses (where else?). If a punctuation mark would normally follow the
word or idea modified by the parenthetical expression (as it would here),
put the punctuation mark after the second parenthesis (as I just did and
as I am just about to do).

Passive Voice.   Passive constructions make the subject the receiver of an
action, rather than the doer of it: "The ball *was pitched* by Lolich." This
construction has several valuable uses. *One*, it indicates that the doer of
the action is unknown: "When I got up this morning, my wallet had been
stolen." *Two*, it emphasizes the action: "The house *was destroyed.*" *Third*,
it makes the receiver of an action more important than the agent: "I *was
hit* by a car." For these purposes and occasionally to avoid awkwardness,
the passive *can be used;* but except for these relatively infrequent reasons,
you *shouldn't use* it. English verbs normally function best in the active
voice: "Lolich *pitched* the ball" is what we expect to hear, not something
as feeble as "The ball *was pitched* by Lolich." The more you use such
passive constructions in your writing, the more lifeless and monotonous
it will become. Use the passive voice on the rare occasions when it is
effective, then, but most of the time, leave it for frightened bureaucrats
who want to hide behind its weak impersonality.

Quotation Marks.   These are sometimes used to call special attention to
a word or to indicate that it is being used in a special sense:

He considers "extremism" one of the major issues in modern politics.

There is no real need for quotation marks here, and this practice is diminishing. Some people use it to sneak slang into formal writing:

Crimes of Passion is a "lousy" book.

Don't do this; it just makes bad writing more obvious.
   The principal uses of quotation marks are to quote some titles (see
Titles) and to indicate the exact words someone has used:

The general said, "The best way to lose national power is to misuse it."

For quotations within quotations, use single marks:

The general testified, "I heard him say, 'I refuse to go.'"

Recently, some people have begun using single marks wherever quotation
marks are needed; don't follow this bad example.
   In using punctuation with quotation marks, *always* put commas and
periods *inside* the marks; *always* put semicolons and colons *outside;* and
put dashes, question marks, and exclamation points *inside* if they belong
to the quotation, but *outside* if they are part of the whole statement:

Arguing against "extremism," the senator praised the President: "He is a man of moderation."

The senator attacked "extremism": he said that "extremists could start a nuclear war"; and, in answer to a question, he called Smith an "extremist."

He asked, "Did Mary call?"

Did he say, "Mary called"?

If both the quoted material and whole statement require a question mark, put it *inside* the quotation marks:

Did he say, "Did Mary call?"

Unless you want to give them special force, you should usually set direct quotations off from the rest of the sentence:

The senator praised the President: "He is a man of moderation."
"The President," said the senator, "is a man of moderation."

Sometimes, however, this can result in awkward or confusing sentences:

He said that, "the President is a man of moderation."
Praising the President, the senator said, "He is a man of moderation."

In such constructions, discard the comma before the quotation:

He said that "the President is a man of moderation."
Praising the President, the senator said "He is a man of moderation."

As usual, let clarity and ease of reading be your guides.

Redundancy.   In general, redundancy means wordiness — using more words than you need to express your ideas. Specifically, however, it can mean two different kinds of wordiness. *Repetition* means the careless and insensitive use of the same word or group of words over and over again until it tolls in the reader's mind like a broken bell (see Repetition). *Tautology* means repeating the same idea in different words without any gain either in meaning or in emphasis: "The Marines *retreated back to the rear*" and "In the *modern* world of *today* —" If you're using that last one, get rid of it, and you'll probably add years to your instructor's life. Watch out, too, for comfortable but tautological pairs: "She is a *true* and *faithful* friend" and "I am *ready* and *available* for work." Not only do such pairs repeat the same idea unnecessarily but they also dilute it. "She is a *faithful* friend" and "I am *ready* for work" are stronger as well as simpler statements.

Repetition.   Repeating a word or group of words several times in the same context usually makes writing awkward and monotonous. Carefully used, however, repetition can be a valuable means of achieving em·phasis. Here, for example, is a famous passage from Winston Churchill's report to Parliament after Britain's epic evacuation from Dunkirk in the summer of 1940:

Even though large tracts of Europe and many old and famous States have fallen or may fall into the grip of the Gestapo and all the odious apparatus of Nazi rule, *we shall not flag or fail. We shall go on* to the end, *we shall fight* in France, *we shall fight* on the seas and oceans, *we shall fight* with *growing* confidence and *growing* strength in the air, *we shall defend* our Island, whatever the cost may be, *we shall fight* on the beaches, *we shall fight* on the landing grounds, *we shall fight* in the fields and in the streets, *we shall fight* in the hills; *we shall never surrender* . . .

Use repetition, then, but use it only for specific purposes, and use it carefully. In avoiding monotonous repetition, however, don't fall into the trap of *strained variation* — the use of increasingly strained synonyms in order to prevent any repetition whatever:

President Jaffe addressed the nation on the Cuban crisis. Speaking in sober tones, *the chief executive* said that we must stay calm. But, added *the nation's leader,* we must also be firm. The *first magistrate* closed his speech with a prayer for guidance for him as *pilot of our ship of state.*

I've managed to keep from repeating *President,* but the result is, if anything, worse than the repetition would have been. Instead of straining so hard for variation, I should have recast my sentences and used a pronoun:

Addressing the nation on the Cuban crisis, *President* Jaffe said soberly that we must stay calm but also be firm. *He* closed with a prayer for guidance.

Semicolon. Don't use a semicolon just to replace a comma whenever you feel like it. A semicolon has its own particular purposes, and you should use it only for these. It combines the functions of a comma and a period: it links ideas like a comma and, at the same time, separates them almost as strongly as a period. Semicolons have *two* main uses. *One,* they separate items in a series if one or more of the items is long or contains internal punctuation:

I bought a blue suit, sharkskin in a slight check; two pairs of shoes, one casual and one for formal wear; and a felt hat.

Semicolons are necessary here because the commas in the two items would dilute the force of commas separating the items, and the reader couldn't distinguish at first between items and parts of items.

Two, semicolons can be used in several ways in compound sentences. As in a series of long or internally punctuated items, a semicolon before the coordinating conjunction gives the stronger separation you usually need when one or more of the main clauses is relatively long or contains internal punctuation. Again, a semicolon can replace the coordinating conjunction when you want to retain the indication of the close relationship between the main clauses but give greater stress to their separate importance: "I think the situation is serious, but no one else does" becomes subtly different when you write it, "I think the situation is serious; no one else does." If you want to indicate the individual importance of the main clauses and at the same time emphasize the relationship between them, you can use a semicolon before the coordinating conjunction: "I think the situation is serious; but no one else does"; or you can replace the conjunction with a semicolon and a conjunctive adverb: "I think the situation is serious; however, no one else does." If you do use a conjunctive adverb here, be sure to put a comma after it.

The semicolon is a versatile tool, then, and you shouldn't waste it. Use it only for its specific purposes and effects, and it will serve you well.

Sentence Length.   A sentence should be as long as it needs to be. There is no ideal length; whatever expresses your meaning most clearly and directly is the right length. Moreover, this principle will protect your style from choppiness or excessive complication. Your ideas will nearly always vary in importance and complexity; therefore, they can seldom be accurately expressed either in a lengthy series of short simple sentences or in a succession of long complicated ones. Watch out for such constructions, then; most of the time, they are not only stylistically ineffective but also logically inexact.

Shift in Viewpoint.   This means a change in grammatical form without any logical change to support it. It usually comes either from simple carelessness or from failure to imagine your audience or your material clearly. Don't begin writing formal English and then, without apparent logical reason, shift to informal expressions or to slang; this suggests either that you don't know whom you are addressing or that you don't care. Similarly, be consistent in the tense, voice, and mood of your verbs. Change the *tense* of a verb only when you want to show that its action occurred at a different time: "The wind *was* strong, and the boats *are having* rough going" is obviously a mistake; but "*I used to fly* frequently, but I *can't afford* it any more" indicates a logical change in time. Don't shift from one *voice* or *mood* to another; it is nearly always awkward: "Lolich *threw* a sinker, and it *was hit* by Howard for a triple." Howard deserves more credit than that: he *hit* the triple. Again, be careful not to write this kind of thing: "*Aim* carefully, and then you *should squeeze* the trigger slowly and steadily." Write, "*Aim* carefully, and *squeeze* the trigger slowly and steadily." Finally, don't shift the *person* or *number* of pronouns; it is often awkward and usually confusing: "*Everyone* should work hard if *you* want to succeed" should be "*Everyone* should work hard if *he* wants to succeed"; and "I always use *a dictionary* when I write because *they* save time" should be "I always use a *dictionary* when I write because *it* saves time." (See Agreement of Pronoun and Antecedent)

Watch your writing carefully for such illogical shifts; they expose you as an indifferent or undiscerning writer.

Slang. Slang is easier to recognize than it is to define. It is a form of linguistic shorthand, a simplifying or emphasizing usage that gives the language a lively energy and a colorful force. There are many kinds of slang, among them mispronunciation: *gal* for *girl*, *tetched* for *touched* (slang for *crazy*); substitution: *heap* for *automobile*, *jack* for *money*; shortening: *vip* from *very important person*, *kayo* from *knockout*, *frosh* from *freshman*; and extension: *lousy* to mean anything *bad* or *unpleasant*, *head* to mean *bathroom*. The richest source of slang, however, is metaphor, as in expressions like *bar fly*, *make a pass*, and *out like a light*. Words and expressions like these are the salt of language, and our informal speech and writing would be much less alive and interesting without them. They have their occasional uses even in formal writing, but in general, the primary purpose of such writing is to organize and use language with greater control and polish than in its everyday patterns Moreover, though some slang lasts — *dad*, *double-header*, *swell* — much of it is fashionable for a short time and then wears out and disappears. Try *sashay*, *razzamatazz*, and *sockdollager* on your friends, and watch their blank expressions. Even slang of such recent vintage as *cool* and *groovy* sounds dated already.

Slang is a vital part of language, then, but don't use it just because you can't think of a more exact term to express what you want to say or because you want to impress people with your knowledge of the latest fashions. Use slang when it can convey your ideas with color and force, but remember that in formal writing, it seldom does this without an awkward shift in tone and in viewpoint.

Spelling. I wish I had an easy and foolproof system to give you to help you spell correctly. I haven't. English is a hard language to spell. The phonetic ambiguity of its alphabet and the multiple sources of its vocabulary make any reliable spelling system almost impossible. Smarter men than I are constantly offering new methods to teach spelling, but as far as I can see, none of them works very well. If they did, smarter men than I wouldn't have to keep contriving new ones. The only way I know to learn to spell English is by constant reading and writing. Seeing words in contexts and then using them is the only way to become reliably familiar with most of them. If you are a constant reader and a frequent writer and you still misspell often, you will have to contrive some personal solution or hire a good professor.

Although I can't offer you a system to teach you to spell correctly, I can suggest a method for correcting misspelling — when you discover it. Keep a list of every word you misspell. Each day, take a few words from the list, and look them up in the dictionary — not just for their spelling, but for their meanings and etymology. Then write them several times, associating their meanings with the patterns of their letters and sounds.

Keep doing this until you are no longer misspelling the words when you use them; then drop them from the list. I realize that this is a long and arduous process, but I know no other way to break the bad habit which a misspelled word represents.

Break that habit you must, one way or another, if you are going to be an effective writer for any purpose. Bad spelling, like flaking paint on a house, is obvious even to a casual glance, and your reader will immediately wonder why you don't paint your house.

Split Infinitive.   The vehement protest that this practice usually provokes has two main sources. *First,* it reflects the Latin precedents used in the first English grammars: you can't split a Latin infinitive; it's only one word. Traditionally, this precedent has been taught in preference to usage, in which infinitives are split commonly in ordinary speech and occasionally in literature. *Second,* supporting this traditional position is the fact that the two words of the English infinitive function as one. For this reason, splitting them usually makes an awkward construction: "I want *to someday read* that book" is certainly awkward compared with "Someday, I want *to read* that book" or "I want *to read* that book someday." Most of the time, therefore, you should avoid such unnatural infinitive splitting.

Occasionally, however, splitting an infinitive is the quickest and smoothest way to say what you mean; sometimes, it is the only way. "I wanted *to* more than just *see* it; I wanted to buy it" could be written, "More than just seeing it, I wanted to buy it"; but the first version seems to me sharper and smoother. Similarly, in "I plan *to* really *read* that book," you can't put the *really* anywhere else without altering the exact meaning.

Such inflexible situations occur infrequently. Don't be afraid to split an infinitive if you are sure it is the smoothest and most exact way to express your thought; but usually, it won't be. And if you don't have to split an infinitive, leave it alone. It isn't harming anybody.

Titles.   The convention for writing or typing titles is a simple one, and I don't understand why so many people have such trouble with it. In print, titles of book-length works, works published separately, or anything of major or separate importance are put in italics; and titles of shorter works or parts of longer works are put in quotation marks. In print then, *Hamlet, For Whom the Bell Tolls,* the *Venus de Milo,* the *Mona Lisa,* the *New York Times,* the *Empire State Building,* and the *U.S.S. Enterprise* would all be italicized. But in writing or in typing, we don't have italics, so we replace them with underlining: <u>Hamlet</u>, <u>For Whom the Bell Tolls</u>, the <u>Venus de Milo</u>, the <u>Mona Lisa</u>, the <u>New York Times</u>, the <u>Empire State Building</u>, and the <u>U.S.S. Enterprise</u>. With shorter works or parts of longer works, there is no problem; in writing or in typing we still put quotation marks around them: "The Killers," "How to Build Your Own Moon Rocket," in the August *Science Monthly* and "Stranger in Paradise" from *Kismet*. This is a simple and a useful distinction. I can't think of a single reason why you shouldn't learn it and use it.

Vague.   You aren't saying what you think you're saying — or, at least, you're not saying it clearly and directly. Rewrite.

Wordiness.   You're letting ten words do the work of one. Try reversing the equation (see Careless Complexity, Flowery Writing, Redundancy, and Repetition).

Wrong Word.   This word doesn't mean what you apparently think it means. Check the dictionary.

Part 4

*A Collection
of Essays*

James Agee

Knoxville: Summer 1915

We are talking now of summer evenings in Knoxville, Tennessee in the time that I lived there so successfully disguised to myself as a child. It was a little bit mixed sort of block, fairly solidly lower middle class, with one or two juts apiece on either side of that. The houses corresponded: middle-sized gracefully fretted wood houses built in the late nineties and early nineteen hundreds, with small front and side and more spacious back yards, and trees in the yards, and porches. These were softwooded trees, poplars, tulip trees, cottonwoods. There were fences around one or two of the houses, but mainly the yards ran into each other with only now and then a low hedge that wasn't doing very well. There were few good friends among the grown people, and they were not poor enough for the other sort of intimate acquaintance, but everyone nodded and spoke, and even might talk short times, trivially, and at the two extremes of the general or the particular, and ordinarily nextdoor neighbors talked quite a bit when they happened to run into each other, and never paid calls. The men were mostly small businessmen, one or two very modestly executives, one or two worked with their hands, most of them clerical, and most of them between thirty and forty-five.

But it is of these evenings, I speak.

Supper was at six and was over by half past. There was still daylight, shining softly and with a tarnish, like the lining of a shell; and the carbon lamps lifted at the corners were on in the light, and the locusts were started, and the fire flies were out, and a few frogs were flopping in the dewy grass, by the time the fathers and the children came out. The children ran out first hell bent and yelling those names by which they were known; then the fathers sank out leisurely in crossed suspenders, their collars removed and their necks looking tall and shy. The mothers stayed back in the kitchen washing and drying, putting things away, recrossing their traceless footsteps like the lifetime journeys of bees, measuring out the dry cocoa for breakfast. When they came out they had taken off their aprons and their skirts were dampened and they sat in rockers on their porches quietly.

It is not of the games children play in the evening that I want to speak now, it is of a contemporaneous atmosphere that has little to do with them: that of the fathers of families, each in his space of lawn, his shirt fishlike pale in the unnatural light and his face nearly anonymous, hosing their lawn. The hoses were attached at spigots that stood out of the brick foundations of the houses. The nozzles were variously set but usually so there was a long sweet stream of spray, the nozzle wet in the hand, the water trickling the right forearm and the peeled-back cuff, and the water whishing out a long loose and low-curved cone, and so gentle a sound. First an insane noise of violence in the nozzle, then the still irregular sound of adjustment, then the smoothing into steadiness and a pitch as accurately tuned to the size and style of stream as any violin. So many qualities of sound out of one hose: so many choral differences out of those several hoses that were in earshot. Out of any one hose, the almost dead silence of the release, and the short still arch of the separate big drops, silent as a held breath, and the only noise the flattering noise on leaves and the slapped grass at the fall of each big drop. That, and the intense hiss with the intense stream; that, and that same intensity not growing less but growing more quiet and delicate with the turn of the nozzle, up to that extreme tender whisper when the water was just a wide bell of film. Chiefly, though, the hoses were set much alike, in a compromise between distance and tenderness of spray, (and quite surely a sense of art behind this compromise, and a quiet deep joy, too real to recognize itself), and the sounds therefore were pitched much alike; pointed by the snorting start of a new hose; decorated by some man playful with the nozzle; left empty, like God by the sparrow's fall, when any single one of them desists: and all, though near alike, of various pitch; and in this unison. These sweet pale streamings in the light lift out their pallors and their voices all together, mothers hushing their children, the hushing unnaturally prolonged, the men gentle and silent and each snail-like withdrawn into the quietude of what he singly is doing, the urination of huge children stood loosely military against an invisible wall, and gentle happy and peaceful, tasting the mean goodness of their living like the last of their suppers in their mouths; while the locusts carry on this noise of hoses on their much higher and sharper key. The noise of the locust is dry, and it seems not to be rasped or vibrated but urged from him as if through a small orifice by a breath that can never give out. Also there is never one locust but an illusion of at least a thousand. The noise of each locust is pitched in some classic locust range out of which none of them varies more than two full tones: and yet you seem to hear each locust discrete from all the rest, and there is a long, slow, pulse in their noise, like the scarcely defined arch of a long and high set bridge. They are all around in every tree, so that the noise seems to come from nowhere and everywhere at once, from the whole shell heaven, shivering in your flesh and teasing your eardrums, the boldest of all the sounds of night. And yet it is habitual to summer nights, and is of the great order of noises, like the noises of the sea and of the blood her precocious grandchild, which you realize you are hearing only when you catch yourself listening. Meantime from low in the dark, just outside the swaying horizons of the hoses, conveying always grass in the damp of dew and its strong green-black smear of smell, the regular yet spaced noises of the crickets, each a sweet cold silver noise threenoted, like the slipping each time of three matched links of a small chain.

But the men by now, one by one, have silenced their hoses and drained and coiled them. Now only two, and now only one, is left, and you see only ghostlike shirt with the sleeve garters, and sober mystery of his mild face like the lifted face of large cattle enquiring of your presence in a pitchdark pool of meadow; and now he too is gone; and it has become that time of evening when people sit on their porches, rocking gently and talking gently and watching the street and the standing up into their sphere of possession of the trees, of birds hung havens, hangars. People go by; things go by. A horse, drawing a buggy, breaking his hollow iron music on the asphalt; a loud auto; a quiet auto; people in pairs, not in a hurry, scuffling, switching their weight of aestival body, talking casually, the taste hovering over them of vanilla, strawberry, pasteboard and starched milk, the image upon them of lovers and horsemen, squared with clowns in hueless amber. A street car raising its iron moan; stopping, belling and starting; stertorous; rousing and raising again its iron increasing moan and swimming its gold windows and straw seats on past and past and past, the bleak spark crackling and cursing above it like a small malignant spirit set to dog its tracks; the iron whine rises on rising speed; still risen, faints; halts; the faint stinging bell; rises again, still fainter; fainting, lifting, lifts, faints forgone: forgotten. Now is the night one blue dew.

Now is the night one blue dew, my father has drained, he has coiled the hose.
Low on the length of lawns, a frailing of fire who breathes.
Content, silver, like peeps of light, each cricket makes his comment over and over in the drowned grass.
A cold toad thumpily flounders.
Within the edges of damp shadows of side yards are hovering children nearly sick with joy of fear, who watch the unguarding of a telephone pole.

Around white carbon corner lamps bugs of all sizes are lifted elliptic, solar systems. Big hardshells bruise themselves, assailant: he is fallen on his back, legs squiggling.
Parents on porches: rock and rock: From damp strings morning glories: hang their ancient faces.
The dry and exalted noise of the locusts from all the air at once enchants my eardrums.

On the rough wet grass of the back yard my father and mother have spread quilts. We all lie there, my mother, my father, my uncle, my aunt, and I too am lying there. First we were sitting up, then one of us lay down, and then we all lay down, on our stomachs, or on our sides, or on our backs, and they have kept on talking. They are not talking much, and the talk is quiet, of nothing in particular, of nothing at all in particular, of nothing at all. The stars are wide and alive, they seem each like a smile of great sweetness, and they seem very near. All my people are larger bodies than mine, quiet, with voices gentle and meaningless like the voices of sleeping birds. One is an artist, he is living at home. One is a musician, she is living at home. One is my mother who is good to me. One is my father who is good to me. By some chance, here they are, all on this earth; and who shall ever tell the sorrow of being on this earth, lying, on quilts, on the grass, in a summer evening, among the sounds of the night. May God bless my people, my uncle, my aunt, my mother, my good father, oh, remember them kindly in their time of trouble, and in the hour of their taking away.

After a little I am taken in and put to bed. Sleep, soft smiling, draws me unto her: and those receive me, who quietly treat me, as one familiar and well-beloved in that home: but will not, oh, will not, not now, not ever; but will not ever tell me who I am.

Kenneth Allsop

Music by Muzak

"Just lemme hear some more of that rock-'n'-roll music, Any old way you choose it," sing the Beatles. In fact there is neither rock-'n'-roll beat nor choice in the music with the biggest audience of all. If one definition of pop music is that which reaches the greatest number of ears, the Liverpool sound and rhythm-and-blues, Tamla Motown and soul, city-billy and protest, and all their later Top Ten modifications, are swamped into insignificance by Muzak.

Muzak is the dreamy drizzle you are vaguely conscious of in assembly plant or cocktail bar. Like the ethereal lilt from the pipes on the doves' tails in Shangri-La, it drifts from the air upon you as you cross a hotel lobby and ambushes you again in the lift. It will probably be subliminally hovering above you in the dentist's chair, at the restaurant table, at the factory bench, in the executive suite, in the supermarket, in a bank's vaults, in a zoo reptile house, in the beauty parlour. If you were privileged to fly in a space capsule, cruise in a nuclear submarine, or attend a Pentagon strategic conference, Muzak would be there murmuring into your brain cells. You are now likely to emerge from the womb into a Muzak environment, for many a labour room is wired-up, and as likely to be shot into the crematorium's final annihilating flames to a requiem of Muzak Honey-Rich Strings oozing *Unforgettable*. If you are so moved in the vicinity of Waterloo Station, you will go to the lavatory to Muzak.

Muzak now seeps vapour-like through almost every cranny of urban life. It is the twilight-sleep gas that pervades the atmosphere wherever human beings congregate. It is a plasma of pacification, administered by drip transfusion from concealed grilles. The distinguishing characteristic of Muzak is its indistinguishability: it is seldom possible to remember the tune that creamy ensemble was playing five seconds ago, which floated on the periphery of familiarity, for it is boned, predigested melodious pap, processed to slide down without gulp or taste, and canned for consumption everywhere.

From the endlessly unspooling 550,000 miles of magnetic tape, it is absorbed by sixty million people a day in America alone, its birthplace, and by twice as many again throughout Europe and Asia. The U.S.S.R. is being equipped with its own system. The franchise company in Britain, Planned Music Ltd. — a wholly-owned subsidiary of A.T.V. — already has a 3,000-mile cable network reaching two million listeners a day. But "listener" is a discordant word, for the fundamental idea is that the brain-washed millions do not *listen* to Muzak: they hear it and are blandished by it. It is *Brave New World* spell-binding for our electronic age; sorcery spooned out of *Moon River*, mass mesmerism by *Mary Poppins*.

Needless to say, the Muzak men themselves don't see their product in quite that light, or at least describe it in those terms. Yet they are surprisingly candid about their aims and achievements, which are paraded with an innocent ardour. In the New York headquarters on Park Avenue South, in a custom-tailored Muzak heaven (silky indirect lighting, apricot walls, frondy tendrils, ceramic lamps, and natch, the faint purl of a mellifluous *pot-pourri*, as pastel-shaded and blank as the walls) I got the straight pitch.

"Muzak is music to be heard but not listened to," explained a young executive. "Once you're conscious of it there's something wrong. No, I wouldn't agree that it's soporific. On the contrary, it's euphoric. It creates a feeling of well-being where people work in conditions of stress or monotony. Muzak gives workers a cohesive feeling of belonging. They share the mood created by Muzak, whether it's in a hospital or a foundry, but it also gives a good sense of privacy and separation. There's now this total environment concept — ergonomics — which figures out how to provide people with the right functional furniture, atmosphere, spatial lighting and colour climate, and Muzak is architected in, just as routine as air-conditioning.

"Every big building going up in New York has the Muzak system as a basic requisite. No communuity in the United States of more than fifty thousand population is now without Muzak. This is scientifically programmed background music. But what we're really marketing is a technique for motivating people in boring or tense situations. We put a smile on the face; we pick up morale; we improve efficiency."

A member of the sales staff had just been dealing with a finicky customer, who, finding that Hawaiian medleys hadn't stimulated appetites with South Sea island magic, had asked for a replacement of standard Muzak in his café — and was now "as happy as a clam." Standing in the transmission studio, beside banks of huge reels silently unwinding their eight hours of happiness into the ether, the sales director explained that if a hitch occurred the computerised control threw the automation into an emergency programme "So really," he added with serene satisfaction, "nothing can stop Muzak."

Don O'Neill, the programme chief who organises the fortnightly recording sessions with the fifty-five arranger-conductors and the groups
ranging from sextets to orchestras thirty-strong, talked of the art of tempering Muzak to exact requirements. "It stresses melody and simplicity,"
he said. "It has no tricks or colour. Of course, carried to an extreme this
could be uninteresting, vapid, without character. Programmes aren't
designed for entertainment, but to eliminate monotony and boredom.
You couldn't do that if the music itself was boring, so we try to find a line
between that and music that dominates or distracts.

"No crescendos, no runs from pianissimo to fortissimo — that would
interfere with the worker's concentration on his task. Nor must it be too
loud. A lot of brass is used, but we score it to be non-intrusive, discreet,
with mutes or delicate playing, so that we get the tonal quality without
the powerful impact. We never put on voices. That doesn't go over too
well. They stop to listen. We couldn't use the Rolling Stones or Elvis
Presley."

Behind Mr. O'Neill hung large coloured graphs: the *Mood Stimulus
Charts*. It should not be supposed that Muzak dribbles over infinite mud
flats of sameness. It is far more subtly constructed, a mosaic dove-tailed
from aerial reconnaissance of the human spirit. Mr. O'Neill guided me
along the first diagram, a roller-coaster of the *Industrial Efficiency Curve*.
The zig-zagging red line illustrated how the typical worker arrives at the
factory in moderately chipper shape, to nose-dive into a steep slump
around ten-thirty. As lunch-time approaches, his morale and output rev
upward, a glow sustained until early afternoon. Then, wham again —
down at about three-thirty into the deepest pit of lassitude and blues,
with a distinct recovery as the clock nears knock-off time. Alongside, the
Muzak Stimulus Curve disclosed how these treacherous human vagaries
are manipulated and ironed out, so that each veer on the first chart is
neatly complemented and counterbalanced. Between 8 a.m. and 9 a.m.
the worker is gently bombarded with a Muzak that is "*Moderate:* to
instil cheerful attitude at start of first half of workday." Between 9 a.m.
and 10 a.m.: "*Moderate to bright:* to combat onset of potential tension."
Between 10 a.m. and 11 a.m.: "*Bright:* to counter maximum potential tension at period of morning when most critical." Between noon and 1 p.m.:
"*Mild and restful:* to provide midday relief." A similar cycle is dialled for
the afternoon, except that the brightness is brighter.

In its pioneer infancy, Muzak made such blunders as programming
Brazil with sambas and tangos, which proved too aggressively attention-
bothering. Thereafter, the identical American-styled tapes were distributed globally: "All music is functional. There is no difference anywhere how people respond to Muzak." In the Muzak world the whole
human race can be plugged into the same circuit. The circuit also pumps
out silence. "Research studies reveal a law of diminishing returns,"

continued Mr. O'Neill. "You can play too much music. If you keep it going continuously it becomes part of the monotony of the job and production rates drop. We alternate fifteen minutes of music with a fifteen-minute interlude. This produces the effect of breaking-up the day. We sell silence."

Nor is the old record incessantly rehashed. Mr. O'Neill is in charge of the Muzak Tune Treasury, a ten million dollar punch-card library from which computers retrieve and juggle 365 programmes a year with no tune repeated more than once every nine days on any premises. "People don't really know they're hearing it, but they scream if it's turned off," Mr. O'Neill said with business-like wizardry.

Those upon whom Muzak has impinged will hazily recall that it calibrates from Victor Sylvester-ish buoyant to Melachrinoesque swoony, adjusted to whether it is intended for, say, high-school examination rooms or that Atlanta motel swimming pool with underwater Muzak, which leaves you with the desperate thought that you couldn't escape it even by drowning yourself. The menu is schemed out with astute relevance to its egress point. *Stormy Weather* and *I Don't Stand a Ghost of a Chance* are banned on airlines. Presumably *It Can't Be That Bad* and *Scarlet Ribbons* have been excised from the tapes for the Houston operating theatre where the Duke of Windsor had hum-along abdominal surgery, and *I've Got a Feeling I'm Falling* from the programmes for President Johnson's ranch. Certainly classical music has been altogether scrubbed. "I love Mozart, Beethoven, Brahms," said another Muzak man, "but I couldn't work to that stuff. Hindemith felt that music could be put to some everyday use but wasn't sure what it could be. Muzak did it. As a matter of fact, if we could invent a subsonic signal that could have the same influence over work-people that Muzak has, we'd broadcast that."

Frank though the spokesmen are, there is an even balder philosophy in Muzak's printed literature. This unashamedly exhorts the employer to boost his profits and stealthily soothe his staff. A Muzak booklet entitled *The Science of Music* says:

Music arouses varied emotional and physical responses in people, both on a conscious and subconscious level. Muzak puts this powerful effect to work for business. . . . In the early 1930's Muzak psychologists and musicologists began harnessing the emotional power of music for the specific purpose of creating pleasant and profitable business environment. Unlike most other forms of music, music by Muzak was designed to be unobtrusive and to require no active listening. Years of research resulted in the present-day Muzak concept of "functional programming," a technique for motivating people with precisely timed and planned musical conditioning. . . . Transmitted via modern communications channels, music by Muzak is employed as a technique of realistic profit-minded management in outstanding businesses throughout the world.

It carries on:

Every year industry loses countless millions of productive hours to inefficiency, mistakes, and absenteeism, most of which start with boredom and monotony. Every year, thousands upon thousands of restaurants and stores fail to reach their potential sales level — because of customer tension and irritation from noise, crowds, long waits or cold atmosphere. Muzak creates an atmosphere beneficial to workers, and produces a sense of well-being among customers and patrons. . . . It puts people in a relaxed frame of mind and enhances their buying moods. . . . Accurate timing is crucial to the Muzak concept, for the music must always be in phase with the emotional needs of its audience. Muzak has invested millions of dollars for research into accurate, automatic, and foolproof timing methods.

Another promotional leaflet emphasizes: "The very nature of functional background music requires that it is not a noticeable factor to those 'hearing' it. It follows that people do not realise the way music is used today or appreciate the size and scope of the industry at work behind the loudspeaker. . . . As each tune is played there is an increase in stimulus value, giving workers a psychological sense of moving forward — making work seem easier and time pass faster." *Can Music Increase the Efficiency of Your Office By Ten Per Cent?* asks one booklet. It describes how Muzak can "create a work mood." Pointing out that all the "ten best-managed companies" and "over eighty per cent of America's largest life insurance companies and banks" shimmer with Muzak, it declares: "When personnel become tense or feel frustrated, they develop an indifference which often results in costly errors, accidents, absenteeism, lateness and non-productive activities such as early departures, idle conversation and daydreaming." Muzak "enhances a company's image, combats tension and fatigue with timed psychological lifts, and masks distracting machine noise, conversation or cold silence."

Testimonials are presented from realistic, profit-minded and silence-hating businessmen. Edward S. Godlewski, of the Levi Case Company, Schenectady, confides: "Our plant is as noisy as ever, but our employees don't realise it." Frank A. Gunther, of Radio Engineering Laboratories Inc., New York, reports: "Increased efficiency, fewer errors, eased tensions, happy, contented employees, and a reduction in absenteeism — a major profit factor." The Muzak Marketing Memos, for internal circulation among the sales force, yield some interesting attitudes: "Profit-minded hotel managers know Muzak warms a cold, impersonal atmosphere, keeps guests on the premises with money to spend. Check-out bills are fatter." A Memphis school principal finds Muzak has "pleasing effects on young children during the cafeteria period when they are somewhat uninhibited." One Marketing Memo introduces Irving Wexler,

Miami Beach franchise vice-president, a completely "Muzakated" man. "He lives the product he sells. He believes in it. He has Music by Muzak in his home, in every room, and it plays twenty-four hours a day. 'I know Muzak has therapeutic, psychological value,' Irving says. 'We sleep with it on, watch television with it on. I never permit it to be shut off.'" Even Irving's "fiery red Thunderbird convertible" is on the beam. "Muzak programming is played continuously on the special automobile tuner."

Yet another Marketing Memo discusses *Togetherness: The Bad Side:*

*Proxemics, the study of human behaviour at varying degrees of prox-
imity, gives Muzakmen another opportunity to show how Muzak programming has proved highly successful as the solution to problems
caused by overcrowding or isolation in offices. The new science concerned with spatial relationships among office workers reveals clearly
that employee performance can suffer if workers are packed too close
together, or, conversely, if they are too widely separated or isolated.
A crowded office atmosphere leads to worker tensions evidenced sooner
or later in tardiness, early departures, absenteeism, idle chatter, water-
cooler visits, rest-room lounging, protracted personal telephone calls and
a high rate of turnover. Conversely, employees situated too far apart
tend to develop feelings of loneliness, being lost. . . . Unobtrusive Muzak
programming forms a kind of screen in the crowded atmosphere, separates workers with an invisible curtain of melody and reduces substantially feelings of fear and oppression. . . . Also it gives isolated employees
a sense of belonging, a unified and cohesive feeling of working together,
because background music by Muzak acts as an invisible but unifying
force.*

There is also a British publication entitled *Muzak In Industry*. Its glossy pages are lucent with smiling contented hands. There are many quotes, straight from the fraternal factory floor: "Muzak takes your mind off your own personal worries." "When we had *Housewives' Choice* the women sang with the records and tended to skylark about. Muzak stopped that." "It seems to pass the time away. When the first quarter of an hour is over there is always the next one to look forward to."

However, this is all rah-rah-rah material for the front-line salesmen. Hardcore Muzak tactics can be tracked down in duller documents, such as *Effects of Muzak on Industrial Efficiency* and *Effects of Muzak on Office Personnel*. These are jingly with diagrams and mathematical equa-tions: sections headed "Calculation of Significance of Performance Change in Test Department," "Manual Dexterity Speed Scores and Pro-ductivity Changes with Muzak," and "Percentage Increase Before Muzak and With Muzak." Even more fascinating is the *Vigilance With Back-ground Music* report prepared by the Human Engineering Laboratories at the Aberdeen Proving Ground, Maryland. This instructs how to conduct music-while-you-press-the-button tests for missile system personnel. The examiner is advised to get it across this way:

Alertness is very important in a lot of military situations — your life, and maybe your buddies' lives, too, can depend on how alert you are. The task you're to do is based on what the officer in charge of a missile site might have to do. . . . The colour of the light tells you what the target's identification is: green — friendly; yellow — unidentified; red — enemy. You press a key to tell the missile system what to do.

Then the examiner switches on Muzak.

It may come as a relief to the civilian population barred from this special Muzak intimacy to learn that the overwhelming majority of missile button-pressers approve of background music while responding alertly to the coloured flashes. In fact most said: "The music was really great." What worries me is the small, but possibly vital, percentage who sulked: "I didn't like the tunes." I hope they work out a programme that keeps them permanently pleased.

In point of fact, this recalcitrant minority isn't confined to Minutemen control centres. Muzak have a problem. There is a last ditch awkward squad who won't be human-engineered. Melvin Cohen, Muzak's research manager, concedes that there are "negative responses from three to five per cent of the population: elderly spinster ladies, just-plain-contrary people and individualists who won't accept any music that others have chosen for them. . . ." One can see how infuriating they must be to Muzak. But my impression was that Muzak feel they can ride out their small irritation; they *know* which is the winning side.

Carlos Baker

The Function of the Critic

"Finders keepers, losers weepers," runs the ancient taunt by which boys justify their acquisitive instincts. Those first two words happen to summarize the whole social duty of the critic: finding and keeping. For if we do not preserve what we already have, we shall not only impoverish ourselves but we shall also lose our grip on those principles by which we measure the perpetual innovations the lively arts thrust upon us. The other half of our duty is to find, among these innovations, all their use and their beauty. Otherwise we may become so stultified among our dusty tomes that our critical progress will amount to nothing but a pretentious parade through terminological changes.

There is no overstating the importance of the critic's obligation as keeper of our ancestral domain, the literary heritage of the Western — to say nothing of the Eastern — tradition. It is the huge plantation to which, individually and collectively, we have fallen heir. We are at once the explorers and the husbandmen. But our first obligation is to preserve. The terrain is crowded with innumerable structures, from the vast temples of Homeric antiquity to the latest split-level novels, and from the Gothic cathedrals of Shakespearean tragedy to the rundown ranch-houses of Zane Grey.

Time is the enemy. A hundred foundations that seemed solid in their day have cracked with the frost of centuries; some of the structures have suffered the fateful burial of Herculaneum; others have crumbled into dust and been blown away, round the world. The critic must clear away the verbal rubble, shore up decaying towers, and mend the walls of demarcation which time and human carelessness have allowed to tumble into disrepair. He must rebuild for modern occupancy any structures that deserve it, and repair broken lines of communication between other ages, other lands and other persuasions than our own.

Like any other keeper he must on occasion destroy. He must oppose the meretricious in whatever form it survives — or arrives: the sensational and the trivial, the idle and the puerile, the cheap and the tawdry. He must fell the soft and punklike trees that have shot up to obscure the noble view of distant spires. He must root out the tough old stumps of former errors. It was Thomas Carew's praise of John Donne that he had purged the Muses' garden of pedantic weeds, and thrown away the lazy seeds of servile imitation. But the purge was not permanent; the work of Donne is never really done.

Another part of his task is to determine what is worth keeping. Ralph Waldo Emerson's advice to the American scholar — "defer never to the popular cry" — is as much an indefensible absolute as its opposite: defer always to the unpopular cry. The middle ground of the critic's personal integrity is perhaps the only absolute of this kind that justifies our belief. Wherever his views run counter to received opinion, it is clearly one of his social obligations to stick to his conviction "that a popgun is a popgun" even though "the ancient and honorable of the earth affirm it to be the crack of doom." And he should be prepared to recognize the accents of thunder in works to which the larger public is obviously tone-deaf. "The best art of our time" as a critic recently observed, "can easily be missed." It is the critic's social responsibility to see that we miss as little of it as possible, and this he can never do if he does not remain receptive to innovation.

The task of finding is the second of the critic's social obligations. It parallels, at one remove, the task of discovery the reputable artist sets himself when he undertakes any significant piece of writing. Matthew Arnold recognized the parallel. Indeed we owe to him a brilliant simile, one which happens to apply, under the general rubric of finding, both to the work of the artist and the work of the critic. He asks us to consider the situation of an Athenian playgoer in attendance at a performance of the Oresteia. "The terrible old mythic story on which the drama was founded," says Arnold, can be presumed to have existed at least in bare outline within the spectator's mind before he entered the theatre. "It stood in his memory as a group of statuary, faintly seen, at the end of a long and dark vista: then came the Poet, embodying outlines, developing situations, not a word wasted, not a sentiment capriciously thrown in: stroke upon stroke, the drama proceeded; the light deepened upon the group; more and more it revealed itself to the riveted gaze of the spectator: until at last, when the final words were spoken, it stood before him in broad sunlight, a model of immortal beauty."

Arnold is here rightly assuming that it is a major office of literature to illumine human experience. Under conditions that are at least imaginable, however seldom they may be achieved in practice, the artist causes his three-dimensional statuary to come fully alive before our eyes. The spectator leaves the theatre, or the reader lays down his book, in something like total possession of all that the artist sought to convey. If such an ideal were invariably achieved, the critic as finder would have far less to do. Yet our experience as readers readily informs us that the artist does not always succeed in the total illumination of his subject. It is perhaps one of the laws of authorship that no one can make his fullest meaning at once intelligible, even to himself. He may even prefer to leave his living statues in some degree of obscurity or ambiguity as a matter of esthetic principle. Even the clearest work of art, while often self-contained, is not necessarily self-explanatory. The multiple relations between its meaning and its form, to take only one example, are ordinarily implicit rather than explicit. The critic as finder would be kept busy enough if his only task were to explore these relations.

Among those who distrust the critic as an intrusive middleman, edging his vast steatopygous bulk between author and audience, it is not uncommon to wish him away, out of the direct line of vision. "It is barely possible," said James Russell Lowell ironically, "that the power of a book resides in the book itself, and that real books somehow compel an audience without extraneous intervention." One wishes that he could believe this wholesome dictum, which was handed down in 1849, a scant two years before a "real book" called "Moby Dick" began its long struggle for the recognition it did not attain until seventy years after publication. The critic's intervention would be needed if only to maintain the reader's receptivity at the highest level of operation. We have merely to consult our own records as readers to recall how frequently the vista between artist and audience can be darkened by extraneous factors. Anything from ignorance to indigestion, or from prejudice to pusillanimity, may, and often does, get in our way.

If, therefore, it is a major office of the artist to illumine human experience, it is assuredly a major office of the critic to illuminate the artist's illumination. As the man of good sense and finer sensibility, he seeks to make the implicit as explicit as possible in any work of art he chooses to explore.

In his function as a finder, the critic may be called the scientist of the unsuspected and the cartographer of the uncircumscribed. He returns from the realms of gold with a relief map of the hills and valleys. He must accept the role of John Keats' Cortez, toiling up the landward slope of some masking range to stand finally upon the peak, seeing for the first time perhaps a broad and heaving expanse whose existence has been known, but whose islands and archipelagos, whose shoals and depths, had not hitherto been adequately charted. He must be prepared for change: what once loomed as a considerable mountain on the horizons of its own epoch may since have been eroded to a minor protuberance by the weathering of successive ages. Like Robert Frost's oven bird, the critic must have some idea of "what to make of a diminished thing."

There is also the opposite effect. The tides of time, receding from a former level, may have exposed an island long hidden and unknown. The critic must give it sea-room on his charts, taking due account of its relationship to those larger land-masses over which critical factions have made war for so many centuries.

Finally, the critic must find power to be fair to the work which engages his attention. Criticism would be of immense social value if it existed for no other reason than the constant exercise it gives to the intellectual morality of the critic himself. In criticism as in religious ethics, there are sins venial and sins deadly.

The seven deadly sins of criticism, if we are to avoid them, and not one of us completely does, require of us a constant reassessment of our motives. There is, for example, the critical sin of covetousness, which may cause the critic to seek fame at the expense of the author whose work he exploits. The closely associated sin of envy leads to the denigration of the work of others for the hidden purpose of self-aggrandizement. To indulge the sin of gluttony is to bite off more than one is prepared to digest, denying others the right to partake. To be lustful is to indulge an inordinate desire for the gratification of one's sense of power. The deadly sin of anger leads to the loss of one's composure and sense of balance during the inevitable exchanges of differing opinion. The deadly sin of sloth is to repeat accepted lies about an author or a body of work because one is too lazy to dig out the truth. The critical sin of pride is to hand down judgments from on high with a godlike assumption of infallibility, and to assume, along with the robes of the judge, the axe of the executioner.

Criticism, in sum, if it is to be socially responsible, ought to begin at home, within the ivory tower of the critic's own cranium, where finding and keeping, if they are to be done at all, must take their origin and prove their worth. And if the finding and the keeping are not done, we shall all be the losers, with every right to weep at the enormity of our loss.

Muse, Spare Me

I beseech the Muse to keep me from ever becoming a Black Humorist. Mind, I don't object to Black Humorists, in their place, but to be numbered with them inspires me to a kind of spiritual White Backlash. For one thing they are in their way *responsible*, like more conventional social satirists: they dramatize — and good for them! — the Madness of Contemporary Society, of Modern Warfare, of Life with the Bomb, of What Have We Nowadays. But I say, Muse spare me (at the desk, I mean) from Social-Historical Responsibility, and in the last analysis from every other kind as well, except Artistic. Your teller of stories will likely be responsive to his time; he needn't be responsible to it. I'm not impressed by the apocalyptic character of the present age — nor is the age by my indifference! — though I note the fact, and will return to it. Joyce figured the writer as Dedalus, Mann as Faust; the best of the Black Humorists are good comical Amoses and Isaiahs.

My own favorite image in this line used to be Cassandra — a *laughing* Cassandra, of course — the darling of many another young writer convinced that he has unhappy truth by the tail, or on his back, and that no one's getting the message. Later, shorn of such vanity, I preferred an image out of Dante: the Florentine assassins alluded to in Canto XIX of the *Inferno*. Head-downwards in a hole and sentenced to be buried alive, the murderer postpones his fate by drawing out his confession to the attendant priest. The beauties of this image are its two nice paradoxes: the more sins he has to confess, the longer retribution is delayed, and since he has nothing to lose anyhow, he may well invent a few good ones to hold the priest's attention.

But as soon as his audience grants absolution, the wretch's mouth is stopped with earth: "Nothing fails like success," as Mr. Fiedler says of our popular novelists. Less satisfactory are the details that his audience is also captive, duty-bound to hear him out whether entertained or not; respite is granted only as long as he talks, not as long as he amuses, and there's no real stay of execution, only a hold in the countdown. More-over, the fact that his tale consists of fabricated or exaggerated misde-meanors of his own, a perverse kind of authorial self-aggrandizement, while it may make the image apter yet for some novelists we know — assassins indeed of the characters they "draw from life," as one draws a man to the gallows — does not, I hope, apply to my own concoctions.

In any case, the image I'm lately fonder of — the aptest, sweetest, hauntingest, hopefullest I know for the storyteller — is Scheherazade. The whole frame of those thousand nights and a night speaks to my heart, directly and intimately — and in many ways at once, personal and technical. The sultan Shahryar, you remember, is so disenchanted with life in general and love in particular that he marries a virgin every night and has her killed in the morning; Scheherazade, who has "perused the books, annals, and legends of preceding kings, and the stories, examples and instances of by-gone men . . . antique races and departed rulers," volunteers herself; the King "abates her virginity" (as if it were an intense condition!), whereafter, with the prearranged assistance of her younger sister Dunyazad — about whose role much might be said — Scheherazade beguiles her deflowerer with a tale, artfully continued, involuted, compounded, and complicated through a thousand and one nocturnal installments, during the invention of which she also bears three sons by her imperious audience. It is on behalf of these offspring that, her inspiration spent at last, she begs for her life, and the King grants her — in honor of her stories — the relative tenure of formal marriage. Scheherazade's tales are published (in 30 volumes) and their author lives happily with her hard-earned family. But not ever after; only until they all are taken by the Destroyer of Delights, whereafter, we're specifically told, "their houses fell waste and their palaces lay in ruins . . . and [other] kings inherited their riches" — including *The Thousand and One Nights*.

My love affair with Scheherazade is an old and continuing one. As an illiterate undergraduate I worked off part of my tuition filing books in the Classics Library at Johns Hopkins, which included the stacks of the Oriental Seminary. One was permitted to get lost for hours in that splendrous labyrinth and intoxicate, engorge oneself with *story*. Espe-cially I became enamored of the great tale-cycles and collections: Somadeva's *Ocean of Story* in ten huge volumes. Burton's *Thousand Nights and a Night* in twelve, the *Panchatantra*, the *Gesta Romanorum*, the *Novellini*, and the *Pent- Hept-* and *Decameron*. If anything ever makes a writer out of me, it will be the digestion of that enormous surreptitious feast of narrative.

Most of those spellbinding liars I have forgotten, but never Schehera-zade. Though the tales she tells aren't my favorites, she remains my favorite teller, and it is a heady paradox that this persistence, being the figure of her literal aim, thereby generates itself, and becomes the emblem as well of my figurative aspiration. When I think of my condition and my hope, Musewise, in the time between now and when I shall run out of ink or otherwise expire it is Scheherazade who comes to mind, for many reasons — not least of which is a technical interest in the ancient device of the framing-story, used more beautifully in the *Nights* than anywhere else I know. Chaucer's frame, for example, the pilgrimage to Canterbury, is an excellent if venerable ground-metaphor — but, having established it, he does nothing with it. Boccaccio's frame — ten wealthy young ladies and gentlemen amusing themselves with clever stories while the great post-Easter plague of 1348 lays waste the countryside — is more arresting for its apocalyptic nature, for the pretty rules with which the company replaces those of their literally dying society, for the hints of growing relationships between the *raconteurs* and *raconteuses* themselves, and for the occasional relevance of the tales to the tellers and to the general situation. On the other hand, the very complex serial frames of the *Ocean of Story*, for example, are full-fledged stories in themselves, but except for the marvelous (and surely fictitious) "history of the text" and the haunting title, they have no apparent meaningfulness beyond their immediate narrative interest.

The story of Scheherazade excels these others, it seems to me, in all respects. For one thing her tales are told at night: an inestimable advantage, for the whole conception, despite its humor, is darker, more magical and dreamish than Boccaccio's or Chaucer's. Consider too the prerequisites for her taletellerhood: not only native endowment and mastery of the tradition, but the sacrifice of her present personal maidenhead to her auditor and absolute critic — whose pleasure, by the way, fertilizes as well as spares her, and who finally rewards her (for what they have in a manner of speaking created together) with official distinctions which *he* will not take away (though her productivity, it seems, ends with the award of tenure), but time will.

Consider finally that in the years of her flourishing, her talent is always on the line: not enough to have satisfied the old cynic once, or twice; she's only as good as her next piece, Scheherazade; night by night it's publish or perish. Thus her situation is no less apocalyptic in its way than the *Decameron's*, and perhaps more pointed, even without regard to the interesting "public" state of affairs: the King's epical despair and the ruin it's bringing his kingdom to. For though the death of one person is not the death of a people, even mankind's demise will have to consist of each of our dyings; in this respect all apocalypses are ultimately personal — an important fact, since it validates apocalyptic visions age after age despite the otherwise awkward circumstance that the world has, so far, persisted.

Even the detail that Scheherazade's stories are drawn from the literal and legendary foretime I find arresting. It reminds me that the eschewing of contemporaneous, "original" material is a basic literary notion, by comparison to which its use is but an occasional anomaly and current fad. Not only classical epic and tragedy and Elizabethan and neo-classical drama, but virtually all folk and heroic narrative, both Eastern and Western, follows Horace's advice: ". . . *safer shall the bard his pen employ/ With yore, to dramatize the Tale of Troy,/Than, venturing trackless regions to explore,/Delineate characters untouched before.*"

Joyce's Dedalus calls history a nightmare from which he's trying to wake; some other writers have found it more a wet-dream (and their readers, perhaps, a soporific). For me, also, the past is a dream — but I laugh in my sleep. The use of historical or legendary material, especially in a farcical spirit, has a number of technical virtues, among which are esthetic distance and the opportunity for counter-realism. Attacked with a long face, the historical muse is likely to give birth to costume romances, adult Westerns, tiresome allegories, and ponderous mythologizings; but she responds to a light-hearted approach. *Magic* is what chiefly saves Scheherazade's tales from these poor categories — a device we may hardly use today, for the realistic tradition and its accompanying cultural history are under our belts, for better or worse, and may not be ignored. They may, however, be come to terms with and got beyond, not by the use of farce alone, surely, but by farce inspired with passion — and with mystery, which, older than magic, still enwraps our lives as it does the whole queer universe. In passionate, mysterious farce, it seems to me, lies also the possibility of transcending categories more profound than Tragedy and Comedy: I mean the distinction between Tragedy and Mystery — or, if you like, tragicism and mysticism, the finest expressions respectively of the Western and Eastern spirits. No matter that the achievement of such a synthesis would want the talents of Scheherazade, Shakespeare, and Schopenhauer combined; it is a polestar that even a middling comic novelist may steer by, without mistaking it for his destination.

Like a parable of Kafka's or a great myth, the story of deflowered Scheherazade, yarning tirelessly through the dark hours to save her neck, corresponds to a number of things at once, and flashes meaning from all its facets. For me its rich dark circumstances, mixing the subtle and the coarse, the comic and the grim, the realistic and the fantastic, the apocalyptic and the hopeful, figure, among other things, both the estate of the fictioner in general and the particular endeavors and aspirations of this one, at least, who can wish nothing better than to spin like that vizier's excellent daughter, through what nights remain to him, tales within tales within tales, full-stored with "description and discourse and rare traits and anecdotes and moral instances and reminiscences . . . proverbs and parables, chronicles and pleasantries, quips and jests, stories and . . . dialogues and histories and elegies and other verses . . ." until he and his scribblings are fetched low by the Destroyer of Delights.

The Sign in Jimmy Breslin's Front Yard

The wife of a new neighbor from up on the corner came down and walked up to my wife and started acting nice, which must have exhausted her.

This woman is one of the people I have to live with. Four years ago, in the true style of an amateur, I "moved out a bit." I moved into a block with a lot of other people who live side by side in houses. Now, people are all right. Get them alone and they're pretty good. But put five of them together and they start conforming and after that all they are is trouble. Put sixteen families on the same block, the way it is on mine, and they become unbelievable. They are not people any more. They are enemies. On my block they sweep the lawn and have the waxer polish the front walk and all of them ring doorbells about kid fights and if everything isn't the same, and everybody doesn't worry about things that show, they bother you as an occupation. Anybody who has his own mind and moves out of a beautiful anonymous Manhattan apartment and goes to a house on a block is crazy.

For four years now, so many of the neighbors have come to the door, or had their kids run up like stool pigeons to report some crime my kids committed, that now I sit at the front window and watch one of them come down the block and as he walks I dream of a big black car pulling up and three guys in big hats jumping out and breaking both my neighbor's legs.

It is this bad to live with these people, and this woman could get first on the whole block.

"I haven't gotten a chance to see you since the baby," the new one said. "How nice. This is, uh, your . . .?"

She knew the number, she knows everything. She knew my take-home pay by the end of the first week she was on the block.

"Fifth," my wife said.

"How wonderful," she said. "And did you plan this one?"

"Oh, yes," my wife said sweetly. "Why, everybody I know plans their fifth baby."

The woman got mad and walked away. Which was great. And I was going to say something to her that she could tell her husband for me, but I didn't have the time. I had to stay on Walter, from the Dazzle Sign Painting Company, who was on my lawn and acting like a coward.

"Put it up, Walter," I told him.

"Not in the daylight," Walter said.

Walter had two big wooden posts and a lot of tools in his arms.

"An argument is an argument, but if you do this it lets everybody know that you're crazy," my wife says.

"Put it up, Walter," I said. "I want these people to read my sign right now."

Walter shook his head. Then he dropped everything and began jamming one of the posts into the lawn. My wife ran inside the house. She is the former Rosemary Dattolico and she is very Italian. She likes knives on black nights, not big posters in broad daylight.

"Let's go, Walter," I said, and Walter, from the Dazzle Sign Painting Company, put in both the stakes and tacked the sign on, and when he was finished, right there on the lawn was the most beautiful sign you ever saw.

It was about three feet high and five feet wide and it was in three bright colors and it read real good. On the top, in two lines of big red upper-case letters, the sign said:

SORRY TO MAKE YOU LOOK AT THIS BECAUSE I KNOW HOW TIRED YOU PEOPLE GET MOVING YOUR LIPS WHEN YOU READ

Underneath this, in smaller, but still real big blue letters, was a line which said: PEOPLE I'M NOT TALKING TO THIS YEAR.

The line was centered. Right under it, in neat columns, like a service honor roll, was the name of everybody who lives on my block. Everybody. All the couples, all the mothers-in-law, and all the kids. Every single person alive on my block had his name printed on that sign by Walter, from the Dazzle Sign Painting Company. And at the end of the list of names, I had Walter put "Dugan" for the bread man and "Stylon" for the dry-cleaning guy and "Borden's" for the fat milkman I don't like.

The best was at the bottom. In clear orange italics, the little passage said: "I also am announcing a special service for people who ring my bell to tell me what my children did. This service includes a man who answers the doorbell. Why don't you come and ring my bell and see what happens to you?"

Walter and I stepped back to look at the sign. The white pasteboard looked nice in the sunlight. It was the greatest sign I ever saw.

"Nobody ever had a sign like this," Walter said. "Nobody. I paint 'Fire Sale' and 'Prices Slashed' and for gin mills I do 'Under New Management' or 'Sunday Cocktail Hour,' but I never in my life done a sign like this."

"Beautiful," I said. I stood back and admired it. This was my message, my own personal message to everybody on the block. How could you find a better way to put it across? For a year now, my wife has been hissing at the neighbors, "He's writing a novel about the block and you're in it because he hid a tape recorder under your kitchen table." But this sign of mine beat any book. And even those Burma Shave signs — "She went wild/When he went woolly" — they never read as good as my personal sign.

"The sign costs $27.50," Walter said.

"Walter, it's worth $100," I said. "Look at that." I grabbed his arm. "Look at that woman up the block, Walter. She just saw the sign. She's dying to come up here and see it, I bet. Look at her, Walter. She's dying. Wait'll she comes up here and sees what it says. Can you imagine the face on her when she does that, Walter? Boy, this takes care of them. Why don't you stay around so we can both look out the window and watch?"

"I think you're sick," Walter said.

"No, I'm not, I just hate those people."

I hate them all. In the whole area where we live, I hate them all. Once I thought we got a break. A big gangster from Brooklyn moved out and tried to live quietly with his two Cadillacs parked in front of the house and his pearl-gray hat stuck on his head even when he came out for the milk. But the guy was in the neighborhood only three months and then he got arrested and he was all over the papers. People began detouring two blocks so they wouldn't go near his house, and the fellow stayed holed up so much that you never could meet him. He finally moved, and left me with all the garbage. One thing you can bet, I wouldn't have had Walter, from the Dazzle, put the gangster's name on my sign.

After I had watched my sign for a while, and Walter left with his truck from the Dazzle, I went into the kitchen and had coffee and waited until this friend of mine called Bad Eddie showed up. Bad Eddie is called this because he doesn't do anything nice, and I had things I wanted him to do to my neighbors that aren't nice.

"There's a lot of people out on the block," Bad Eddie said.

"That's good, we're going to get rid of them all," I said.

"Oh, dear Lord, look at this," my wife said. "They're coming from the other block, too."

"They could get hurt, too, and I wouldn't complain," I said.

Then I got down to business with Bad Eddie. "Now look," I said, "we're going to do this big-time. We'll get white mice and put them in someone's house. That'll fix them. Now, look out the window. See that guy up there in his back yard? Walking around the bushes? We don't even mess with him. He goes."

"What do you mean, he goes?" Bad Eddie said.

"Any way you want to do it," I said. "But he goes. We're going to do this right, just like Capone. We'll use mice, threats, beatings, anything we want."

Bad Eddie did not look up from his coffee.

"Don't that joint of his give him any vacation?" he asked my wife. "He needs a rest." Nobody answered.

"It's going to be crowded out there," my wife said. "Almost like the day Jason Robards and Lauren Bacall were across the street."

That was the biggest day in the history of the block and the people did just what you'd expect them to do. They acted like jerks. They walked back and forth, then back and forth again, or they stood on the sidewalk and gaped at Mr. Robards and his wife. They were visiting their accountant, who lives across the street and doesn't talk to me, but they should have charged admission for coming out in the front of the house.

When they left, the block went back to normal. Which means all that ever happens is some grown man, pushed out by his wife with an adolescent's mind, comes up to the door and tells you, "Your Jimmy tried to strangle my son the other day," And you tell him, "I'm awfully sorry. I'm awfully sorry Jimmy messed up the job and didn't kill your kid."

Now, for the rest of this day, I sat over coffee with Eddie and plotted doing things to people, and, outside, the people stopped to look at the sign and they stumbled through the reading and then went on. And in one day everybody got my personal message.

They never did get Bad Eddie's message because he spent the whole day sitting at the kitchen table and shaking his head and when he left he only said one thing. "Get yourself a good rest," Bad Eddie said.

Since then the sign has come down, but it's in the garage and it can go up any time, just like a flag. That is, if there is a garage left. As a precaution against a slow real-estate market when we find something in town and put the house up for sale, I had Marvin the Torch over one day. He is a man who burns down things for a living.

He went out in the front and dug a fingernail into the wood and looked around.

"Not too good," he said. "The wood is green. Too green. To do this sure, I might have to load it up, and that would mean taking out half the block."

"Don't let that stand in your way," I told him. The new one was right up the block looking at us.

Charles S. Brooks

On the Difference Between Wit and Humor

I am not sure that I can draw an exact line between wit and humor. Perhaps the distinction is so subtle that only those persons can decide who have long white beards. But even an ignorant man, so long as he is clear of Bedlam, may have an opinion.

I am quite positive that of the two, humor is the more comfortable and more livable quality. Humorous persons, if their gift is genuine and not a mere shine upon the surface, are always agreeable companions and they sit through the evening best. They have pleasant mouths turned up at the corners. To these corners the great Master of marionettes has fixed the strings and he holds them in his nimblest fingers to twitch them at the slightest jest. But the mouth of a merely witty man is hard and sour until the moment of its discharge. Nor is the flash from a witty man always comforting, whereas a humorous man radiates a general pleasure and is like another candle in the room.

I admire wit, but I have no real liking for it. It has been too often employed against me, whereas humor is always an ally. It never points an impertinent finger into my defects. Humorous persons do not sit like explosives on a fuse. They are safe and easy comrades. But a wit's tongue is as sharp as a donkey's stick. I may gallop the faster for its prodding, yet the touch behind is too persuasive for any comfort.

Wit is a lean creature with sharp inquiring nose, whereas humor has a kindly eye and comfortable girth. Wit, if it be necessary, uses malice to score a point — like a cat it is quick to jump — but humor keeps the peace in an easy chair. Wit has a better voice in a solo, but humor comes into the chorus best. Wit is as sharp as a stroke of lightning, whereas humor is diffuse like sunlight. Wit keeps the season's fashions and is precise in the phrases and judgments of the day, but humor is concerned with the homely eternal things. Wit wears silk, but humor in homespun endures the wind. Wit sets a snare, whereas humor goes off whistling without a victim in its mind. Wit is sharper company at table, but humor serves better in mischance and in the rain. When it tumbles wit is sour, but humor goes uncomplaining without its dinner. Humor laughs at another's jest and holds its sides, while wit sits wrapped in study for a lively answer. But it is a workaday world in which we live, where we get mud upon our boots and come weary to the twilight — it is a world that grieves and suffers from many wounds in these years of war: and therefore as I think of my acquaintances, it is those who are humorous in its best and truest meaning rather than those who are witty who give the more profitable companionship.

And then, also, there is wit that is not wit. As someone has written:

Nor ever noise for wit on me could pass,
When thro' the braying I discern'd the ass.

I sat lately at dinner with a notoriously witty person (a really witty man) whom our hostess had introduced to provide the entertainment. I had read many of his reviews of books and plays, and while I confess their wit and brilliancy, I had thought them to be hard and intellectual and lacking in all that broader base of humor which aims at truth. His writing — catching the bad habit of the time — is too ready to proclaim a paradox and to assert the unusual, to throw aside in contempt the valuable haystack in a fine search for a paltry needle. His reviews are seldom right — as most of us see the right — but they sparkle and hold one's interest for their perversity and unexpected turns.

In conversation I found him much as I had found him in his writing — although, strictly speaking, it was not a conversation, which requires an interchange of word and idea and is turn about. A conversation should not be a market where one sells and another buys. Rather, it should be a bargaining back and forth, and each person should be both merchant and buyer. My rubber plant for your Victrola, each offering what he has and seeking his deficiency. It was my friend B——— who fairly put the case when he said that he liked so much to talk that he was willing to pay for his audience by listening in his turn.

But this was a speech and a lecture. He loosed on us from the cold spigot of his intellect a steady flow of literary allusion — a practice which he professes to hold in scorn — and wit and epigram. He seemed torn from the page of Meredith. He talked like ink. I had believed before that only people in books could talk as he did, and then only when their author had blotted and scratched their performance for a seventh time before he sent it to the printer. To me it was an entirely new experience, for my usual acquaintances are good common honest daytime woollen folk and they seldom average better than one bright thing in an evening.

At first I feared that there might be a break in his flow of speech which I should be obliged to fill. Once, when there was a slight pause — a truffle was engaging him — I launched a frail remark; but it was swept off at once in the renewed torrent. And seriously it does not seem fair. If one speaker insists — to change the figure — on laying all the cobbles of a conversation, he should at least allow another to carry the tarpot and fill in the chinks. When the evening was over, although I recalled two or three clever stories, which I shall botch in the telling, I came away tired and dissatisfied, my tongue dry with disuse.

Now I would not seek that kind of man as a companion with whom to be becalmed in a sailboat, and I would not wish to go to the country with him, least of all to the North Woods or any place outside of civilization. I am sure that he would sulk if he were deprived of an audience. He would be crotchety at breakfast across his bacon. Certainly for the woods a humorous man is better company, for his humor in mischance comforts both him and you. A humorous man — and here lies the heart of the matter — a humorous man has the high gift of regarding an annoyance in the very stroke of it as another man shall regard it when the annoyance is long past. If a humorous person falls out of a canoe he knows the exquisite jest while his head is still bobbing in the cold water. A witty man, on the contrary, is sour until he is changed and dry, but in a week's time when company is about, he will make a comic story of it.

My friend A——— with whom I went once into the Canadian woods has genuine humor, and no one can be a more satisfactory comrade. I do not recall that he said many comic things, and at bottom he was serious as the best humorists are. But in him there was a kind of joy and exaltation that lasted throughout the day. If the duffle were piled too high and fell about his ears, if the dinner was burned or the tent blew down in a driving storm at night, he met these mishaps as though they were the very things he had come north to get, as though without them the trip would have lacked its spice. This is an easy philosophy in retrospect but hard when the wet canvas falls across you and the rain beats in. A——— laughed at the very moment of disaster as another man will laugh later in an easy chair. I see him now swinging his axe for firewood to dry ourselves when we were spilled in a rapids; and again, while pitching our tent on a sandy beach when another storm had drowned us. And there is a certain cry of his (dully, *Wow!* on paper) expressive to the initiated of all things gay, which could never issue from the mouth of a merely witty man.

Real humor is primarily human — or divine, to be exact — and after that the fun may follow naturally in its order. Not long ago I saw Louis Jouvet of the French Company play Sir Andrew Ague-Cheek. It was a most humorous performance of the part, and the reason is that the actor made no primary effort to be funny. It was the humanity of his playing, making his audience love him first of all, that provoked the comedy. His long thin legs were comical and so was his drawling talk, but the very heart and essence was this love he started in his audience. Poor fellow! how delightfully he smoothed the feathers in his hat! How he feared to fight the duel! It was easy to love such a dear silly human fellow. A merely witty player might have drawn as many laughs, but there would not have been the catching at the heart.

As for books and the wit or humor of their pages, it appears that wit fades, whereas humor lasts. Humor uses permanent nutgalls. But is there anything more melancholy than the wit of another generation? In the first place, this wit is intertwined with forgotten circumstance. It hangs on a fashion — on the style of a coat. It arose from a forgotten bit of gossip. In the play of words the sources of the pun are lost. It is like a local jest in a narrow coterie, barren to an outsider. Sydney Smith was the most celebrated wit of his day, but he is dull reading now. Blackwood's at its first issue was a witty daring sheet, but for us the pages are stagnant. I suppose that no one now laughs at the witticisms of Thomas Hood. Where are the wits of yesteryear? Yet the humor of Falstaff and Lamb and Fielding remains and is a reminder to us that humor, to be real, must be founded on humanity and on truth.

Rachel L. Carson

The Long Snowfall

Every part of the earth or air or sea has an atmosphere peculiarly its own, a quality or characteristic that sets it apart from all others. When I think of the floor of the deep sea, the single, overwhelming fact that possesses my imagination is the accumulation of sediments. I see always the steady, unremitting, downward drift of materials from above, flake upon flake, layer upon layer — drift that has continued for hundreds of millions of years, that will go on as long as there are seas and continents.

For the sediments are the materials of the most stupendous 'snowfall' the earth has ever seen. It began when the first rains fell on the barren rocks and set in motion the forces of erosion. It was accelerated when living creatures developed in the surface waters and the discarded little shells of lime or silica that had encased them in life began to drift downward to the bottom. Silently, endlessly, with the deliberation of earth processes that can afford to be slow because they have so much time for completion, the accumulation of the sediments has proceeded. So little in a year, or in a human lifetime, but so enormous an amount in the life of earth and sea.

The rains, the eroding away of the earth, the rush of sediment-laden waters have continued, with varying pulse and tempo, throughout all of geologic time. In addition to the silt load of every river that finds its way to the sea, there are other materials that compose the sediments. Volcanic dust, blown perhaps half way around the earth in the upper atmosphere, comes eventually to rest on the ocean, drifts in the currents, becomes waterlogged, and sinks. Sands from coastal deserts are carried seaward on off-shore winds, fall to the sea, and sink. Gravel, pebbles, small boulders, and shells are carried by icebergs and drift ice to be released to the water when the ice melts. Fragments of iron, nickel, and other meteoric debris that enter the earth's atmosphere over the sea — these, too, become flakes of the great snowfall. But most widely distributed of

194

all are the billions upon billions of tiny shells and skeletons, the limy or silicious remains of all the minute creatures that once lived in the upper waters.

The sediments are a sort of epic poem of the earth. When we are wise enough, perhaps we can read in them all of past history. For all is written here. In the nature of the materials that compose them and in the arrangement of their successive layers the sediments reflect all that has happened in the waters above them and on the surrounding lands. The dramatic and the catastrophic in earth history have left their trace in the sediments — the outpourings of volcanoes, the advance and retreat of the ice, the searing aridity of desert lands, the sweeping destruction of floods.

The book of the sediments has been opened only within the lifetime of the present generation of scientists, with the most exciting progress in collecting and deciphering samples made since 1945. Early oceanographers could scrape up surface layers of sediment from the sea bottom with dredges. But what was needed was an instrument, operated on the principle of an apple corer, that could be driven vertically into the bottom to remove a long sample or 'core' in which the order of the different layers was undisturbed. Such an instrument was invented by Dr. C. S. Piggot in 1935, and with the aid of this 'gun' he obtained a series of cores across the deep Atlantic from Newfoundland to Ireland. These cores averaged about 10 feet long. A piston core sampler, developed by the Swedish oceanographer Kullenberg about 10 years later, now takes undisturbed cores 70 feet long. The rate of sedimentation in the different parts of the ocean is not definitely known, but it is very slow; certainly such a sample represents millions of years of geologic history.

Another ingenious method for studying the sediments has been used by Professor W. Maurice Ewing of Columbia University and the Woods Hole Oceanographic Institution. Professor Ewing found that he could measure the thickness of the carpeting layer of sediments that overlies the rock of the ocean floor by exploding depth charges and recording their echoes; one echo is received from the top of the sediment layer (the apparent bottom of the sea), another from the 'bottom below the bottom' or the true rock floor. The carrying and use of explosives at sea is hazardous and cannot be attempted by all vessels, but this method was used by the Swedish *Albatross* as well as by the *Atlantis* in its exploration of the Atlantic Ridge. Ewing on the *Atlantis* also used a seismic refraction technique by which sound waves are made to travel horizontally through the rock layers of the ocean floor, providing information about the nature of the rock.

Before these techniques were developed, we could only guess at the thickness of the sediment blanket over the floor of the sea. We might have expected the amount to be vast, if we thought back through the ages of gentle, unending fall — one sand grain at a time, one fragile shell after another, here a shark's tooth, there a meteorite fragment — the whole continuing persistently, relentlessly, endlessly. It is, of course, a process similar to that which has built up the layers of rock that help to make our mountains, for they too, were once soft sediments under the shallow seas that have overflowed the continents from time to time. The sediments eventually became consolidated and cemented and, as the seas retreated again, gave the continents their thick, covering layers of sedimentary rocks — layers which we can see uplifted, tilted, compressed, and broken by the vast earth movements. And we know that in places the sedimentary rocks are many thousands of feet thick. Yet most people felt a shock of surprise and wonder when Hans Pettersson, leader of the Swedish Deep Sea Expedition, announced that the *Albatross* measurements taken in the open Atlantic basin showed sediment layers as much as 12,000 feet thick.

If more than two miles of sediments have been deposited on the floor of the Atlantic, an interesting question arises: has the rocky floor sagged a corresponding distance under the terrific weight of the sediments? Geologists hold conflicting opinions. The recently discovered Pacific sea mounts may offer one piece of evidence that it has. If they are, as their discoverer called them, 'drowned ancient islands,' then they may have reached their present stand a mile or so below sea level through the sinking of the ocean floor. Hess believed the islands had been formed so long ago that coral animals had not yet evolved; otherwise the corals would presumably have settled on the flat, planed surfaces of the sea mounts and built them up as fast as their bases sank. In any event, it is hard to see how they could have been worn down so far below 'wave base' unless the crust of the earth sagged under its load.

One thing seems probable — the sediments have been unevenly distributed both in place and time. In contrast to the 12,000-foot thickness found in parts of the Atlantic, the Swedish oceanographers never found sediments thicker than 1,000 feet in the Pacific or in the Indian Ocean. Perhaps a deep layer of lava, from ancient submarine eruptions on a stupendous scale, underlies the upper layers of the sediments in these places and intercepts the sound waves.

Interesting variations in the thickness of the sediment layer on the Atlantic Ridge and the approaches to the Ridge from the American side were reported by Ewing. As the bottom contours became less even and began to slope up into the foothills of the Ridge, the sediments thickened, as though piling up into mammoth drifts 1,000 to 2,000 feet deep against the slopes of the hills. Farther up in the mountains of the Ridge, where there are many level terraces from a few to a score of miles wide, the sediments were even deeper, measuring up to 3,000 feet. But along the backbone of the Ridge, on the steep slopes and peaks and pinnacles, the bare rock emerged, swept clean of sediments.

Reflecting on these differences in thickness and distribution, our minds return inevitably to the simile of the long snowfall. We may think of the abyssal snowstorm in terms of a bleak and blizzard-ridden arctic tundra. Long days of storm visit this place, when driving snow fills the air; then a lull comes in the blizzard, and the snowfall is light. In the snowfall of the sediments, also, there is an alternation of light and heavy falls. The heavy falls correspond to the period of mountain building on the continents, when the lands are lifted high and the rain rushes down their slopes, carrying mud and rock fragments to the sea; the light falls mark the lulls between the mountain-building periods, when the continents are flat and erosion is slowed. And again, on our imaginary tundra, the winds blow the snow into deep drifts, filling in all the valleys between the ridges, piling the snow up and up until the contours of the land are obliterated, but scouring the ridges clear. In the drifting sediments on the floor of the ocean we see the work of the 'winds,' which may be the deep ocean currents, distributing the sediments according to laws of their own, not as yet grasped by human minds.

We have known the general pattern of the sediment carpet, however, for a good many years. Around the foundations of the continents, in the deep waters off the borders of the continental slopes, are the muds of terrestrial origin. There are muds of many colors — blue, green, red, black, and white — apparently varying with climatic changes as well as with the dominant soils and rocks of the lands of their origin. Farther at sea are the oozes of predominantly marine origin — the remains of the trillions of tiny sea creatures. Over great areas of the temperate oceans the sea floor is largely covered with the remains of unicellular creatures known as foraminifera, of which the most abundant genus is Globigerina. The shells of Globigerina may be recognized in very ancient sediments as well as in modern ones, but over the ages the species have varied. Knowing this, we can date approximately the deposits in which they occur. But always they have been simple animals, living in an intricately sculptured shell of carbonate of lime, the whole so small you would need a microscope to see its details. After the fashion of unicellular beings, the individual Globigerina normally did not die, but by the division of its substance became two. At each division, the old shell was abandoned, and two new ones were formed. In warm, lime-rich seas these tiny creatures have always multiplied prodigiously, and so, although each is so minute, their innumerable shells blanket millions of square miles of ocean bottom, and to a depth of thousands of feet.

In the great depths of the ocean, however, the immense pressures and the high carbon-dioxide content of deep water dissolve much of the lime long before it reaches the bottom and return it to the great chemical reservoir of the sea. Silica is more resistant to solution. It is one of the curious paradoxes of the ocean that the bulk of the organic remains that reach the great depths intact belong to unicellular creatures seemingly of the most delicate construction. The radiolarians remind us irresistibly of snow flakes, as infinitely varied in pattern, as lacy, and as intricately made. Yet because their shells are fashioned of silica instead of carbonate of lime, they can descend unchanged into the abyssal depths. So there are broad bands of radiolarian ooze in the deep tropical waters of the North Pacific, underlying the surface zones where the living radiolarians occur most numerously.

Tow other kinds of organic sediments are named for the creatures whose remains compose them. Diatoms, the microscopic plant life of the sea, flourish most abundantly in cold waters. There is a broad belt of diatom ooze on the floor of the Antarctic Ocean, outside the zone of glacial debris dropped by the ice pack. There is another across the North Pacific, along the chain of great deeps that run from Alaska to Japan. Both are zones where nutrient-laden water wells up from the depths, sustaining a rich growth of plants. The diatoms, like the radiolaria, are encased in silicious coverings — small, boxlike cases of varied shape and meticulously etched design.

Then, in relatively shallow parts of the open Atlantic, there are patches of ooze composed of the remains of delicate swimming snails, called pteropods. These winged mollusks, possessing transparent shells of great beauty, are here and there incredibly abundant. Pteropod ooze is the characteristic bottom deposit in the vicinity of Bermuda, and a large patch occurs in the South Atlantic.

Mysterious and eerie are the immense areas, especially in the North Pacific, carpeted with a soft, red sediment in which there are no organic remains except sharks' teeth and the ear bones of whales. This red clay occurs at great depths. Perhaps all the materials of the other sediments are dissolved before they can reach this zone of immense pressures and glacial cold.

The reading of the story contained in the sediments has only begun. When more cores are collected and examined we shall certainly decipher many exciting chapters. Geologists have pointed out that a series of cores from the Mediterranean might settle several controversial problems concerning the history of the ocean and of the lands around the Mediterranean basin. For example, somewhere in the layers of sediment under this sea there must be evidence, in a sharply defined layer of sand, of the time when the deserts of the Sahara were formed and the hot, dry winds began to skim off the shifting surface layers and carry them seaward. Long cores recently obtained in the western Mediterranean off Algeria have given a record of volcanic activity extending back through thousands of years, and including great prehistoric eruptions of which we know nothing.

The Atlantic cores taken more than a decade ago by Piggot from the cable ship *Lord Kevin* have been thoroughly studied by geologists. From their analysis it is possible to look back into the past 10,000 years or so and to sense the pulse of the earth's climatic rhythms; for the cores were composed of layers of cold-water globigerina faunas (and hence glacial stage sediments), alternating with globigerina ooze characteristic of warmer waters. From the clues furnished by these cores we can visualize inter-glacial stages when there were periods of mild climates, with warm water overlying the sea bottom and warmth-loving creatures living in the ocean. Between these periods the sea grew chill. Clouds gathered, the snows fell, and on the North American continent the great ice sheets grew and the ice mountains moved out to the coast. The glaciers reached the sea along a wide front; there they produced icebergs by the thousand. The slow-moving, majestic processions of the bergs passed out to sea, and because of the coldness of much of the earth they penetrated farther south than any but stray bergs do today. When finally they melted, they relinquished their loads of silt and sand and gravel and rock fragments that had become frozen into their under surfaces as they made their grinding way over the land. And so a layer of glacial sediment came to overlie the normal globigerina ooze, and the record of an Ice Age was inscribed.

Then the sea grew warmer again, the glaciers melted and retreated, and once more the warmer-water species of Globigerina lived in the sea — lived and died and drifted down to build another layer of globigerina ooze, this time over the clays and gravels from the glaciers. And the record of warmth and mildness was again written in the sediments. From the Piggot cores it has been possible to reconstruct four different periods of the advance of the ice, separated by periods of warm climate.

It is interesting to think that even now, in our own lifetime, the flakes of a new snow storm are falling, falling, one by one, out there on the ocean floor. The billions of Globigerina are drifting down, writing their unequivocal record that this, our present world, is on the whole a world of mild and temperate climate. Who will read their record, ten thousand years from now?

G. K. Chesterton

A Piece of Chalk

I remember one splendid morning, all blue and silver, in the summer holidays, when I reluctantly tore myself away from the task of doing nothing in particular, and put on a hat of some sort and picked up a walking-stick, and put six very bright-coloured chalks in my pocket. I then went into the kitchen (which, along with the rest of the house, belonged to a very square and sensible old woman in a Sussex village), and asked the owner and occupant of the kitchen if she had any brown paper. She had a great deal; in fact, she had too much; and she mistook the purpose and the rationale of the existence of brown paper. She seemed to have an idea that if a person wanted brown paper he must be wanting to tie up parcels; which was the last thing I wanted to do; indeed, it is a thing which I have found to be beyond my mental capacity. Hence she dwelt very much on the varying qualities of toughness and endurance in the material. I explained to her that I only wanted to draw pictures on it, and that I did not want them to endure in the least; and that from my point of view, therefore, it was a question not of tough consistency, but of responsive surface, a thing comparatively irrelevant in a parcel. When she understood that I wanted to draw she offered to overwhelm me with note-paper, apparently supposing that I did my notes and correspondence on old brown paper wrappers from motives of economy.

I then tried to explain the rather delicate logical shade, that I not only like brown paper, but liked the quality of brownness in paper, just as I liked the quality of brownness in October woods, or in beer, or in the peat-streams of the North. Brown paper represents the primal twilight of the first toil of creation, and with a bright-coloured chalk or two you can pick out points of fire in it, sparks of gold, and blood red, and sea-green, like the first fierce stars that sprang out of divine darkness. All this I said (in an off-hand way) to the old woman; and I put the brown paper in my pocket along with the chalks, and possibly other things. I suppose every one must have reflected how primeval and how poetical are the things that one carries in one's pocket; the pocket-knife, for instance, the type of all human tools, the infant of the sword. Once I planned to write a book of poems entirely about the things in my pocket. But I found it would be too long; and the age of the great epics is past.

With my stick and my knife, my chalks and my brown paper, I went out on to the great downs. I crawled across those colossal contours that express the best quality of England, because they are at the same time soft and strong. The smoothness of them has the same meaning as the smoothness of great cart-horses, or the smoothness of the beech-tree; it declares in the teeth of our timid and cruel theories that the mighty are merciful. As my eye swept the landscape, the landscape was as kindly as any of its cottages, but for power it was like an earthquake. The villages in the immense valley were safe, one could see, for centuries; yet the lifting of the whole land was like the lifting of one enormous wave to wash them all away.

I crossed one swell of living turf after another, looking for a place to sit down and draw. Do not, for heaven's sake, imagine I was going to sketch from Nature. I was going to draw devils and seraphim, and blind old gods that men worshipped before the dawn of right, and saints in robes of angry crimson, and seas of strange green, and all the sacred or monstrous symbols that look so well in bright colours on brown paper. They are much better worth drawing than Nature; also they are much easier to draw. When a cow came slouching by in the field next to me, a mere artist might have drawn it; but I always get wrong in the hind legs of quadrupeds. So I drew the soul of a cow; which I saw there plainly walking before me in the sunlight; and the soul was all purple and silver, and had seven horns and the mystery that belongs to all the beasts. But though I could not with a crayon get the best out of the landscape, it does not follow that the landscape was not getting the best out of me. And this, I think, is the mistake that people make about the old poets who lived before Wordsworth, and were supposed not to care very much about Nature because they did not describe it much.

They preferred writing about great men to writing about great hills; but they sat on the great hills to write it. They gave out much less about Nature, but they drank in, perhaps, much more. They painted the white robes of their holy virgins with the blinding snow, at which they had stared all day. They blazoned the shields of their paladins with the purple and gold of many heraldic sunsets. The greenness of a thousand green leaves clustered into the live green figure of Robin Hood. The blueness of a score of forgotten skies became the blue robes of the Virgin. The inspiration went in like sunbeams and came out like Apollo.

But as I sat scrawling these silly figures on the brown paper, it began to dawn on me, to my great disgust, that I had left one chalk, and that a most exquisite and essential chalk, behind. I searched all my pockets, but I could not find any white chalk. Now, those who are acquainted with all the philosophy (nay, religion) which is typified in the art of drawing on brown paper, know that white is positive and essential. I cannot avoid remarking here upon a moral significance. One of the wise and awful truths which this brown-paper art reveals, is that, that white is a colour. It is not a mere absence of colour; it is a shining and affirmative thing, as fierce as red, as definite as black. When (so to speak) your pencil grows red-hot, it draws roses; when it grows white-hot, it draws stars. And one of the two or three defiant verities of the best religious morality, of real Christianity for example, is exactly the same thing; the chief assertion of religious morality is that white is a colour. Virtue is not the absence of vices or the avoidance of moral dangers; virtue is a vivid and separate thing, like pain or a particular smell. Mercy does not mean not being cruel or sparing people revenge or punishment; it means a plain and positive thing like the sun, which one has either seen or not seen. Chastity does not mean abstention from sexual wrong; it means something flaming, like Joan of Arc. In a word, God paints in many colours; but He never paints so gorgeously, I had almost said so gaudily, as when He paints in white. In a sense our age has realized this fact, and expressed it in our sullen costume. For if it were really true that white was a blank and colourless thing, negative and non-committal, then white would be used instead of black and grey for the funeral dress of this pessimistic period. We should see city gentlemen in frock coats of spotless silver satin, with top hats as white as wonderful arum lilies. Which is not the case.

Meanwhile I could not find my chalk.

I sat on the hill in a sort of despair. There was no town nearer than Chichester at which it was even remotely probable that there would be such a thing as an artist's colourman. And yet, without white, my absurd little pictures would be as pointless as the world would be if there were no good people in it. I stared stupidly round, racking my brain for expedients. Then I suddenly stood up and roared with laughter, again and again, so that the cows stared at me and called a committee. Imagine a man in the Sahara regretting that he had no sand for his hourglass. Imagine a gentleman in mid-ocean wishing that he had brought some salt water with him for his chemical experiments. I was sitting on an immense warehouse of white chalk. The landscape was made entirely out of white chalk. White chalk was piled mere miles until it met the sky. I stooped and broke a piece off the rock I sat on: it did not mark so well as the shop chalks do; but it gave the effect. And I stood there in a trance of pleasure, realizing that this Southern England is not only a grand peninsula, and a tradition and a civilization; it is something even more admirable. It is a piece of chalk.

John Ciardi

The Unfading Beauty: A Well-filled Mind

Anatole France once observed of his countrymen that they raised their daughters in convents and then married them to pirates. Most of today's college girls will find themselves married not long after graduation, and whether or not they later think of their college days as having been passed in a convent, few of them will find themselves married to anything quite as dramatic as a real pirate, or quite as revolting as a late-nineteenth-century French pirate of finance. The present-day standard model husband is more likely to come out as a serious suburban gardener who flies his week-end flag from the patio of a split-level, and who does his daily cruising in a car pool or on the 7:45 local in the morning and on the 4:40 in the afternoon. The girls are headed for a well-advertised and basically well-padded way of life, but the gist of Anatole France's observation may still apply: it may still be that what the girls do in school is no real preparation for what they will be doing after graduation.

What a liberal arts college is supposed to do in theory is certainly clear enough and can be summarized in the single phrase: "To see life steadily and see it whole." The college exists to teach some sense of the dimensions of a meaningful life. Were our college infallibly fulfilling that purpose, there would be nothing to say to college girls, today's or yesterday's, except to congratulate, to admire them, and to envy them happily.

World as it is, however, being in college is no occasion for unreserved congratulation. Hundreds of bachelor's degrees are being conferred annually by American colleges, and not one of them serves as any real evidence in itself that a reasonably adequate education has taken place, or that the holder of the degree has some viable sense of the whole dimension of the life that starts next.

True, it is still possible for an able and willing student to get something like an education in almost any college in the land, but the fact seems to be that no college any longer insists upon it. The educational insistence of a college is defined by its minimum standards, and the minimum standards of American colleges are everywhere too low. Even Harvard, proud as it is of its scholarly tradition, will grant a Bachelor's degree on a four-year scholastic average of three C's and a D. "Three C's and a D and keep your name out of the papers," the rule runs: practical sounding, certainly, but a bit smaller in scale than "To see life steadily and see it whole."

The colleges, for their part, can educate only up to the level permitted by society, and our society has been reluctant as a general thing to support "egghead institutions" that think Aristotle is more important than a well-rounded social life that somehow develops a quality called "leadership," a quality that seems to be best developed by doing exactly the same thing everyone else does.

I do not know by what confusion of the national mores we are so insistent on this idea of leadership, but I have received hundreds of application forms in the last year or two, and there is hardly a one that does not contain a dotted line labeled "Leadership?" Certainly as things are, no man need be an intellectual explorer to do well in American business. The chances are, in fact, that he will go further on a little common sense and a lot of social manner than he will on enthusiasm for Chaucer. No salesman who has made the mistake of acquiring a Phi Beta Kappa key can afford to make the mistake of wearing it when he goes to call on a customer.

Nor is it likely that the affable young man with his destiny in an attaché-case is going to scour the *summa cum laude* list when he starts looking for a wife. He wants her pretty, easy to get along with, a good mixer, a good dancer, and without any freakishly high-brow ideas. Besides, there really isn't room for more than a small decorative bookcase in the rumpus-room of a split-level — not once you have put in the bar, the TV set, the TV chairs, and the card table.

The girls know all this very well, and to the extent that they know it, they have before them no such transition as Anatole France saw from the convent to the pirate's bed. They know the advertised standard and most of them will slip into it eagerly and without a hitch. The chance they must take, however, is that the dreary gist of that advertised standard will eventually trap them into dullness. A few years ago one of our largest corporations prepared for distribution in the Ivy League colleges a pamphlet advising the boys how to behave as undergraduates if they wanted a corporation career after graduation. One sentence from that pamphlet could not be improved as a summary of the necessary intellectual tone. "Personal opinions," it read, "can cause a lot of trouble." The student editor of the Princeton newspaper assaulted the pamphlet and especially that sentence as a desecration of the free mind, and the corporation sent down as trouble-shooters the man who had written the pamphlet and a vice-president in charge of public relations. As I have the story, the pamphlet writer could not see what there was to argue. Personal opinions *can* cause a lot of trouble; everyone knows that. The vice-president, on the other hand, granted the student's point and the pamphlet was withdrawn and later rewritten. Victory for the free mind, perhaps, but there still remains one speculation: did the vice-president really see that a great principle was involved, or was he simply acting as a good public relations man soothing a possibly troublesome crackpot?

Wherever the speculation comes out, the girls are reasonably well aware of what is required of a successful corporate wife, and while they have enough public-relations sense on their own to get along with the fuddy-duddy faculty they are certainly not going to ruin their chances by getting themselves reputations as bookworm intellectuals.

So it happens that our colleges are divided into two cultural groups whose values tend to meet only in the most tangential ways. The faculty group is made up of men and women not particularly distinguished as smooth dancers but, rather, dedicated to books; so dedicated, in fact, that they are willing to live on academic salaries in return for the freedom of having their reading interfered with by students, most of whom are only taking the course because they have to. The student group does share the same campus with the faculty group, but tends to center around the jukebox in the snack bar rather than around the library. Professor Jones is eager to explain the Greek aorist and to show its connection with the Latin ablative absolute, but what the girls really want out of Greek Week is a good date for the dance. Let the faculty praise great minds; the girls are there to get married, most of them as per the advertised standard.

And were that advertised standard a sufficient and a lasting truth, the colleges would be more than justified in becoming finishing schools of the minor social graces. And may the graces flourish: the least thing the world needs is ungainly and ungracious women. The trouble with the advertised standard is that it simply is not true enough. It does to lounge in; it cannot do to live by. Its plot starts well, but the later chapters have an alarming tendency to fall to pieces.

It is those later chapters the girls generally fail to foresee, and it is that failure that still gives point to Anatole France's observation. For it may well be argued that we are raising our daughters in some sort of illusory heaven and then turning them loose to be mortal. Americans have always tended to be a bit surprised at their own deaths; it all seems so unprogressive. It almost seems that the Constitution, or at least General Motors, should have taken care of that.

But why should the girls be thinking of mortality? They have better things to foresee, glorious things. They see the excitement of the wedding, of the honeymoon, of setting up housekeeping, of the children arriving, and of the busy happy years of raising a family. It seems a paradise, and it is. It seems an eternity, and it is not. But who needs Plato among the nursery babble? As Yeats put it, beginning with what might very reasonably be taken as a reference to the faculty:

> *That is no country for old men. The young*
> *In one another's arms, birds in the trees*
> *— Those dying generations — at their song,*
> *The salmon-falls, the mackerel crowded seas,*
> *Fish, flesh, or fowl, command all summer long*
> *Whatever is begotten, born, or dies.*
> *Caught in that sensual music, all neglect*
> *Monuments of unageing intellect.*

The faculty has no place in paradise. Their monuments of unaging intellect are meaningless to those caught up in that sensual music. The monuments have point only in the silence that follows the music.

And that silence comes. By the time today's college girl has reached thirty-five and forty, having spent fifteen or twenty years busily and happily rearing a family that has needed her, she will find that the children have grown free. There will come a morning after the last of them has moved out to his own life. She will get up at 7:30 for a strangely silent breakfast with her husband who eight years ago was promoted from the 7:45 local to the 8:50. She would like to talk to him, but through her busy years she will have lost touch with his business affairs. And he, doggedly working away at his thrombosis, has his own thoughts to think.

By 8:30 he will have left, and there is the day stretching ahead. Dawdle as she will, the breakfast dishes are in the dishwasher by 9:00. The cleaning woman will be in tomorrow to do the house, which is immaculate anyhow. And the ironing woman will be in the day after to do the clothes. She could write that letter to Mary, but 10:00 o'clock is still a long way off. And 11:00. And is lunch worth bothering with just for yourself? Well, maybe a really fancy dinner. But that is hours ahead and the push-button oven will do most of that anyhow. And what is there to do? Today, tomorrow, and the next day? What will there ever be to do?

She will have entered the First Loneliness. Statistically, too, she will have entered the circle of possible widowhood. The years that follow are those in which her husband is more and more likely to achieve the final thrombosis of his success. American women outlive their husbands by an average of six years. Six years is perhaps not an alarming figure, but to begin with it is a bit higher among the wives of professional men And if the average for all is six years, it must follow that the average for half will be more nearly twelve, and that for a quarter of them it will be more nearly twenty-four. May it be later rather than sooner, but there can be no doubt that the unadvertised years also lie ahead.

And what will today's college girls take into those long, well-padded and lonely years? There is touring, of course. And there is bridge. And there is TV. And there are community projects, and gardening, and gay little shopping trips with the other girls. But is it enough? Ernest Hemingway once said to Marlene Dietrich, "Daughter, never confuse motion with action." Our better suburbs — and by this time most of the girls will have graduated from the split-level to the custom-built house — are full of little organizations devoted to making motions for the girls to go through. But there still remains that force at the core of the unstultified psyche that cries for a more meaningful and more human thing to do, that cries for action rather than motion.

Many such women make sudden awkward gestures of turning to the arts again. They used to play the piano rather well. Or they used to write for the college magazine. Now that they no longer have the P.T.A. on their hands, why not start again?

Many of them turn to poetry; and because a poet is easily taken as some sort of summonable clergyman, many have sent their poems to me, as if I had no more to do than to spend a day reading and criticizing them. At that, one would somehow make the time if the poems were not so hopeless. For invariably it is too late. There is that about an art form that will not survive being held in abeyance for a decade or two. They should have had enough devotion to have kept it alive. If only in a stolen hour of the day. If only at the expense of sleep. It can be done. As Salvador Dali once declared: "One always has time to do what he really wants to do." One may have to pay a price for it, but one does pay the price for his true hungers. It is not easy, but to quote Yeats once again:

> To be born woman is to know,
> Though it's not taught to us at school,
> That we must labor to be beautiful.

No, it is not easy. It is something better than easy: it is joyous. It is as Frost put it, "The pleasure of taking pains." That gracious lady, distinguished biographer, and my good friend, Catherine Drinker Bowen, raised her family and managed her household for years while turning out a series of meticulously researched biographies, stealing one piece of every day at whatever cost, putting herself through the routine busyness of her day on the excitement of anticipating that hour at her own particular work. She had, in fact, had two books selected by the Book of the Month Club before she dared label her income-tax form "author" rather than "housewife."

A human being is finally defined by what he does with his attention.

It is difficult to keep one's attention in order; difficult and demanding. How much easier it is to let one's mind into a lawn chair of the advertised life and to tune it there to Hollywood scenarios, or to let it drift into what Aldous Huxley called "the endless idiot gibberish of the reverie." It is easier to be inane; but the price is boredom, emptiness, and finally the inability to communicate meaningfully with any human being. How many mothers are there in America today who have begotten sons of their own body and pain and are now unable to speak to them except in the stereotype of "Mom" and "Dicky-boy," rather than as human being to human being, open to both joys and distresses but bound together by a love that includes understanding. It was a better thing than stereotypes that Adam and Eve began, and whoever allows that better thing to be lessened in himself lessens the possibility of the race.

It is what one does with his attention that defines him, and because art is the best ordering we have of human attention, there can be no truly meaningful life without the dimension of art. The arts — and I take them to include religion, philsosphy, and history at those points where they are least dogmatic and most speculative — teach us not only ideas but the very dimension of possibility in idea. There is a resonance in a great line of poetry without which the mind cannot truly tune itself. Listen to your own mind. Think the best thing you know. Then measure it against such a line as Wallace Stevens' "The major abstraction is the idea of man." Who can permit himself to think that what was in his mind before he read that line was as good as what was in his mind as he read it? Or listen to John Donne: "And now goodmorrow to our waking souls/Which watch not one another out of fear." Those lines may take a bit of mental focusing, but what a concept of love they speak? Whatever mental effort they require is indistinguishable from joy, and what the effort leaves behind it is a better human being.

Art is the resonance of inseeing joy, but that resonance is only the beginning. Every work of art is a piece of life one may have for the taking. It is not a thing said about an experience, it is the experience itself, not only re-enacted but given form, and therefore, value. Art is the best memory of the race. Art stores up in everlasting form the most meaningful experiences of the most perceptive minds of the past, and because there is such a thing as vicarious experience any man is free to relive those experiences, which is to say, he is free to take those lives into his life. May heaven defend those people who live no lives but their own. Imagine being only Susie Jones when one could also be Penelope, and Cleopatra, and Ophelia, and Madame DuBarry, and Emma Bovary, and Anna Karenina. And may heaven defend the man married to the woman who has not tried all those other necessary lives into herself. Nothing will defend monogamy sooner than a wife who — this side of schizophrenia, to be sure — contains her pluralities. "Age cannot wither her, nor custom stale/Her infinite variety."

And that finally is what any good book is about. A good book offers the reader a life he has not time for on the clock-as-it-ticks, and a world he may enter *as if* in actual fact. A great book is distinguished from a good book only by the size of the life and the world it offers, but no novel or book of poems is worth the reading unless it has that basic fact of experience to offer.

Art cannot fend loss and loneliness from any life. Loss and loneliness will fall as they must, and for many people they will fall inevitably. But let the meaningful woman look at the statistical probability of that loss and loneliness that lies before her, and let her ask what she will take into those years. Can a mind with Mozart in it ever be as lost as a mind with nothing in it? If girls now in college, just out of college, or even several years away from it do no more than set themselves a twenty-year program of reading meaningfully and carrying alive in their minds one passage a day from the English poets, can they fail to see that they will be more valuable to their families as mothers, and more valuable to themselves as widows?

One of Hemingway's characters in *Winner Take Nothing* is told that so-and-so is a coward and he answers, "He didn't invent it." The line is underplayed but a great understanding and a great mercy shine through it. One could do worse than to store a bit of that understanding and mercy for himself. So stored, one may learn in time that whatever happens to him is not his own invention. He may learn to see then that there is such a thing as the experience of the race on this planet, and learning that he will learn that one who takes that experience into himself has joined himself to the ever-uncertain but ever-hopeful and sometimes glorious continuum of man-and-woman born of man-and-woman.

It is that one must say to today's college girls. That they are beautiful, and ignorant, and illusory. And that only as they learn to shape their attention to the long memory we call the humanities, can they be beautiful after the bloom is off, and understandingly compassionate as time furrows them, and real to the lives they labor to make shapely.

Eldridge Cleaver

Soul on Ice

Folsom Prison
October 9, 1965

I'm perfectly aware that I'm in prison, that I'm a Negro, that I've been a rapist, and that I have a Higher Uneducation. I never know what significance I'm supposed to attach to these factors. But I have a suspicion that, because of these aspects of my character, "free-normal-educated" people rather expect me to be more reserved, penitent, remorseful, and not to quick to shoot off my mouth on certain subjects. But I let them down, disappoint them, make them gape at me in a sort of stupor, as if they're thinking: "You've got your nerve! Don't you realize that you owe a debt to society?" My answer to all such thoughts lurking in their split-level heads, crouching behind their squinting bombardier eyes, is that the blood of Vietnamese peasants has paid off all my debts; that the Vietnamese people, afflicted with a rampant disease called Yankees, through their sufferings — as opposed to the "frustration" of fat-assed American geeks safe at home worrying over whether to have bacon, ham, or sausage with their grade-A eggs in the morning, while Vietnamese worry each morning whether the Yankees will gas them, burn them up, or blow away their humble pads in a hail of bombs — have cancelled all my IOUs.

In beginning this letter I could just as easily have mentioned other aspects of my situation; I could have said: "I'm perfectly aware that I'm tall, that I'm skinny, that I need a shave, that I'm hard-up enough to suck my grandmother's old withered tits, and that I would dig (deeper than deeply) getting *clean* once more — not only in the steam-bath sense, but in getting sharp as an *Esquire* square with a Harlem touch — or that I would like to put on a pair of bib overalls and become a Snicker, or that I'd like to leap the whole last mile and grow a beard and don whatever threads the local nationalism might require and comrade with Che Guevara, and share his fate, blazing a new pathfinder's trail through the stymied upbeat brain of the New Left, or how I'd just love to be in Berkeley right now, to roll in that mud, frolic in that sty of funky revolution, to breathe in its heady fumes, and look with roving eyes for a new John Brown, Eugene Debs, a blacker-meaner-keener Malcolm X, a Robert Franklin Williams with less rabbit in his hot blood, an American Lenin, Fidel, a Mao-Mao, A MAO MAO, A MAO MAO, A MAO MAO, A MAO MAO, A MAO MAO, A MAO MAO . . . All of which is true.

But what matters is that I have fallen in love with my lawyer! Is that surprising? A convict is expected to have a high regard for *anyone* who comes to his aid, who tries to help him and who expends time, energy, and money in an effort to set him free. But can a convict really love a lawyer? It goes against the grain. Convicts hate lawyers. To walk around a prison yard and speak well of a lawyer is to raise the downcast eyebrows of felons who've been bitten by members of the Bar and Grill. Convicts are convinced that lawyers must have a secret little black book which no one else is ever allowed to see, a book that schools lawyers in an esoteric morality in which the Highest Good is treachery and crossing one's dumb and trusting client the noblest of deeds. It was learned by the convicts that I'd gotten busted with some magazines given to me by my lawyer and that I was thrown in the Hole for it. Convicts smiled knowingly and told me that I had gone for the greasy pig, that my lawyer had set me up, and that if I couldn't see through the plot I was so stupid that I would buy not only the Golden Gate Bridge but some fried ice cream.

It was my turn to smile knowingly. A convict's paranoia is as thick as the prison wall — and just as necessary. Why should we have faith in anyone? Even our wives and lovers whose beds we have shared, with whom we have shared the tenderest moments and most delicate relations, leave us after a while, put us down, cut us clean aloose and treat us like they hate us, won't even write us a letter, send us a Christmas card every other year or a quarter for a pack of cigarettes or a tube of toothpaste now and then. All society shows the convict its ass and expects him to kiss it: the convict feels like kicking it or putting a bullet in it. A convict sees man's fangs and claws and learns quickly to bare and unsheath his own, for real and final. To maintain a hold on the ideals and sentiments of civilization in such circumstances is probably impossible. How much more incredible is it, then, while rooted in this pit, to fall in love, and with a lawyer! Use a lawyer, yes: use anybody. Even tell the lawyer that you're in love. But you will always know when you are lying and even if you could manage to fool the lawyer you could never manage to fool yourself.

And why does it make you sad to see how everything hangs by such thin and whimsical threads? Because you're a dreamer, an incredible dreamer, with a tiny spark hidden somewhere inside you which cannot die, which even you cannot kill or quench and which tortures you horribly because all the odds are against its continual burning. In the midst of the foulest decay and putrid savagery, this spark speaks to you of beauty, of human warmth and kindness, of goodness, of greatness, of heroism, of martyrdom, and it speaks to you of love.

So I love my lawyer. My lawyer is not an ordinary person. My lawyer is a rebel, a revolutionary who is alienated fundamentally from the *status quo*, probably with as great an intensity, conviction, and irretrievability as I am alienated from it — and probably with more intelligence, compassion, and humanity. If you read the papers, you are no doubt aware of my lawyer's incessant involvement in agitation against all manifestations of the monstrous evil of our system, such as our intervention in the internal affairs of the Vietnamese people or the invasion of the Dominican Republic by U.S. Marines. And my lawyer defends civil rights demonstrators, sit-iners, and the Free Speech students who rebelled against the Kerr–Strong machine at the University of California. My love for my lawyer is due, in part, to these activities and involvements, because we are always on the same side of the issues. And I love all my allies. But this, which may be the beginning of an explanation, does not nearly explain what goes on between my lawyer and me.

I suppose that I should be honest and, before going any further, admit that my lawyer is a woman — or maybe I should have held back with that piece of the puzzle — a very excellent, unusual and beautiful woman. I know that *she* believes that I do not really love her and that I am confusing a combination of lust and gratitude for love. Lust and gratitude I feel abundantly, but I also love this woman. And I fear that, believing that I do not love her, she will act according to that belief.

At night, I talk with her in my sleep, long dialogues in which she answers back. We alternate in speaking, like in the script of a play. And let me say that I don't believe a word she says. While we are talking, I participate and believe everything, taking her word as her bond. But when I awake, I repudiate the conversation and disbelieve her. I awake refreshed, and though my sleep has been restless, I am not tired. Except for a few lost hours in which she slips away and I fall into a deep sleep, I hover on a level between consciousness and peace, and the dialogue ensues. It does not bother me now. I have often gone through this when something seizes my mind.

I place a great deal of emphasis on people really listening to each other, to what the other person has to say, because you very seldom encounter a person who is capable of taking either you or himself seriously. Of course, when I was out of prison I was not really like this; the seeds were there, but there was too much confusion and madness mixed in. I had a profound desire for communicating with and getting to know other people, but I was incapable of doing so. I didn't know how.

Getting to know someone, entering that new world, is an ultimate, irretrievable leap into the unknown. The prospect is terrifying. The stakes are high. The emotions are overwhelming. The two people are reluctant really to strip themselves naked in front of each other, because in doing so they make themselves vulnerable and give enormous power over themselves one to the other. How often they inflict pain and torment upon each other! Better to maintain shallow, superficial affairs; that way the scars are not too deep. No blood is hacked from the soul.

But I do not believe a beautiful relationship has to end always in carnage, or that we have to be fraudulent and pretentious with one another. If we project fraudulent, pretentious images, or if we fantasize each other into distorted caricatures of what we really are, then, when we awake from the trance and see beyond the sham and front, all will dissolve, all will die or be transformed into bitterness and hate. I know that sometimes people fake on each other out of genuine motives to hold onto the object of their tenderest feelings. They see themselves as so inadequate that they feel forced to wear a mask in order continuously to impress the second party.

If a man is free — not in prison, the Army, a monastery, hospital, spaceship, submarine — and living a normal life with the usual multiplicity of social relations with individuals of both sexes, it may be that he is incapable of experiencing the total impact of another individual upon himself. The competing influences and conflicting forces of other personalities may dilute one's psychic and emotional perception to the extent that one does not and cannot receive all that the other person is capable of sending.

Yet I may believe that a man whose soul or emotional apparatus had lain dormant in a deadening limbo of desuetude is capable of responding from some great sunken well of his being, as though a potent catalyst had been tossed into a critical mass, when an exciting, lovely, and lovable woman enters the range of his feelings. What a deep, slow, tortuous, reluctant, frightened stirring! He feels a certain part of himself in a state of flux, as if a bodiless stranger had stolen inside his body, startling him by doing calisthenics, and he feels himself coming slowly back to life. His body chemistry changes and he is flushed with new strength.

When she first comes to him his heart is empty, a desolate place, a dehydrated oasis, unsolaced, and he's craving womanfood, without which sustenance the tension of his manhood has unwound and relaxed. He has imepartive need of the kindness, sympathy, understanding, and conversation of a woman, to hear a woman's laughter at his words, to answer her questions and be answered by her, to look into her eyes, to sniff her primeval fragrance, to hear — with slaughtered ears — the sensuous rustling of frivolous garments as legs are crossed and uncrossed beneath a table, to feel the delicate, shy weight of her hand in his — how painfully and totally aware is he of her presence, her every movement! It is as if one had been left to die beneath a bush on a lonely trail. The sun is hot and the shade of the bush, if not offering an extension of life, offers at least a slowing-down of death. And just when one feels the next breath will surely be the last, a rare and rainbow-colored bird settles on a delicate twig of the bush and, with the magic of melodious trillings and beauty of plumage, charms the dying one back to life. The dying man feels the strength flowing into and through the conduits of his body from the charged atmosphere created by the presence of the bird, and he knows intuitively in his clinging to life that if the bird remains he will regain his strength and health — and live.

Seeing her image slipping away from the weak fingers of his mind as soon as she has gone, his mind fights for a token of her on which to peg memory. Jealously, he hoards the fading memory of their encounter, like a miser gloating over a folio of blue-chip stock. The unfathomable machinery of the subconscious projects an image onto the conscious mind: her bare right arm, from curve of shoulder to fingertip. (Had his lips quivered with desire to brand that soft, cool-looking flesh with a kiss of fire, had his fingers itched to caress?) Such is the magic of a woman, the female principle of nature which she embodies, and her power to resurrect and revitalize a long-isolated and lonely man.

I was twenty-two when I came to prison and of course I have changed tremendously over the years. But I had always had a strong sense of myself and in the last few years I felt I was losing my identity. There was a deadness in my body that eluded me, as though I could not exactly locate its site. I would be aware of this numbness, this feeling of atrophy, and it haunted the back of my mind. Because of this numb spot, I felt peculiarly off balance, the awareness of something missing, of a blank spot, a certain intimation of emptiness. Now I know what it was. After eight years in prison I was visited by a woman, a woman who was interested in my work and cared about what happened to me. And since encountering her, I feel life, strength flowing back into that spot. My step, the tread of my stride, which was becoming tentative and uncertain, has begun to recover a definiteness, a confidence, a boldness which makes me want to kick over a few tables. I may even swagger a little, and, as I read in a book somewhere, "push myself forward like a train."

Bernard Cohan

Mister Marvel and the Little People

We called him Mister Marvel, and he was indeed marvelous. We little people looked up at his broad frame and wide grin, and could only see the trees beyond him as being taller or stronger. But they didn't count, for they could hardly perform the many tricks of Mister Marvel, and weren't half as nice to be with.

I can't really remember the first time I saw Mister Marvel. I thought about it at the time, and decided that he was just *always* there, pushing his cart through the streets, always followed by dozens of little people. My friends would crowd around him as he walked, making him look as if he were waist-deep in choppy water. But he'd push his cart through the waves, ringing his bells, laughing and singing.

His ringing bells were my cue. I always heard them a block away. "It's Mister Marvel! Mister Marvel! Can I go out now? Please? Can I?" And my mother would smile and give me a dime for the ice cream he would bring.

I'd bound down the stairs, clutching my dime tightly in my fist. Then I was out the door and running down the sidewalk toward the sound of his bells.

Many other little people were already near him, shouting and laughing. I'd pour my sweat-wet dime into his huge, hairy hand, and receive my "usual." He'd always ask the others, "On a cone or a stick?," but he knew what I wanted, and had it ready when I arrived.

When the procession reached the end of the block, cries of "magic! magic!" would echo and re-echo down the street. Mister Marvel's eyes would become thin slits and his shoulders would shake up and down as he laughed his loud, hearty "ho ho ho." And then he'd put up his hands for silence, looking around as if he were in a great auditorium, inspecting each seat. On the porches of nearby houses, mothers would stand and watch. Then Mister Marvel would begin his performance. Pennies flowed from noses, little balls would multiply by themselves in his hand. A grin on his lips, he would go on and on, his tie changing colors before our eyes, rings appearing on his fingers.

And then it would be time for him to go. We would protest, but he'd have to move on, and we'd stand on the corner as he jingled his bells and strolled down the street into the next block and the next group of little people. A few of the older ones would follow him, but could only go so far. When asked where he finally went, they could only answer that his bells would fade in the distance, and then he'd disappear. So he came from nowhere and left the same way. *He* was magic himself.

And he was big and strong as well, and would perform many great feats of strength before us. He once walked across Niagara Falls — he *told* us so. And there was the time he saved a safari from mortal danger by fighting with three savage lions at the same time, and he never even got *cut*!

He was a fine specimen of a man: big, muscular arms, a wide face complemented by his shiny, black, curly hair made him the perfect hero. True, he was dressed in a worn and faded coat, but that was because he had worn it through his many adventures. When he'd juggle oranges, we'd stand there in awe of his power, and then applaud wildly. He'd laugh his special laugh all the while, and then do another trick.

One day some big kids came on the block while Mister Marvel was telling us a story. They stood on the opposite side of the street and made noises at him, but he never turned around or interrupted his tale.

Soon they were crossing the street, coming toward us while we were listening to Mister Marvel tell us about the time he swam the English Channel.

"Hey, fella, you really a strong man?" one of the boys asked.

Mister Marvel looked down at the boy for a few seconds. Then, flashing his smile, he answered:

"You bet, son! Strong as an ox, that's me!"

"Let's see ya do some push-ups, ox."

We all looked up at Mister Marvel expectantly. A bird sang in a tree nearby. A car horn went off somewhere. Mister Marvel's eyes blinked a little. He just looked at the boy, just stared at him with no expression. It was the first time I had seen him so quiet.

"Sure, kid," he said finally, and got right down on the ground. One, two, three pushups, four, five, six, and we stood there as he proved himself before those disbelievers. Mister Marvel was our hero. *Of course* he could do it. He was the greatest — better than Superman and Santa Claus put together. That night at dinner my father told me something about Mister Marvel that really convinced me of all this. "Gosh," I thought, "I hope I'll be able to do pushups when *I'm* seventy."

And then the bells stopped ringing. The next day the street was quiet.

Where was Mister Marvel? Many days passed. The street finally became a barren canyon, a canyon with new and strange echoes, a canyon never again to be filled with the sound of bells or laughter.

Was he just an ordinary man, who lived and died and was nice to us little people in between? No. He was Mister Marvel, our champion, our knight in shaggy armor. I'm sure that his spirit still pushes a cart on that old street.

And what is the point in this tale? Is it just a re-telling of a fond memory? No, it means more than that. To me, remembering Mister Marvel means that for a few short years there was a magical man whose only purpose in life was to make little people laugh. That in itself is a rare and wonderful phenomenon worth remembering. And little people everywhere, unable to fight lions or swim the English Channel, trapped inside a body that must take naps and be indoors by four o'clock, were, for a few marvelous moments, transported to a world where freedom and adventure were real. Mister Marvel was our hero who took us there. Every child should have one. It gives those early years of growing up a little purpose, a little romance, and dissolves a great part of the loneliness. To me, this combination was a cornerstone for living. Mister Marvel was an era in my life; without that era, I would have missed much of what living is all about.

"Gee, Mister Marvel, that was great!"

"Wow, Mister Marvel, you're terrific!"

"Mister Marvel, when I grow up, I want to be just like you!"

Marilyn Collins

Death in the Morning

When I was young and the world was bathed in lavender and rose, I saw the birth of many things. A slender baby water bird not wholly certain of its wings finally felt its courage and drifted with the wind. A scented lily, like an infant opening its eyes for the first time, stretched its tender petals and blinked in wonder at the morning sun. I saw a growing bluebell rise out of the garden soil and a wild bird's egg part its shell to reveal new life. God was garbed in hospital white, delivering the April morning and the bright ribbons of hyacinth, giving birth and beauty to the warm rising sun and cool violet skies.

Nothing ever died in the lovely world of childhood; all was new and green, bathed in the fresh morning dew of life. The last snowfall was not the death of winter, but the birth of spring; the setting sun not the death of day, but the birth of night. Mothers and fathers never died. Nothing was buried underground but the tender seeds of life waiting to burst through the earth to breathe scented air. Cemeteries were pretty parks with dark green grass, awfully nice for walking, I should have thought. "Daddy," I asked one day, "can we take a walk through there? The grass looks so pretty and soft." He said no and I wondered why.

No one died that ever really mattered in childhood's realm. Puppies died, but after the first few tears were shed, I guessed it didn't really matter that much; there were other puppies just as cute for sale at the corner pet shop. Puppies were buried underground in back yards, but I never knew. Daddy had a little box in his arms and Mommy said, "Go in the house and play, dear, and everything will be all right again."

Grandmas died, but that didn't matter much either, except that Mommy cried and mothers aren't supposed to cry. Men in trucks brought flowers to the house, big lovely flowers, far prettier than any bouquet I could ever have picked. I remembered Grandma only because her house had been nice to visit on Sunday afternoons with its musty smell and big rooms. The couch in the living room was scarlet with thick cushions that sank and felt prickly when I sat on it and exploring the big brown desk with its many drawers and secret compartments was like visiting a castle, very old and very dark. But most of all I liked the bedrooms because they looked like a fairy-tale and smelled of rose water. The beds, like golden thrones in a mystical kingdom, were big and soft to jump on, and the satin comforter reminded me of pansies because it was so smooth. Yes, grandmas died in childhood's realm, but they were just sweet old ladies who lived in storybook castles, and could easily be said never to have lived at all.

The world still bloomed as I grew in youth to ripeness. The slender leaves in the bedwarm woods exposed their shapes and flirted on a branch with a hummingbird. A majestic elm stood straight and tall, winked at a squirrel and beckoned him to climb. Lady April lowered her eyelids bringing her cool rains and running brooks, hints of May blossoms and whispers of spring. A ripened fruit, red with desire, dangled from a branch and smiled while a warm heart, longing for air, opened in excitement to spring. I learned to love. I found the warmth of a mother's voice and the strength of a father's will, the humbleness of prayer and the wisdom of a book. I took a deep lingering kiss out of a brimming mouth, and feeling the joyous pain of too much tenderness, I could not leave. Life was the cool crushed mint of a wood and the warm lavish promise of love. The world was still green because no one ever died that mattered. Husbands or lovers never died.

A tender pink rose ripened to a wild scarlet flower and I found myself a woman. Cool winds began from out of the west bringing me hints from the other side of happiness. The restless winds blew stronger until a word of lavender and rose met a thunderstorm in the sky and a May morning was turned to grey. I saw a budding violet with petals barely opened swept away by a gusty wind before it had seen the sky. A towering locust dropped white blossoms to the ground and a baby water bird fell in fright while trying to fly. I opened my eyes in womanhood and saw that lavender could be dulled to grey, that golden leaves could be brown at the edges, that love could be less than wonderful. While lightning struck in a thunderstorm, I learned that people who matter die.

Low-hung clouds in a dull grey sky dropped cold rain as if they had known all along. The world sang a funeral chant for loss of innocence to all like me who had passed from childhood's lovely realm. A mother's caring voice was silenced and a father's will was lost. A lover's sweet breath that had whispered endearments was caught in the lung and vanished. A warm promise of love hovered in the air to ring the heart and knock upon the mind of the living beloved. A lost hope was lowered into the ground with the once living dead to shake the earth with silence.

Perhaps I'll take a stroll someday holding the hand of my daughter.

The month will be April and the grass will be green and she'll say, "What's underground, Mommy? What's under the soft green grass we're walking on?" Perhaps I'll shock her sweet innocence and tell the truth. "Cold hands and dead promises, darling, cold hands and dead promises."

Malcolm Cowley

Papa and the Parricides

"Great men die twice," Paul Valéry said, "once as men and once as great." Their second death, in the public mind, may be no more than a forgetting, but in other cases it becomes a noisy spectacle that makes one think of a very old tree assaulted by a band of savages. The tree is the great man's reputation, which had hidden the sky and prevented lesser reputations from growing in its shade. Now it must be destroyed by tribal necessity, but the tribesmen have only stone axes that shatter against its enormous trunk. So they start by hacking off roots and branches one by one, then wait for the weakened tree to crash in the first gale.

That process of severing roots and lopping off branches is known in the critical world as "reassessment." If the critic is also a teacher, he is likely to speak of "establishing a canon," which means choosing the works that his students will be required to read and, in effect, abolishing the others. For some years I have been taking notes on a classical or, as the critics now prefer to write, a paradigmatic example of that operation, in this case performed on the works of Ernest Hemingway.

"At the time of his death, in 1961," says one critic, John Thompson, who is or was Visiting Associate Professor of English at the State University of New York at Stony Brook, Hemingway "was probably the best-known writer in the world, and one of the most popular. But his writing no longer exerted an influence on literature, and serious critics usually disposed of his work as being of minor interest compared to that of writers like Fitzgerald and Faulkner whom he had once completely overshadowed.

"Such questions as may arise about his writing today," Mr. Thompson continues in the tone of a Supreme Court justice reading an almost unanimous opinion "are only manifestations of the slow and uneven filtering down of accepted opinion, or of the uneven rates at which the glamour

221

of his settings evaporates in different minds. Nearly everyone agrees now on the order of quality in the canon of his work. *The Sun Also Rises* and many of his short stories are absolutely first-rate, surpassed in scope by other novelists of his time but unsurpassed by anyone in their perfection." Nothing else that Hemingway wrote is really worth the trouble of rereading. "Thus, while he is still recognized clearly enough as an artist of occasional success," the critic concludes in *The New York Review of Books*, "his work no longer seems to contain promises for others, and his books are not much regarded by writers anymore."

I envy the assurance with which Mr. Thompson, never speaking in the first person, repeats what he thinks that other people think who he thinks are serious critics. He might not regard Vance Bourjaily as one of them, since Bourjaily makes the critical *gaffe* of speaking for himself and in any case is not a critic primarily. His profession is writing novels, and he owes a substantial debt to Hemingway, as do other writers of talent in his World War II generation. In an article contributed to the Book Review section of the New York *Times*, Bourjaily acknowledges the debt, but he also engages in what seems to be the inevitable business of drawing up a canon. "As a reader," he says, "and claiming to speak for other readers, I suppose I rank the works quite simply according to the frequency with which it occurs to me that I would now enjoy rereading a given one. By this test, *The Sun Also Rises* is incomparably the best novel; I reread it every fourth or fifth year. There are between fifteen and twenty short stories, mostly early but including *Macomber* and *Kilimanjaro*, which I read as often and feel to be of the same extraordinary merit. *A Farewell to Arms* is somewhat below these, but not far — perhaps on a seven-year or eight-year cycle. I suspect that *Green Hills of Africa*, which I discovered quite recently, will come in next."

From other books Mr. Bourjaily recalls "a few moving things," but he does not propose to reread them. Thus, even in his favorable report, the Hemingway canon is reduced to fifteen or twenty short stories, most of them early ones, two novels, and a travel book. But all the Hemingway critics are engaged in critical canoneering, and most of them carry it to greater extreme — as does, for example, Stanley Edgar Hyman, who says in *The New Leader*, ". . . at his best Hemingway left us, in *The Sun Also Rises* and a handful of short stories, authentic masterpieces, small-scale but immortal." How many stories make a handful? Certainly fewer than the fifteen or twenty that Mr. Bourjaily delights in rereading. Robert Emmet Long, writing in *The North American Review*, wants to shorten the list of canonical works to a few of those produced in the early or vintage years. "Almost all of his best work," Mr. Long says, "was done while he was still in his twenties. . . . *The Sun Also Rises*, *A Farewell to Arms* and half a dozen short stories present Hemingway at his best." Having added a novel to Mr. Hyman's version of the canon, Mr. Long subtracts from it three or four stories — unless "half a dozen" and "a handful" are synonyms.

Leslie A. Fiedler places the same emphasis on the early work, which he admires for a curious reason, as Hemingway's celebration of "the bleak truth it had been given him to know." That truth was "death and the void," or so we learn in Mr. Fiedler's recent book, *Waiting for the End*, where we are also told that "after the first two novels and the early stories, he was able only to echo, in the end parody, himself." Other critics want to reject even those first two novels. "The fact is Hemingway is a short-story writer and not a novelist," Dwight Macdonald says in *Against The American Grain*. "He has little understanding of the subject matter of the novel: character, social setting, politics, money matters, human relations, all the prose of life. . . . In a novel he gets lost, wandering aimlessly in a circle as lost people are said to do, and the alive parts are really short stories, such as the lynching of the Fascists and the blowing up of the bridge in *For Whom the Bell Tolls*."

I will resist the temptation to argue with Mr. Macdonald, though it would be easy to cite passages from Hemingway's novels that reveal his understanding of character, social setting, politics, money matters, human relations, and — if only by implication, since he does not burden the story with extraneous material — all the prose of life. It would be still easier to show that instead of getting lost in a novel he marches ahead in a straight-line narrative that appears to be simple, but is actually a difficult type of writing, since it avoids all the tricks by which novelists are enabled to impart or withhold information at their own convenience. Those citations and proofs, however, can wait for another occasion. At present what interests me is that Mr. Macdonald's judgment, however debatable, seems to have been accepted by segments of the academic world. I remember a recent comment by a professor of American literature on an anthology I was helping to revise. "Why not include Hemingway's two or three best stories," he said, "and omit any reference to his novels? Hemingway is beginning to be taught chiefly as a short-story writer." Here was the critical canon again, this time reduced to two or three stories. "Pretty soon," I said to myself, "they will have him chipped down to *Big Two-Hearted River*." The next step would be to chip that story down to a single paragraph presented by critics as the only true essence of his work, from which they could infer the rest of it much in the fashion that paleontologists reconstruct the skeleton of an extinct animal from a single bone. Perhaps it would be the paragraph that reads:

"He watched them holding themselves with their noses into the current, many trout in deep, fast moving water, slightly distorted as he watched them far down through the glassy convex surface of the pool, its surface pushing and swelling smooth against the resistance of the log-driven piles of the bridge. At the bottom of the pool were the big trout.

Nick did not see them at first. Then he saw them at the bottom of the pool, big trout looking to hold themselves on the gravel bottom in a varying mist of gravel and sand, raised in spurts by the current."

Or would the critics choose another paragraph for fear of having to confess that they had never seen the big trout? I respect most of those whose judgments I have quoted, and some of them are my friends, but in the present connection they evoke a mental picture I should like to forget. This time the picture is not of a tree being felled, but of a dead lion surrounded by a pack of jackals. At first they gather round him cautiously, ready to take flight at any sign of life, and then, gaining courage from one another, they rush in to tear the flesh from the bones. I suppose the bones are the critical canon, but they will not remain undisturbed; soon the hyenas will come to crack them for their marrow. There will be nothing left but a white skull on the wide African plain and hunters will say as they look at it, "Why, it wasn't such a big lion after all."

But Hemingway for most of his life was our biggest lion. In the midst of these posthumous assaults on his reputation, I should like to interject a few remarks about the lasting values in his work and about the whole business of setting up a critical canon by exclusion.

It seems to me a snobbish business essentially. Each critic is tempted to display his superior discrimination by excluding a little more than other critics excluded. The process is exactly similar to the one by which drinkers some years ago used to display their superior taste by insisting on less and less vermouth in their Martinis: the man who ordered eight parts of gin to one of vermouth was obviously twice as high in the social-drinking scale as the man who was satisfied with four parts to one. Just so in the critical scale, Vance Bourjaily, who admits to liking two Hemingway novels and fifteen or twenty stories, is only half as discriminating as Stanley Hyman, who praises only one novel and "a handful" of stories — would it be a single or a double handful? — while Hyman in turn must bow to Dwight Macdonald, who retains a few stories but completely excudes the novels. They can each be assigned a rank, but it has nothing to do with their sense of literary values.

There are other reasons for distrusting the process of critical canoneering when it is applied to an author of any standing. Of course it has the practical justification that students can't be expected to read everything; the instructor has to make choices. But when he chooses a book for them to read, he shouldn't imply, except in special cases, that nothing else by the same author is worth their attention. The special cases are those of one-book authors, a genus that has some famous members; Hemingway isn't one of them. Some of his books are immensely better than others. Some I should surrender without regret, as notably *Across the River and into the Trees*; perhaps that is the only one. *Green Hills of Africa* and

To Have and Have Not fall short of their mark, each for a different reason, but both contain passages I should hate to relinquish.

For Whom the Bell Tolls does not belong among those partial failures. It seems to me the most complicated and powerful of Hemingway's works, as it is certainly the longest. Often it is dismissed by critics as if they had reached a tacit agreement, but that appears to be the result of circumstances quite apart from its literary value. One circumstance is its popular success; critics always distrust a novel that has had an enormous sale — in this case eight hundred thousand hardbound copies in the first few years — after being announced as a masterpiece by the daily reviewers. *For Whom the Bell Tolls* has suffered from the additional handicaps of dealing with the Spanish civil war, a subject that many critics wanted to forget, and of dealing with it in a fashion that offended most of the political factions: Fascists, Stalinists, Trotskyites, pacifists, Spanish patriots on both sides, almost the whole spectrum. As time passed the book was so bitterly condemned on political grounds that critics did not feel they had to read it with close attention. Nothing they said against it was likely to be challenged, even if their judgments were based on an obvious misinterpretation.

Take for example Dwight Macdonald's judgment, already quoted, that "the alive parts are really short stories such as the lynching of the Fascists and the blowing up of the bridge in *For Whom the Bell Tolls*." His notion that the parts would be better if separated from the whole is not supported by the text. Conceivably the lynching of the Fascists might stand alone, but it is an essential shadow in the picture that Hemingway has been presenting all through the novel. The blowing up of a bridge, with Robert Jordan's death as recounted in the last forty pages, clearly depends for its power on the tensions that have been created in the preceding four hundred pages. It is no more a short story than the fifth act of *Hamlet* is a one-act play.

There is more to be said about Jordan's fight at the bridge. In addition to being the end of the novel, it is also the last in a series of events that had continued through several books. Most of Hemingway's early heroes are aspects of the same person, whether we call him Nick Adams or Frederic Henry or Jake Barnes, and of course he reappears in Robert Jordan. The hero's adventures began in Michigan, but reached their first climax in *A Farewell to Arms*, when, falsely charged with being a spy, he deserted from the Italian army (and also, in a sense, from organized society). The fight at the bridge is a sequel to that earlier climax, which had taken place at another bridge; this time the hero accepts the fate from which he had escaped, in *A Farewell to Arms*, by plunging into a flooded river. Hemingway's books are interconnected in several fashions; the connections are what so many critics miss by their cannoneering. Though a story in itself may be an authentic masterpiece, small-scale but immortal — to quote Mr. Hyman — the scale is magnified when we read it with other stories, which in turn are enhanced in value by the novels. Everything is part of the same pattern.

In the background of the pattern are death, loneliness, and fear of the void, but these are not Hemingway's subject — Mr. Fiedler to the contrary — except in two or three of the early vignettes and in a few stories written during the Thirties. In *A Clean, Well-Lighted Place*, for example, the old waiter says, "What did he fear? It was not fear or dread. It was a nothing that he knew too well." But although the old waiter seems to speak from the depths of nihilism, he suggests a remedy against that feeling of nothingness; it is for the lonely man to sit all night in a bright, pleasant café where he will be surrounded with order and decorum. That appears to be an essential statement, and we can see more clearly in other stories that Hemingway's real subject is the barriers that can be erected against death and loneliness and the void.

Decorum in the broadest sense, in which it becomes the discipline of one's calling and the further discipline required of every human being if he is to live as a man, not collapse into a jelly of emotions, is the strongest of those barriers, "Be a man, my son," a priest in one of the early vignettes says to Sam Cardinella when he loses control of his sphincter muscle as he is being strapped for the gallows. Sam is the specter of fear that seems more repulsive to Hemingway than death itself. To maintain discipline in the face of death requires a strict control of the imagination, lest it get to racing "like a flywheel with the weight gone," as Robert Jordan says in *For Whom the Bell Tolls*. It also requires complete attention to every action in its proper sequence, as if that single action, at the moment, were the whole of life. Meanwhile the sequence of actions is being reported in a disciplined style that is in harmony with the subject matter and that also becomes a method of suggesting — while at the same time warding off — fears that are not directly expressed.

Besides imposing a discipline, the implied or actual presence of death in Hemingway's fiction has compensations that are also part of his subject. This feature of his work, not often discussed, is one that I found easy to recognize from a memory of youth; there must be many others with a similar memory. In my case it goes back to Paris in the early summer of 1917. I was on leave from driving a truck for the French army, not a proud occupation in those days when one's friends were enlisting in various flying corps and getting killed with astonishing dispatch. In the Lafayette Escadrille, for example, the average expectancy of life was something like three months. I decided on that June morning to enlist in American aviation, knowing that I should make an incompetent pilot and should certainly be killed with greater dispatch than the others; nevertheless the decision was made. Suddenly everything changed for me. The chestnut trees in the Champs Elysées seemed greener, their blossoms pinker, the girls on the sidewalk more beautiful, and the sky an unprecedented shade of blue, as if my senses had been sharpened and my capacity for enjoyment vastly increased by the imminence of death. Humming a silly wartime song, stumbling at the curb, smiling to passersby, I went to a restaurant and ordered what seemed to me the best meal I had ever eaten, washed down with a bottle of miraculous wine.

The experience had no sequel in life, since I was rejected by the Army doctors, but much later it helped me to recognize a lasting quality in Hemingway's prose. Because death seems to hover in the air while he is writing, like an obscene bird — or moves silently in pairs, on bicycles, like French policemen, or has a wide snout like a hyena and prowls outside his tent, as in *The Snows of Kilimanjaro* — because of that wordless presence, he feels and transmits a special cleanness and freshness in the physical world that has been rendered by no other novelist of our time. It is a quality one finds in many poems of the Middle Ages, also written by men whose enjoyment of nature was sharpened by their feeling that death lay in ambush at the turn of the road.

Landscape, the weather, fishing and hunting, eating and drinking, talking round the fire and making love: those are the wonderful things in Hemingway. The ideas are interesting too, even though merely implied, for he was always more of an intellectual than he pretended to be; but he was best at describing natural scenes and activities. Indeed, he described them with such gusto that the young men of more than one generation were determined to share in his exploits. Years ago, when I was gathering material for a profile, I talked to Jakie Key, a charter-boat captain in Key West. "If you want to say anything bad about Hemingway," he told me, "don't talk to me. Hemingway made this charter-boat business — he brought the fishermen down." That set me to thinking about his importance as an economic force. Charter boats in Key West and Bimini, ski resorts, bullfights, restaurants: he enjoyed them all, he told what they had to offer, and the crowds followed.

That side of his career is not what interests me. Most writers were inclined to resent it, on the ground that there seemed to be no place in it for books and bookmen. Not sharing that resentment, I still find that Hemingway the writer paid a high price for his activities as a sportsman and war correspondent. His real excuse for engaging in them, implicit in everything he wrote, was that he liked them. That was not the same as his public excuse, which was that they furnished him with material. "In going where you have to go, and doing what you have to do, and seeing what you have to see," he said in his preface to *The Fifth Column and the First Forty-nine Stories*, "you dull and blunt the instrument you write with. But I would rather have it bent and dulled and know I had to put it on the grindstone again and hammer it into shape, and put a whetstone to it, and know that I had something to write about, than to have it bright and shining and nothing to say, or smooth and well-oiled in the closet, but unused."

Long before the end, and in fact before World War II, he had gathered more material than he could ever put into his writing. In *The Snows of Kilimanjaro* (1936), he deliberately threw away material for a dozen stories, each of which was reduced to one or two paragraphs of the dying hero's recollections, as if both hero and author were trying to get rid of compulsive memories. "He had sold vitality, in one form or another, all his life," they both complain. As for "the instrument you write with" — if Hemingway meant his head — it was scarred and battered like a boxer's head in a dozen serious accidents, from one of which, the second airplane crash in Africa, he never recovered. That was our loss, but we should remember that in all those costly adventures there was something on the other side of the ledger too, not for literature, but for the world. The public career was in itself an artistic creation. By the enormous zest with which he studied the rules of every game, including those of love and war and the chase, he made our world more dramatic than it would have been without him, and something went out of it when he died.

But the work is what interests me, not the career, and that is why I am disturbed by the recent sapping and pruning of his literary reputation. Does nothing survive of the work but a few short stories? Why not toss them out with the novels and finally reduce the Hemingway canon to a blank page? As yet that gesture of total rejection hasn't been made by any reputable critic. Even Dwight Macdonald, who comes nearest to making it, still finds a few things he would like to save. There were, however, premonitory hints of the gesture in a few newspaper reviews of *A Moveable Feast,* mixed in with favorable comments by others. ". . . aging boy that he became," Glendy Culligan said in The Washington *Post,* "Hemingway was finally surpassed by his own imitators." I wonder what books by which imitators she had in mind. The anonymous reviewer for the Harrisburg *Patriot News* wanted to dismiss Hemingway's readers along with the books and their author. "The reputation he built up studiously," the reviewer said "will linger among the middle-aged generation that naturally clings to the illusions of youth."

What this cry from Harrisburg, Pennsylvania, suggests — when taken with other evidence — is the broader scope of the operation that had seemed to be directed against Hemingway and no one else. He isn't the only victim; he isn't even the first. Thomas Wolfe has already gone down under repeated assaults — for which there was more excuse in his case — and Dos Passos, though not stoned to death, has been loaded with the sins of the literary community and driven into the desert. Of course the ultimate goal of the operation is the whole age-group of which Hemingway was a member. A few of his contemporaries have escaped the recent attacks, notably Faulkner and Fitzgerald and Edmund Wilson, but it is not hard to foresee that their turn is coming. What we are witnessing is a crucial stage in an event that has been delayed beyond expectations, that is, the ritual murder of the literary fathers.

To cast some light on that ceremony revived from ancient times, I might quote a famous passage from the last chapter of *Totem and Taboo*. Freud introduces the passage by recalling Darwin's notion that the first form of human society may have been a primal horde in which a violent, jealous father kept all the females for himself and drove away the growing sons. The notion has never been confirmed by anthropologists, but Sigmund Freud accepts it as the basis for a more dramatic picture of his own.

"One day [he says] the expelled brothers joined forces, slew and ate the father, and thus put an end to the father horde. Together they dared and accomplished what would have remained impossible for them singly. . . . This violent primal father had surely been the envied and feared model for each of the brothers. Now they accomplished their identification with him by devouring him and each acquired a part of his strength."

Freud goes on to explain that the original parricide, or *Vatermord*, was the original sin and hence was the beginning of religion. I shall not follow him in those later conjectures. All I wanted to suggest is that a ritual murder of the fathers has become a custom in the literary world. Each new generation provides admired, then feared and envied models for the generation that follows. The new men, however, have their own sense of life, which they are bent on expressing in their own fashion, and therefore they have to break free from the models. Often they do so by denying that the models have any virtues, by rejecting their works one after another, and, in effect, by killing them as men of letters. Of course they eat them too, in the sense of absorbing what they can from the slaughtered parents.

For the new generation of parricides, Hemingway becomes an especially tempting victim, partly because he had been so abundantly paternal. All the social novelists of the Thirties were his sons, in one way or another, and so were almost all the war novelists of the Forties. He had been extremely kind to them in the beginning, so long as they did not threaten his preeminence, but later, when they promised to become rivals, he expelled them one by one from the primal horde. No wonder that many of the sons joined forces against him. Hemingway, in fact, had offered them a model of filial ingratitude in his early career, since his third book, *The Torrents of Spring*, was a ritual murder of Sherwood Anderson, from whom he had learned valuable lessons. The young men might argue that they were paying him back a death for a death.

If I deplore the recent attacks on Hemingway's reputation, it is not because I think that the critics are guilty of more than the customary measure of ingratitude. It is not for personal reasons, because I want to defend my own generation or the man who for thirty years and more embodied so many of its perceptions; and it is not because I think the attacks will be successful in the end. With the necessary subtractions made, Hemingway's work as a whole is so clearly permanent that, even if his reputation were destroyed for the moment and the work buried, it would be exhumed after a hundred years, as Melville's was. My protest is simply in defense of American literature. It is vastly richer now than it was when Hemingway started writing but it is not yet so rich that it can afford to disown and devalue one of its lasting treasures.

Loren Eiseley

The Judgment of the Birds

It is a commonplace of all religious thought, even the most primitive, that the man seeking visions and insight must go apart from his fellows and live for a time in the wilderness. If he is of the proper sort, he will return with a message. It may not be a message from the god he set out to seek, but even if he has failed in that particular, he will have had a vision or seen a marvel, and these are always worth listening to and thinking about.

The world, I have come to believe, is a very queer place, but we have been part of this queerness for so long that we tend to take it for granted. We rush to and fro like Mad Hatters upon our peculiar errands, all the time imagining our surroundings to be dull and ourselves quite ordinary creatures. Actually, there is nothing in the world to encourage this idea, but such is the mind of man, and this is why he finds it necessary from time to time to send emissaries into the wilderness in the hope of learning of great events, or plans in store for him, that will resuscitate his waning taste for life. His great news services, his world-wide radio network, he knows with a last remnant of healthy distrust will be of no use to him in this matter. No miracle can withstand a radio broadcast, and it is certain that it would be no miracle if it could. One must seek, then, what only the solitary approach can give — a natural revelation.

Let it be understood that I am not the sort of man to whom is entrusted direct knowledge of great events or prophecies. A naturalist, however, spends much of his life alone, and my life is no exception. Even in New York City there are patches of wilderness, and a man by himself is bound to undergo certain experiences falling into the class of which I speak. I set mine down, therefore: a matter of pigeons, a flight of chemicals, and a judgment of birds, in the hope that they will come to the eye of those who have retained a true taste for the marvelous and who are capable of discerning in the flow of ordinary events the point at which the mundane world gives way to quite another dimension.

New York is not, on the whole, the best place to enjoy the downright miraculous nature of the planet. There are, I do not doubt, many remarkable stories to be heard there and many strange sights to be seen, but to grasp a marvel fully it must be savored from all aspects. This cannot be done while one is being jostled and hustled along a crowded street. Nevertheless, in any city there are true wildernesses where a man can be alone. It can happen in a hotel room, or on the high roofs at dawn.

One night on the twentieth floor of a midtown hotel I awoke in the dark and grew restless. On an impulse I climbed upon the broad old-fashioned window sill, opened the curtains and peered out. It was the hour just before dawn, the hour when men sigh in their sleep, or, if awake, strive to focus their wavering eyesight upon a world emerging from the shadows. I leaned out sleepily through the open window. I had expected depths, but not the sight I saw.

I found I was looking down from that great height into a series of curious cupolas or lofts that I could just barely make out in the darkness. As I looked, the outlines of these lofts became more distinct because the light was being reflected from the wings of pigeons who, in utter silence, were beginning to float outward upon the city. In and out through the open slits in the cupolas passed the white-winged birds on their mysterious errands. At this hour the city was theirs, and quietly, without the brush of a single wing tip against stone in that high, eerie place, they were taking over the spires of Manhattan. They were pouring upward in a light that was not yet perceptible to human eyes, while far down in the black darkness of the alleys it was still midnight.

As I crouched half asleep across the sill, I had a moment's illusion that the world had changed in the night, as in some immense snowfall, and that if I were to leave, it would have to be as these other inhabitants were doing, by the window. I should have to launch out into the great bottomless void with the simple confidence of young birds reared high up there among the familiar chimney pots and interposed horrors of the abyss.

I leaned farther out. To and fro went the white wings, to and fro. There were no sounds from any of them. They knew man was asleep and this light for a little while was theirs. Or perhaps I had only dreamed about man in this city of wings — which he could surely never have built. Perhaps I, myself, was one of these birds dreaming unpleasantly a moment of old dangers far below as I teetered on a window ledge.

Around and around went the wings. It needed only a little courage, only a little shove from the window ledge to enter that city of light. The muscles of my hands were already making little premonitory lunges. I wanted to enter that city and go away over the roofs in the first dawn. I wanted to enter it so badly that I drew back carefully into the room and opened the hall door. I found my coat on the chair, and it slowly became clear to me that there was a way down through the floors, that I was, after all, only a man.

I dressed then and went back to my own kind, and I have been rather more than usually careful ever since not to look into the city of light. I had seen, just once, man's greatest creation from a strange inverted angle, and it was not really his at all. I will never forget how those wings went round and round, and how, by the merest pressure of the fingers and a feeling for air, one might go away over the roofs. It is a knowledge, however, that is better kept to oneself. I think of it sometimes in such a way that the wings, beginning far down in the black depths of the mind, begin to rise and whirl till all the mind is lit by their spinning, and there is a sense of things passing away, but lightly, as a wing might veer over an obstacle.

To see from an inverted angle, however, is not a gift allotted merely to the human imagination. I have come to suspect that within their degree it is sensed by animals, though perhaps as rarely as among men. The time has to be right; one has to be, by chance or intention, upon the border of two worlds. And sometimes these two borders may shift or interpenetrate and one sees the miraculous.

I once saw this happen to a crow.

This crow lives near my house, and though I have never injured him, he takes good care to stay up in the very highest trees and, in general, to avoid humanity. His world begins at about the limit of my eyesight.

On the particular morning when this episode occurred, the whole countryside was buried in one of the thickest fogs in years. The ceiling was absolutely zero. All planes were grounded, and even a pedestrian could hardly see his outstretched hand before him.

I was groping across a field in the general direction of the railroad station, following a dimly outlined path. Suddenly out of the fog, at about the level of my eyes, and so closely that I flinched, there flashed a pair of immense black wings and a huge beak. The whole bird rushed over my head with a frantic cawing outcry of such hideous terror as I have never heard in a crow's voice before, and never expect to hear again.

He was lost and startled, I thought, as I recovered my poise. He ought not to have flown out in this fog. He'd knock his silly brains out.

All afternoon that great awkward cry rang in my head. Merely being lost in a fog seemed scarcely to account for it — especially in a tough, intelligent old bandit such as I knew that particular crow to be. I even looked once in the mirror to see what it might be about me that had so revolted him that he had cried out in protest to the very stones.

Finally, as I worked my way homeward along the path, the solution came to me. It should have been clear before. The borders of our worlds had shifted. It was the fog that had done it. That crow, and I knew him well, never under normal circumstances flew low near men. He had been lost all right, but it was more than that. He had thought he was high up, and when he encountered me looming gigantically through the fog, he had perceived a ghastly and, to the crow mind, unnatural sight. He had seen a man walking on air, desecrating the very heart of the crow kingdom, a harbinger of the most profound evil a crow mind could conceive of — air-walking men. The encounter, he must have thought, had taken place a hundred feet over the roofs.

He caws now when he sees me leaving for the station in the morning, and I fancy that in that note I catch the uncertainty of a mind that has come to know things are not always what they seem. He has seen a marvel in his heights of air and is no longer as other crows. He has experienced the human world from an unlikely perspective. He and I share a viewpoint in common: our worlds have interpenetrated, and we both have faith in the miraculous.

It is a faith that in my own case has been augmented by two remarkable sights. As I have hinted previously, I once saw some very odd chemicals fly across a waste so dead it might have been upon the moon, and once, by an even more fantastic piece of luck, I was present when a group of birds passed a judgment upon life.

On the maps of the old voyageurs it is called *Mauvaises Terres*, the evil lands, and, slurred a little with the passage through many minds, it has come down to us anglicized as the Badlands. The soft shuffle of moccasins has passed through its canyons on the grim business of war and flight, but the last of those slight disturbances of immemorial silences died out almost a century ago. The land, if one can call it a land, is a waste as lifeless as that valley in which lie the kings of Egypt. Like the Valley of the Kings, it is a mausoleum, a place of dry bones in what once was a place of life. Now it has silences as deep as those in the moon's airless chasms.

Nothing grows among its pinnacles; there is no shade except under great toadstools of sandstone whose bases have been eaten to the shape of wine glasses by the wind. Everything is flaking, cracking, disintegrating, wearing away in the long, imperceptible weather of time. The ash of ancient volcanic outbursts still sterilizes its soil, and its colors in that waste are the colors that flame in the lonely sunsets on dead planets. Men came there but rarely, and for one purpose only, the collection of bones.

It was a late hour on a cold, wind-bitten autumn day when I climbed a great hill spined like a dinosaur's back and tried to take my bearings. The tumbled waste fell away in waves in all directions. Blue air was darkening into purple along the bases of the hills. I shifted my knapsack, heavy with the petrified bones of long-vanished creatures, and studied my compass. I wanted to be out of there by nightfall, and already the sun was going sullenly down in the west.

It was then that I saw the flight coming on. It was moving like a little close-knit body of black specks that danced and darted and closed again. It was pouring from the north and heading toward me with the undeviating relentlessness of a compass needle. It streamed through the shadows rising out of monstrous gorges. It rushed over towering pinnacles in the red light of the sun, or momentarily sank from sight within their shade. Across that desert of eroding clay and wind-worn stone they came with a faint wild twittering that filled all the air about me as those tiny living bullets hurtled past into the night.

It may not strike you as a marvel. It would not, perhaps, unless you stood in the middle of a dead word at sunset, but that was where I stood. Fifty million years lay under my feet, fifty million years of bellowing monsters moving in a green world now gone so utterly that its very light was travelling on the farther edge of space. The chemicals of all that vanished age lay about me in the ground. Around me still lay the shearing molars of dead titanotheres, the delicate sabers of soft-stepping cats, the hollow sockets that had held the eyes of many a strange, outmoded beast. Those eyes had looked out upon a world as real as ours; dark, savage brains had roamed and roared their challenges into the streaming night.

Now they were still here, or, put it as you will, the chemicals that made them were here about me in the ground. The carbon that had driven them ran blackly in the eroding stone. The stain of iron was in the clays. The iron did not remember the blood it had once moved within, the phosphorous had forgot the savage brain. The little individual moment had ebbed from all those strange combinations of chemicals as it would ebb from our living bodies into the sinks and runnels of oncoming time.

I had lifted up a fistful of that ground. I held it while that wild flight of south-bound warblers hurtled over me into the oncoming dark. There went phosphorous, there went iron, there went carbon, there beat the calcium in those hurrying wings. Alone on a dead planet I watched that incredible miracle speeding past. It ran by some true compass over field and waste land. It cried its individual ecstacies into the air until the gullies rang. It swerved like a single body, it knew itself and, lonely, it bunched close in the racing darkness, its individual entities feeling about them the rising night. And so, crying to each other their identity, they passed away out of my view.

I dropped my fistful of earth. I heard it roll inanimate back into the gully at the base of the hill: iron, carbon, the chemicals of life. Like men from those wild tribes who had haunted these hills before me seeking visions, I made my sign to the great darkness. It was not a mocking sign, and I was not mocked. As I walked into my camp late that night, one man, rousing from his blankets beside the fire, asked sleepily, "What did you see?"

"I think, a miracle," I said softly, but I said it to myself. Behind me that vast waste began to glow under the rising moon.

I have said that I saw a judgment upon life, and that it was not passed by men. Those who stare at birds in cages or who test minds by their closeness to our own may not care for it. It comes from far away out of my past, in a place of pouring waters and green leaves. I shall never see an episode like it again if I live to be a hundred, nor do I think that one man in a million has ever seen it, because man is an intruder into such silences. The light must be right, and the observer must remain unseen. No man sets up such an experiment. What he sees, he sees by chance.

You may put it that I had come over a mountain, that I had slogged through fern and pine needles for half a long day, and that on the edge of a little glade with one long, crooked branch extending across it, I had sat down to rest with my back against a stump. Through accident I was concealed from the glade, although I could see into it perfectly.

The sun was warm there, and the murmurs of forest life blurred softly into my sleep. When I awoke, dimly aware of some commotion and outcry in the clearing, the light was slanting down through the pines in such a way that the glade was lit like some vast cathedral. I could see the dust motes of wood pollen in the long shaft of light, and there on the extended branch sat an enormous raven with a red and squirming nestling in his beak.

The sound that awoke me was the outraged cries of the nestling's parents, who flew helplessly in circles about the clearing. The sleek black monster was indifferent to them. He gulped, whetted his beak on the dead branch a moment and sat still. Up to that point the little tragedy had followed the usual pattern. But suddenly, out of all that area of woodland, a soft sound of complaint began to rise. Into the glade fluttered small birds of half a dozen varieties drawn by the anguished outcries of the tiny parents.

No one dared to attack the raven. But they cried in some instinctive common misery, the bereaved and the unbereaved. The glade filled with their soft rustling and their cries. They fluttered as though to point their wings at the murderer. There was a dim intangible ethic he had violated, that they knew. He was a bird of death.

And he, the murderer, the black bird at the heart of life, sat on there, glistening in the common light, formidable, unmoving, unperturbed, untouchable.

The sighing died. It was then I saw the judgment. It was the judgment of life against death. I will never see it again so forcefully presented. I will never hear it again in notes so tragically prolonged. For in the midst of protest, they forgot the violence. There, in that clearing, the crystal note of a song sparrow lifted hesitantly in the hush. And finally, after painful fluttering, another took the song, and then another, the song passing from one bird to another, doubtfully at first, as though some evil thing were being slowly forgotten. Till suddenly they took heart and sang from many throats joyously together as birds are known to sing. They sang because life is sweet and sunlight beautiful. They sang under the brooding shadow of the raven. In simple truth they had forgotten the raven, for they were the singers of life, and not of death.

I was not of that airy company. My limbs were the heavy limbs of an earthbound creature who could climb mountains, even the mountains of the mind, only by a great effort of will. I knew I had seen a marvel and observed a judgment, but the mind which was my human endowment was sure to question it and to be at me day by day with its heresies until I grew to doubt the meaning of what I had seen. Eventually darkness and subtleties would ring me round once more.

And so it proved until, on top of a stepladder, I made one more observation upon life. It was cold that autumn evening, and, standing under a suburban street light in a spate of leaves and beginning snow, I was suddenly conscious of some huge and hairy shadows dancing over the pavement. They seemed attached to an odd, globular shape that was magnified above me. There was no mistaking it. I was standing under the shadow of an orb-weaving spider. Gigantically projected against the street, she was about her spinning when everything was going underground. Even her cables were magnified upon the sidewalk and already I was half-entangled in their shadows.

"Good Lord," I thought, "she has found herself a kind of minor sun and is going to upset the course of nature."

I procured a ladder from my yard and climbed up to inspect the situation. There she was, the universe running down around her, warmly arranged among her guy ropes attached to the lamp supports — a great black and yellow embodiment of the life force, not giving up to either frost or step ladders. She ignored me and went on tightening and improving her web.

I stood over her on the ladder, a faint snow touching my cheeks, and surveyed her universe. There were a couple of iridescent green beetle cases turning slowly on a loose strand of web, a fragment of luminescent eye from a moth's wing and a large indeterminable object, perhaps a cicada, that had struggled and been wrapped in silk. There were also little bits and slivers, little red and blue flashes from the scales of anonymous wings that had crashed there.

Some days, I thought, they will be dull and gray and the shine will be out of them; then the dew will polish them again and drops hang on the silk until everything is gleaming and turning in the light. It is like a mind, really, where everything changes but remains, and in the end you have these eaten-out bits of experience like beetle wings.

I stood over her a moment longer, comprehending somewhat reluctantly that her adventure against the great blind forces of winter, her seizure of this warming globe of light, would come to nothing and was hopeless. Nevertheless it brought the birds back into my mind, and that faraway song which had traveled with growing strength around a forest clearing years ago — a kind of heroism, a world where even a spider refuses to lie down and die if a rope can still be spun on to a star. Maybe man himself will fight like this in the end, I thought, slowly realizing that the web and its threatening yellow occupant had been added to some luminous store of experience, shining for a moment in the fogbound reaches of my brain.

The mind, it came to me as I slowly descended the ladder, is a very remarkable thing; it has gotten itself a kind of courage by looking at a spider in a street lamp. Here was something that ought to be passed on to those who will fight our final freezing battle with the void. I thought of setting it down carefully as a message to the future: *In the days of the frost seek a minor sun.*

But as I hesitated, it became plain that something was wrong. The marvel was escaping — a sense of bigness beyond man's power to grasp, the essence of life in its great dealings with the universe. It was better, I decided, for the emissaries returning from the wilderness, even if they were merely descending from a stepladder, to record their mavel, not to define its meaning. In that way it would go echoing on through the minds of men, each grasping at that beyond out of which the miracles emerge, and which, once defined, ceases to satisfy the human need for symbols.

In the end I merely made a mental note: One specimen of Epeira observed building a web in a street light. Late autumn and cold for spiders. Cold for men, too. I shivered and left the lamp glowing there in my mind. The last I saw of Epeira she was hauling steadily on a cable. I stepped carefully over her shadow as I walked away.

Erich Fromm

Is Love an Art?

Is love an art? Then it requires knowledge and effort. Or is love a pleasant sensation, which to experience is a matter of chance, something one "falls into" if one is lucky? This little book is based on the former premise, while undoubtedly the majority of people today believe in the latter.

Not that people think that love is not important. They are starved for it; they watch endless numbers of films about happy and unhappy love stories, they listen to hundreds of trashy songs about love — yet hardly anyone thinks that there is anything that needs to be learned about love.

This peculiar attitude is based on several premises which either singly or combined tend to uphold it. Most people see the problem of love primarily as that of *being loved*, rather than that of *loving*, of one's capacity to love. Hence the problem to them is how to be loved, how to be lovable. In pursuit of this aim they follow several paths. One, which is especially used by men, is to be successful, to be as powerful and rich as the social margin of one's position permits. Another, used especially by women, is to make oneself attractive, by cultivating one's body, dress, etc. Other ways of making oneself attractive, used both by men and women, are to develop pleasant manners, interesting conversation, to be helpful, modest, inoffensive. Many of the ways to make oneself lovable are the same as those used to make oneself successful, "to win friends and influence people." As a matter of fact, what most people in our culture mean by being lovable is essentially a mixture between being popular and having sex appeal.

A second premise behind the attitude that there is nothing to be learned about love is the assumption that the problem of love is the problem of an *object*, not the problem of a *faculty*. People think that to *love* is simple, but that to find the right object to love — or to be loved by — is difficult. This attitude has several reasons rooted in the development of modern society. One reason is the great change which occurred in the twentieth century with respect to the choice of a "love object." In the Victorian age, as in many traditional cultures, love was mostly not a spontaneous personal experience which then might lead to marriage. On the contrary, marriage was contracted by convention — either by the respective families, or by a marriage broker, or without the help of such intermediaries; it was concluded on the basis of social considerations, and love was supposed to develop once the marriage had been concluded. In the last few generations the concept of romantic love has become almost universal in the Western world. In the United States, while considerations of a conventional nature are not entirely absent, to a vast extent people are in search of "romantic love," of the personal experience of love which then should lead to marriage. This new concept of freedom in love must have greatly enhanced the importance of the *object* as against the importance of the *function*.

Closely related to this factor is another feature characteristic of contemporary culture. Our whole culture is based on the appetite for buying, on the idea of a mutually favorable exchange. Modern man's happiness consists in the thrill of looking at the shop windows, and in buying all that he can afford to buy, either for cash or on installments. He (or she) looks at people in a similar way. For the man an attractive girl — and for the woman an attractive man — are the prizes they are after. "Attractive" usually means a nice package of qualities which are popular and sought after on the personality market. What specifically makes a person attractive depends on the fashion of the time, physically as well as mentally. During the twenties, a drinking and smoking girl, tough and sexy, was attractive; today the fashion demands more domesticity and coyness. At the end of the nineteenth and the beginning of this century, a man had to be aggressive and ambitious — today he has to be social and tolerant — in order to be an attractive "package." At any rate, the sense of falling in love develops usually only with regard to such human commodities as are within reach of one's own possibilities for exchange. I am out for a bargain; the object should be desirable from the standpoint of its social value, and at the same time should want me, considering my overt and hidden assets and potentialities. Two persons thus fall in love when they feel they have found the best object available on the market, considering the limitations of their own exchange values. Often, as in buying real estate, the hidden potentialities which can be developed play a considerable role in this bargain. In a culture in which the marketing orientation prevails, and in which material success is the outstanding value, there is little reason to be surprised that human love relations follow the same pattern of exchange which governs the commodity and the labor market.

The third error leading to the assumption that there is nothing to be learned about love lies in the confusion between the initial experience of *"falling"* in love, and the permanent state of *being* in love, or as we might better say, of "standing" in love. If two people who have been strangers, as all of us are, suddenly let the wall between them break down, and feel close, feel one, this moment of oneness is one of the most exhilarating, most exciting experiences in life. It is all the more wonderful and miraculous for persons who have been shut off, isolated, without love. This miracle of sudden intimacy is often facilitated if it is combined with, or initiated by, sexual attraction and consummation. However, this type of love is by its very nature not lasting. The two persons become well acquainted, their intimacy loses more and more its miraculous character, until their antagonism, their disappointments, their mutual boredom kill whatever is left of the initial excitement. Yet, in the beginning they do not know all this: in fact, they take the intensity of the infatuation, this being "crazy" about each other, for proof of the intensity of their love, while it may only prove the degree of their preceding loneliness.

This attitude — that nothing is easier than to love — has continued to be the prevalent idea about love in spite of the overwhelming evidence to the contrary. There is hardly any activity, any enterprise, which is started with such tremendous hopes and expectations, and yet, which fails so regularly, as love. If this were the case with any other activity, people would be eager to know the reasons for the failure, and to learn how one could do better — or they would give up the activity. Since the latter is impossible in the case of love, there seems to be only one adequate way to overcome the failure of love — to examine the reasons for this failure, and to proceed to study the meaning of love.

The first step to take is to become aware that *love is an art*, just as living is an art; if we want to learn how to love we must proceed in the same way we have to proceed if we want to learn any other art, say music, painting, carpentry, or the art of medicine or engineering.

What are the necessary steps in learning any art?

The process of learning an art can be divided conveniently into two parts: one, the mastery of the theory; the other, the mastery of the practice. If I want to learn the art of medicine, I must first know the facts about the human body, and about various diseases. When I have all this theoretical knowledge, I am by no means competent in the art of medicine. I shall become a master in this art only after a great deal of practice, until eventually the results of my theoretical knowledge and the results of my practice are blended into one — my intuition, the essence of the mastery of any art. But, aside from learning the theory and practice, there is a third factor necessary to becoming a master in any art — the mastery of the art must be a matter of ultimate concern; there must be nothing else in the world more important than the art. This holds true for music, for medicine, for carpentry — and for love. And, maybe, here lies the answer to the question of why people in our culture try so rarely to learn this art, in spite of their obvious failures: in spite of the deep-seated craving for love, almost everything else is considered to be more important than love: success, prestige, money, power — almost all our energy is used for the learning of how to achieve these aims, and almost none to learn the art of loving.

Could it be that only those things are considered worthy of being learned with which one can earn money or prestige, and that love, which "only" profits the soul, but is profitless in the modern sense, is a luxury we have no right to spend much energy on? However this may be, the following discussion will treat the art of loving in the sense of the foregoing divisions: first I shall discuss the theory of love — and this will comprise the greater part of the book; and secondly I shall discuss the practice of love — little as can be *said* about practice in this, as in any other field.

J. B. S. Haldane

On Being the Right Size

The most obvious differences between different animals are differences of size, but for some reason the zoologists have paid singularly little attention to them. In a large textbook of zoology before me I find no indication that the eagle is larger than the sparrow, or the hippopotamus bigger than the hare, though some grudging admissions are made in the case of the mouse and the whale. But yet it is easy to show that a hare could not be as large as a hippopotamus, or a whale as small as a herring. For every type of animal there is a most convenient size, and a large change in size inevitably carries with it a change of form.

Let us take the most obvious of possible cases, and consider a giant man sixty feet high — about the height of Giant Pope and Giant Pagan in the illustrated *Pilgrim's Progress* of my childhood. These monsters were not only ten times as high as Christian, but ten times as wide and ten times as thick, so that their total weight was a thousand times his, or about eighty to ninety tons. Unfortunately the cross sections of their bones were only a hundred times those of Christian, so that every square inch of giant bone had to support ten times the weight borne by a square inch of human bone. As the human thigh-bone breaks under about ten times the human weight, Pope and Pagan would have broken their thighs every time they took a step. This was doubtless why they were sitting down in the picture I remember. But it lessens one's respect for Christian and Jack the Giant Killer.

To turn to zoology, suppose that a gazelle, a graceful little creature with long thin legs, is to become large; it will break its bones unless it does one of two things. It may make its legs short and thick, like the rhinoceros, so that every pound of weight has still about the same area of bone to support it. Or it can compress its body and stretch out its legs obliquely to gain stability, like the giraffe. I mention these two beasts because they happen to belong to the same order as the gazelle, and both are quite successful mechanically, being remarkably fast runners.

Gravity, a mere nuisance to Christian, was a terror to Pope, Pagan, and Despair. To the mouse and any smaller animal it presents practically no dangers. You can drop a mouse down a thousand-yard mine shaft; and, on arriving at the bottom, it gets a slight shock and walks away, provided that the ground is fairly soft. A rat is killed, a man is broken, a horse splashes. For the resistance presented to movement by the air is proportional to the surface of the moving object. Divide an animal's length, breadth, and height each by ten; its weight is reduced to a thousandth, but its surface only to a hundredth. So the resistance to falling in the case of the small animal is relatively ten times greater than the driving force.

An insect, therefore, is not afraid of gravity; it can fall without danger, and can cling to the ceiling with remarkably little trouble. It can go in for elegant and fantastic forms of support like that of the daddy-long-legs. But there is a force which is as formidable to an insect as gravitation to a mammal. This is surface tension. A man coming out of a bath carries with him a film of water of about one-fiftieth of an inch in thickness. This weighs roughly a pound. A wet mouse has to carry about its own weight of water. A wet fly has to lift many times its own weight and, as every one knows, a fly once wetted by water or any other liquid is in a very serious position indeed. An insect going for a drink is in as great danger as a man leaning out over a precipice in search of food. If it once falls into the grip of the surface tension of the water — that is to say, gets wet — it is likely to remain so until it drowns. A few insects, such as water-beetles, contrive to be unwettable; the majority keep well away from their drink by means of a long proboscis.

Of course tall land animals have other difficulties. They have to pump their blood to greater heights than a man and, therefore, require a larger blood pressure and tougher blood-vessels. A great many men die from burst arteries, especially in the brain, and this danger is presumably still greater for an elephant or a giraffe. But animals of all kinds find difficulties in size for the following reason. A typical small animal, say a microscopic worm or rotifer, has a smooth skin through which all the oxygen it requires can soak in, a straight gut with sufficient surface to absorb its food, and a simple kidney. Increase its dimensions tenfold in every direction, and its weight is increased a thousand times, so that if it is to use its muscles as efficiently as its miniature counterpart, it will need a thousand times as much food and oxygen per day and will excrete a thousand times as much of waste products.

Now if its shape is unaltered its surface will be increased only a hundredfold, and ten times as much oxygen must enter per minute through each square millimetre of skin, ten times as much food through each square millimetre of intestine. When a limit is reached to their absorptive powers their surface has to be increased by some special device. For example, a part of the skin may be drawn out into tufts to make gills or pushed in to make lungs, thus increasing the oxygen-absorbing surface in proportion to the animal's bulk. A man, for example, has a hundred square yards of lung. Similarly, the gut, instead of being smooth and straight, becomes coiled and develops a velvety surface, and other organs increase in complication. The higher animals are not larger than the lower because they are more complicated. They are more complicated because they are larger. Just the same is true of plants. The simplest plants, such as the green algae growing in stagnant water or on the bark of trees, are mere round cells. The higher plants increase their surface by putting out leaves and roots. Comparative anatomy is largely the story of the struggle to increase surface in proportion to volume.

Some of the methods of increasing the surface are useful up to a point, but not capable of a very wide adaptation. For example, while vertebrates carry the oxygen from the gills or lungs all over the body in the blood, insects take air directly to every part of their body by tiny blind tubes called tracheae which open to the surface at many different points. Now, although by their breathing movements they can renew the air in the outer part of the tracheal system, the oxygen has to penetrate the finer branches by means of diffusion. Gases can diffuse easily through very small distances, not many times larger than the average length travelled by a gas molecule between collisions with other molecules. But when such vast journeys — from the point of view of a molecule — as a quarter of an inch have to be made, the process becomes slow. So the portions of an insect's body more than a quarter of an inch from the air would always be short of oxygen. In consequence hardly any insects are much more than half an inch thick. Land crabs are built on the same general plan as insects, but are much clumsier. Yet like ourselves they carry oxygen around in their blood, and are therefore able to grow far larger than any insects. If the insects had hit on a plan for driving air through their tissues instead of letting it soak in, they might well have become as large as lobsters, though other considerations would have prevented them from becoming as large as man.

Exactly the same difficulties attach to flying. It is an elementary principle of aeronautics that the minimum speed needed to keep an aeroplane of a given shape in the air varies as the square root of its length. If its linear dimensions are increased four times, it must fly twice as fast. Now the power needed for the minimum speed increases more rapidly than the weight of the machine. So the larger aeroplane which weighs sixty-four times as much as the smaller, needs one hundred and twenty-eight times its horsepower to keep up. Applying the same principles to the birds, we find that the limit to their size is soon reached. An angel whose muscles developed no more power weight for weight than those of an eagle or a pigeon would require a breast projecting for about four feet to house the muscles engaged in working its wings, while to economize in weight, its legs would have to be reduced to mere stilts. Actually a large bird such as an eagle or kite does not keep in the air mainly by moving its wings. It is generally to be seen soaring, that is to say balanced on a rising column of air. And even soaring becomes more and more difficult with increasing size. Were this not the case eagles might be as large as tigers and as formidable to man as hostile aeroplanes.

But it is time that we passed to some of the advantages of size. One of the most obvious is that it enables one to keep warm. All warm-blooded animals at rest lose the same amount of heat from a unit area of skin, for which purpose they need a food-supply proportional to their surface and not to their weight. Five thousand mice weigh as much as a man. Their combined surface and food or oxygen consumption are about seventeen times a man's. In fact a mouse eats about one quarter its own weight of food every day, which is mainly used in keeping it warm. For the same reason small animals cannot live in cold countries. In the arctic regions there are no reptiles or amphibians, and no small mammals. The smallest mammal in Spitzbergen is the fox. The small birds fly away in the winter, while the insects die, though their eggs can survive six months or more of frost. The most successful mammals are bears, seals, and walruses.

Similarly, the eye is a rather inefficient organ until it reaches a large size. The back of the human eye on which an image of the outside world is thrown, and which corresponds to the film of a camera, is composed of a mosaic of 'rods and cones' whose diameter is little more than a length of an average light wave. Each eye has about half a million, and for two objects to be distinguishable their images must fall on separate rods or cones. It is obvious that with fewer but larger rods and cones we should see less distinctly. If they were twice as broad two points would have to be twice as far apart before we could distinguish them at a given distance. But if their size were diminished and their number increased we should see no better. For it is impossible to form a definite image smaller than a wave-length of light. Hence a mouse's eye is not a small-scale model of a human eye. Its rods and cones are not much smaller than ours, and therefore there are far fewer of them. A mouse could not distinguish one human face from another six feet away. In order that they should be of any use at all the eyes of small animals have to be much larger in proportion to their bodies than our own. Large animals on the other hand only require relatively small eyes, and those of the whale and elephant are little larger than our own.

For rather more recondite reasons the same general principle holds true of the brain. If we compare the brain-weights of a set of very similar animals such as the cat, cheetah, leopard, and tiger, we find that as we quadruple the body-weight the brain-weight is only doubled. The larger animal with proportionately larger bones can economize on brain, eyes, and certain other organs.

Such are a very few of the considerations which show that for every type of animal there is an optimum size. Yet athough Galileo demonstrated the contrary more than three hundred years ago, people still believe that if a flea were as large as a man it could jump a thousand feet into the air. As a matter of fact the height to which an animal can jump is more nearly independent of its size than proportional to it. A flea can jump about two feet, a man about five. To jump a given height, if we neglect the resistance of the air, requires an expenditure of energy proportional to the jumper's weight. But if the jumping muscles form a constant fraction of the animal's body, the energy developed per ounce of muscle is independent of the size, provided it can be developed quickly enough in the small animal. As a matter of fact an insect's muscles, although they can contract more quickly than our own, appear to be less efficient; as otherwise a flea or grasshopper could rise six feet into the air.

And just as there is a best size for every animal, so the same is true for every human institution. In the Greek type of democracy all the citizens could listen to a series of orators and vote directly on questions of legislation. Hence their philosophers held that a small city was the largest possible democratic state. The English invention of representative government made a democratic nation possible, and the possibility was first realized in the United States, and later elsewhere. With the development of broadcasting it has once more become possible for every citizen to listen to the political views of representative orators, and the future may perhaps see the return of the national state to the Greek form of democracy. Even the referendum has been made possible only by the institution of daily newspapers.

To the biologist the problem of socialism appears largely as a problem of size. The extreme socialists desire to run every nation as a single business concern. I do not suppose that Henry Ford would find much difficulty in running Andorra or Luxembourg on a socialistic basis. He has already more men on his pay-roll than their population. It is conceivable that a syndicate of Fords, if we could find them, would make Belgium Ltd. or Denmark Inc. pay their way. But while nationalization of certain industries is an obvious possibility in the largest of states, I find it no easier to picture a completely socialized British Empire or United States than an elephant turning somersaults or a hippopotamus jumping a hedge.

Susan Hepler

_____

Secret Places

They always find my secret places and ruin them. Secret places are never allowed to pass quietly away, either, but must be drawn and quartered, mutilated beyond recognition before they are allowed to die as best they can. My first secret place died like that. It was a stand of virgin oak and maple across the street from my house that enchanted all my childhood tomorrows. I had a kitten's ransom in marbles and grey 1943 pennies buried in there beneath the fourth tree off the school path. I had sole ownership of a hepatica patch that came up faithfully for me every Mayday. I also had two flimsy stick huts roofed by vines of curling green leaves that hung limp in the hot summer sun or chattered apprehensively under the severe fall sky. One summer when I was old enough to care, giant cranes and bull-dozers plowed up my pink-flowered playground and replaced it with brick and glass and prying eyes. There's some justice, though. Over my dead hepatica patch stands a Creative Arts Room.

One of the best secret places I had was a leaf-lined ledge overlooking the city millpond. I could ride my bicycle down near the algae-covered water and from there climb twenty feet to the ledge. In the spring, ducklings paraded beneath my ledge in fuzzy yellow aquacades, sending the tiny bits of green algae and my imagination swirling into fanciful patterns of shimmering light. All down the steep embankment violets grew together in opulent purple gangs. To the sonorous accompaniment of the Bullfrog Chorus I could lean back and watch the clouds amble by chased by dragonflies and redwing blackbirds. The last time I was home, though, there was talk of draining the millpond to build a shopping center.

When I went to college, I just happened to discover a secret place. Out walking one day I came upon the beginning construction of a maintenance building and alongside the excavation were seven large lovely drainpipes. Some were faced the wrong way so if I sat in them, I could still see the parking lots. But when I sat in the third one, all I could see were the trees and the grass and cottony clouds that the sparrows seemed intent upon lacing together. The third drainpipe and I became good friends as we studied together. And when my mind wandered from rock structures and the War of the Roses, I'd tell him my troubles and he'd listen but sometimes not very courteously. If I got overly emotional, he'd start to roll. I learned from him that one doesn't take advantage of the good nature of his friends. Anyhow, as all friendships must, this one came abruptly to an end when they buried my friend and his six brothers side by side. I don't go walking much in that field anymore. I hate the feeling of walking on someone.

My highway interchange died that way too. It was long and smooth and the silver cement sparkled and gleamed as it soared out over a field of brown-green brush. They hadn't opened the interchange yet, but on Saturdays the workmen stopped at noon so I had the whole highway to myself. (And if occasionally I had to share it with an excursion of two or three dogs sent by the neighborhood to map out the territory, I didn't really mind.) I endured the pedaling up the steep cloverleaf turns because I knew that eventually I'd get to come down. I chugged ever so slowly up the grade to where the real road began and then relaxed my feet to fly out over the concrete. Nothing mattered but the wind in my hair and the smoky smell of fall. The shining road was so perfect, so clean that it somehow didn't seem sacrilegious for the workman to have hewn a path so rudely through the middle of the fall-colored field. But they opened it last spring, and now growling Mack trucks with "No Riders" signs on their windshields downshift where I used to soar and sing.

I've still got my woodlot, though. I discovered it last spring and I know where the best leaning-and-thinking tree is and where the best spot is to watch the ducks arrive in time for the premiere of spring. Blindfolded I can slip straight to the lightning-struck tree with the squeaky bouncing branches. They'll take this one away from me slowly. . . . but they'll take it away. Last fall my swinging vine was torn down and they plowed a path through my trillium bed. And there's an impudent chain of fat rusty links hanging between two impersonal white posts to block my path into the woodlot.

I don't really regret it, though, because once you get to know a place, it's time to push on. So, I'll find another secret place. I always do.

_____

Excerpt from *Lady Sings the Blues*

I've been told that nobody sings the word "hunger" like I do. Or the word "love."

Maybe I remember what those words are all about. Maybe I'm proud enough to *want* to remember Baltimore and Welfare Island, the Catholic institution and the Jefferson Market Court, the sheriff in front of our place in Harlem and the towns from coast to coast where I got my lumps and my scars, Philly and Alderson, Hollywood and San Francisco — every damn bit of it.

All the Cadillacs and minks in the world — and I've had a few — can't make it up or make me forget it. All I've learned in all those places from all those people is wrapped up in those two words. You've got to have something to eat and a little love in your life before you can hold still for any damn body's sermon on how to behave.

Everything I am and everything I want out of life goes smack back to that.

Look at my big dream! It's always been to have a big place of my own out in the country someplace where I could take care of stray dogs and orphan kids, kids that didn't ask to be born; kids that didn't ask to be black, blue, or green or something in between.

I'd only want to be sure of one thing — that nobody in the world wanted these kids. Then I would take them. They'd have to be illegit, no mama, no papa.

I'd have room for twenty-five or thirty, with three or four big buxom women just like my mom to take care of them, feed them, see to it the little bastards go to school; knock them in the head when they're wrong, but love them whether they're good or bad.

We'd have a crazy big kitchen with a chartreuse stove and a refrigerator to match, and I'd supervise the cooking and baking. We might have a doctor and a nurse and a couple of tutors. But I'd always be around to teach them my kind of teaching — not the kind that tells them how to spell Mississippi, but how to be glad to be who you are and what you are.

When they grow up enough to go out and do babysitting and take little jobs or start on their own, away they'd go. And then there would always be more.

Grownups can make it some kind of way. They might have a little more or a little less to eat than the next guy — a little more or a little less love, and it isn't fatal.

But kids? Take me, I didn't ask Clarence Holiday and Sadie Fagan to get together in that Baltimore hallway and have me and then have to leave me to get pushed around and hassle with life on my own. Sure, my old lady took care of me the best she could and she was the greatest. But she was only a kid herself. Her hassle was worse than mine. She was just a young kid trying to raise a young kid.

Anyway, that's my dream and there is another dream too.

All my life I've wanted my own club. A small place where I can walk in, have my own piano, drums, and a swinging guitar. I'd want it to be crowded if there were one hundred and twenty-five people there — that's how intimate I want it.

I've fought all my life to be able to sing what I wanted the way I wanted to sing it. Before I die I want a place of my own where nobody can tell me *when* to go on. I might go on at nine, or four in the morning; I might sing forty-nine songs or one song. I might even get up and stop the band in the middle of a number and sing something I felt like singing.

But it would be a place where my friends could come and really relax and enjoy themselves — sleep if they wanted to sleep, and eat if they wanted to eat.

And I'd run that kitchen myself. I might not actually cook everything, but I'd oversee it and taste it and see that it's my kind of cooking and that it's straight. I used to laugh when Mom talked about having her own place, but look at me now.

I could have had a dozen clubs in my time, but I'd always have been fronting for something else. Even today there are promoters willing to get behind a club of mine. But I wouldn't take somebody else's money even if they were fool enough to give it me. I'd always be scared someone would come in and plant some stuff in my place, have me raided and busted.

Besides, it would have to be proven to me that it was mine, all mine, before the law would let me sing in it. And I would have to know it was mine before I could sing in it anyway.

Although people sometimes act like they think so, a singer is not like a saxophone. If you don't sound right, you can't go out and get some new reeds, split them just right. A singer is only a voice and a voice is completely dependent on the body God gave you. When you walk out there and open your mouth, you never know what's going to happen.

I'm not supposed to get a toothache, I'm not supposed to get nervous; I can't throw up or get sick to my stomach; I'm not supposed to get the flu or have a sore throat. I'm supposed to go out there and look pretty and sing good and smile and I'd just better.

Why? Because I'm Billie Holiday and I've been in trouble.

Louis and I have made plenty of miles together, by train, plane, every kind of way. But I'll never forget one night when we were coming in by plane from the Coast.

When we took our seats in this big fancy air liner I knew the man next to me was going to cause a scene. I could just smell him. He started fidgeting and peeking and staring at me and Louis. He made it perfectly clear he wished he'd taken the train where he wouldn't have had to sit next to no damn Negroes.

I didn't pay any attention. This has happened to me too many times. But it bothered Louis.

We hadn't been out thirty minutes, when one of the engines caught fire. Before long the whole wing was blazing and everybody thought we'd had it.

You should have seen this dicty neighbour of ours. He got religion in a hurry. He wanted to hold Louis' hand. He wanted to be nice. He even wanted to say he hadn't meant to be nasty, he was sorry and couldn't we all pray together?

Louis had been a preacher when he was fifteen and he was ready to go along. I flipped.

"This man didn't even want to sit next to me until he thought he was going to die," I told Louis.

"You die in your seat, mister," I told him, "and we'll die in ours."

We rode out the fire someway and made the airport.

When we got on the ground, the man was so ashamed of himself he cut right on by Louis without even speaking.

"Mr. McKay," I told him, "you've had your lesson today. Some people is and some people ain't, and this man ain't."

That's the way I've found it, and that's still the way it is.

James Simon Kunen

Excerpt from *The Strawberry Statement*

INTRO 1
ABOUT THE BOOK

My question is a simple one; who am I to write a book? I don't know. I'm just writing it. You're just reading it. Let's not worry about it.

INTRO 2
WHO WROTE THE BOOK

I wrote the Book.

I should like to point out immediately that just because I happened to be born in 1948, it doesn't mean that what I have to say as a nineteen-year-old is worth any more than what nineteen-year-olds had to say in, to pick a year at random, 1920. To say that youth is what's happening is absurd. It's always been happening. Everyone is nineteen, only at different times. This youth-cult scene is a disservice to everyone. I'm anticipating a severe psychological set-back when I turn twenty, and I don't know what I'm going to do when my youth-fare card runs out. As for this "don't-trust-anyone-over-30" shit, I agree in principle, but I think they ought to drop the zero.

What sort of man gets busted at Columbia? I don't know. I got busted at Columbia and I, for one, strongly support trees (and, in the larger sense, forests), flowers, mountains and hills, also valleys, the ocean, wiliness (when used for good), good, little children, people, tremendous record-setting snowstorms, hurricanes, swimming underwater, nice policemen, unicorns, extra-inning ball games up to twelve innings, pneumatic jackhammers (when they're not too close), the dunes in North Truro on Cape Cod, liberalized abortion laws, and Raggedy Ann dolls, among other things.

I do not like Texas, people who go to the zoo to be arty, the Defense Department, the name "Defense Department," the fly buzzing around me as I write this, protective tariffs, little snowstorms that turn to slush, the short days of winter, extra-inning ball games over twelve innings, calling people consumers, pneumatic jackhammers immediately next to the window, and G.I. Joe dolls. Also racism, poverty and war. The latter three I'm trying to do something about.

But I am not a nihilist. I do like some things.

I should add that I have never been able to stand at a high place without thinking about jumping off.

INTRO 3
WHO WE ARE

People want to know who we are, and some think they know who we are. Some think we're a bunch of snot-nosed brats. It's difficult to say really who we are. We don't have snots on our noses. What we do have is hopes and fears, or ups and downs, as they are called.

A lot of the time we are very unhappy, and we try to cheer ourselves up by thinking. We think how lucky we are to be able to go to school, to have nice clothes and fine things and to eat well and have money and be healthy. How lucky we are really. But we remain unhappy. Then we attack ourselves for self-pity, and become more unhappy, and still more unhappy over being sad.

We're unhappy because of the war, and because of poverty and the hopelessness of politics, but also because we sometimes get put down by girls or boys, as the case may be, or feel lonely and alone and lost.

And who we are is people in New York City.

New York is the most exciting city in the world, and also the cruddiest place to be that I can conceive of. The city, where when you see someone on the subway you know you will never see him again. The city, where the streets are dead with the movement of people brushing by, like silt in a now-dry riverbed, stirred by the rush of a dirty wind. The city, where you walk along on the hard floor of a giant maze with walls much taller than people and full of them. The city is an island and feels that way; not enough room, very separate. You have to walk on right-angle routes, can't see where you're going to, only where you are, can only see a narrow part of sky, and never any stars. It's a giant maze you have to fight through, like a rat, but unlike the rat you have no reward awaiting you at the end. There is no end, and you don't know what you're supposed to be looking for.

And unlike the rat, you are not alone. You are instead lonely. There is loneliness as can exist only in the midst of numbers and numbers of people who don't know you, who don't care about you, who won't let you care about them.

Everywhere you walk you hear a click-clack. The click-clack of your walking never leaves you, reminding you all the time that you are at the bottom of a box. The earth is trapped beneath concrete and tar and you are locked away from it. Nothing grows.

All of this makes us sad. And all of this is at Columbia, is Columbia, for Columbia is New York. Leaving the school or its city really doesn't help. Once you live in New York you are locked in the city, and the city is locked in you.

On the beach or in the woods the click-clack follows you, and you carry pavement beneath your feet. The walls are all around, for you have lived with people and away from them. You know the story on the world; you see how far people are. And you feel quite sad.

But sadness is not despair so long as you can get angry. And we have become angry at Columbia. Not having despaired, we are able to see things that need to be fought, and we fight. We have fought, we are fighting, we will fight.

INTRO 4
HOW THE BOOK WAS WRITTEN

Writing a book is a lot like having a baby; they both involve bringing something into the world that wasn't there before, and they're both a pain in the ass.

This book was written on napkins and cigarette packs and hitchhiking signs. It was spread all over, but so is my mind. I exhibit a marked tendency to forget things. I can remember only three things at a time. If I think of a fourth thing, I forget the first. Like a cigarette machine. You take one pack out — all the rest fall down a notch. Exactly analogous in every salient detail.

The best, truest way to read this book would be to rip it up and throw the scraps all over the house. Then, later, should you come across a piece, read it, or don't read it, depending upon how you feel. Or, better, save it until four o'clock in the morning when you would rather do almost anything else, and read it then. Above all, don't spend too much time reading it because I didn't spend much time writing it.

You will notice that a great deal of this book simply relates little things I've done and thought. It may seem completely irrelevant to Columbia. That's the way it goes.

Carnival

Dusk falls, and with it, the deepening dark settles over the usually silent countryside. But in one commonly peaceful straw-colored field laced with quiet asphalt paths, the flickering kaleidoscope of the carnival sizzles against the richening sky. The noise of the carnival draws and builds to a billowing blare of a thousand metal megaphones blasting their asynchronous throb into the moving air, the clatter of feet and the turnstiles with their flashing chromium posts counting the human noises into dollars and cents.

Colors flash in multiple exposures of green and red and blue and yellow in erratic motion on countless retinas of glinting mirror eyes. Multicolored beasts with screaming prey in their metal maws wrench themselves in demented patterns to shake their neon tethers off so they may hurl themselves into the blackness. Insane jointed monsters yank their angularity over slippery metal rails in smooth curves, buckling and jerking to fit.

Cotton candy leaves its pink stickiness in globs about the concession stands, making the thick air heavy with the scent. Chalky white popcorn and syrupy carmelcorn crunch and stick in flashing white teeth reflecting green and blue neon in twisted tubes. The jagged asphalt dances with multicolored light and flickering black shadow as the jagged teeth of the human machine grind back and forth in uneven rows at erratic speeds. And between the teeth, laughter spits in controlled uneasiness and uncontrolled exhilaration.

But the carnival is a fifty-foot world, and even that only with self-imposed mental blinders. This unreal world will not hold up to examination. The carnival is paced to rush by the shabbiness and flimsiness without a second, or long first, look.

The flashing lights in rows which depict astrological signs are only common lightbulbs, covered with layers of dust and grime, hung on a taped black vine of wire. The swirling pinwheels are illusions made of many neon-filled tubes, with dirt and dead insects, burned to brittle stillness, at the lower end of each, fastened to rotating metal wheels lubricated with heavy black grease. And as the wheels rotate, and the chairs with their dents and peeling paint swivel and tilt, the sediment in the colored tubes slides and sifts.

The music, whose original sequences are distorted and mocked by the metal-mouthed speaker system, originates from a dirty turntable and a warped and fingerprinted shellac disc, dull black in color, hidden under the dark and patched side of brightly painted canvas, among trampled straw and fieldmouse burrows. The music bounces off sweaty foreheads glistening in the din of swirling light, off painted tin and moulded papier-mache heads with chicken-wire skulls etched with rust.

Grimy hands, connected to grizzled, anonymous faces, transfer warm coins and cardboard tickets, pull worn levers, and wait, feeling the scratchy damp of the dirty coveralls and smelling the mingled grease and sweat, for the monotony of the screams and laughter to end. Arms and legs and teeth flicker past the grey stubble faces with dead eyes, the faintly warm static elements in a whirling fantasy world in chipped red and yellow paint.

And the groaning mechanisms, whose endless wear is lost in the metallic human noises: the creaking of soft metal bearings oozing their black blood, and the regular, friction sounds of the recirculating chain drives are drowned by the clatter of laughter like shattering glass.

The sweetness of the cotton candy is packed into the blackness of oily metal drums on the unpainted side of the concession stands. Wet stains are splattered across the aprons of the hardened women in the stands: ketchup and thick cola syrup and stickypink cotton candy strands. The damp faces and underarms and smeared lipstick.

Who are they? the bristling spines of a cactus carpet with reflecting eyes and sweaty hands. Are they people? these flashing torsos doubling and clutching in the neon heat. Why are they here? among the grinding mechanisms and hoarse-voiced barkers. Who do they laugh at? Why do they scream? Why do they cling to the roller coaster bars and the candy apples and each other?

Why?

Because it is the carnival. Because it is a chance to fool yourself without really taking the chance of being fooled. Because it is a chance to laugh without a real reason and go unquestioned. Because it is a chance to fear, without the anxiety of real fear.

The carnival is a simple fantasy to some of them. It is an unreal land of Oz where the fantasy is false but touchable. It is a walk-in dream, without the ordeal of falling asleep. The tastes and smells are all fantasy, and the pity for the worn face at the lever of the breathless ride is no more real than the laughter following.

It is exhilaration for some of them, though first they must believe in the reality of the fantasy, believe in the false dangers and forget the real fears. These flashing teeth grin out of a sweat-beaded face with hair flowing in the wind and laugh at the possibility of catastrophe, carefully imagined and vividly depicted in the fantasy now in the mind. Here is the fear one can see and face reflected in these eyes, these same eyes that will stare, wide and trembling, out of a body in cold sweat at night, safe in bed, as they behold the real dangers somewhere in the sifting vagueness of the mind.

But for most, it is more than this. It is the temporary answer to the constant fear of the unknown and of the known. It is an escape from fear by creating fear, calculated fear, and calculated laughter. It is experiencing a known experience, being picked up by a brightly painted mechanism and carried swiftly through angular patterns and seeing the ground far enough below for justification of fear and being set down afterward and feeling the exhilaration of meeting fear, if falsely. What seems to be fear is really security. It is the manifestation of a child's, an adult's, fantasies, where the self is omnipotent and invulnerable. Dangerous situations are imagined for excitement, but the outcome is never in doubt, so the emotions can explode with no fear of the unexpected. It is the ability, if only for a few hours, to control life completely and be fearless master over pseudo-frightening situations. The carnival is what every person who knows the uncertainty and aimlessness of reality needs: a self-controlled nightmare.

Donald Lori

The Home of America

If you leave the steel and glass shopping center that forms the heart of
Ridgefield and drive north on the patched concrete of Route 35, you seem
to travel down the maple-lined corridors of time, following the history of
New England in the half-hidden homes amidst the trees that fence the
road. First you pass the sporadic clusters of over-mortgaged split levels
which spring up overnight like tasteless pastel mushrooms, rows of
identical prefabricated toadstools that are occupied only in the evenings
when the diurnal migrations from Madison Avenue and the local schools
turn Connecticut into the world's only landscaped bedroom. Next, the
highway winds among the more conservative neo-colonials and two-story
Cape Cods built during the nineteen twenties and early thirties, and preferred by the middle-class natives who attend DAR meetings and run
the stores in town. Then, where the road forks at the old cemetery, the
shuttered baronial mansions of the eighteen-hundreds begin to appear
and stare haughtily at you with blank windows from the exact, geo-
metrical center of their acres of man-high azaleas; the occasional bit of
stained glass is as pretentious as the monocles of the long-dead merchants
and rum-runners who built these Victorian Gothic palaces from orange
brick and whitewash. Now they're occupied by the retired Cadillac
owners of our local upper class — the aristocratic descendants of all those
people who came over on that phenomenally spacious Mayflower and
have lived in Fairfield County ever since.

Finally, your car leaves all the traces of modern man behind. The
macadammed side roads give way to rutted, weed-paved dirt trails, and
the TV antennas on chimneys become wild grape vines, clinging with
their surprisingly strong maze of tentacles and tendrils to the sagging
shingle and cedar-shake roofs of abandoned barns. The houses out here
are pre-revolutionary farms, their weathered grey siding innocent of the

artificial paints of Twentieth-Century civilization and their austere interiors spared the reforming efforts of interior decorators or antique-happy housewives.

I took such a drive once, and because I was intrigued by this progression of architectures, I went past my usual turn-off toward home. A few bends in the road later, I discovered it. I never knew it was there before, hidden in its clump of dying elms a little distance back from the two-lane state highway. I parked the car to study it better — and I haven't felt the same since.

There was really nothing remarkable about the old house, squatting forlornly in its ghostly patch of moonlight. I pushed my way through the beer-can littered sea of dry autumn grass surrounding it to the wide, railing-free porch that ran along three sides. From the crumbling stone pillars of what once had been a gate, it looked like an immense two-story shoe box of unfinished pine boards, but as I approached the rotted remains of the well house beside the slate steps, its size seemed more modest, less exaggerated — perhaps because the paneless windows were so small, or because the afterthoughts of collapsing utility sheds clustered along the sides and back walls broke up its monolithic appearance. I crossed the worm-eaten flooring of the porch carefully to the massive, split-log door and walked into a different, spectral world.

The rooms were tiny, almost cozy, beneath two centuries of undisturbed dust — but I could almost see the hand-hewn furniture that once filled them, resting on the scrubbed and polished oak floor which now was pitted by the gaping entrances that time and gravity had improvised to the root cellar. There would have been a rag rug (not stainless Acrilan, and certainly not wall to wall) in front of the blazing granite hearth that now supported my weight and kept me from joining the field mice scurrying furtively through the basement. A teenaged girl would have sat in a corner of the front parlor and spun wool or darned clothes — and the only music she would have listened to was the symphony of birds in the meadows outside.

Her mother would be making candles in a chromeless kitchen, or putting up preserves to fill the floor-to-wood-beamed-ceiling shelves that covered one wall in lieu of an installment-plan freezer. She'd be more worried about dinner than the PTA or why her husband was working late at the office. I made my way there, but the only monument to her non-push-button life was the grimy pile of kindling that once held her jars — and a cloudy sliver of museum glass thrust up through it. The once spotless counter beside the back door sloped to the floor like a ski run; the numerous sitz marks from a paring knife showed a brown spider the easiest trail up the hill. He'd used it many times before, because the silk-shrouded boulders of former meals lined the way.

The stairway had long since fed the termites, so I couldn't go upstairs.

Maybe it was just as well, for the sparse decorations, the down mattresses, cotton curtains, and hand-hewn wall mottoes would all have lined rats' nests for decades. I might have stacked the rubbish in the hall high enough to grab the second floor landing, but somehow it seemed like sacrilege to explore those haunted Puritan bedrooms with a flashlight; the back of my neck told me there was a chance I'd meet with an outraged and ectoplasmic grandparent who'd quote Calvin in a voice like noiseless thunder at the agnostic intruder from a Godless age.

In the front room again, I leaned gingerly against the loose frame of a window that undoubtedly had held waxed, yellow paper (instead of the fabulously expensive luxurious plate glass of the early 1700's) and let warm golden sunlight into a room white with plaster walls. The plaster was patches and dust now, and rain poured in the perpetually open sashes as often as the sun: "Sic transit, gloria mundi."

Outside, my mind superimposed a spring scene on the silent, shriveled stalks of goldenrod. A small army of barefoot kids were running across the dried-mud drive and green lawn, closely cropped by a nondescript herd of sheep and goats, hunting squirrels with stick rifles instead of plastic bazookas that fire nuclear-cap shells, and feeling between their toes the remote ancestors of those same dandelions I'd crushed beneath my machine-made Italian loafers fifteen minutes before. Families were closer knit then, so their great-grandparents would be sitting on the porch and keeping an eye on them.

An unpedigreed pack of watchdogs chased the housecat around the corner of the building, where the older boys (sans switchblades) were varnishing or whitewashing the age-silvered wood and caulking the cracks of the rock foundation. The size of the house implied that it was a prosperous farm, so I mentally placed a few hired hands in the distant fields — pulling the omnipresent glacial debris from the earth and piling it into those mysterious stone walls that dissect New England's second-growth forests and so intrigued Robert Frost.

A diesel fuel delivery truck rumbled by on the highway, and the stench of it startled me back to the present. I glanced at my watch. I was an hour late for dinner, so I began to run back to the car. About halfway to the gate, I tripped over something big and hard. Rubbing my skinned knee and standing on the unhurt foot, I turned my flashlight down. The beam hit a cement highway memorial marker that some historically minded vandal had uprooted and dragged there. I turned it over rather clumsily with my foot. It was dedicated to "General David Wooster, who died of wounds suffered during the Battle of Ridgefield, April 17, 1777." He might have watered his horse at the well behind me during that long trek to the arsenal at Danbury — or perhaps it had been his home in the first place.

His world may not have been better than mine or easier to live in, but his values were clear-cut and his goals uncompromised. The people on that farm had something we seem to have lost on the road up to the A & P shopping center. It may have been a sort of serenity, or perhaps merely Thoreau's "simplicity, simplicity, simplicity" — I don't pretend to know. Maybe it doesn't matter.

I left Mr. Wooster with the four and eight-legged inhabitants of that anonymous place, and climbed back into the car.

Dinner was cold when I got home, but somehow I didn't care.

Norman Mailer

Excerpt from *Miami and the Siege of Chicago*

CHICAGO, AUGUST 24–29

Chicago is the great American city. New York is one of the capitals of the world and Los Angeles is a constellation of plastic, San Francisco is a lady, Boston has become Urban Renewal, Philadelphia and Baltimore and Washington wink like dull diamonds in the smog of Eastern Megalopolis, and New Orleans is unremarkable past the French Quarter. Detroit is a one-trade town, Pittsburgh has lost its golden triangle, St. Louis has become the golden arch of the corporation, and nights in Kansas City close early. The oil depletion allowance makes Houston and Dallas naught but checkerboards for this sort of game. But Chicago is a great American city. Perhaps it is the last of the great American cities.

The reporter was sentimental about the town. Since he had grown up in Brooklyn, it took him no time to recognize, whenever he was in Chicago again, that the urbanites here were like the good people of Brooklyn — they were simple, strong, warm-spirited, sly, rough, compassionate, jostling, tricky and extraordinarily good-natured because they had sex in their pockets, muscles on their back, hot eats around the corner, neighborhoods which dripped with the sauce of local legend, and real city architecture, brownstones with different windows on every floor, vistas for miles of red-brick and two-family wood-frame houses with balconies and porches, runty stunted trees rich as farmland in their promise of tenderness the first city evenings of spring, streets where kids played stick-ball and roller-hockey, lots of smoke and iron twilight. The clangor of the late nineteenth century, the very hope of greed, was in these streets. London one hundred years ago could not have looked much better.

Brooklyn, however, beautiful Brooklyn, grew beneath the skyscrapers of Manhattan, so it never became a great city, merely an asphalt herbarium for talent destined to cross the river. Chicago did not have Manhattan to preempt top branches, so it grew up from the savory of its neighborhoods to some of the best high-rise architecture in the world, and because its people were Poles and Ukrainians and Czechs as well as Irish and the rest, the city had Byzantine corners worthy of Prague or Moscow, odd tortured attractive drawbridges over the Chicago River, huge Gothic spires like the skyscraper which held the Chicago *Tribune,* curves and abutments and balconies in cylindrical structures thirty stories high twisting in and out of the curves of the river, and fine balustrades in its parks. Chicago had a North Side on Lake Shore Drive where the most elegant apartment buildings in the world could be found — Sutton Place in New York betrayed the cost analyst in the eye of the architect next to these palaces of glass and charcoal colored steel. In superb back streets behind the towers on the lake were brownstones which spoke of ironies, cupidities and intricate ambition in the fists of the robber barons who commissioned them —substantiality, hard work, heavy drinking, carnal meats of pleasure, and a Midwestern sense of how to arrive at upper-class decorum were also in the American grandeur of these few streets. If there was a fine American aristocracy of deportment, it was probably in the clean tough keen-eyed ladies of Chicago one saw on the streets off Lake Shore Drive on the near North Side of Chicago.

Not here for a travelogue — no need then to detail the Loop, in death like the center of every other American city, but what a dying! Old department stores, old burlesque houses, avenues, dirty avenues, the El with its nineteenth-century dialogue of iron screeching against iron about a turn, and caverns of shadow on the pavement beneath, the grand hotels with their massive lobbies, barouque ceilings, resplendent as Roman bordellos, names like Sheraton-Blackstone, Palmer House, red fields of carpet, a golden cage for elevator, the unheard crash of giant mills stamping new shapes on large and obdurate materials is always pounding in one's inner ear — Dreiser had not written about Chicago for nothing.

To the West of the Lake were factories and Ciceros, Mafia-lands and immigrant lands; to the North, the suburbs, the Evanstons; to the South were Negro ghettos of the South Side — belts of Black men amplifying each the resonance of the other's cause — the Black belt had the Blackstone Rangers, the largest gang of juvenile delinquents on earth, 2,000 by some count — one could be certain the gang had leaders as large in potential as Hannibal or Attila the Hun — how else account for the strength and wit of a stud who would try to rise so high in the Blackstone Rangers?

Further South and West were enclaves for the University of Chicago, more factories, more neighborhoods for Poles, some measure of more good hotels on the lake, and endless neighborhoods — white neighborhoods which went for miles of ubiquitous dingy wood houses with back yards, neighborhoods to hint of Eastern Europe, Ireland, Tennessee, a gathering of all the clans of the Midwest, the Indians and Scotch–Irish, Swedes, some Germans, Italians, Hungarians, Rumanians, Finns, Slovaks, Slovenes — it was only the French who did not travel. In the Midwest, land spread out; not five miles from the Loop were areas as empty, deserted, enormous and mournful by night as the outer freight yards of Omaha. Some industrial desert or marsh would lie low on the horizon, an area squalling by day, deserted by night, except for the hulking Midwestern names of the boxcars and the low sheds, the warehouse buildings, the wire fences which went along the side of unpaved roads for thousands of yards.

The stockyards were like this, the famous stockyards of Chicago were at night as empty as the railroad sidings of the moon. Long before the Democratic Convention of 1968 came to the Chicago Amphitheatre, indeed eighteen years ago when the reporter had paid his only previous visit, the area was even then deserted at night, empty as the mudholes on a battlefield after a war has passed. West of the Amphitheatre, railroad sidings seemed to continue on for miles, accompanied by those same massive low sheds larger than armories, with pens for tens of thousands of frantic beasts, cattle, sheep, and pigs, animals in an orgy of gorging and dropping and waiting and smelling blood. In the slaughterhouses, during the day, a carnage worthy of the Disasters of War took place each morning and afternoon. Endless files of animals were led through pens to be stunned on the head by hammers, and then hind legs trussed, be hoisted up on hooks to hang head down, and ride along head down on an overhead trolley which brought them to Negroes or whites, usually huge, the whites most often Polish or Hunkies (hence the etymology of Honkie — a Chicago word) the Negroes up from the South, huge men built for the shock of the work, slash of a knife on the neck of the beast and gouts of blood to bathe their torso (stripped of necessity to the waist) and blood to splash their legs. The animals passed a psychic current back along the overhead trolley — each cut throat released its scream of death into the throat not yet cut and just behind, and that penultimate throat would push the voltage up, drive the current back and further back into the screams of every animal upside down and hanging from that clanking overhead trolley, bare electric bulbs screaming into the animal eye and brain, gurglings and awesome hollows of sound coming back from the open plumbing ahead of the cut jugular as if death were indeed a rapids along some underground river, and the fear and absolute anguish of beasts dying upside down further ahead passed back along the line, back all the way to the corrals and the pens, back even to the siding with the animals still in boxcars, back, who knew — so high might be the psychic voltage of the beast — back to the farm where first they were pushed into the truck which would take them into the train. What an awful odor the fear of absolute and unavoidable death gave to the stool and stuffing and pure vomitous shit of the beasts waiting in the pens in the stockyard, what a sweat of hell-leather, and yet the odor, no, the titanic stench, which rose from the yards was not so simple as the collective diarrhetics of an hysterical army of beasts, no, for after the throats were cut and the blood ran in rich gutters, red light on the sweating back of the red throat-cutters, the dying and some just-dead animals clanked along the overhead, arterial blood spurting like the nip-ups of a little boy urinating in public, the red-hot carcass quickly encountered another Black or Hunkie with a long knife on a long stick who would cut the belly from chest to groin and a stew and a stink of two hundred pounds of stomach, lungs, intestines, mucosities, spleen, exploded cowflop and pigshit, blood, silver lining, liver, mother-of-pearl tissue, and general gag-all would flop and slither over the floor, the man with the knife getting a good blood-splatting as he dug and twisted with his blade to liberate the roots of the organ, intestine and impedimenta still integrated into the meat and bone of the excavated existence he was working on.

Well, the smell of the entrails and that agonized blood electrified by all the outer neons of ultimate fear got right into the grit of the stockyard stench. Let us pass over into the carving and the slicing, the boiling and scraping, annealing and curing of the flesh in sugars and honeys and smoke, the cooking of the cow carcass, stamp of the inspector, singeing of the hair, boiling of hooves, grinding of gristle, the wax-papering and the packaging, the foiling and the canning, the burning of the residue, and the last slobber of the last unusable guts as it went into the stockyard furnace, and up as stockyard smoke, burnt blood and burnt bone and burnt hair to add their properties of specific stench to fresh blood, fresh entrails, fresh fecalities already all over the air. It is the smell of the stockyards, all of it taken together, a smell so bad one must go down to visit the killing of the animals or never eat meat again. Watching the animals be slaughtered, one knows the human case — no matter how close to angel we may become, the butcher is equally there. So be it. Chicago makes for hard minds. On any given night, the smell may go anywhere — down to Gary to fight with the smog and the coke, out to Cicero to quiet the gangs with their dreams of gung ho and mop-up, North to Evanston to remind the polite that *inter faeces et urinam* are we born, and East on out to Lake Michigan where the super felicities in the stench of such earth-bound miseries and corruptions might cheer the fish with the clean spermy deep waters of their fate.

Yes, Chicago was a town where nobody could ever forget how the money was made. It was picked up from floors still slippery with blood, and if one did not protest and take a vow of vegetables, one knew at least that life was hard, life was in the flesh and in the massacre of the flesh — one breathed the last agonies of beasts. So something of the entrails and the secrets of the gut got into the faces of native Chicagoans. A great city, a strong city was faces tough as leather hide and pavement, it was also a city where the faces took on the broad beastiness of ears which were dull enough to ignore the bleatings of the doomed, noses battered enough to smell no more the stench of every unhappy end, mouths — fat mouths or slit mouths — ready to taste the gravies which were the reward of every massacre, and eyes, simple pig eyes, which could look the pig truth in the face. In any other city, they would have found technologies to silence the beasts with needles, quarter them with machines, lull them with Muzak, and have stainless steel for floors, aluminum beds to take over the old overhead trolley — animals would be given a shot of vitamin-enrichment before they took the last ride. But in Chicago, they did it straight, they cut the animals right out of their hearts — which is why it was the last of the great American cities, and people had great faces, carnal as blood, greedy, direct, too impatient for hypocrisy, in love with honest plunder. They were big and human and their brother in heaven was the slaughtered pig — they did not ignore him. If the yowls and moans of his extinction was the broth of their strength, still they had honest guts to smell him to the end — they did not flush the city with Odorono or Pinex or No-Scent, they swilled the beer and assigned the hits and gave America its last chance at straight-out drama. Only a great city provides honest spectacle, for that is the salvation of the schizophrenic soul. Chicago may have beasts on the street, it may have a giant of fortitude for Mayor who grew into a beast — a man with the very face of Chicago — but it is an honest town, it does not look to incubate psychotics along an air-conditioned corridor with a vinyl floor.

Nightmare

When my mother was pregnant with me, she told me later, a party of hooded Ku Klux Klan riders galloped up to our home in Omaha, Nebraska, one night. Surrounding the house, brandishing their shotguns and rifles, they shouted for my father to come out. My mother went to the front door and opened it. Standing where they could see her pregnant condition, she told them that she was alone with her three small children, and that my father was away, preaching, in Milwaukee. The Klansmen shouted threats and warnings at her that we had better get out of town because "the good Christian white people" were not going to stand for my father's "spreading trouble" among the "good" Negroes of Omaha with the "back to Africa" preachings of Marcus Garvey.

My father, the Reverend Earl Little, was a Baptist minister, a dedicated organizer for Marcus Aurelius Garvey's U.N.I.A. (Universal Negro Improvement Association). With the help of such disciples as my father, Garvey, from his headquarters in New York City's Harlem, was raising the banner of black-race purity and exhorting the Negro masses to return to their ancestral African homeland — a cause which had made Garvey the most controversial black man on earth.

Still shouting threats, the Klansmen finally spurred their horses and galloped around the house, shattering every window pane with their gun butts. Then they rode off into the night, their torches flaring, as suddenly as they had come.

My father was enraged when he returned. He decided to wait until I was born — which would be soon — and then the family would move. I am not sure why he made this decision, for he was not a frightened Negro, as most then were, and many still are today. My father was a big, six-foot-four, very black man. He had only one eye. How he lost the other one I have never known. He was from Reynolds, Georgia, where he had left school after the third or maybe fourth grade. He believed, as did Marcus Garvey, that freedom, independence and self-respect could never be achieved by the Negro in America, and that therefore the Negro should leave America to the white man and return to his African land of origin. Among the reasons my father had decided to risk and dedicate his life to help disseminate this philosophy among his people was that he had seen four of his six brothers die by violence, three of them killed by white men, including one by lynching. What my father could not know then was that of the remaining three, including himself, only one, my Uncle Jim, would die in bed, of natural causes. Northern white police were later to shoot my Uncle Oscar. And my father was finally himself to die by the white man's hands.

It has always been my belief that I, too, will die by violence. I have done all that I can to be prepared.

I was my father's seventh child. He had three children by a previous marriage — Ella, Earl, and Mary, who lived in Boston. He had met and married my mother in Philadelphia, where their first child, my oldest full brother, Wilfred, was born. They moved from Philadelphia to Omaha, where Hilda and then Philbert were born.

I was next in line. My mother was twenty-eight when I was born on May 19, 1925, in an Omaha hospital. Then we moved to Milwaukee, where Reginald was born. From infancy, he had some kind of hernia condition which was to handicap him physically for the rest of his life.

Louise Little, my mother, who was born in Grenada in the British West Indies, looked like a white woman. Her father *was* white. She had straight black hair, and her accent did not sound like a Negro's. Of this white father of hers, I know nothing except her shame about it. I remember hearing her say she was glad that she had never seen him. It was, of course, because of him that I got my reddish-brown "mariny" color of skin, and my hair of the same color. I was the lightest child in our family. (Out in the world later on, in Boston and New York, I was among the millions of Negroes who were insane enough to feel that it was some kind of status symbol to be light-complexioned — that one was actually fortunate to be born thus. But, still later, I learned to hate every drop of that white rapist's blood that is in me.)

Our family stayed only briefly in Milwaukee, for my father wanted to find a place where he could raise our own food and perhaps build a business. The teaching of Marcus Garvey stressed becoming independent of the white man. We went next, for some reason, to Lansing, Michigan. My father bought a house and soon, as had been his pattern, he was doing free-lance Christian preaching in local Negro Baptist churches, and during the week he was roaming about spreading word of Marcus Garvey.

He had begun to lay away savings for the store he had always wanted to own when, as always, some stupid local Uncle Tom Negroes began to funnel stories about his revolutionary beliefs to the local white people. This time, the get-out-of-town threats came from a local hate society called The Black Legion. They wore black robes instead of white. Soon, nearly everywhere my father went, Black Legionnaires were reviling him as an "uppity nigger" for wanting to own a store, for living outside the Lansing Negro district, for spreading unrest and dissension among "the good niggers."

As in Omaha, my mother was pregnant again, this time with my youngest sister. Shortly after Yvonne was born came the nightmare night in 1929, my earliest vivid memory. I remember being suddenly snatched awake into a frightening confusion of pistol shots and shouting and smoke and flames. My father had shouted and shot at the two white men who had set the fire and were running away. Our home was burning down around us. We were lunging and bumping and tumbling all over each other trying to escape. My mother, with the baby in her arms, just made it into the yard before the house crashed in, showering sparks. I remember we were outside in the night in our underwear, crying and yelling our heads off. The white police and firemen came and stood around watching as the house burned down to the ground.

My father prevailed on some friends to clothe and house us temporarily; then he moved us into another house on the outskirts of East Lansing. In those days Negroes weren't allowed after dark in East Lansing proper. There's where Michigan State University is located; I related all of this to an audience of students when I spoke there in January, 1963 (and had the first reunion in a long while with my younger brother, Robert, who was there doing postgraduate studies in psychology). I told them how East Lansing harassed us so much that we had to move again, this time two miles out of town, into the country. This was where my father built for us with his own hands a four-room house. This is where I really begin to remember things — this home where I started to grow up.

After the fire, I remember that my father was called in and questioned about a permit for the pistol with which he had shot at the white men who set the fire. I remember that the police were always dropping by our house, showing things around, "just checking" or "looking for a gun." The pistol they were looking for — which they never found, and for which they wouldn't issue a permit — was sewed up inside a pillow. My father's .22 rifle and his shotgun, though, were right out in the open; everyone had them for hunting birds and rabbits and other game.

After that, my memories are of the friction between my father and mother. They seemed to be nearly always at odds. Sometimes my father would beat her. It might have had something to do with the fact that my mother had a pretty good education. Where she got it I don't know.

But an educated woman, I suppose, can't resist the temptation to correct an uneducated man. Every now and then, when she put those smooth words on him, he would grab her.

My father was also belligerent toward all of the children, except me. The older ones he would beat almost savagely if they broke any of his rules — and he had so many rules it was hard to know them all. Nearly all my whippings came from my mother. I've thought a lot about why. I actually believe that as anti-white as my father was, he was subconsciously so afflicted with the white man's brainwashing of Negroes that he inclined to favor the light ones, and I was his lightest child. Most Negro parents in those days would almost instinctively treat any lighter children better than they did the darker ones. It came directly from the slavery tradition that the "mulatto," because he was visibly nearer to white, was therefore "better."

My two other images of my father are both outside the home. One was his role as a Baptist preacher. He never pastored in any regular church of his own; he was always a "visiting preacher." I remember especially his favorite sermon: "That little *black* train is a-comin' . . . an' you better get all your business right!" I guess this also fit his association with the back-to-Africa movement, with Marcus Garvey's "Black Train Homeward." My brother Philbert, the one just older than me, loved church, but it confused and amazed me. I would sit goggle-eyed at my father jumping and shouting as he preached, with congregation jumping and shouting behind him, their souls and bodies devoted to singing and praying. Even at that young age, I just couldn't believe in the Christian concept of Jesus as someone divine. And no religious person, until I was a man in my twenties — and then in prison — could tell me anything. I had very little respect for most people who represented religion.

It was in his role as a preacher that my father had most contact with the Negroes of Lansing. Believe me when I tell you that those Negroes were in bad shape then. They are still in bad shape — though in a different way. By that I mean that I don't know a town with a higher percentage of complacent and misguided so-called "middle-class" Negroes — the typical status-symbol-oriented, integration-seeking type of Negroes. Just recently, I was standing in a lobby at the United Nations talking with an African ambassador and his wife, when a Negro came up to me and said, "You know me?" I was a little embarrassed because I thought he was someone I should remember. It turned out that he was one of those bragging, self-satisfied, "middle-class" Lansing Negroes. I wasn't ingratiated. He was the type who would never have been associated with Africa, until the fad of having African friends became a status-symbol for "middle-class" Negroes.

Back when I was growing up, the "successful" Lansing Negroes were such as waiters and bootblacks. To be a janitor at some downtown store was to be highly respected. The real "elite," the "big shots," the "voices of the race," were the waiters at the Lansing Country Club and the shoe-shine boys at the state capital. The only Negroes who really had any money were the ones in the numbers racket, or who ran the gambling houses, or who in some other way lived parasitically off the poorest ones, who were the masses. No Negroes were hired then by Lansing's big Oldsmobile plant, or the Reo plant. (Do you remember the Reo? It was manufactured in Lansing, and R. E. Olds, the man after whom it was named, also lived in Lansing. When the war came along, they hired some Negro janitors.) The bulk of the Negroes were either on Welfare, or W.P.A., or they starved.

The day was to come when our family was so poor that we would eat the hole out of a doughnut; but at that time we were much better off than most town Negroes. The reason was we raised much of our own food out there in the country where we were. We were much better off than the town Negroes who would shout, as my father preached, for the pie-in-the-sky and their heaven in the hereafter while the white man had his here on earth.

I knew that the collections my father got for his preaching were mainly what fed and clothed us, and he also did other odd jobs, but still the image of him that made me proudest was his crusading and militant campaigning with the words of Marcus Garvey. As young as I was then, I knew from what I overheard that my father was saying something that made him a "tough" man. I remember an old lady, grinning and saying to my father, "You're scaring these white folks to death!"

One of the reasons I've always felt that my father favored me was that to the best of my remembrance, it was only me that he sometimes took with him to the Garvey U.N.I.A. meetings which he held quietly in different people's homes. There were never more than a few people at any one time — twenty at most. But that was a lot, packed into some-one's living room. I noticed how differently they all acted, although sometimes they were the same people who jumped and shouted in church. But in these meetings both they and my father were more intense, more intelligent and down to earth. It made me feel the same way.

I can remember hearing of "Adam driven out of the garden into the caves of Europe," "Africa for the Africans," "Ethiopians, Awake!" And my father would talk about how it would not be much longer before Africa would be completely run by Negroes — "by black men," was the phrase he always used. "No one knows when the hour of Africa's redemption cometh. It is in the wind. It is coming. One day, like a storm, it will be here."

I remember seeing the big shiny photographs of Marcus Garvey that were passed from hand to hand. My father had a big envelope of them that he always took to these meetings. The pictures showed what seemed to me millions of Negroes thronged in parade behind Garvey riding in a fine car, a big black man dressed in a dazzling uniform with gold braid on it, and he was wearing a thrilling hat with tall plumes. I remember hearing that he had black followers not only in the United States but all around the world, and I remember how the meeting always closed with my father saying, several times, and the people chanting after him, "Up, you mighty race, you can accomplish what you will!"

I have never understood why, after hearing as much as I did of these kinds of things, I somehow never thought, then, of the black people in Africa. My image of Africa, at that time, was of naked savages, cannibals, monkeys and tigers and steaming jungles.

My father would drive in his old black touring car, sometimes taking me, to meeting places all around the Lansing area. I remember one daytime meeting (most were at night) in the town of Owosso, forty miles from Lansing, which the Negroes called "White City." (Owosso's greatest claim to fame is that it is the home town of Thomas E. Dewey.) As in East Lansing, no Negroes were allowed on the streets there after dark — hence the daytime meeting. In point of fact, in those days lots of Michigan towns were like that. Every town had a few "home" Negroes who lived there. Sometimes it would be just one family, as in the nearby county seat, Mason, which had a single Negro family named Lyons. Mr. Lyons had been a famous football star at Mason High School, was highly thought of in Mason, and consequently he now worked around that town in menial jobs.

My mother at this time seemed to be always working — cooking, washing, ironing, cleaning, and fussing over us eight children. And she was usually either arguing with or not speaking to my father. One cause of friction was that she had strong ideas about what she wouldn't eat — and didn't want *us* to eat — including pork and rabbit, both of which my father loved dearly. He was a real Georgia Negro, and he believed in eating plenty of what we in Harlem today call "soul food."

I've said that my mother was the one who whipped me — at least she did whenever she wasn't ashamed to let the neighbors think she was killing me. For if she even acted as though she was about to raise her hand to me, I would open my mouth and let the world know about it. If anybody was passing by out on the road, she would either change her mind or just give me a few licks.

Thinking about it now, I feel definitely that just as my father favored me for being lighter than the other children, my mother gave me more hell for the same reason. She was very light herself but she favored the ones who were darker. Wilfred, I know, was particularly her angel. I remember that she would tell me to get out of the house and "Let the sun shine on you so you can get some color." She went out of her way never to let me become afflicted with a sense of color-superiority. I am sure that she treated me this way partly because of how she came to be light herself.

I learned early that crying out in protest could accomplish things. My older brothers and sister had started to school when, sometimes, they would come in and ask for a buttered biscuit or something and my mother, impatiently, would tell them no. But I would cry out and make a fuss until I got what I wanted. I remember well how my mother asked me why I couldn't be a nice boy like Wilfred; but I would think to myself that Wilfred, for being so nice and quiet, often stayed hungry. So early in life, I had learned that if you want something, you had better make some noise.

Not only did we have our big garden, but we raised chickens. My father would buy some baby chicks and my mother would raise them. We all loved chicken. That was one dish there was no argument with my father about. One thing in particular that I remember made me feel grateful toward my mother was that one day I went and asked her for my own garden, and she did let me have my own little plot. I loved it and took care of it well. I loved especially to grow peas. I was proud when we had them on our table. I would pull out the grass in my garden by hand when the first little blades came up. I would patrol the rows on my hands and knees for any worms and bugs, and I would kill and bury them. And sometimes when I had everything straight and clean for my things to grow, I would lie down on my back between two rows, and I would gaze up in the blue sky at the clouds moving and think all kinds of things.

At five, I, too, began to go to school, leaving home in the morning along with Wilfred, Hilda, and Philbert. It was the Pleasant Grove School that went from kindergarten through the eighth grade. It was two miles outside the city limits, and I guess there was no problem about our attending because we were the only Negroes in the area. In those days white people in the North usually would "adopt" just a few Negroes; they didn't see them as any threat. The white kids didn't make any great thing about us, either. They called us "nigger" and "darkie" and "Rastus" so much that we thought those were our natural names. But they didn't think of it as an insult; it was just the way they thought about us.

One afternoon in 1931 when Wilfred, Hilda, Philbert, and I came home, my mother and father were having one of their arguments. There had lately been a lot of tension around the house because of Black Legion threats. Anyway, my father had taken one of the rabbits which we were raising, and ordered my mother to cook it. We raised rabbits, but sold them to whites. My father had taken a rabbit from the rabbit pen. He had pulled off the rabbit's head. He was so strong, he needed no knife to behead chickens or rabbits. With one twist of his big black hands he simply twisted off the head and threw the bleeding-necked thing back at my mother's feet.

My mother was crying. She started to skin the rabbit, preparatory to cooking it. But my father was so angry he slammed on out of the front door and started walking up the road toward town.

It was then that my mother had this vision. She had always been a strange woman in this sense, and had always had a strong intuition of things about to happen. And most of her children are the same way, I think. When something is about to happen, I can feel something, sense something. I never have known something to happen that has caught me completely off guard — except once. And that was when, years later, I discovered facts I couldn't believe about a man who, up until that dis-covery, I would gladly have given my life for.

My father was well up the road when my mother ran screaming out onto the porch. *"Early! Early!"* She screamed his name. She clutched up her apron in one hand, and ran down across the yard and into the road. My father turned around. He saw her. For some reason, considering how angry he had been when he left, he waved at her. But he kept on going.

She told me later, my mother did, that she had a vision of my father's end. All the rest of the afternoon, she was not herself, crying and ner-vous and upset. She finished cooking the rabbit and put the whole thing in the warmer part of the black stove. When my father was not back home by our bedtime, my mother hugged and clutched us, and we felt strange, not knowing what to do, because she had never acted like that.

I remember waking up to the sound of my mother's screaming again. When I scrambled out, I saw the police in the living room; they were trying to calm her down. She had snatched on her clothes to go with them. And all of us children who were staring knew without anyone having to say it that something terrible had happened to our father.

My mother was taken by the police to the hospital, and to a room where a sheet was over my father in a bed, and she wouldn't look, she was afraid to look. Probably it was wise that she didn't. My father's skull, on one side, was crushed in, I was told later. Negroes in Lansing have always whispered that he was attacked, and then laid across some tracks for a streetcar to run over him. His body was cut almost in half.

He lived two and a half hours in that condition. Negroes then were stronger than they are now, especially Georgia Negroes. Negroes born in Georgia had to be strong simply to survive.

It was morning when we children at home got the word that he was dead. I was six. I can remember a vague commotion, the house filled up with people crying, saying bitterly that the white Black Legion had finally gotten him. My mother was hysterical. In the bedroom, women were holding smelling salts under her nose. She was still hysterical at the funeral.

I don't have a very clear memory of the funeral, either. Oddly, the main thing I remember is that it wasn't in a church, and that surprised me, since my father was a preacher, and I had been where he preached people's funerals in churches. But this was in a funeral home.

And I remember that during the service a big black fly came down and landed on my father's face, and Wilfred sprang up from his chair and he shooed the fly away, and he came groping back to his chair — there were folding chairs for us to sit on — and the tears were streaming down his face. When we went by the casket, I remember that I thought that it looked as if my father's strong black face had been dusted with flour, and I wished they hadn't put on such a lot of it.

.   .   .

Joseph Morgenstern

Stay? No Stay?

Once his first words were behind him, very nice first words that he tossed off with the air of faintly self-conscious valedictorian, the first man was free to do his first deed. He dug a toe of his boot into the ashen-cocoa surface to find out just where he stood, to make sure his first foothold was firm. He was free as a prisoner can be in utterly solitary confinement, living out a whole small life on a small planet with a small ration of air for his lungs. Neither Armstrong nor Aldrin was free to set foot on the moon. They could only set boot on it, or landing pad on it, but that was more than good enough. They could never stand naked on it, as they could on their own genial earth, but they were naked enough, more than vulnerable enough.

Two *dei ex machina*, two modern men of module born, and their existence depending entirely upon the machine. The first pictures they took of themselves were simply too good to seem true. They were artistic to a fault: diagonal strut in the foreground, skeletal shadows below, a dangling leg from some ancient Chinese shadow play. But not Chinese! American. United States of American, and a weirdly starched Stars and Stripes to prove it, a flag flying flaplessly in a black solar wind. A black-and-white still life, frequently and joyously animated by two strapping 28-pound specimens of American manhood taking their first baby steps in one-sixth gravity — you can go to the moon, but don't cross any craters — learning quickly how to walk, glide, dodge, lope, hop like kangaroos and run like slightly tipsy cat burglars. They were *supposed* to move around a lot. They were supposed to star, for scientific purposes, in a lunar version of "The Running, Jumping, Standing Still Movie." But they still bespoke wordless jubilance as they tripped the dark fantastic in the white liquefaction of their clothes.

"THEN THEY RESUMED THEIR GAMBOLS"

Their clothes turned them into fat men who could not bend down to touch their toes (fat men are often wonderful dancers) but they sounded downright cozy inside. I remembered how cozy I used to feel in the winter when my mother would zip me into my snowsuit. They stood fatly at attention while President Nixon took on the role of the stuffy speaker who stops a swinging banquet dead in its tracks. Then they resumed their gambols across crusty fields and made us forget for a while that they were exceedingly fragile fellows whose lives could be ended in an instant by a random bolt from the black.

I was pleased that the first man on the moon was an American rather than an Andorran, but I was thrilled that we shared the same language, that I could savor the direct delights of Armstrong's hippie talk upon going into lunar orbit ("It was like perfect"), of their "happy home" in space, of their minimum impulses and their Stay-No Stays. The Greeks have Homer and Aeschylus, the Italians have Dante and Petrarch, the French have Molière and Voltaire and the Americans have Armstrong and Aldrin. Neither of them was an entirely satisfactory substitute for Marianne Moore, but I bet Miss Moore thought well of their taciturn landing technique. "The Eagle Has Landed," Armstrong announced, and it sounded like a code message in a Resistance broadcast from London. What did it mean? What was he trying to tell us about the future of the species? Would it be Stay or No Stay for us here on earth?

After that landing, in which Armstrong was forced by an implacable computer to give himself and Aldrin a helping human hand, a little boy was interviewed on television from Disneyland and asked what he thought of the whole thing. Trying to use as fancy a word as possible, the little boy replied that it was "sort of fantastic, sort of incorrigible that they could do it." And so it was. It made you sort of gape your mouth and shake your head at humanity's crazy, incorrigible yearning to do and to know.

What they did and what we shall know as a result of it may not matter in the slightest to the rest of the cosmos. Nobody else out there may have been watching. But we were watching, from their lift-off at Cape Kennedy to their happy home in space to their happy landing in the Sea of Tranquility. We were watching, though not always comprehending, and to many of us it mattered desperately. I went to Cape Kennedy to be where the action was so I could understand it better and when I got there two days before the launch I couldn't find any action to understand.

I kept wishing as I wandered, free as a goony bird on a sand spit, for a television set to tell me what it was all about. Happenings kept happening, of course. The local Sears store in Searstown Mall announced a "Moonshot Madness Sale" with "out-of-this-world prices." A million visitors came, give or take a half million. Cars assembled and overheated. The Rev. Ralph Abernathy, gentle and strong, obtained the admission of some of his flock to the VIP stands at the launch site and gave new meaning to an old acronym. Henceforth VIP will also mean Very Important Poor.

Closer to the main event, though, the action was abstract to the point of complete distraction. Numbers provided the only sense of movement, flashing green numbers on the countdown clocks all over the Cape, odometers on a used car being driven at full tilt backward. The world was watching, but where were the watchers and what were they watching? Thousands of technicians across the country were at the astronauts' service, but you couldn't see them. You couldn't see the rocket from the firing room because of a black fire shutter over the window. You couldn't see Houston from the Cape, though voices from Houston brayed out of loudspeakers. Worst of all, you couldn't see the moon. Where was it? The nights were clear but the moon was absent. I asked several Apollo people where the moon was, asked them to point to its position, and they couldn't. They were low-echelon Apollo people, to be sure. Certainly high-echelon Apollo people knew where the moon was at any given moment before the launch. Surely high-echelon Apollo computers did.

"A GRAVELLY LAND LANDSCAPED WITH CONCRETE"

The Kennedy Space Center is a civilian installation, strictly speaking, but civilian in an intensely military way. It is flat and still. It sprawls with a military–industrial sprawl that is not so different from an urban sprawl, though much less garish. It sprawls as if there were all the space in the world to sprawl across. It is peaceful, sprawling and supremely ugly to the eye, a gravelly land landscaped with concrete. Monotony without harmony. Abstract monotony of concrete. I looked for beauty in the monoliths that house the rockets or the towers that prop them up, in the deep-dish antennas that keep track of them aloft, in the spherical fuel tanks and radomes that lie scattered about like planetoids on the encircling horizon. But it wasn't beautiful. It seemed scattered, random, disconnected. It has simply occurred and then proceeded to amplify itself. Amplification. Electronic amplification. It was then that I began to understand something about the Cape and the age we're beginning to live in: not much, but something. Kennedy Space Center is laid out with a beauty that is invisible to the eye. It is laid out like a printed circuit board in a transistor radio.

"THE ESSENCE IS INVISIBLE TO THE EYE"

All the connections are invisible. Spatial relations have no bearing on the beauty. There is no place for a Place de la Concorde. Buildings are indeed placed at random, and what they look like to the eye doesn't matter at all. The only thing that matters is the secret, synaptic connections that bring the whole thing to life. "It's very simple," says the fox in "The Little Prince." "The essence is invisible to the eye." The fox was referring to love, not to electrons chasing each other along wires or waves. But an invisible essence informs Cape Kennedy with its own mysterious beauty. Rocket, firing room, Houston, countdown clocks, press center, television networks — all were on one circuit, the space circuit. And when you measured the white rocket against space it was suddenly a tiny thing, and it was tender and touching to think of three tiny men climbing into that tiny white dart and being flung away to scratch the surface of the moon.

By the morning of the launch I thought I had things fairly well in hand and mind. But I was not prepared for the sight of that rocket before dawn. It was anything but tiny. Pristine, silent, proud, it stood at the center of all visible creation. Arc lights played on it from all sides, spilled over it and past it to form an immense fan, the white fan of an albino peacock. There was nothing else, nothing at all anywhere. No sign of the unsuspecting moon. Was the moon where it was supposed to be? The rocket sustained itself in motionless grandeur. There was nothing else. Then heat lightning started to lick at it. Had the designers remembered a lightning rod? The sky softened. Dawn dawned. A water bird barked. More lightning came. A cloud cover trundled in on Caterpillar treads. As the new day grew, the rocket once again shrank. The rocket stood still and proud and white, but shrinking. The first big event of the morning was morning, the vast and entire redemption of failed sunlight.

"THE WHOLE WORLD WAS NOT WATCHING"

The whole world was watching this rocket, I reminded myself. But it wasn't. The rocket wasn't doing anything worth watching. Reporters in the press grandstands turned their binoculars on girls with miniskirts or on television reporters talking to themselves as they rehearsed their broadcasts to come. The whole world was not watching. A spider hung from a weed on his own bosun's chair, but not for a view of the rocket. Lightning still coursed through the sky, but not in search of the rocket. The cloud cover slid back slowly, but not from fear of the rocket. The rocket stood still, doing nothing.

At 6:30, slightly more than three hours before launch, a stern-faced reporter dictated his lead into a telephone: "With a teeth-rattling roar heard round the world comma . . ." I sat still on the sandy bank of a pond between the grandstand and the rocket, staring at the rocket, trying hard to commune with unnature. A small panel truck loaded with astronauts drove past, blue dome lights flashing. It reached the rocket, perhaps 5,000 yards away, discharged its precious load. Now that the rocket was inhabited I watched it more carefully for a while. I tried to care more about it. I wanted to feel something about it or the crew inside it, anything but this feeling of sitting idly on a sandy bank and staring senselessly at a silent rocket. If you call a rocket a bird, I wondered, what do you call a bird? An article in the previous day's paper had announced an increased bag limit for the 1969 dove-hunting season. And a veteran reporter of these launchings had told me that a bald eagle who used to live in the neighborhood was nowhere to be seen. So you call a bird unlucky. At four minutes, fifteen seconds from launch time a small fish launched himself briefly out of the pond, gulping the alien gas and not finding it good. Finally it was 9:32.

The rich are different from the rest of humanity, and so are people who have traveled in space, and so are people who have seen rocket launches. Or so they should be. It is a seductive and a shattering experience. I can understand now why congressmen are brought to Cape Kennedy as skeptics and shipped back as true believers, ready to fork over somebody else's tax dollar for the advancement of space science. A launching blasts away all doubt, at least for a while.

I expected the smoke and the flames and therefore remained on top of the event for at least five seconds. But then the sound reached me, as loud a sound as I would ever hope to survive, and with it came blows on the face and the chest, blows on the earth, blows of atrocious force, while through it all rose the marauding rocket, smashing its way into the heavens with a violence that could only be halted by the greater violence of self-destruction. I sat cross-legged and weeping, now, weeping and watching the damned thing go forth, not thinking at all about the men on board but only about the rocket's irresistible unstoppability. I was taken out of myself, blasted out of myself by the primitive ecstasy of being in the presence of whatever raw, blinding power it took to hurl a titanic weight toward the moon. In the wake of the blast stood a blackened launching pad, a gray-brown cloud and a bereft crowd of onlookers trying, I hope no more successfully than I, to collect their thoughts and slow their hearts.

"THE CAPABILITY TO HAVE THE CAPABILITY"

What are we to make of power that can do such things to people? What *will* we make of it? The terrifying part is the irrationality such power evokes, but the beauty part is the rationality it represents, the sweet reason with which the invisible connections were devised and the first foothold won. The fate of an individual mission is a transfixing thing, a heart-shredding thing, but not a final thing. We have the capability, as the space people say, to have the capability. We can make further and better connections among ourselves and the planet we live on. We can explore space and put our own house in brilliant order and bring every last one of the Very Important Poor through the front door. But will we? There is a Cape Kennedy joke to the effect that the colossal Vehicle Assembly Building stands on another Vehicle Assembly Building that sank beneath the sand. But the space age to come stands on a civilization that is itself sinking beneath the sand, and it remains to be seen if those on top will be good enough and wise enough to help those below.

Newsweek

Home is the Soldier...

A chill breeze swept in off the Hudson River, pewter gray in the patchy afternoon light, and rustled in the dogwood on the plains of West Point high above. Down Washington Road, a cadet band, all in black, played "Lead, Kindly Light," and then there was only the drear cadence of the muffled drums. They moved in slow procession to the cemetery: the band, the honor guard from C-2 Company, the colors, the family, the flag-draped coffin. It was another spring, another Memorial Day was at hand, and Second Lt. Frank Rybicki, Jr. was home from the war.

Frank Rybicki's career as a cadet had not been the Point's most distinguished: he was graduated, only last June, as the 212th in a class of 579. Nor was his death its most glorious: he had spent most of his scant three and a half months in Vietnam chafing for combat, and he had not really tasted it when he was accidentally felled, by his own rifle, while struggling through a jungle swamp half a world from home. And so, on 9 May 1967, he became an abstraction, an integer in the unending statistics of an unending war. He was the second to die in West Point's class of '66, the 101st Academy graduate, one of 10,000 Americans lost in what has now become the fifth costliest war in U.S. history.

Frank Rybicki, like most men of 23, had little to leave in worldly goods or formal biography.

There is the yearbook photo in the 1966 "Howitzer," a photo that catches a slender face, not quite handsome, plainly most comfortable in a broad, flashing smile. And, with the photo, a catalogue of extracurricular activities ("Glee Club, 4,3,2,1, President 1; Chapel Acolyte, 2,1: Spanish Club, 4,3,2,1 . . ."). And, with the catalogue, an inadequate sketch: "FRANK ANTHONY RYBICKI JR., Balboa, Canal Zone. C-2. 'Ask not what your country can do for you, but what you can do for your country.' These are the words Frank lives by . . . Frank's dedication to duty, together with his ceaseless wit, will always gain him respect and friendship. He will always be known as a leader of men as he proudly wears the crossed rifles down the trail of life chanting, 'Follow me.' "

Memory. There is also on file the stock, 8-by-10 glossy of the cadet, in dress whites and say-cheese smile, standing with a pretty date under a giant, mock-up West Point ring at an Academy hop. There is the guitar that came home from Vietnam, and a well-thumbed copy of John Kennedy's "Profiles in Courage." There is the marker now in the West Point cemetery, one on a lengthening gray line of 41 of the Vietnam dead. And there are the bright scattered mosaic tiles of memory.

Frank Rybicki is remembered, first, as a man of bubbling, musical gaiety. He was born in the Canal Zone, one of four children of an old Army Air Corps man who served and settled there and took a Panamanian bride. Frank grew up with an underlying streak of seriousness: he won a VFW essay contest, made the National Honor Society, commanded his high-school ROTC unit and spent more spare time than he had to with one of his kid brothers, Robert, now 12, who is afflicted with cerebral palsy. But West Point recalls him best as a youth who burst on the Academy in 1962, relentlessly gung-ho, invincibly cheery, fluent in the speech and song of two cultures.

"Everybody else was worried to death our plebe year," says Second Lt. Terry G. Stull, a Georgian who was Rybicki's best buddy at the Point and, later, in Vietnam. "But not Frank — he didn't let things bother him. When I met him, I talked to him an hour and I felt I'd known him all my life. He might have blown a test worse than you had, and he'd still be cheering you up. He had a smile for everybody." He had a song for everybody, too. "Frankie started a sing-out wherever he went," his father recalls. "Whenever he saw anybody with their head low, he'd grab the guitar and cheer 'em up."

And everybody remembers Frank Rybicki's girls, endlessly changing, unfailingly pretty, the datebook of a ladies' man but not a lady-killer. Terry Stull was a one-woman man; the woman he chose and made his fiancée was Rybicki's sister, Annette. But Rybicki was different. "He couldn't see himself settling down with one girl till he had time to meet 'em all," Stull reminisces. Rybicki was a first-class dancer, a talent he lavished on everyone from the commandant's wife ("He was the best jitterbug at the Academy") to the palest wallflowers. "Once," says a friend, "he showed me a little notebook he kept with the names of the Miss America nominees in all the states. He'd find out what states the Glee Club was going to on tour, then write to Miss So-and-so and send her free tickets. I know he got a date with Miss Texas that way."

Volunteer. Yet he kept a solemnity of purpose about him. He revered John F. Kennedy; he read a book about PT-109 while still a teen-ager, built a little Kennedy library around it, bought a desk blotter with the famous "ask-not" quote so he could always see it. What could he do for his country? He chose a military career, hoped someday to be assigned to Latin America because he knew it so well. But the country's first order of business, in 1966, was Vietnam, and Rybicki volunteered for infantry duty there.

On 10 January 1967, he and Stull shipped out together. "Gettin' on the boat," says Stull, "he was the funniest thing you ever saw in your life, comin' up the gangplank with two duffel bags, two 'AWOL' bags, his rifle — and his guitar." While Stull went off into the Mekong Delta and was wounded in the leg, Rybicki put in a restless tour running a Ninth Infantry platoon assigned to security duty around the base camp. His men liked his easy, deferential ways; he had scarcely joined the unit when his platoon sergeant dropped in on Alpha Company's topkick and paid Rybicki that rarest of NCO's compliments: "Looks like I lucked out and got a good lieutenant." But Rybicki hankered for action.

Stuck.   His marching orders came after his buddy Stull's own platoon was decimated in a six-hour battle with two Viet Cong companies. "We're coming down to help you out," Rybicki exulted over the phone. " 'Bout time we worked together again." They never got the chance. Moving out on a five-day search-and-destroy mission, Alpha Company knifed into the Rang Sat special zone — a steaming mangrove swamp southeast of Saigon that had once been a VC sanctuary. The first day out, the march bogged down in calf-deep water and ankle-deep mud. Stuck fast, Rybicki thrust his rifle, stock first, toward one of his men for help. The man tugged. The rifle went off. And Frank Rybicki fell dying in the mud.

Terry Stull and Frank Rybicki flew home together, the quick and the dead, for one last day at the Point. At Holy Trinity Chapel, Father Edwin O'Brien celebrated the mysteries of youth and death at Calvary, and the Glee Club sang: "They are here in ghostly assemblage/The men of the Corps long dead/ And our hearts are standing attention/While we wait for their passing tread . . ." And then the slow pilgrimage to graveside, Frank Sr. mashing a handkerchief, mother Cecilia staring blankly into the grass, sister Annette's dark eyes flashing out of a frame of white lace, 10-year-old brother James trailing, tiny and frail.

They sat at the edge of the grave. Thrushes sang; the grass shimmered in the broken sunlight; there were the ritual words, the three rifle volleys, the last lingering notes of "Taps." The honor guard lifted the flag from the coffin and folded it, and Terry Stull handed it to Mrs. Rybicki. A breeze scented with lilac crossed the Hudson plains. Frank Rybicki was home from the war.

Eric Nicol

The White Knight

Once upon a time there was a knight who lived in a little castle on the edge of the forest of Life. One day this knight looked in the mirror and saw that he was a White Knight.

"Lo!" he cried. "I am a White Knight and therefore represent good. I am the champion of virtue and honour and justice, and I must ride into the forest and slay the Black Knight, who is evil."

So the White Knight mounted his snow-white horse and rode into the forest to find the Black Knight and slay him in single combat.

Many miles he rode the first day, without so much as a glimpse of the Black Knight. The second day he rode even farther, still without sighting the ebony armour of mischief. Day after day he rode, deeper and deeper into the forest of Life, searching thicket and gully and even the tree-tops. The Black Knight was nowhere to be seen.

Yet the White Knight found many signs of the Black Knight's presence. Again and again he passed a village in which the Black Knight had struck — a baker's shop robbed, a horse stolen, an innkeeper's daughter ravished. But always he just missed catching the doer of these deeds.

At last the White Knight had spent all his gold in the cause of his search. He was forced to steal some buns from a bakeshop. His horse went lame, so that he was forced to replace it, silently and by darkness, with another white horse in somebody's stable. And when he stumbled, faint and exhausted, into an inn, the innkeeper's daughter gave him her bed, and because he was the White Knight in shining armour, she gave him her love, and when he was strong enough to leave the inn she cried bitterly because she could not understand that he had to go and find the Black Knight and slay him.

Through many months, under hot sun, over frosty paths, the White Knight pressed on his search, yet all the knights he met in the forest were, like himself, fairly white. They were knights of varying shades of whiteness, depending on how long they, too, had been hunting the Black Knight.

Some were sparkling white. These had just started hunting that day and irritated the White Knight by innocently asking directions to the nearest Black Knight.

Others were tattle-tale grey. And still others were so grubby, horse and rider, that the mirror in their castle would never have recognized them.

Yet the White Knight was shocked the day a knight of gleaming whiteness confronted him suddenly in the forest and with a wild whoop thundered towards him with levelled lance. The White Knight barely had time to draw his sword and, ducking under the deadly steel, plunge it into the attacker's breast.

The White Knight dismounted and kneeled beside his mortally wounded assailant, whose visor had fallen back to reveal blond curls and a youthful face. He heard the words, whispered in anguish: "Is evil then triumphant?" And holding the dead knight in his arms he saw that beside the bright armour of the youth his own, besmirched by the long quest, looked black in the darkness of the forest.

His heart heavy with horror and grief, the White Knight who was white no more buried the boy, then slowly stripped off his own soiled mail, turned his grimy horse free to the forest, and stood naked and alone in the quiet dusk.

Before him lay a path which he slowly took, which led him to his castle on the edge of the forest. He went into the castle and closed the door behind him. He went to the mirror and saw that it no more gave back the White Knight, but only a middle-aged, naked man, a man who had stolen and ravished and killed in pursuit of evil.

Thereafter when he walked abroad from his castle he wore a coat of simple colours, a cheerful motley, and never looked for more than he could see. And his hair grew slowly white, as did his fine, full beard, and the people all around called him the Good White Knight.

Charlton Ogburn, Jr.

Catastrophe by the Numbers

The poet, who a century and a quarter ago, "dipt into the future, far as human eye could see" and "saw the Vision of the world, and all the wonder that would be," would, if he dipt into it today, find disaster for the human race squarely ahead down the road our species is travelling with gathering speed. Even in 1842, however, when Tennyson's paean of optimism and affirmation was published, there was no need to have been unprepared for the fate mankind now appears bent on bringing on itself. More than forty years earlier, the professor of history and political economy at East India College in Haileybury, England, the Reverend Thomas Malthus, had called attention to the fact that the power of the human race to reproduce itself is infinite, while the capacity of the earth to support its numbers is finite. By 1842 birth rates and death rates in England, which had been in a rough balance a century before, showed a wide disparity. Owing to a fall in the death rate, the annual excess of births over deaths had reached thirteen per thousand persons, which meant that in another fifty years the population would double.

Death rates for the human race as a whole have been tumbling ever since, as science has been bringing the big killers of mankind under control and extending its beneficent sway from the advanced parts of the world to the less favored. The paradoxical result has been that human existence is threatened. Scientists concerned with the world's future have for a decade and more been urging mankind to grasp and be guided by the ominous statistics — so far with little response. The figures cannot be too often rehearsed.

The population of the world, from an estimated five million 8,000 years ago, reached 500 million about 300 years ago, having doubled about every 1,000 years. It reached one billion before 1850, having doubled in less than 200 years. Two billion was reached about 1930 — the doubling period having been reduced to about eighty years. The population of the world is now over 3.5 billion, and the doubling period is now down to about thirty-five years. *Every day* the population goes up by 190,000 — the equivalent of a fair-sized city.

The joker in the population pack — the terrible, cruel joker — is that with a rate of population increase that is constant, or even somewhat declining, the population will not only continue to grow, but the amount by which it grows will *every year become greater*. The principle is that of compound interest. If the present rate of population increase were to continue, at the end of only 650 years there would be one person for every square foot of the earth's surface. Such a horror could not, of course, actually come to pass. If birth rates had not long since been sufficiently reduced to bring them back into balance with death rates, nature would have achieved the same end by scourging mankind with one of the traditional mass killers — war, famine, and plague — or with a more modern agent, crippling psychic ills.

The rate of population increase is highest in the poorer countries. What most of us have failed to grasp, however, is that the rate of increase is menacing in the United States — menacing to ourselves and, because of our disproportionate demands on the world environment, menacing to everyone else. As in other technologically advanced countries, though less so than in some others, the birth rate in the United States has markedly declined in the past century. Nevertheless, our population, having passed 100 million in 1917, passed 200 million in 1967. Even at the present low fertility rate (the birth rate for women of childbearing age), which is the lowest since the 1930's, it will reach 400 million before a child born today is seventy years old (by which time the population of the world will have reached fifteen billion). When the Republic is as old again as it is now, in 2162, the number of Americans will be getting on toward 1.5 billion, while many children born that year may live to see the equivalent of the entire population of the world today jammed into the United States.

To picture what is in store for us as the population mounts we do not have to peer into the future far as human eye can see. We need only apply a little imagination to the effects of population pressure that we are already enduring. Nearly all of the problems we are wrestling with today are being rendered far more difficult of solution by the addition of nearly 5,500 lodgers to the national boardinghouse every day — such problems as providing adequate education and job training, housing, medical services, parks, playgrounds, sports fields and swimming pools, highways, airports and rapid mass-transit, and the wherewithal to relieve the plight of the poor in slums and rural backwaters. If we are finding urban problems today almost more than we can manage, how are we going to handle them as the cities are swelled by ever more millions? Our streams and lakes are already so befouled with human, industrial, and agricultural wastes that to clean them up will cost one hundred billion dollars, we are told. Our garbage is piling up around us: a million tons more every day, according to specialists at the Massachusetts Institute of Technology. Noise, taking a toll in health and efficiency and generally adding to the strain of life, has been doubling in volume every ten years. The cost of maintaining a nation of 200 million in the ever more expansive style to which we are accustomed comes high, and it bears not on the American people alone. With one seventeenth of the world's population, we consume two fifths of its production of raw materials, and, even with allowance made for the finished products we return, the disparity is enormous. Into the common atmosphere of the earth we Americans annually pour 140 million tons of pollutants, of which some ninety million come from transport (we burn more gasoline in motorcars than the rest of the world put together) and more than fifteen million from electric-power generation (of which our share of the world's total is a third). Our contribution to the carbon-dioxide content of the atmosphere, which has gone up by over 10 per cent in the past century (and which by creating a "greenhouse effect" could result in the melting of the polar ice caps and the inundation of all the world's ports and coastal plains) is comparable to our share of the world's fossil fuel combustion — 34 per cent.

Within thirty or thirty-five years we may expect to have 100 million more Americans generating refuse, water pollutants, and toxic gases; demanding their share of the world's resources and of our own — forests and minerals, soil and water. We shall have the same 100 million more taxing those services which already the nation is supplying with difficulty — where, indeed, it is not already woefully in arrears. As the population continues to soar, the costs of providing for its needs will far outpace it. For example, to supply water-deficient areas of the western part of the continent there is already being proposed a North American Water and Power Alliance to redirect southward the flow of several large Canadian rivers now emptying in the north — at a price of one hundred billion dollars: just to have water come out of the faucets.

And that will be only part of it. The inflation of any commodity results in its devaluation, and so must it be with human life. Humanity, from having been an object to be loved and cherished, will become one to be escaped, which will scarcely be possible as the teeming hordes press in on the resorts of privacy, convert the cities into the psychological equivalent of concentration camps, and necessitate a regimentation and computerization of life in order to manage the packed masses. Human inflation must also strike at the individual's estimate of his importance. The average American, from having been one hundredth or one thousandth part of a rural community or town two centuries ago, has become one two-hundred-thousandth part of a city today; if he is on the young side of middle age, he can expect to be reduced to one thirty-millionth part of a megalopolis. As the individual is overwhelmed by and lost in a society of ever more monstrous and inhuman forms, we must anticipate a progressive multiplication of the symptoms of anomie and alienation, which range from apathy and despondency to aggression and violence.

We shall also witness the desolation of what remains of the natural world around us and the closing of avenues of escape from the mounting tensions of an increasingly overwrought, high-pressure civilization. Beaches, lakes, mountains — the green kingdoms that have always stood for the living world in our eyes and have been the matrix of every human culture — will be overrun, debased, and obliterated by the products of that civilization, human and material. The process accelerates rapidly today. The cottages crowd rank on rank along the shores and lakesides. The suburbs spread like a skin eruption ever farther into farm land, and with them come the shopping centers and industrial plants, converting fields and forests to asphalt, masonry, and neon lights in eighty- and hundred-acre swoops. To the rear, even as they spread outward, the cities are cut to pieces by freeways on which, beneath thickening palls of smog, swelling streams of motorcars race eight abreast.

Of course, events in the world at large may preclude the climax of this spoilage. Despite our poor, the average American can purchase nine times as much in the way of goods and services as the average Latin American, and more than twenty times as much as the average Asian or African. And the have-not peoples are ill content with this dispensation. There has been let loose in the world a so-called "revolution of rising expectations." Actually, those expectations only *aim* at revolution. They amount to a demand, affecting billions, for the health and comforts the West has shown to be attainable. We might ask ourselves what course those billions are likely to take as they see the disparity between what they have and what we have grow wider — as it is doing — and if they see no prospect of substantial relief from their poverty under the institutions they are accustomed to. At the same time we might ask ourselves what the consequences would be if their expectations of the more abundant life were met: what overwhelming demands would be made on the resources of the globe, and what damage done to the environment of life if the incomes of the disadvantaged billions should approach our own and all peoples began to live on the American model — felling forests for paper as we do, burning fuels and pouring pollutants into the air and the rivers and the sea as we do, and consuming an equivalent share of the earth's minerals. "The ecology of the earth," says Harvard nutritional expert Jean Mayer, " — its streams, woods, animals — can accommodate itself better to a rising *poor* population than to a rising *rich* population."

What remains clear is that the higher the rate of population growth among the economically laggard peoples — and, to repeat, it is now the highest in the world — the slower any improvement in their lot is likely to be, and the more costly to the earth and its ecology would be the dramatic improvement we have taught them to expect. Year by year the alternatives ahead grow more dangerous. With a continuation of present rates of world population growth, either progress or lack of progress in satisfying the wants of the multiplying billions will alike become ever more hazardous, ever more certain to be destructive of world order.

How vast a human multitude the planet can feed is moot. Fanatic agriculturalists speak of 50 billion and more and present us a graphic picture of the world's forests being "sheared off at ground level" by "a huge steel blade . . . pushed by a heavy crawler-type tractor" to provide farm land. That forests are indispensable in preserving watersheds and water tables and tempering climates, that the need will be for more forests in the future to provide lumber and pulp, does not seem to concern them. But at least they point up the insanity of devoting our energies, not to creating conditions in which man's potentialities may be realized, but to converting this splendid earth into a dreary food-factory to provide a mere subsistence for overflowing billions with whom no one in his right mind could wish to see the planet burdened.

The nightmare that the population explosion has in store for their descendants has been persistently pictured for the American people. Congress, no longer palsied before native obscurantism or the medieval theology of the Vatican, has — admirably — appropriated substantial funds for research into human reproduction and for the dissemination of information on contraceptive techniques. Yet the public on the whole continues to show itself passively or actively on the side of catastrophe — not on the side of its prevention.

In the face of all warnings, we Americans brought over 3.5 million new human beings into the world last year, to send the population of the United States up by 1.5 million. And with each of these added lives representing a burden on the earth equal to a half dozen or more Asians or Africans, we should perhaps not expect those unenlightened folk to be much moved by our exhortations to them to reproduce less. A Gallup poll in November a year ago showed that 41 per cent of Americans considered *four or more* children ideal for a family, the percentage being 50 among Roman Catholics, 56 among Negroes, and higher than average among the poor — 47.

Admittedly, there were once good reasons for large families. At the time of the American Revolution, only half of the children born lived to sixteen. Most of us were farmers, and on the farm children were an asset. In any case, land and resources appeared inexhaustible. Let it be acknowledged too that while times have changed drastically, asking couples to limit the number of their children is asking a great deal.

Watching a human personality gradually take shape, one that you have helped bring out of nothing, is an incomparable satisfaction. Children lend a kind of charm to life that nothing else can.

That the traditional indulgent view of large families should die hard is not surprising. The fact remains — and it is a fact of which there is no excuse for ignorance — that those who reproduce as if they were living in the past are preparing for the children of the future a world in which life will scarcely be worth living. Yet evidently little stigma attaches to their doing so. If suburban mothers hesitate to traipse across the shopping center with a train of offspring, nothing in their bearing betrays it. A father of ten grins with self-satisfaction out of the television tube on "Generation Gap," while another parent beside him appologizes for being, by comparison, an underachiever. A prominent clergyman of the nation's capital and his wife are evidently unembarrassed at having brought nine children into the world. Newspapers regularly report the plight — and complaints — of parents of twelve on relief, without any suggestion that society has rights in the matter, rights which have been grossly violated. Public figures who have become known partly because of their concern with the nation's future, like columnist Jack Anderson and entertainer Dick Gregory, can have nine and seven children, respectively, and not feel that they owe the public an apology any more than John Wayne, who also has seven children. The governor of New Jersey, Richard J. Hughes, had three children by one wife, acquired three more with a second wife, and by her had an additional three. Presumably his career has not been impaired as a result — or Governor Nelson Rockefeller's by his having six children, or ex-Congressman Hugh L. Carey's by his having had fourteen.

The crucial test of public opinion on the issue came last year when a strong bid for the presidential nomination was made by a dynamic and appealing young politician whose ten children (with an eleventh on the way) marked him as entirely disqualified to address himself to the problem that Dwight Eisenhower had called one of the most critical of our time. During his campaign for a Senate seat Robert Kennedy had indeed lightheartedly confessed to this disqualification. The next year he had gone further. Speaking in a country in which one of the world's most rapidly growing populations had for two decades been outstripping an already inadequate food production by 10 per cent — Peru — he gaily challenged his audience to outbreed him. ("Deadly dangerous," the Washington *Post* termed the ploy, and with reason. If all the speaker's eleven children and their descendants reproduced as he had, there would be over 214 million descendants of the Robert Kennedys in the ninth generation, and seven times as many as there are people in the entire world today in the eleventh.) Not only, however, did Senator Kennedy's exemplification of the procreative irresponsibility that is pushing the world toward catastrophe create no bar to his political ambitions; no public figure, editorialist, or columnist that I know of deemed it important enough to mention as bearing on his eligibility for the supreme office.

In a statement hailed by family-planning groups, the heads of thirty governments in the United Nations have announced "that the opportunity to decide the number and spacing of children is a basic human right." Not to limit but to *decide* the number. What this "right" is, of course, is the "right" of any part of the human race to make the planet uninhabitable for the whole. It is the "right" of any passenger in a lifeboat to help himself to as much of the provisions as he wants, regardless of the consequences to his fellows.

Just as early humanoids were probably unaware of any connection between sexual intercourse and its subsequent issue, so their descendants today, one could almost believe, are unaware of any between the number of children individual couples have and the growth of the population as a whole. That would explain how the *Reader's Digest* can run an excellent article hammering home the implications of the problem, and in an advertisement a few months later, beam upon John and Mary Ann Forristal of Houston and their nine children as a representative *Digest* family. It would explain the report issued in November, 1968, by a committee of highly qualified citizens set up by the President to recommend steps to deal with population pressure. On one page the report tells us that the current rate of growth of the American population "cannot be maintained indefinitely," on the opposite that the national objective is "a society in which all parents can have the number of children they want when they want them." What we do if the number of children parents want must produce a rate of population growth impossible to maintain, which is the case at present, the committee does not say. Last July, in the strongest public statement on population yet made by an American President, Mr. Nixon detailed the enormous scope of the problem and proposed the creation by Congress of a "Commission on Population Growth and the American Future"; then he went on to vitiate all he had been urging with the pious pronouncement that the government's pursuit of the goal of population control would "in no circumstances . . . be allowed to infringe upon the religious convictions or personal wishes and freedom of any individual, nor . . . to impair the absolute right of all individuals to have such matters of conscience respected by public authorities." One wonders how close to final debacle we shall have to come before a President summons up the nerve to do what is clearly imperative now and gives the American people to understand that if they care anything for posterity, for their country, and for the handiwork of the Creator that has made North America so hospitable and inspiring to human habitation, they are going to have to accept a ceiling on the number of children per couple, and that the national interest will be best served if that ceiling for the present is no more than two.

Even if such a national policy were enunciated, however — as sooner or later it will have to be — there will remain the question of how individual couples are to be brought to conform to it. What results could be expected from a mere appeal to conscience?

Harmful ones, Garret Hardin of the University of California argues persuasively. The person whose conscience is appealed to, says Professor Hardin, is caught in a "double bind" of a kind that can induce schizophrenia. For he is damned if he does and damned if he doesn't. If he ignores the appeal and has three or four children, he stands to be publicly condemned as selfish, irresponsible, and antisocial. If he obeys it while others ignore it,. he can only feel he has been had — one whom others "secretly condemn . . . for a simpleton."

Of course, we should not have to fear these consequences if an appeal to conscience were *uniformly* acceded to. But one thing that experience of this world should teach us is the futility of expecting human beings in the aggregate to curb their instincts or desires for any length of time just for the general good. Were it otherwise, we could have government by exhortation instead of by laws — laws with teeth in them. Can it be imagined that wartime rationing that depended on voluntary compliance would be of any effect? And rationing is what we are talking about.

To move human beings to what is uncongenial and unnatural to them requires the carrot and/or the stick. For the great majority of us over the long run, nothing else will serve. The question is, what sort of carrot and what sort of stick would be most likely to prove effective in preventing the earth from being swamped by people and at the same time provide an equitable apportionment of the right to bear children? That is the question to which those most concerned with the future of life on earth should address themselves — or show how these ends may otherwise be achieved.

Professor Hardin favors coercion — but "mutual coercion, mutually agreed upon by the majority of the people affected." Social sanctions could perhaps meet the need. If anyone with three or four children automatically brought obloquy and ostracism on himself as an antipatriot and an offender against the Deity (who presumably would have some interest in the preservation of his magnificent creation, the earth), we might have the answer. But the world might be close to irreversible disaster, or over the line, before such an effective consensus could form, even in the United States.

Meanwhile, economic levers are available. Federal and state income-tax exemptions now authorized for every minor child could be denied in the case of children over the number of two, born nine months or more after the enactment of the legislation. Annual payments could be made to sexually mature females who refrain from bearing children, and in lesser amounts to those who stop with two. Fines, proportionate to the offender's capacity to pay, could be levied against parents for each child they produce in excess of two; beyond a certain limit the offenders could be deprived of the right to vote. (Why should those indifferent to society's future be given a voice in it?) At the same time, of course, anti-abortion laws — which in any case represent a tyrannical denial by the state of the rights of an individual — should be repealed; contraceptives should be made freely available to all, and every effort should be made to devise simpler, surer, safer methods of contraception.

Obviously, strong opposition to any program equal to arresting the population explosion is to be expected, especially on the part of the Roman Catholic hierarchy. But public opinion can be swayed. The Vatican has changed its mind in the past, and can and must change it again. The more public discussion there is, the sooner the public will become accustomed to and will accept measures to deal effectively with a crisis that four thousand scientists at a recent meeting of the American Association for the Advancement of Science termed — along with the related crisis of pollution — the most serious facing mankind. Too-long delay in meeting it can result only in having the issue taken out of our hands, for under the strains to which the population explosion must increasingly subject civilization, the institutions of representative self-government will be among the surest to give way.

George Orwell

Some Thoughts on the Common Toad

Before the swallow, before the daffodil, and not much later than the snow drop, the common toad salutes the coming of spring after his own fashion, which is to emerge from a hole in the ground, where he has lain buried since the previous autumn, and crawl as rapidly as possible towards the nearest suitable patch of water. Something — some kind of shudder in the earth, or perhaps merely a rise of a few degrees in the temperature — has told him that it is time to wake up: though a few toads appear to sleep the clock round and miss out a year from time to time — at any rate, I have more than once dug them up, alive and apparently well, in the middle of the summer.

At this period, after his long fast, the toad has a very spiritual look, like a strict Anglo-Catholic toward the end of Lent. His movements are languid but purposeful, his body is shrunken, and by contrast his eyes look abnormally large. This allows one to notice, what one might not at another time, that a toad has about the most beautiful eye of any living creature. It is like gold, or more exactly it is like the golden-colored semi-precious stone which one sometimes sees in signet rings, and which I think is called a chrysoberyl.

For a few days after getting into the water the toad concentrates on building up his strength by eating small insects. Presently he has swollen to his normal size again, and then he goes through a phase of intense sexiness. All he knows, at least if he is a male toad, is that he wants to get his arms round something, and if you offer him a stick, or even your finger, he will cling to it with surprising strength and take a long time to discover that it is not a female toad. Frequently one comes upon shapeless masses of ten or twenty toads rolling over and over in the water, one clinging to another without distinction of sex. By degrees, however, they sort themselves out into couples, with the male duly sitting on the female's back. You can now distinguish males from females, because the male is smaller, darker and sits on top, with his arms tightly clasped round the female's neck. After a day or two the spawn is laid in long strings which wind themselves in and out of the reeds and soon become invisible. A few more weeks, and the water is alive with masses of tiny tadpoles which rapidly grow larger, sprout hind legs, then forelegs, then shed their tails: and finally, about the middle of the summer, the new generation of toads, smaller than one's thumbnail but perfect in every particular, crawl out of the water to begin the game anew.

I mention the spawning of the toads because it is one of the phenomena of spring which most deeply appeal to me, and because the toad, unlike the skylark and the primrose, has never had much of a boost from the poets. But I am aware that many people do not like reptiles or amphibians, and I am not suggesting that in order to enjoy the spring you have to take an interest in toads. There are also the crocus, the missel thrush, the cuckoo, the blackthorn, etc. The point is that the pleasures of spring are available to everybody, and cost nothing. Even in the most sordid street the coming of spring will register itself by some sign or other, if it is only a brighter blue between the chimney pots or the vivid green of an elder sprouting on a blitzed site. Indeed it is remarkable how Nature goes on existing unofficially, as it were, in the very heart of London. I have seen a kestrel flying over the Deptford gasworks, and I have heard a first-rate performance by a blackbird in the Euston Road. There must be some hundreds of thousands, if not millions, of birds living inside the four-mile radius, and it is rather a pleasing thought that none of them pays a half-penny of rent.

As for spring, not even the narrow and gloomy streets round the Bank of England are quite able to exclude it. It comes seeping in everywhere, like one of those new poison gases which pass through all filters. The spring is commonly referred to as "a miracle," and during the past five or six years this worn-out figure of speech has taken on a new lease of life. After the sort of winters we have had to endure recently, the spring does seem miraculous, because it has become gradually harder and harder to believe that it is actually going to happen. Every February since 1940 I have found myself thinking that this time winter is going to be permanent. But Persephone, like the toads, always rises from the dead at about the same moment. Suddenly, toward the end of March, the miracle happens and the decaying slum in which I live is transfigured. Down in the square the sooty privets have turned bright green, the leaves are thickening on the chestnut trees, the daffodils are out, the wallflowers are budding, the policeman's tunic looks positively a pleasant shade of blue, the fish-monger greets his customers with a smile, and even the sparrows are quite a different color, having felt the balminess of the air and nerved themselves to take a bath, their first since last September.

Is it wicked to take a pleasure in spring, and other seasonal changes?

To put it more precisely, is it politically reprehensible, while we are all groaning under the shackles of the capitalist system, to point out that life is frequently more worth living because of a blackbird's song, a yellow elm tree in October or some other natural phenomenon which does not cost money and does not have what the editors of the left-wing newspapers call a class angle? There is no doubt that many people think so. I know by experience that a favorable reference to "Nature" in one of my articles is liable to bring me abusive letters, and though the keyword in these letters is usually "sentimental," two ideas seem to be mixed up in them. One is that any pleasure in the actual process of life encourages a sort of political quietism. People, so the thought runs, ought to be discontented, and it is our job to multiply our wants and not simply to increase our enjoyment of the things we have already. The other idea is that this is the age of machines and that to dislike the machine, or even to want to limit its domination, is backward-looking, reactionary, and slightly ridiculous. This is often backed up by the statement that a love of Nature is a foible of urbanized people who have no notion what Nature is really like. Those who really have to deal with the soil, so it is argued, do not love the soil, and do not take the faintest interest in birds or flowers, except from a strictly utilitarian point of view. To love the country one must live in the town, merely taking an occasional week-end ramble at the warmer times of year.

This last idea is demonstrably false. Medieval literature, for instance, including the popular ballads, is full of an almost Georgian enthusiasm for Nature, and the art of agricultural peoples such as the Chinese and Japanese centers always round trees, birds, flowers, rivers, mountains. The other idea seems to me to be wrong in a subtler way. Certainly we ought to be discontented, we ought not simply to find out ways of making the best of a bad job, and yet if we kill all pleasure in the actual process of life, what sort of future are we preparing for ourselves? If a man cannot enjoy the return of spring, why should he be happy in a labor-saving Utopia? What will he do with the leisure that the machine will give him? I have always suspected that if our economic and political problems are ever really solved, life will become simpler instead of more complex, and that the sort of pleasure one gets from finding the first primrose will loom larger than the sort of pleasure one gets from eating an ice to the tune of a Wurlitzer. I think that by retaining one's childhood love of such things as trees, fishes, butterflies, and — to return to my first instance — toads, one makes a peaceful and decent future a little more probable, and that by preaching the doctrine that nothing is to be admired except steel and concrete, one merely makes it a little surer that human beings will have no outlet for their surplus energy except in hatred and leader-worship.

At any rate, spring is here, even in London, N.1, and they can't stop you enjoying it. This is a satisfying reflection. How many a time have I stood watching the toads mating, or a pair of hares having a boxing match in the young corn, and thought of all the important persons who would stop me enjoying this if they could. But luckily they can't. So long as you are not actually ill, hungry, frightened, or immured in a prison or a holiday camp, spring is still spring. The atom bombs are piling up in the factories, the police are prowling through the cities, the lies are streaming from the loudspeakers, but the earth is still going round the sun, and neither the dictators nor the bureaucrats, deeply as they disapprove of the process, are able to prevent it.

Daniel Rosochacki

Herbie

We met Herbie in the town where he lived. We moved into our apart-ment over the grocery store on a spring day as the sun dazzled and danced over the whitewashed buildings, and the trees leaned to a light wind blowing across the empty fields behind the stores. We carried our furniture up the flight of stairs leading to our rooms and on each trip down we saw a thin, sparse-looking man wearing soiled and baggy khaki-colored pants, a tail-out and faded plaid flannel shirt and a crushed and sweatstained tan baseball cap. He watched us with a wide grin and gestured vigorously with his arms, pausing spasmodically to catch a line of saliva drooling out of the corner of his mouth and failing to get it before it ran dripping down the plaids of his shirt. His gray and matted hair edged from his cap in clumps, and beads of sweat ran through it and splashed onto a flannel shoulder and vanished. His eyes rested deep in their sockets and occasionally blinked out the sun. Not a tall man and slightly bent at the spine, he looked as if he had let age catch him all at once in that minute we saw him. This was Herbie.

We lived in the small town all that spring and summer and saw Herbie often as he ran his errands and did his chores for the store owners, who in turn saw to it he had food and a place to sleep. Nobody knew for sure where he had come from or when; one day he had appeared and stayed. He could not talk and the only answer anyone ever received was a gurgle and a murmur and always a wide grin. After a short while most people learned to communicate with him through signs and word suggestions. In this way they took care of Herbie.

The town was on a highway that bridged two larger cities and was a popular gas and food stop for travelers to the cities. The merchants of the town depended on the highway business for a living and treated every car that stopped with care and courtesy so they might be remembered as a friendly town and a good place to stop. The stores were clean and orderly and had a quaint, country atmosphere the townspeople worked hard to promote and maintain.

It was the quaintness that had prompted us to leave the city for awhile and relax in the country. It was the orderliness that had drawn us out of the confusion of city life. It was the friendliness of the people that had turned us against the cold and aloof city. We enjoyed going to the simple white church on Sunday mornings and on picnics in the afternoons; we found it calming to take winding walks through the narrow roads in the evenings; we thought how reassuring and peaceful it was to look out the window and see a deserted and quiet street. Everything seemed to fall in place — except Herbie.

Whenever he wandered into one of the stores while a passing motorist happened to be there, the owner would graciously excuse himself and quietly whisk Herbie through the back door and return wiping his hands and smiling. If the restaurant had any patrons and Herbie came in for his meal, he would be served on the back porch or in the kitchen, and if he was doing his chores at the gas station and a car pulled in, he would be given an errand to run until the car had driven away. Once customers had gone on their way Herbie was allowed to come out of hiding and roam about the town until another traveler stopped. We wondered whether Herbie ever felt more deeply than his wide grins and monotonous murmurs suggested, but when we watched him wander in and out of the stores and shuffle down the street in no apparent direction we knew he was childishly content.

One day in late summer Herbie did not show up for his morning chores at the grocery store nor did he go to the restaurant for lunch. People thought it odd because he had never missed his chores before, but they dismissed the fact as only curious, for Herbie was not normal and certainly not above flightiness or forgetfulness. When he didn't come to supper, a feeling that they should be worried came over the people, and a few of them decided to check his room to see if he might be there. They found him sitting in an old easy chair facing the window and figured he had been dead since the night before. His clothes were crumped and his stained cap was tilted down over his eyes, shadowing his face. He had died peacefully. The townspeople heaved a sigh, and a small collection was taken up. He was buried in an overgrown corner of the cemetery without a marker or much of a service. In this way they took care of Herbie.

Shortly after Herbie's death we left the town and went back to the city. We loaded the car and paused for a last look around. The buildings stood white and gleaming in the sun and we felt a breeze from the fields flush our cheeks with the first whisper of fall. Everything was quiet and quaintly in place and the town had an air of sublime orderliness about it. We got into our car and drove down the road toward the city.

George Santayana

Cervantes

Cervantes is known to the world as the author of *Don Quixote*, and although his other works are numerous and creditable, and his pathetic life is carefully recorded, yet it is as the author of *Don Quixote* alone that he deserves to be generally known or considered. Had his wit not come by chance on the idea of the Ingenious Hidalgo, Cervantes would never have attained his universal renown, even if his other works and the interest of his career should have sufficed to give him a place in the literary history of his country. Here, then, where our task is to present in miniature only what has the greatest and most universal value, we may treat our author as playwrights are advised to treat their heroes, saying of him only what is necessary to the understanding of the single action with which we are concerned. This single action is the writing of *Don Quixote;* and what we shall try to understand is what there was in the life and environment of Cervantes that enabled him to compose that great book, and that remained imbedded in its characters, its episodes, and its moral.

There was in vogue in the Spain of the sixteenth century a species of romance called books of chivalry. They were developments of the legends dealing with King Arthur and the Knights of the Table Round, and their numerous descendants and emulators. These stories had appealed in the first place to what we should still think of as the spirit of chivalry: they were full of tourneys and single combats, desperate adventures and romantic loves. The setting was in the same vague and wonderful region as the Coast of Bohemia, where to the known mountains, seas, and cities that have poetic names, was added a prodigious number of caverns, castles, islands, and forests of the romancer's invention. With time and popularity this kind of story had naturally intensified its characteristics until it had reached the greatest extravagance and absurdity and combined in a way the unreality of the fairy tale with the bombast of the melodrama.

Cervantes had apparently read these books with avidity and was not without a great sympathy with the kind of imagination they embodied. His own last and most carefully written book, the *Travails of Persiles and Sigismunda*, is in many respects an imitation of them; it abounds in savage islands, furious tyrants, prodigious feats of arms, disguised maidens whose discretion is as marvelous as their beauty, and happy deliverances from intricate and hopeless situations. His first book also, the *Galatea*, was an embodiment of a kind of pastoral idealism: sentimental verses being interspersed with euphuistic prose, the whole describing the lovelorn shepherds and heartless sheperdesses of Arcadia.

But while these books, which were the author's favorites among his own works, expressed perhaps Cervantes's natural taste and ambition, the events of his life and the real bent of his talent, which in time he came himself to recognize, drove him to a very different sort of composition. His family was ancient but impoverished, and he was forced throughout his life to turn his hand to anything that could promise him a livelihood. His existence was a continuous series of experiments, vexations, and disappointments. He adopted at first the profession of arms, and followed his colors as a private soldier upon several foreign expeditions. He was long quartered in Italy; he fought at Lepanto against the Turks, where among other wounds he received one that maimed his left hand, to the greater glory, as he tells us, of his right; he was captured by Barbary pirates and remained for five years a slave in Algiers; he was ransomed, and returned to Spain only to find official favors and recognitions denied him; and finally, at the age of thirty-seven, he abandoned the army for literature.

His first thought as a writer does not seem to have been to make direct use of his rich experience and varied observation; he was rather possessed by an obstinate longing for that poetic gift which, as he confesses in one place, Heaven had denied him. He began with the idyllic romance, the *Galatea*, already mentioned, and various times during the rest of his life wrote poems, plays, and stories of a romantic and sentimental type. In the course of these labors, however, he struck one vein of much richer promise. It was what the Spanish call the *picaresque*; that is, the description of the life and character of rogues, pickpockets, vagabonds, and all those wretches and sorry wits that might be found about the highways, in the country inns, or in the slums of cities. Of this kind is much of what is best in his collected stories, the *Novelas Exemplares*. The talent and the experience which he betrays in these amusing narratives were to be invaluable to him later as the author of *Don Quixote*, where they enabled him to supply a foil to the fine world of his poor hero's imagination.

We have now mentioned what were perhaps the chief elements of the preparation of Cervantes for his great task. They were a great familiarity with the romances of chivalry, and a natural liking for them; a life of honorable but unrewarded endeavor both in war and in the higher literature; and much experience of Vagabondia, with the art of taking down and reproducing in amusing profusion the typical scenes and languages of low life. Out of these elements a single spark, which we may attribute to genius, to chance, or to inspiration, was enough to produce a new and happy conception: that of a parody on the romances of chivalry, in which the extravagances of the fables of knighthood should be contrasted with the sordid realities of life. This is done by the ingenious device of representing a country gentleman whose naturally generous mind, unhinged by much reading of the books of chivalry, should lead him to undertake the office of knight-errant, and induce him to ride about the country clad in ancient armor, to right wrongs, to succor defenseless maidens, to kill giants, and to win empires at least as vast as that of Alexander.

This is the subject of *Don Quixote*. But happy as the conception is, it could not have produced a book of enduring charm and well-seasoned wisdom, had it not been filled in with a great number of amusing and lifelike episodes, and verified by two admirable figures, Don Quixote and Sancho Panza, characters at once intimately individual and truly universal.

Don Quixote at first appears to the reader, and probably appeared to the author as well, as primarily a madman, — a thin and gaunt old village squire, whose brain has been turned by the nonsense he has read and taken for gospel truth; and who is punished for his ridiculous mania by an uninterrupted series of beatings, falls, indignities, and insults. But the hero and the author together, with the ingenuity proper to madness and the inevitableness proper to genius, soon begin to disclose the fund of intelligence and ideal passion which underlies this superficial insanity. We see that Don Quixote is only mad north-north-west, when the wind blows from the quarter of his chivalrous preoccupation. At other times he shows himself a man of great goodness and fineness of wit; virtuous, courageous, courteous, and generous, and in fact the perfect ideal of a gentleman. When he takes, for instance, a handful of acorns from the goat-herds' table and begins a grandiloquent discourse upon the Golden Age, we feel how cultivated the man is, how easily the little things of life suggest to him the great things, and with what delight he dwells on what is beautiful and happy. The truth and pathos of the character become all the more compelling when we consider how naturally the hero's madness and calamities flow from this same exquisite sense of what is good.

The contrast to this figure is furnished by that of Sancho Panza, who embodies all that is matter-of-fact, gross, and plebeian. Yet he is willing to become Don Quixote's esquire, and by his credulity and devotion shows what an ascendency a heroic and enthusiastic nature can gain over the most sluggish of men. Sancho has none of the instincts of his master. He never read the books of chivalry or desired to right the wrongs of the world. He is naturally satisfied with his crust and his onions, if they can be washed down with enough bad wine. His good drudge of a wife never transformed herself in his fancy into a peerless Dulcinea. Yet Sancho follows his master into every danger, shares his discomfiture and the many blows that rain down upon him, and hopes to the end for the governorship of that Insula with with Don Quixote is some day to reward his faithful esquire.

As the madness of Don Quixote is humanized by his natural intelligence and courage, so the grossness and credulity of Sancho are relieved by his homely wit. He abounds in proverbs. He never fails to see the reality of a situation, and to protest doggedly against his master's visionary flights. He holds fast as long as he can to the evidence of his senses, and to his little weaknesses of flesh and spirit. But finally he surrenders to the authority of Don Quixote, and of the historians of chivalry, although not with a certain reluctance and some surviving doubts.

The character of Sancho is admirable for the veracity with which its details are drawn. The traits of the boor, the glutton, and the coward come most naturally to the surface upon occasion, yet Sancho remains a patient, good-natured peasant, a devoted servant, and a humble Christian. Under the cover of such lifelike incongruities, and of a pervasive humor, the author has given us a satirical picture of human nature not inferior, perhaps, to that furnished by Don Quixote himself. For instance: Don Quixote, after mending his helmet, tries its strength with a blow that smashes it to pieces. He mends it a second time, but now, without trial, deputes it to be henceforth a strong and perfect helmet. Sancho, when he is sent to bear a letter to Dulcinea, neglects to deliver it, and invents an account of his interview with the imaginary lady for the satisfaction of his master. But before long, by dint of repeating the story, he comes himself to believe his own lies. Thus self-deception in the knight is the ridiculous effect of courage, and in the esquire the not less ridiculous effect of sloth.

The adventures these two heroes encounter are naturally only such as travelers along the Spanish roads would then have been likely to come upon. The point of the story depends on the familiarity and commonness of the situations in which Don Quixote finds himself, so that the absurdity of his pretensions may be overwhelmingly shown. Critics are agreed in blaming the exceptions which Cervantes allowed himself to make to the realism of his scenes, where he introduced romantic tales into the narrative of the first part. The tales are in themselves unworthy of their setting, and contrary to the spirit of the whole book. Cervantes doubtless yielded here partly to his story-telling habits, partly to a fear of monotony in the uninterrupted description of Don Quixote's adventures. He avoided this mistake in the second part, and devised the visit to the Duke's palace, and the intentional sport there made of the hero, to give variety to the story.

More variety and more unity may still, perhaps, seem desirable in the book. The episodes are strung together without much coherence, and without any attempt to develop either the plot or the characters. Sancho, to be sure, at last tastes the governorship of his Insula, and Don Quixote on his death-bed recovers his wits. But this conclusion, appropriate and touching as it is, might have come almost anywhere in the course of the story. The whole book has, in fact, rather the quality of an improvisation. The episodes suggest themselves to the author's fancy as he proceeds; a fact which gives them the same unexpectedness and sometimes the same incompleteness which the events of a journey naturally have. It is in the genius of this kind of narrative to be a sort of imaginary diary, without a general dramatic structure. The interest depends on the characters and the incidents alone; on the fertility of the author's invention, on the ingenuity of the turns he gives to the story, and on the incidental scenes and figures he describes.

When we have once accepted this manner of writing fiction — which might be called that of the novelist before the days of the novel — we can only admire the execution of *Don Quixote* as masterly in its kind. We find here an abundance of fancy that is never at a loss for some probable and interesting incident; we find a graphic power that makes living and unforgettable many a minor character, even if slightly sketched; we find the charm of the country rendered by little touches without any formal descriptions; and we find a humorous and minute reproduction of the manners of the time. All this is rendered in flowing and easy style, abounding in both characterization and parody of diverse types of speech and composition; and the whole is still but the background for the figures of Don Quixote and Sancho, and for their pleasant discourse, the quality and savor of which is maintained to the end. These excellences unite to make the book one of the most permanently delightful in the world, as well as one of the most diverting. Seldom has laughter been so well justified as that which the reading of *Don Quixote* continually provokes; seldom has it found its causes in such genuine fancy, such profound and real contrast, and such victorious good-humor.

We sometimes wish, perhaps, that our heroes were spared some of their bruises, and that we were not asked to delight so much in promiscuous beatings and floggings. But we must remember that these three hundred years have made the European race much more sensitive to physical suffering. Our ancestors took that doubtful pleasure in the idea of corporal writhings which we still take in the description of the tortures of the spirit. The idea of both evils is naturally distasteful to a refined mind; but we admit more willingly the kind which habit has accustomed us to regard as inevitable, and which personal experience very probably has made an old friend.

Don Quixote has accordingly enjoyed a universal popularity, and has had the singular privilege of accomplishing the object for which it was written, which was to recall fiction from the extravagances of the books of chivalry to the study of real life. This is the simple object which Cervantes had and avowed. He was a literary man with literary interests, and the idea which came to him was to ridicule the absurdities of the prevalent literary mode. The rich vein which he struck in the conception of Don Quixote's madness and topsy-turvy adventures encouraged him to go on. The subject and the characters deepened under his hands, until from a parody of a certain kind of romances the story threatened to become a satire on human idealism. At the same time Cervantes grew fond of his hero, and made him, as we must feel, in some sort a representative of his own chivalrous enthusiasms and constant disappointments.

We need not, however, see in this transformation any deep-laid malice or remote significance. As the tale opened out before the author's fancy and enlisted his closer and more loving attention, he naturally enriched it with all the wealth of his experience. Just as he diversified it with pictures of common life and manners, so he weighted it with the burden of human tragedy. He left upon it an impress of his own nobility and misfortunes side by side with a record of his time and country. But in this there was nothing intentional. He only spoke out of the fullness of his heart. The highest motives and characters had been revealed to him by his own impulses, and the lowest by his daily experience.

There is nothing in the book that suggests a premeditated satire upon faith and enthusiasm in general. The author's evident purpose is to amuse, not to upbraid or to discourage. There is no bitterness in his pathos or despair in his disenchantment; partly because he retains a healthy fondness for this naughty world, and partly because his heart is profoundly and entirely Christian. He would have rejected with indignation an interpretation of his work that would see in it an attack on religion or even on chivalry. His birth and nurture had made him religious and chivalrous from the beginning, and he remained so by conviction to the end. He was still full of plans and hopes when death overtook him, but he greeted it with perfect simplicity, without lamentations over the past or anxiety for the future.

If we could have asked Cervantes what the moral of Don Quixote was to his own mind, he would have told us perhaps that it was this: that the force of idealism is wasted when it does not recognize the reality of things. Neglect of the facts of daily life made the absurdity of the romances of chivalry and of the enterprise of Don Quixote. What is needed is not, of course, that idealism should be surrendered, either in literature or in life; but that in both it should be made efficacious by a better adjustment to the reality it would transform.

Something of this kind would have been, we may believe, Cervantes's own reading of his parable. But when parables are such direct and full transcripts of life as is the story of Don Quixote, they offer almost as much occasion for diversity of interpretation as does the personal experience of men in the world. That the moral of Don Quixote should be doubtful and that each man should be tempted to see in it the expression of his own convictions, is after all the greatest possible encomium of the book. For we may infer that the truth has been rendered in it, and that men may return to it always, as to Nature herself, to renew their theories or to forget them, and to refresh their fancy with the spectacle of a living world.

William Serrin

The Incredible World of Barney Stutesman

Hey, Charlie. A helicopter. Isn't that Barney Stutesman? Yeah. Yeah, it is. Blink your light. You're supposed to blink your lights at him. Hey. Look. He's blinking back.

It's Barney Stutesman, all right, the chunky Barney Stutesman, George Gobel in a blue flight jacket, a radio personality. The WIXIE promotion people think Barney is the greatest thing since the Bloody Mary. Barney is an Institution, they say. Actually, Barney is a steal. All the big towns had an airborne traffic reporter — Chicago, New York, LA, San Francisco, even Kansas City, Pittsburgh, Houston, Milwaukee. The WIXIE execs said Detroit was just as big as those towns, by golly, so they brought Barney in.

Things are looking pretty good right now. We're out here on the West Side. Driving conditions have improved quite a bit. Traffic is getting just a little heavier now. I felt a few sprinkles of rain just before I took off. So kind of watch your driving, won't you?

He's up in the air four hours a day, old Barney is, two in the morning, two at night. Here he is one minute over the Lodge-Davison interchange, here he is another over the Ford, Telegraph, the Southfield. He orbits, slides, flaps, wheels, hunkers like his ship is wearing Keds.

Barney starts at seven in the morning, revving his $35,000, white-carpeted, Naugahyde-upholstered Bell chopper, then zooming off the hardstand at National Airport. The rest of the town is . . . waking up . . . stretching, shaving, making its beds, eating breakfast, dressing, getting into its cars, driving to work. In the afternoon, he goes up at 3:45, and now everything is reversed, the jams in the opposite lanes, the opposite directions. And here they come again, the commuters, businessmen, ad men, cops, clerks, all rushing home, tense, nervous, teed-off, maybe a bit in the bag from a couple of stiff martinis.

Either way, thousands upon thousands of cars, Pontiacs, Fords, VWs, Chevrolets, Mercs, Citroens, Volvos, Buicks, Cadillacs, Dodges, Jags, Imperials. Streaks of color, a pitchman's palette of color, sierra fawn, madeira maroon, tahoe turquoise, aquamarine, grenada gold, marine blue, capri cream, tomato soup red, inverness green, trafalgar blue, cumberland beige, persian white, desert dune, daffodil yellow, twilight turquoise, pebble beige, raven black, candyapple red. Always bumper to bumper, grill to trunk, stop, jerk, breeze off, hit the brakes, slide in, slip out.

Millions, just millions of people, their adrenal glands pumping like hell to cope with the tension, ulcers enlarging to the size of half dollars, headaches thumping just like the Bufferin ads, cancer, kidney, liver failures shooting up like Business Week graphs during inflation, half a ton of aspirin a day down the hatch.

Each day, 160,000 to 180,000 cars on the Lodge, 160,000 to 180,000 more on the Ford, 80,000 more on the Southfield. The Freeway . . . the chute, the DITCH . . . walled, bridged, fenced . . . 14 to 20 inches of sand, three-quarters of an inch of compacted gravel, four inches of concrete, three-quarters inch of steel mesh, six more inches of concrete.

Every thousand feet there's a drain, every 99 feet a joint, eight contraction joints, then an expansion joint, all filled with Neoprene, rubberized cement. Concrete conveyors are what the freeways are, as much of the commuter's life as food, sex, and sleep. An experienced commuter can drive the Lodge or the Ford for 40 minutes and not remember a minute of it, not the suburbs, scrapyards, factories, slums, litter, abandoned cars.

Always there is NOISE . . . exhaust, brakes, fast starts, airplanes, pneumatic drills, pile drivers, excavators . . . and after dusk neon lights, all kinds of NEON LIGHTS, the whole city a juke box of lights, And the Radio, always the RADIO . . . Sonny and Cher, the Association, housewife-on-the-phone yeast ads, Nelson Riddle, Paul Revere and the Raiders, Sinatra, Conniff, the SUpremes, Kenner 13, Golden Oldies, Contact News, Headlines by Dateline, interviews with the Tigers, Mike Maus, J. P. McCarthy, Dr. Golden's Optometric Clinic with young adult credit plans, Sta-Flo Starch with super silicones, Heckman's Bakeries, Donovan, Lesley Gore, Ringo Starr, the Mamas and the Papas, 20-20 News, Specs and Hare, Dave Prince.

Hopefully Specs and Hare, and Dave Prince, the Princer. At least for WXYZ. These are the WIXIE jocks when Barney comes on. It's always the same, the lead-in with the old theme from the Broderick Crawford "Highway Patrol" TV show, the voice of Barney from his chopper, a little repartee between Barney and Specs and Hare or the Princer, then Barney's report on the traffic, Barney all the time floating that chopper 600 feet in the air.

We're over the Southfield now, in the Six Mile Road and Outer Drive area. Northbound and southbound Southfield are both doing pretty well. Six mile, Seven Mile, Outer Drive and Eight mile are all doing well . . . moving along without any problems. The northbound Lodge is getting heavier now, from Davison to Eight Mile. But it's still moving along at a pretty good pace. Past that, it's moving at maximum speed. Grand River is just a little heavier right now. But still no problems anywhere we can find . . .

Stutesman is part of a national phenomenon, part of radio's huckstering to rebuild its image, cracked by TV, flicks, the barbecue, the fall of the networks. Radio is stressing public service. It is emphasizing editorials, measle-shot campaigns, nationwide news hookups, remote local news, talk shows.

For years radio was nothing but hard rock, but now stations all over America are striving for respectability. Traffic reporters are up all over the place, in whirly-birds, small Cessnas. WCBS in New York has two watchers, Bob Richardson and Neal Busch. They call themselves "Orville" and "Wilbur" and their helicopters "help-o-copters." KAGC in Los Angeles has female traffic reporters, Kelly Lange and Lorrie Ross, Beach Bingolike starlets in silver costumes that show their brassieres. The traffic reporter in KGIL in Los Angeles is Bruce Payne, an ex-Army major. In New York and LA they have regular whirlybird wars, the choppers hovering over accidents like turkey buzzards, the pilots manipulating their electronic gear like Strategic Air Command technicians to get the news on the air.

It can, of course, be hazardous. Ice can accumulate on chopper blades, wings, and windshields. Wash from big jets can upend choppers like canoes. Since 1957, reports Time Magazine, at least 10 traffic reporters have died in on-the-job crashes. When one went down in Chicago, the idea was so funny it became something of a town joke. In Houston, thousands of commuters watched a chopper fall from the sky like a stone. The crash killed two.

Stutesman is one of thousands of helicopter pilots who learned to fly in the Army, then got out and went into the chopper business on their own. Like everybody else, Stutesman was trained at Ft. Rucker, Ala., the Army chopper school, then spent a couple of years flying intelligence officers over bivouacs to check camouflage, ferrying troops into mock battles, chauffeuring around some dude general. Of course, Vietnam has changed the casual aspect of it all, and now Army chopper pilots get zapped in droves, some ignorant VC in shower clogs shooting down a $100,000 chopper with a 79-cent Czech rifle left over from World War II.

Still, then and now, chopper pilots couldn't get past field grade. So, like Stutesman, they got out. Barney quit in 1957, and now owns and operates Hi-Lift Helicopters Inc., and does a sweet business. He does aerial photography work, is Michigan's only licensed helicopter examiner. He has his own helicopter school, has logged over 7,000 hours. He can put you on a dime almost anywhere in North America, no terminals, holding patterns, hour rides from the airport. He can cart you to Cleveland, put a newsman over a sinking ship, take you fishing for Lake Trout in Great Slave Lake.

We're over the Edsel Ford right now. Traffic is heavy. The northbound Southfield is heavy right now from Michigan Avenue, and remains that way up past Grand River. The Edsel Ford is heavy from the interchange past Livernois. Michigan Avenue, Warren, Grand River . . . all the surface routes are heavy . . . Still, we can't find anything wrong with the driving. Everybody is doing a fine job. But the weather is picking up . . . so kind of watch your driving . . .

So there is Barney, whipping here, zooming there, reporting accidents, tie-ups, detours and flats; warning of this and cautioning of that, guiding us home like the Great Whirlybird in the Sky. What would we do, what would we ever do, without him?

Nothing. We would do nothing at all. Because none of it, none of it at all, makes any difference. There is Barney, swooping and tooting and telling how it really is . . . and IT MAKES NO DIFFERENCE AT ALL.

Once you are in the ditch, in the Freeway, it's all over. There is no where else to go. Stutesman could report hydrogen warfare over the Interchange and you would keep right on driving. Even if you'd rather quit than try, the guy next door won't let you in his lane and the guy behind you is honking you on to disaster and the guy in front couldn't care less because he, he is listening to WWJ. The Joint Chiefs of Staff in a massed flight of Huey-16s couldn't shave a minute off Joe Glotz's driving time. And everybody, or almost everybody, knows it.

Oh, the WIXIE biggies say he helps. Even Time Magazine says that, because Time is written in New York and published in Chicago and they probably have never been, not once, on the John Lodge Expressway.

The John Lodge was built to handle 90,000 cars a day and it was behind, out-of-date, a monster, the day they finished it all. It handles twice the traffic it's supposed to right now and things are going to get worse, not better.

Barney can't even reroute you because once you are thudding down the Lodge or the Ford you can't go anywhere else because anywhere else is fouled up, too. Barney can tell you to squeeze right (so you hit a truck) or squeeze left (you hit the other truck) or not get on the freeway at all (you get hit by a bicycle) but he hardly ever does. And anyhow, nobody knows where the surface roads go. People are so used to the freeway they've forgotten about the rest of town. A State Highway Department official says commuters are like the rats in the Skinner boxes; the maze has got them hooked. "If they had to use surface routes," he says, "I suspect a hell of a lot of them would just get lost."

We're out on the northeast side. The northbound Lodge is heavy now, beginning from the interchange, and is slow-moving to the Davison, where it gradually begins to loosen up. But it remains heavy from there on to the Wyoming area. The eastbound Ford is clear out past Mt. Elliot. The westbound Ford is still just a little bit heavy, picking up maximum speed past Livernois. The surface routes are all heavy now, and slow-moving in spots. Still, we've found no real accidents or tie-ups. . .

What is striking about Stutesman and his Whirlybird Watch is the sheer contrast of it all. Here is Stutesman, 600 feet above the millions of bilious commuters, above the smokestacks crapping streams of green, blue, red smoke; above the cement, the tinkertoy houses, the millions of miles of telephone wire, the scrapyards. Stutesman, above it all, but not a part of it, always connected. He has an RCA portable radio plugged in his left ear, so he can hear WIXIE and its chicken rock; he has two other receivers, one over each ear like an earmuff, so he can hear City Airport, and old Specs and Hare and the Princer when they talk to him. Then he has two transmitters, one to talk to City Airport, one to chat with the WIXIE jocks. Barney Stutesman, tacking through the brilliant sunshine, slipping through rain and snow squalls, some of them hundreds of feet high, black, airy masses in the sun; Barney Stutesman, not a bird, but a kite.

Even Barney admits to some of the impossibility of his job, telling about the time he was cruising the East Ford, and seeing this guy walking across an exit ramp. A car zoomed up, and ran him over. "I felt like the most helpless guy in the world," Barney says. "He disappeared under the car, then came out the back end. He got up, went around to the driver's side. They talked awhile, then he got in and they drove away."

But whose job is all two-hour lunches, Tanqueray gin and tonics? Barney loves flying, loves his capacity as a radio personality. He does a fine job stressing safety, he often reports accidents to the police department. And sure enough. There is a Barney Stutesman Fan Club.

What Barney is, is WIXIE PR — good, solid WXYZ promotion. How about the time he got chased by the Red Baron? Wixie got permission from Charles Schulz, the cartoonist, to send up an old World War I biplane. They billed it as flown by the Red Baron, Snoopy's nemesis in "Peanuts."

WIXIE pretended the Red Baron had come all the way from Germany — "from Stutesgart," says Ray Koepper, WIXIE writer and producer, "linking it with Barney's name." The idea was the Red Barson was going to shoot down Barney and take over the Detroit skyways. "We had spottings from Schulz, Mike Douglas in Philly, Gary Collins in Cleveland," says Koepper. "Collins plays end for the Cleveland Browns." It lasted 10 days. At the end, the Red Baron found out Barney was of German ancestry, and didn't have the heart to down him. He zoomed away. Harry Martin was the voice of the Red Baron. It was a honey of a bit, Koepper says.

Another time Stutesman was orbiting around, issuing his spot reports plus his eight regular 30-second-or-so bits a day, and bantering with Specs and Hare. The thermometer on the Bell Telephone Building said eight degrees. Barney says, "It's cold up here in the bird." And Specs and Hare, whichever is which, says, "Yeah, when it gets cold, I hear you freeze your bird." What Specs and Hare were doing was using an old Sinatra line, like, "Hey, Dean, how's your bird?" One time Sinatra even put it into a song, singing, ". . . We'll take our birds down to Acapulco Bay . . ." It is Las Vegas hipster, not so obscurely obscene.

Later the same day, Specs and Hare, usually a Mexican League Bob and Ray, get off one of their best lines of their four months in Detroit. "Okay," says Specs and Hare. "At the count of three, everybody in the sound of Barney Stutesman's voice change lanes." It is great, just great.

Then, after the morning stint, Barney slips on down to the WIXIE Broadcast House, and has coffee with the WIXIE people: Shirley Eder, the Free Press columnist, Frank Tomlinson, the news director, Bill Axtell, the promo man, a couple of lacquered women, beautiful broadcast types, assorted others. It wasn't Barney's idea, because Stutesman is still more bush pilot, more loner than radio star. But he is there. In two layers of clothing and boots he is there. Barney Stutesman, part of the scene.

I Hear America Singing; or "Leaves of Grass" Revisited, Like

The nuttiness is spreading in our land.

I get on this plane recently. An emergency trip — out to Chicago and back again. No time to make reservations, and it seems that when you're really in a hurry the only seat you can ever get is on the Champagne — Red Carpet Flight. The others are all booked up weeks ahead of time.

And so I find myself going through this great big chute. You don't walk into airplanes any more; they inject you into them. The airplane is mainlining people. You walk through this tube — the same air-conditioning and Muzak that is in the terminal — you never know you're on a plane. It's like a big tunnel that runs from the Time-Life Building straight to Chicago.

This really is the Jet Age. In order to Keep Your Finger on the Pulse of Life you've got to do it at 700 miles per hour, or slightly below the sonic barrier. Because, Dad, that's where it's happening. That is where the story is being spelled out.

But one thing — at subsonic speeds you've got to really look at it hard in order to see it, because sometimes it's moving so fast it's just a blur. Trailing smoke.

You've got the picture. I am injected into this enormous silver monster, floating gently on a sea of barely audible Muzak, the sweet Karo Syrup of Existence. I am strapped into my seat. My safety belt is a delicate baby-blue shade, matching the cloud-blue and spun-silver interior décor of this about-to-hurtle projectile.

Muzak rises to crescendo and we take off. Instantly we are high over this big chunk of land, and the world has become a blurred Kodachrome slide.

A man today never feels so alive as when he is hurtling from one point to another on the azimuth. My nerves are tingling. I'm ready to devour

Life in great chunks. In the Champagne — Red Carpet — First Class — VIP — Very Expensive Section.

Silently the red velour is rolled out and baby-blue and silver *houris* are plying me with stuff to eat — which if my mother knew I was eating she would really know I have gone to hell. By God, caviar and Moët *brut* and diced lamb's-liver pâté at 8:17 A.M., over Altoona.

Suddenly, with no warning, from behind me I hear the sound. I have never heard anything like this ever in a jet plane. Or in a biplane for that matter. Or even a Fokker trimotor. I'm sitting there knocking down the caviar, slurping up the champagne, when from behind me I hear the sound, the unmistakable twang, the soul-searing biting buzz of a *guitar!*

A plaintive G-minor chord mingled with the sounds of ice cubes and plastic swizzle sticks . . .

Boing . . . boing . . . twaaannng . . .

And then, a heartbroken voice. It's the voice of America Singing:

500 Miles! ! ! !

It echoes through the pressurized cabin, bouncing from one curved baby-blue bulkhead to the next, and finally fading out somewhere near the "Occupied" sign at the far end of our sealed capsule:

500 Miles! ! ! !

For crying out loud! A Lonesome Traveler! On a jet flight for Chicago, Meat Packer to the World, City of the Broad Shoulders, where the fog creeps in on little cat's feet. A Lonesome Traveler in the Champagne — Red Carpet — First Class — VIP — Very Expensive Section!

I turn around. And here's this angry, beat-looking kid sprawled out there in his foam rubber seat, his safety belt unhooked, a battered guitar case beside him. This angry kid, all tanned from Fire Island where the Crusade for Truth is swelling like a mighty organ chord that cannot be ignored. He's tanned, and wearing a pair of Levis carefully torn in all the right places. It cost his old man a lot of bucks for that pair of Levis — torn, faded, and worn as if they've been worn building the Union Pacific by hand, fighting the Terrible Depression of the Thirties, scrabbling out of the stony soil a hard crust of bread for a poor, honest man, just a-livin' in This Land, just a-tryin' to Love and a-tryin' to Understand and Live as a simple, pure Heart with his Fellows, his Brothers and Sisters all over This Land. A pure White Dove, a-sailin', a-sailin', a-sailin' . . .

The Times They Are a-Changin'

This guy's singing there and the tears are just a-streamin' down between the champagne glasses and the olive picks. . . . There was hardly a dry eye in the house. I am surrounded by a horde of college students, all empathizing like mad with the plight of the Common Man Fighting Against the Forces of Evil, the forces of a rotten, decadent Society.

This kid is on his way to his junior year at the University of Iowa, all the way Champagne Flight, all the way it's been all of his life.

If I Had a Hammer

There he sat, honest tears a-coursin' down those hardened, tan cheeks of his, hardened by so many hard, terrible, awful, wrenchin' scrabblin' weeks at Bar Harbor.

WE SHALL OVERCOME

He's getting *real* bugged now.

WE SHALL NOT BE MOVED

The stewardess bends over to say, "More champagne, sir?"

"Yeah, fill it up . . ."

If I Had My Way

I'm sitting there and all of sudden I realize that today's Lonesome Traveler travels *only* First Class. And more and more I realized that the plight of the Common Man is now in the hands of the Uncommon Man. With plenty of jack.

One of the wildest things about this whole new Suffering Traveler bit that is spreading throughout the campuses today is that the higher a guy is in *actual* social status, the more he empathizes with the real strugglers. More and more you'll find that the "folk" groups are the most clean-scrubbed, most obviously well-heeled people you'll ever see in your life. You just can't imagine Peter, Paul and Mary *ever* hungry. Or Joan Baez, either, for that matter.

There I sit with champagne glass in hand, trying to figure out just exactly why all this vaguely bugged me. It reminded me of something else that I couldn't quite remember. Sort of like trying to remember just how *Swan Lake* goes, or something.

The guitar hit a lovely A-minor chord as the feckless youth behind me plumbed even deeper into his social consciousness. The stewardess's baby-blue bottom undulated up the aisle, toward Chicago. And suddenly I knew. Marie Antoinette! And then I recalled something out of my almost completely forgotten European history courses.

Marie Antoinette — now it came back. Just before the French Revolution . . . I could even remember a few pedantic phrases from my European History II textbook:

"Just before the French Revolution there was a tremendous upsurge of interest in and empathy for the peasant on the part of the idle nobility. It reached the point where Marie Antoinette and her ladies-in-waiting, with selected noblemen and their pages, would spend weekends in the country, dressed as milkmaids and simple peasants of the field."

Aha!

"In the forests around Versailles the decadent French court built simple peasant cottages in which to live the 'rough' life and to sing the praises of the rough singular man living his hard, stony life, tilling from the soil of France the barest essentials of existence. They actually *did* empathize with him. There was a movement led by Rousseau, the Rousseau Naturalism Movement . . ."

I toyed moodily with a morsel of Belgian mint jelly as behind me the Simple Peasant of the Field once again raised his sorrowful voice:

This Land Is Your Land

My left hand made the chord changes instinctively as he sang out.

Another section of European history came floating back to me on the scent of delicate candied baby yams:

"It is difficult to imagine what the *real* peasants and laborers and milkmaids of France thought when they observed Marie Antoinette and the noblemen at play. Some French writers believe that the sight so enraged them that the course of Revolution was then truly set."

Nervously, I signaled for more wine. I thought, high over Ohio, of the folk music audiences and singers I had seen. There hadn't been many Downtrodden and Defeated people in those crowds. Could it be that the lower down a man really is on the social scale, the less he identifies with the Folk Freedom Fighters, until finally, in the actual slums themselves, you'll find *no* guys singing:

This Land Is Your Land

I looked down through 37,500 feet of cumulus mist. I wondered how many guys were looking up out of tenements at this whistlin' lonesome jet carrying all these guys in the Champagne Section, winging on their way toward Northwestern, Indiana University, U.C.L.A., the University of Michigan. First Class.

A big blonde across the aisle, with an O.S.U. sticker on her Pan-Am flight bag, had joined in. Another white dove a-sailin' and a-sailin'. I wondered if that chick knew what a tumbrel was. Hard to say. American people are not historically minded. She probably thinks that a tumbrel is a seven-letter word (46 Across) meaning "a small cart."

A tall, skinny, crewcut kid, tweed jacket, Daks slacks, with a "Ban the Bomb" button in his lapel, bumped past me, trailing the scent of Brandy and Benedictine. He was heading for the john.

Ban the bomb. I guess that kid figures that history started in 1945. Everything before that was some kind of bad TV show starring Rip Torn as the company commander who chickened out.

I started in on the mousse. Not bad. Ladyfingers soaked in Virgin Islands rum. The big blonde grinned at me over her copy of *The Realist*. Yes, by God, I was surrounded by Realists.

Another phrase from Eur. His. II jiggled into form:

"One school of thought holds that what happened in France can happen in any society at a certain point in that society's existence, when life becomes so unreal, abstract, to so many people that they begin to long hungrily for the life that they *imagine* is 'Real,' usually the life of men who are tilling the soil or suffering social injustices at the hands of the imaginers themselves."

Hmmmm. Seven or eight pilgrims had joined in the singing, led by a thin, sharp-faced, dark-haired, high-cheekboned girl in a burlap skirt from Jax. A nice bottom. I wondered if she knew what a tumbrel was.

This crowd was as much at home in a jet plane as they were in a taxicab. Belting it out:

> *I'm a lonesome, lonesome traveler*
> *along the hard, rocky road of life . . .*

sitting in the back seat of a Yellow Cab, the meter ticking away.

> *I'm a lonesome, lonesome Yellow Cab*
> *Rider a-travelin' on the old man's*
> *Diners' Club card.*

One thing I've noticed about jet flying is that once you're at cross-country altitude, you rarely feel the slightest bump of a transient air pocket or rough crosswind. At 600 miles per hour plus, you just hang there, suspended. And it is easy to lose all sense of time, space, and reality. The old DC-3's and 4's and even the 6's bumped and banged along, and you knew damn well that something was out there battering at that fuselage, trying to get in. I guess the place to have a fantasy, if you don't want Reality to come creeping in on gnarled vulture claws, is in a jet, just hanging there.

I felt vaguely drunk. Every junky and pothead I've ever known, as well as drinkers of all variety, somehow always use the word "high." By God, we really *were* high! Half a snootful at 37,500 feet is *high*, Dad! Just look out of the misty, ovoid window and there it is, big, fat, and luscious — that fat old earth. I knew one guy who said every time he smoked a joint or two he felt as though he were slowly volplaning around, doing an easy Immelmann, looking down at everybody. He could see it *all*. Of course, the truth is he was five feet six and a very nervous cat. In real life he didn't look down at much, except maybe a gopher or two, and it all scared him. Maybe that's part of the key, too. I don't know.

The hostess began serving brandies and liqueurs. Our little First Class section was now a tightly knit, jet-propelled hootenanny. Bagged to the gills and feeling the rich, heady hot blood of Social Protest coursing through our veins. Solidarity! Love! Ah, it was good to be alive. And not only alive, but a vibrant, sensitive, Aware person who knew where injustice and human misery were. And we knew what to do about it. *Sing* about it.

I could no longer fight back the urge to join in with my fellow men. Yes, we had been through hell together. Together we had seen it.

A thin, pale young man stood in the aisle. His crystal-clear boy soprano quivering with exultation, he led us on to further glories. True, he reminded me of Audrey Hepburn, who never was exactly my type. His little-boy bangs carelessly brushed down over his forehead, his clearly symbolic denim-blue work-shirt open, nay, *ripped* open, à la fist-fightin' Millhand, he was the very image of a Master Sufferer Singer of our time. In the overheated air of our First Class cabin you could almost see his head starkly outlined in a grainy black and white photograph — towering above the rubble of an American street — a perfect Album Cover head. One of the New Breed — the New Breed of fiction artists edging out the old crowd who had used writing as a medium to create fictional characters in novels and plays and short stories, characters that were clearly recognized as make-believe.

The New Breed has gone one important step farther. They use their own lives as a medium for fiction and their own persons as fictional characters. The New Breed can imagine himself to be anything, and believe it — Cowhand, Lumberjack, Negro, Itinerant Fruit-Picker, Bull-fighter — any romantic figure that fits his fancy. So, at 19 or 20, a man can have lived a full, rich, dangerous life and feel that he is a worn-out, misery-scarred pilgrim. And what's more, his followers believe him, because they work in the same medium.

Denim Shirt's China-blue eyes burned with the feverish light of the Creative Artist, believing himself to be a rough-hewn hunk who had traveled many roads, "rode freight trains for kicks and got beat up for laughs, cut grass for quarters and sang for dimes," and now he was singing out all the pain of all those old wounds, a spent, scarred Singer for Truth who had been there and known it all. At 22.

If I Had a Hammer

sang the pale, wispy lad.

Up near the forward bulkhead two shaggy-browed 45-year-old tractor salesmen with the obvious tribal markings of retired paratroopers raised their snouts from the champagne trough. The port-side ex-sergeant glared backward down the aisle.

"For God's sake, sonny, will you keep it down?" With which the old battler went back to his jug.

For a brief moment the plane became very aggressive. A classical — if you will excuse the expression — pregnant moment.

And then, bravely, as he had always done, Young Audrey sang on. . . .

I looked at the bulging back of Old Sarge, and I wondered how many roads *that* old son of a gun had walked down. From Bizerte to Remagen, up the Po Valley and back; 7,000 miles, from Kiska to Iwo. And still on the Goddamn road.

Beat up for laughs! The grizzled specimen next to Old Sarge had the chewed ears of a guy who had fist-fought his way through every Off Limits bar from Camp Kilmer to the Kit Kat Klub on the Potzdamer Platz, and all for laughs.

The dark chick glowered up the cabin at the back of Old Sarge's head. He and his buddy were boffing it up. She glanced meltingly, at young Denim Shirt, her blue and white "Fight for Freedom" button gleaming like an angry shield above her tiny black-T-shirted bosom.

Her glance spoke volumes: "Those clods! What do they know of Suffering, of fighting for Good, for Ideals? What do they know of the hard, flinty back alley of Life, of Injustice? Only Youth *understands* and knows. Do not be afraid. I, an angry Girl-Type Lonesome Traveler, will protect you."

The lissome lad, taking heart, began again with renewed spirit and passion.

She was right. What *did* Old Sarge know about true Suffering? His swarthy, grizzled neck bent defiantly forward, back to the trough, that neck which still bore a permanent mahogany stain of 10,000 suns, the Libyan Desert, Tinian, the Solomons, Burma Road, Corregidor . . .

Chewed Ear glanced over his hunched shoulder for a brief instant at the button-wearer, the leer that had impaled broad-beamed, ripe-bosomed females from Dakar to Adelaide, a glance primeval and unmistakable. She flushed. She obviously was not used to heavy artillery.

Blowin' in the Wind

The black-T-shirted White Dove fluttered, confused, in the sand for a few wing beats and then scurried out of range.

The undergrad hootenanny swung into the chorus. Someone had produced a Kentucky mandolin, jangling high above the passionate Ovaltine voices. . . . The cabin was filled with joyous sound. Old Sarge, after the last note died echoing in the soft light-blue carpeting, turned suddenly. "Hey kid, do any of you guys know 'Dirty Gertie from Bizerte'?"

He laughed obscenely, not realizing he was disrupting a Religious service. The congregation plunked, embarrassed.

"How 'bout 'Lili Marlene'?" Without any warning, Chewed Ear tuned up — *a cappella.*

I've been workin' on the railroad,
all the Goddamned day . . .

He sang in the cracked voice that had sung itself out over 9,000 miles of Canadian-Pacific track, laying every spike in the frozen tundra personally.

> *I've been workin' on the railroad,*
> *just to pass the time away . . .*

he bellowed.

Blue Jeans in the seat behind me, in a put-down stage whisper to O.S.U. Bag:

"For God sake, 'I've Been Working on the Railroad'! This old guy wouldn't know a Work Song if he heard it."

The apple-cheeked youth, his fingers calloused by countless hours of guitar-pick-clutching, slumped knowingly against the cushions of his seat.

> *Can't you hear those whistles blowin' . . .*

The whiskey-cracked calliope, honed and sharpened against the cold winds blowing over countless flatbed coal cars and short-coupled reefers, ground to a stop.

FASTEN YOUR SEAT BELTS. NO SMOKING PLEASE. The soft yellow warning broke up the action.

"This is the Captain speaking. We are making our final approach to O'Hare Airport. We should be on the ground in three minutes. The ground temperature in Chicago — fifty-seven degrees. There is a slight crosswind. I hope you've enjoyed your trip. We hope to see you soon. Please fasten your seat belts."

Our great silver arrow knifed down through the thick underlayer of cloud and smoke. Red-roofed houses and lines of crawling blue Fords rose up toward us. The great flaps creaked and clanked into position. The bird paused for a brief instant, and we touched the runway.

"This is your stewardess. It has been a pleasure to have you aboard. Please keep your seat belts fastened until we come to a full stop. We hope you had a pleasant trip, and hope to see you again soon."

The jet stopped rolling, and outside my porthole I could see the Chicago end of the Great Tube being inserted into our bird. Behind me, the angry snap of a guitar case clasp. We moved up the aisle. From somewhere ahead, a piping adolescent voice:

"Hey Freddie, I'll see ya next weekend at the big hoot in Ann Arbor. Dylan's gonna make the scene. Maybe Baez!"

Old Sarge, hat jammed down over his ears, made one last verbal swipe at the stewardess who stood by the exit as we filed out. She smiled blandly.

"I hope you enjoyed your trip, sir."

Our little band of Lonesome Travelers toiled up the chute toward the City of the Broad Shoulders, Meat Packer to the World. The party was over.

Craig Starnaman

One That Got Away

Walking into a restaurant, he cannot help but attract attention. He is a seasoned hood: long swept-back hair; skin-tight black pants; ankle-height pointed boots. Over a black turtle-neck sweater rests a cracked and discolored black leather jacket, like a battered coat of chain mail. He walks loosely, under perfect control, ready to lash out at any time, in any direction. Leather creaks faintly as his arms swing loosely. His approach is heralded by the metallic clank of his steel heel-plates striking the floor in a slow, rhythmic pattern.

Crossing the room, he seats himself in a far corner, his back to the wall, facing the door. As he sits, his pants stretch tighter around his thighs and buttocks, revealing the long slim shape of a stiletto in his side pocket. His jacket is zipped only an inch or two at the bottom, and bulges away from his chest. From above, a motorcycle chain can be seen wrapped tightly around his waist. His belt buckle has been filed to rough, jagged edges — a vicious weapon in knowledgeable hands.

After ordering the standard fare of hamburgers and coffee, he waits nervously for his order to come. His eyes scan the crowd, probing for tell-tale weapon-bulges among the youthful patrons. He is constantly thinking, weighing possibilities. The blond guy by the door has a knife — he feels he can handle him. The two older hoods near the juke box are a different story. The long bulges under their left armpits conceal guns. He knows he is no match for them. If there is trouble, he'll have to go through a window.

His order arrives, and he eats out of duty rather than enjoyment. His eyes keep flicking around the room, seldom coming to rest, seeing everything, watching nothing. He is more conscious of motion than of individual objects. Any sudden movement attracts his eyes as a tall tree attracts lightning — swiftly, positively.

He drops the last bit of empty crust, swallows the last mouthful of bitter coffee, and slowly rises to his feet. Walking to the cash register, he is conscious of every sound, every movement, for he has left the protection of his corner stronghold and is vulnerable to attack from all sides. He pays his bill, still studying the room. The walk to the door is a terror that must be accepted, for he must pass close to the gun-wielding torpedoes. He gains the door without trouble and is lost from sight.

I know this hood. I was this hood.

Why? Did I grow up in a "pocket of poverty?" Was my education sparse, perhaps only to the sixth grade? Did I lack the entertainment facilities to keep me "off the streets?"

My father was vice-president of a thriving tool company. We lived in a spacious ranch-style house in one of the exclusive suburbs. We bought two new Oldsmobiles every year, and when I was old enough to drive, my father bought me a car of my own.

The high school I went to was the best that money could build and equip; the language labs boasted a phalanx of chrome-covered tape recorders, and the math department took pride in its light-flashing computer. The school was rated in the top ten in the United States, and I graduated in the top third of my class.

We spent our time sitting in drive-in restaurants, going to expensive and elaborate parties, working on our four-hundred-horsepower cars, getting drunk, or making love in the drive-in movies. We were the jaded youths of the high-income suburbs.

The rules of conformity were so strictly enforced by the social structure that no one would dare come to school in anything but a V-neck sweater and pin-stripe shirt. And all through school I was a good example of mass-produced mediocrity, never rising to the top of the society, never falling to the bottom. I was one of the mindless, woolly flock that provided the momentum to keep the system going. I bought the right things, went to the right places, attended the right parties, and drove the right car.

The fight for social status was the only thing that could prod us from our jaded lethargy. High grades were one of the more important status symbols. To increase the competition, there was a rule among the faculty that if there was more than one "A" in the class, they were going too slowly. This pressure whipped us into an academic frenzy.

But good grades were only a part of the status structure, and there was nothing that wasn't done for the sake of status. No one could be sure of a friend, for if he could raise his status by obliterating yours, he was expected to do it. There was nothing sacred in the fight for social acceptance.

At the beginning of the tenth grade, I was dating a girl at the top of the social ladder. I was sure I was in love, and the world was a chromium amphitheatre — life a play for my benefit. Everything was wonderful until the day I found my best friend at her house, the one place that was "Off Limits" to him. It wasn't long before Sue announced that she and Ed were going steady, neatly leaving me out. This drama was not unique. It has been enacted by different trios since the stone axe was the latest in super-weapons. Ed later admitted that he started dating Sue to get invited to the "right" parties. Ed's new Thunderbird convertible had something to do with Sue's decision.

I saw the superficiality of the whole society, and it sickened me. The shock of losing "the only girl in the world," coupled with the distaste I had for the society made me a rebel, a lone wolf.

One night as I sat in the local drive-in restaurant, I was shaken from my pastime of self-pity by the roar of a supercharged engine. A '57 Chevrolet nosed into the open space next to me, and I began discussing the car with its driver. It was a meeting on common ground, and the beginning of a friendship.

I got to know Jim DeLand better, and I was drawn to his circle of friends. I joined their group, and found myself in the world of the hoods, and it seemed to me "the best of all possible worlds." I felt accepted for what I was, not for what everyone said I had to be. I felt free to do the things I wanted to do, say what I wanted to say, and never worried that what I said or did would be "wrong."

Three years later I saw the other side of the coin. The world of the hoods led nowhere. At best, it led to a monotonous job on an assembly line, and at worst, to society's displaced persons camps, the slum ghettos.

Ignorant of the pain and suffering that lay at the dead end of this life, I reveled in the new-found freedom and friends I had among the hoods. I loved the way of life, though it was a hard and sometimes dangerous existence. The ground rules were taught to me one night by Little Tony, a blond Sicilian.

We were in front of Gelly's Drug Store, with its cracked plate glass and chipped marble facade. There was Deland, with his black boots, black pants and shirt, and the white turtle-neck under the shirt that made him look like an unholy priest. With him was Steele, tall and thin in comparison with DeLand's stocky build. He was dressed in a turtle-neck sweater and faded blue levis, stuffed carelessly into the tops of motor-cycle boots. The night was warm, and my own thin cotton shirt was enough to make me sticky and uncomfortable.

We were standing around like characters in a Marlon Brando movie, just killing time. There is nothing to do when you have no money, and as usual, we were broke. I'd spent my last coins for a bottle of cheap Thunderbird wine at about noon, and when it was gone the warm feeling went with it.

Little Tony and three of his friends materialized out of the shadows like deadly spectres, walking toward us with the swagger they get when they're drunk. Tony can't fight very well, and he never has an original idea, but his mean disposition and stark looks make him the leader. He's the only blond Italian I've ever seen — not the yellow blond you see every day, but the kind of white hair you see on ninety-year-old women, stringy, and growing in thin tufts. It looked odd, and he knew it, and it made him mean.

That night he was drunk, and meaner than usual. He spotted me first, and knew from the "grapevine" that I was the new guy, the one who'd never been in a street fight. He'd been bragging to his friends about how tough he was, and now he had a chance to prove it, with the cards stacked in his favor.

He came wandering over, with that mean look on his thin face, when the muscles on the jawline tighten, the nostrils flare, and the eyelids almost close. Three buttons were open on his fluorescent yellow shirt, exposing his hairless chest. He was sweating, and the neon lights reflected off his skin like headlights on wet pavement. He took a long pull on his bottle of half-and-half, a mixture of wine and cheap whiskey.

He took a quick look at DeLand and Steele, and decided that the odds were with him and his three friends. His head swiveled slowly toward me, like the turret of a snow-covered tank. Looking me straight in the eye he said, "So you're the new cat. You don't look so goddam' tough."

I was scared. I was afraid to fight, and too proud to back down. I'd rather be hurt than humiliated. I found a small measure of courage — from where I don't know. "Think so, Fuzz-head?"

It wasn't very original, but it set him off like a land-mine. He kicked me in the groin, and when I doubled over, his knee slammed into my face, dropping me to the sidewalk. I lay there, numb, not quite knowing what had happened. But I could feel the burn each time he kicked me. I wanted to get up and hit him, but I couldn't.

Suddenly the pain stopped. I turned my head and found Tony face-to-face with me on the sidewalk. Beyond him were two legs, silhouetted against the neon lights that twitched in silent agony. My eyes went up the standing form. It was DeLand. Agamemnon with a blackjack. His shirt was mottled with wet darkness, and the white turtle-neck was spotted in a pattern of red from his split lip. Beyond him I saw Steele rise from a groaning figure in the pool of darkness beside the drug store. There was no sign of Tony's other two friends.

I looked up at DeLand and mumbled, "Well, it looks like you guys did all right."

He regarded me silently for a few moments, then said, "Ya. Kinda looks like we won, didn' we."

It took some time to understand what he meant when he said "we won." I was included, even though I had lost my fight with Tony. I had fought and lost, when I knew from the start I had no chance, but I had not run away, and I was respected for it.

Now, though I have left the dead-end world of the hoods, I still carry the traits that, to me, made their society worthwhile. I still live by my code of honor. I still believe that friendship and loyalty, once given, should not be easily set aside. I often wonder if there isn't much that the society of the status symbol can learn from the society of the switchblade. . . .

Mary Sweers

Prejudice

News spread fast that Negroes had moved to our small town. They had come on a grocery-shopping, new-shoes-buying, hair-cut-getting, gossip's Saturday and the town's people were too busy to do more than pass the word on to anyone they met. Not until Sunday night after the town had raised its voice in hymn and prayer and tithed ten-percent of the week's income at morning and evening Church Services; not until this neighbor called on that one and the foamy beer and red, white and blue poker chips were hauled out and the Bibles were stuck away under the kitchen phone book where they would be handy for after-meal devotions; not until the shades were pulled down to shut out the eyes of the old widowed saint across the street and the wayward traveller who might not be in sympathy; not until then did the town start to stew and anger over the niggers.

I had seen Negroes in the city, ridden through their district, amazed at the close, dirty, humble houses and the tattered black children playing everywhere along the busy city streets. Once, when I was small, I asked Daddy why they didn't live in the country, like us, where there were wildflowers, berries and grapes; vegetable and flower gardens; trees to climb; and everything was green and clean and roomy. Daddy answered, "They have their parks in the city." I had been taught in Sunday School that "Jesus loves the little children . . . red and yellow, black and white." But I had also been taught that sin was black, lies were black, night was black and death was black. I decided long ago that things like bare city parks were good enough for people with black skin.

The town didn't wait long to give the Negroes a welcome. That very night some teenaged boys, still dressed in their Sunday suits, put a bullet through a stray cat's head and stuffed it in the Negroes' mailbox. I cried when I heard about that . . . . for the fate of the poor, soft-haired, tiny-pawed, innocent cat.

It took two weeks to get rid of them. The town's people had been transformed into an evil body that struck in the night, silently dumping accumulated garbage on the Negroes' dirt yard, blasting cherry bombs below the Negroes' cardboard-patched windows, flashing headlights and spot lights for hours on the brown-shingled shack with the sagging roof, playing "taps" at midnight at the door of the condemned house with the grassless yard and the flowerless edges along the driveway. Everyone in town had grass and flowers but the Negroes. And they didn't need them.

Then the final Saturday night of the two weeks vigilance — the night I've tried to believe was unreal — came. The town assembled quietly an hour before midnight in the Negroes' yard, armed with gunny sacks full of rocks and corn-cobs. A deacon of the church was the first to throw a stone through a partially glassed window and yell, "Get out of town, niggers!" Others reached into the sacks and others until rocks and cobs flew through the air and thumped on the sides of the house and crashed windows that tinkled like bells as they fell to the ground. I looked at the faces around me and saw set jaws, watery, flashing eyes and flushed cheeks. Around me, the dull rumbling chant rose to the heavens, "Get out of town, niggers. Get out of town. . . ." I thought of Stephan from the Bible and I could feel the rocks bruising my soul. For the first time in my life I doubted that God exists.

Excitement arose in my chest and my hands shook. They had done this, I thought, those people in that house. They had brought the hate into our town and it had spread like an epidemic of measles, changing my friends and the town's good people into faces that forgot how to laugh and minds that could not plan picnics and Fourth-of-July fireworks displays. These were the people — in that shambled house — who had made God a stranger to me. I grasped a rock and flung it with my young strength against the old house and cried hysterically, "Get out of town, niggers!"

The ruined shack is a showplace now and it's pointed out to visitors as the place where "those niggers once lived." That shack is one reason why the people of our town go to church three times a week and sleep through the sermon, then tithe twice as much during the offering. It's one reason they pull down the shades to live their private lives.

In my heart, I've often wanted to set fire to that shack and watch it burn to the ground with all the shameful and hypocritical memories it has for me. But my mind, oh, my mind, has taught me to turn indifferently away from my shame and to pull the shade down on decency and morality, to stretch the canvas of prejudice across the window of my heart and shut out the sunlight of understanding and truth.

Henry David Thoreau

Where I Lived and What I Lived for

At a certain season of our life we are accustomed to consider every spot as the possible site of a house. I have thus surveyed the country on every side within a dozen miles of where I live. In imagination I have bought all the farms in succession, for all were to be bought, and I knew their price. I walked over each farmer's premises, tasted his wild apples, discoursed on husbandry with him, took his farm at his price, at any price, mortgaging it to him in my mind; even put a higher price on it, — took everything but a deed for it, — took his word for his deed, for I dearly love to talk, — cultivated it, and him too to some extent, I trust, and withdrew when I had enjoyed it long enough, leaving him to carry it on. This experience entitled me to be regarded as a sort of real-estate broker by my friends. Wherever I sat, there I might live, and the landscape radiated from me accordingly. What is a house but a *sedes*, a seat? — better if a country seat. I discovered many a site for a house not likely to be soon improved, which some might have thought too far from the village, but to my eyes the village was too far from it. Well, there I might live, I said; and there I did live, for an hour, a summer and a winter life; saw how I could let the years run off, buffet the winter through, and see the spring come in. The future inhabitants of this region, wherever they may place their houses, may be sure that they have been anticipated. An afternoon sufficed to lay out the land into orchard, woodlot, and pasture, and to decide what fine oaks or pines should be left to stand before the door, and whence each blasted tree could be seen to the best advantage; and then I let it lie, fallow perchance, for a man is rich in proportion to the number of things which he can afford to let alone.

My imagination carried me so far that I even had the refusal of several farms, — the refusal was all I wanted, — but I never got my fingers burned by actual possession. The nearest that I came to actual possession was when I bought the Hollowell place, and had begun to sort my seeds, and collected materials with which to make a wheelbarrow to carry it on or off with; but before the owner gave me a deed of it, his wife — every man has such a wife — changed her mind and wished to keep it, and he offered me ten dollars to release him. Now, to speak the truth, I had but ten cents in the world, and it surpassed my arithmetic to tell, if I was the man who had ten cents, or who had a farm, or ten dollars, or all together. However, I let him keep the ten dollars and the farm too, for I had carried it far enough; or rather, to be generous, I sold him the farm for just what I gave for it, and, as he was not a rich man, made him a present of ten dollars, and still had my ten cents, and seeds, and materials for a wheelbarrow left. I found thus that I had been a rich man without any damage to my poverty. But I retained the landscape, and I have since annually carried off what it yielded without a wheelbarrow. With respect to landscapes, —

> *"I am monarch of all I* survey,
> *My right there is none to dispute."*

I have frequently seen a poet withdraw, having enjoyed the most valuable part of a farm, while the crusty farmer supposed that he had got a few wild apples only. Why, the owner does not know it for many years when a poet has put his farm in rhyme, the most admirable kind of invisible fence, has fairly impounded it, milked it, skimmed it, and got all the cream, and left the farmer only the skimmed milk.

The real attractions of the Hollowell farm, to me, were: its complete retirement, being about two miles from the village, half a mile from the nearest neighbor, and separated from the highway by a broad field; its bounding on the river, which the owner said protected it by its fogs from frosts in the spring, though that was nothing to me; the gray color and ruinous state of the house and barn, and the dilapidated fences, which put such an interval between me and the last occupant; the hollow and lichen-covered apple trees, gnawed by rabbits, showing what kind of neighbors I should have; but above all, the recollection I had of it from my earliest voyages up the river, when the house was concealed behind a dense grove of red maples, through which I heard the house-dog bark. I was in haste to buy it, before the proprietor finished getting out some rocks, cutting down the hollow apple trees, and grubbing up some young birches which had sprung up in the pasture, or, in short, had made any more of his improvements. To enjoy these advantages I was ready to carry it on; like Atlas, to take the world on my shoulders, — I never heard what compensation he received for that, — and do all those things which had no other motive or excuse but that I might pay for it and be unmolested in my possession of it; for I knew all the while that it would yield the most abundant crop of the kind I wanted if I could only afford to let it alone. But it turned out as I have said.

All that I could say, then, with respect to farming on a large scale, (I have always cultivated a garden,) was, that I had had my seeds ready. Many think that seeds improve with age. I have no doubt that time discriminates between the good and the bad; and when at last I shall plant, I shall be less likely to be disappointed. But I would say to my fellows, once for all, As long as possible live free and uncommitted. It makes but little difference whether you are committed to a farm or the county jail.

Old Cato, whose "De Re Rustica" is my "Cultivator," says, and the only translation I have seen makes sheer nonsense of the passage, "When you think of getting a farm turn it thus in your mind, not to buy greedily; nor spare your pains to look at it, and do not think it enough to go round it once. The oftener you go there the more it will please you, if it is good." I think I shall not buy greedily, but go round and round it as long as I live, and be buried in it first, that it may please me the more at last.

The present was my next experiment of this kind, which I purpose to describe more at length, for convenience, putting the experience of two years into one. As I have said, I do not propose to write an ode to dejection, but to brag as lustily as chanticleer in the morning, standing on his roost, if only to wake my neighbors up.

When first I took up my abode in the woods, that is, began to spend my nights as well as days there, which, by accident, was on Independence Day, or the Fourth of July, 1845, my house was not finished for winter, but was merely a defence against the rain, without plastering or chimney, the walls being of rough weather-stained boards, with wide chinks, which made it cool at night. The upright white hewn studs and freshly planed door and window casings gave it a clean and airy look, especially in the morning, when its timbers were saturated with dew, so that I fancied that by noon some sweet gum would exude from them. To my imagination it retained throughout the day more or less of this auroral character, reminding me of a certain house on a mountain which I had visited a year before. This was an airy and unplastered cabin, fit to entertain a travelling god, and where a goddess might trail her garments. The winds which passed over my dwelling were such as sweep over the ridges of mountains, bearing the broken strains, or celestial parts only, of terrestrial music. The morning wind forever blows, the poem of creation is uninterrupted; but few are the ears that hear it. Olympus is but the outside of the earth everywhere.

The only house I had been the owner of before, if I except a boat, was a tent, which I used occasionally when making excursions in the summer, and this is still rolled up in my garret; but the boat, after passing from hand to hand, has gone down the stream of time. With this more substantial shelter about me, I had made some progress toward settling in the world.

This frame, so slightly clad, was a sort of crystallization around me, and reacted on the builder. It was suggestive somewhat as a picture in outlines. I did not need to go out doors to take the air, for the atmosphere within had lost none of its freshness. It was not so much within doors as behind a door where I sat, even in the rainiest weather. The Harivansa says, "An abode without birds is like a meat without seasoning." Such was not my abode, for I found myself suddenly neighbor to the birds; not by having imprisoned one, but having caged myself near them. I was not only nearer to some of those which commonly frequent the garden and the orchard, but to those wilder and more thrilling songsters of the forest which never, or rarely, serenade a villager, — the wood-thrush, the veery, the scarlet tanager, the field sparrow, the whippoorwill, and many others.

I was seated by the shore of a small pond, about a mile and a half south of the village of Concord and somewhat higher than it, in the midst of an extensive wood between that town and Lincoln, and about two miles south of that our only field known to fame, Concord Battle Ground; but I was so low in the woods that the opposite shore, half a mile off, like the rest, covered with wood, was my most distant horizon. For the first week, whenever I looked out on the pond it impressed me like a tarn high up on the side of a mountain, its bottom far above the surface of other lakes, and, as the sun arose, I saw it throwing off its nightly clothing of mist, and here and there, by degrees, its soft ripples or its smooth reflecting surface was revealed, while the mists, like ghosts, were stealthily withdrawing in every direction into the woods, as at the breaking up of some nocturnal conventicle. The very dew seemed to hang upon the trees later into the day than usual, as on the sides of mountains.

This small lake was of most value as a neighbor in the intervals of a gentle rain storm in August, when, both air and water being perfectly still, but the sky overcast, mid-afternoon had all the serenity of evening, and the wood-thrush sang around, and was heard from shore to shore. A lake like this is never smoother than at such a time; and the clear portion of the air above it being shallow and darkened by clouds, the water, full of light and reflections, becomes a lower heaven itself so much the more important. From a hill top near by, where the wood had been recently cut off, there was a pleasing vista southward across the pond, through a wide indentation in the hills which form the shore there, where their opposite sides sloping toward each other suggested a stream flowing out in that direction through a wooded valley, but stream there was none. That way I looked between and over the near green hills to some distant and higher ones in the horizon, tinged with blue. Indeed, by standing on tiptoe I could catch a glimpse of some of the peaks of the still bluer and more distant mountain ranges in the north-west, those true-blue coins from heaven's own mint, and also of some portion of the village.

But in other directions, even from this point, I could not see over or beyond the woods which surrounded me. It is well to have some water in your neighborhood, to give buoyancy to and float the earth. One value even of the smallest well is, that when you look into it you see that earth is not continent but insular. This is as important as that it keeps butter cool. When I looked across the pond from this peak toward the Sudbury meadows, which in time of flood I distinguished elevated perhaps by a mirage in their seething valley, like a coin in a basin, all the earth beyond the pond appeared like a thin crust insulated and floated even by this small sheet of intervening water, and I was reminded that this on which I dwelt was but *dry land*.

Though the view from my door was still more contracted, I did not feel crowded or confined in the least. There was pasture enough for my imagination. The low shrub-oak plateau to which the opposite shore arose, stretched away toward the prairies of the West and the steppes of Tartary, affording ample room for all the roving families of men. "There are none happy in the world but beings who enjoy freely a vast horizon," — said Damodara, when his herds required new and larger pastures.

Both place and time were changed, and I dwelt nearer to those parts of the universe and to those eras in history which had most attracted me. Where I lived was as far off as many a region viewed nightly by astronomers. We are wont to imagine rare and delectable places in some remote and more celestial corner of the system, behind the constellation of Cassiopeia's Chair, far from noise and disturbance. I discovered that my house actually had its site in such a withdrawn, but forever new and unprofaned, part of the universe. If it were worth the while to settle in those parts near to the Pleiades or the Hyades, to Aldebaran or Altair, then I was really there, or at an equal remoteness from the life which I had left behind, dwindled and twinkling with as fine a ray to my nearest neighbor, and to be seen only in moonless nights by him. Such was that part of creation where I had squatted; —

> "There was a shepherd that did live,
>   And held his thoughts as high
>   As were the mounts whereon his flocks
>   Did hourly feed him by."

What should we think of the shepherd's life if his flocks always wandered to higher pastures than his thoughts?

Every morning was a cheerful invitation to make my life of equal simplicity, and I may say innocence, with Nature herself. I have been as sincere a worshipper of Aurora as the Greeks. I got up early and bathed in the pond; that was a religious exercise, and one of the best things which I did. They say that characters were engraven on the bathing tub of king Tching-thang to this effect: "Renew thyself completely each day;

do it again, and again, and forever again." I can understand that. Morning brings back the heroic ages. I was as much affected by the faint hum of a mosquito making its invisible and unimaginable tour through my apartment at earliest dawn, when I was sitting with door and windows open, as I could be by any trumpet that ever sang of fame. It was Homer's requiem; itself an Iliad and Odyssey in the air, singing its own wrath and wanderings. There was something cosmical about it; a standing advertisement, till forbidden, of the everlasting vigor and fertility of the world. The morning, which is the most memorable season of the day, is the awakening hour. Then there is least somnolence in us; and for an hour, at least, some part of us awakes which slumbers all the rest of the day and night. Little is to be expected of that day, if it can be called a day, to which we are not awakened by our Genius, but by the mechanical nudgings of some servitor, are not awakened by our own newly-acquired force and aspirations from within, accompanied by the undulations of celestial music, instead of factory bells, and a fragrance filling the air — to a higher life than we fell asleep from; and thus the darkness bear its fruit, and prove itself to be good, no less than the light. That man who does not believe that each day contains an earlier, more sacred, and auroral hour than he has yet profaned, has despaired of life, and is pursuing a descending and darkening way. After a partial cessation of his sensuous life, the soul of man, or its organs rather, are reinvigorated each day, and his Genius tries again what noble life it can make. All memorable events, I should say, transpire in morning time and in a morning atmosphere. The Vedas say, "All intelligences awake with the morning." Poetry and art, and the fairest and most memorable of the actions of men, date from such an hour. All poets and heroes, like Memnon, are the children of Aurora, and emit their music at sunrise. To him whose elastic and vigorous thought keeps pace with the sun, the day is a perpetual morning. It matters not what the clocks say or the attitudes and labors of men. Morning is when I am awake and there is a dawn in me. Moral reform is the effort to throw off sleep. Why is it that men give so poor an account of their day if they have not been slumbering? They are not such poor calculators. If they had not been overcome with drowsiness they would have performed something. The millions are awake enough for physical labor; but only one in a million is awake enough for effective intellectual exertion, only one in a hundred millions to a poetic or divine life. To be awake is to be alive. I have never yet met a man who was quite awake. How could I have looked him in the face?

We must learn to reawaken and keep ourselves awake, not by mechanical aids, but by an infinite expectation of the dawn, which does not forsake us in our soundest sleep. I know of no more encouraging fact than the unquestionable ability of man to elevate his life by a conscious endeavor. It is something to be able to paint a particular picture, or to carve a statue, and so to make a few objects beautiful; but it is far more glorious to carve and paint the very atmosphere and medium through which we look, which morally we can do. To affect the quality of the day, that is the highest of arts. Every man is tasked to make his life, even in its details, worthy of the contemplation of his most elevated and critical hour. If we refused, or rather used up, such paltry information as we get, the oracles would distinctly inform us how this might be done.

I went to the woods because I wished to live deliberately, to front only the essential facts of life, and see if I could not learn what it had to teach, and not, when I came to die, discover that I had not lived. I did not wish to live what was not life, living is so dear; nor did I wish to practise resignation, unless it was quite necessary. I wanted to live deep and suck out all the marrow of life, to live so sturdily and Spartan-like as to put to rout all that was not life, to cut a broad swath and shave close, to drive life into a corner, and reduce it to its lowest terms, and, if it proved to be mean, why then to get the whole and genuine mean-ness of it, and publish its meanness to the world; or if it were sublime, to know it by experience, and be able to give a true account of it in my next excursion. For most men, it appears to me, are in a strange uncer-tainty about it, whether it is of the devil or of God, and have *somewhat hastily* concluded that it is the chief end of man here to "glorify God and enjoy him forever."

Still we live meanly, like ants; though the fable tells us that we were long ago changed into men; like pygmies we fight with cranes; it is error upon error, and clout upon clout, and our best virtue has for its occasion a superfluous and evitable wretchedness. Our life is frittered away by detail. An honest man has hardly need to count more than his ten fingers, or in extreme cases he may add his ten toes, and lump the rest. Sim-plicity, simplicity, simplicity! I say, let your affairs be as two or three, and not a hundred or a thousand; instead of a million count half a dozen, and keep your accounts on your thumb nail. In the midst of this chopping sea of civilized life, such are the clouds and storms and quicksands and thousand-and-one items to be allowed for, that a man has to live, if he would not founder and go to the bottom and not make his port at all, by dead reckoning, and he must be a great calculator indeed who succeeds. Simplify, simplify. Instead of three meals a day, if it be necessary eat but one; instead of a hundred dishes, five; and reduce other things in pro-portion. Our life is like a German Confederacy, made up of petty states, with its boundary forever fluctuating, so that even a German cannot tell you how it is bounded at any moment. The nation itself, with all its so-called internal improvements, which, by the way are all external and superficial, is just such an unwieldy and overgrown establishment, clut-tered with furniture and tripped up by its own traps, ruined by luxury and heedless expense, by want of calculation and a worthy aim, as the million households in the land; and the only cure for it as for them is in a rigid economy, a stern and more than Spartan simplicity of life and elevation of purpose. It lives too fast. Men think that it is essential that the *Nation* have commerce, and export ice, and talk through a telegraph, and ride thirty miles an hour, without a doubt, whether *they* do or not; but whether we should live like baboons or like men, is a little uncertain. If we do not get out sleepers, and forge rails, and devote days and nights to the work, but go to tinkering upon our *lives* to improve *them*, who will build railroads? And if railroads are not built, how shall we get to heaven in season? But if we stay at home and mind our business, who will want railroads? We do not ride on the railroad; it rides upon us. Did you ever think what those sleepers are that underlie the railroad? Each one is a man, an Irishman, or a Yankee man. The rails are laid on them, and they are covered with sand, and the cars run smoothly over them. They are sound sleepers, I assure you. And every few years a new lot is laid down and run over; so that, if some have the pleasure of riding on a rail, others have the misfortune to be ridden upon. And when they run over a man that is walking in his sleep, a supernumerary sleeper in the wrong position, and wake him up, they suddenly stop the cars, and make a hue and cry about it, as if this were an exception. I am glad to know that it takes a gang of men for every five miles to keep the sleepers down and level in their beds as it is, for this is a sign that they may sometime get up again.

Why should we live with such hurry and waste of life? We are determined to be starved before we are hungry. Men say that a stitch in time saves nine, and so they take a thousand stitches to-day to save nine to-morrow. As for *work*, we haven't any of any consequence. We have the Saint Vitus' dance, and cannot possibly keep our heads still. If I should only give a few pulls at the parish bell-rope, as for a fire, that is, without setting the bell, there is hardly a man on his farm in the outskirts of Concord, notwithstanding that press of engagements which was his excuse so many times this morning, nor a boy, nor a woman, I might almost say, but would forsake all and follow that sound, not mainly to save property from the flames, but, if we will confess the truth, much more to see it burn, since burn it must, and we, be it known, did not set it on fire, — or to see it put out, and have a hand in it, if that is done as handsomely; yes, even if it were the parish church itself. Hardly a man takes a half hour's nap after dinner, but when he wakes he holds up his head and asks, "What's the news?" as if the rest of mankind had stood his sentinels. Some give directions to be waked every half hour doubtless for no other purpose; and then, to pay for it, they tell what they have dreamed. After a night's sleep the news is as indispensable as the breakfast. "Pray tell me anything new that has happened to a man anywhere on this globe," — and he reads it over his coffee and rolls, that a man had his eyes gouged out this morning on the Wachito River; never dreaming the while that he lives in the dark unfathomed mammoth cave of this world, and has but the rudiment of an eye himself.

For my part, I could easily do without the post-office. I think that there are very few important communications made through it. To speak critically, I never received more than one or two letters in my life — I wrote this some years ago — that were worth the postage. The penny-post is, commonly, an institution through which you seriously offer a man that penny for his thoughts which is so often safely offered in jest. And I am sure that I never read any memorable news in a newspaper. If we read of one man robbed, or murdered, or killed by accident, or one house burned, or one vessel wrecked, or one steamboat blown up, or one cow run over on the Western Railroad, or one mad dog killed, or one lot of grasshoppers in the winter, — we never need read of another. One is enough. If you are acquainted with the principle, what do you care for a myriad instances and applications? To a philosophy all *news*, as it is called, is gossip, and they who edit and read it are old women over their tea. Yet not a few are greedy after this gossip. There was such a rush, as I hear, the other day at one of the offices to learn the foreign news by the last arrival, that several large squares of plate glass belonging to the establishment were broken by the pressure, — news which I seriously think a ready wit might write a twelvemonth or twelve years beforehand with sufficient accuracy. As for Spain, for instance, if you know how to throw in Don Carlos and the Infanta, and Don Pedro and Seville and Granada, from time to time in the right proportions, — they may have changed the names a little since I saw the papers, — and serve up a bull-fight when other entertainments fail, it will be true to the letter, and give us as good an idea of the exact state or ruin of things in Spain as the most succinct and lucid reports under this head in the newspapers: and as for England, almost the last significant scrap of news from that quarter was the revolution of 1649; and if you have learned the history of her crops for an average year, you never need attend to that thing again, unless your speculations are of a merely pecuniary character. If one may judge who rarely looks into the newspapers, nothing new does ever happen in foreign parts, a French revolution not excepted.

What news! how much more important to know what that is which was never old! "Kieou-he-yu (great dignitary of the state of Wei) sent a man to Khoung-tseu to know his news. Khoung-tseu caused the messenger to be seated near him, and questioned him in these terms: What is your master doing? The messenger answered with respect: My master desires to diminish the number of his faults, but he cannot come to the end of them. The messenger being gone, the philosopher remarked: What a worthy messenger! What a worthy messenger!" The preacher, instead of vexing the ears of drowsy farmers on their day of rest at the end of the week, — for Sunday is the fit conclusion of an ill-spent week, and not the fresh and brave beginning of a new one, — with this one other draggle-tail of a sermon, should shout with thundering voice, — "Pause! Avast! Why so seeming fast but deadly slow?"

Shams and delusions are esteemed for soundest truths, while reality is fabulous. If men would steadily observe realities only, and not allow themselves to be deluded, life, to compare it with such things as we know, would be like a fairy tale and the Arabian Nights' Entertainments. If we respected only what is inevitable and has a right to be, music and poetry would resound along the streets. When we are unhurried and wise, we perceive that only great and worthy things have any permanent and absolute existence, — that petty fears and petty pleasures are but the shadow of the reality. This is always exhilarating and sublime. By closing the eyes and slumbering, and consenting to be deceived by shows, men establish and confirm their daily life of routine and habit everywhere, which still is built on purely illusory foundations. Children, who play life, discern its true law and relations more clearly than men, who fail to live it worthily, but who think that they are wiser by experience, that is, by failure. I have read in a Hindoo book, that "there was a king's son, who, being expelled in infancy from his native city, was brought up by a forester, and, growing up to maturity in that state, imagined himself to belong to the barbarous race with which he lived. One of his father's ministers having discovered him, revealed to him what he was, and the misconception of his character was removed, and he knew himself to be a prince. So soul," continues the Hindoo philosopher, "from the circumstances in which it is placed, mistakes its own character, until the truth is revealed to it by some holy teacher, and then it knows itself to be *Brahme*." I perceive that we inhabitants of New England live this mean life that we do because our vision does not penetrate the surface of things. We think that that *is* which *appears* to be. If a man should walk through this town and see only the reality, where, think you, would the "Mill-dam" go to? If he should give us an account of the realities he beheld there, we would not recognize the place in his description. Look at a meeting-house, or a courthouse, or a jail, or a shop, or a dwelling-house, and say what that thing really is before a true gaze, and they would all go to pieces in your account of them. Men esteem truth remote, in the outskirts of the system, behind the farthest star, before Adam and after the last man. In eternity there is indeed something true and sublime. But all these times and places and occasions are now and here. God himself culminates in the present moment, and will never be more divine in the lapse of all the ages. And we are enabled to apprehend at all what is sublime and noble only by the perpetual instilling and drenching of the reality that surrounds us. The universe constantly and obediently answers to our conceptions; whether we travel fast or slow, the track is laid for us. Let us spend our lives in conceiving then. The poet or the artist never yet had so fair and noble a design but some of his posterity at least could accomplish it.

Let us spend one day as deliberately as Nature, and not be thrown off the track by every nutshell and mosquito's wing that falls on the rails. Let us rise early and fast, or break fast, gently and without perturbation; let company come and let company go, let the bells ring and the children cry, — determined to make a day of it. Why should we knock under and go with the stream? Let us not be upset and overwhelmed in that terrible rapid and whirlpool called a dinner, situated in the meridian shallows. Weather this danger and you are safe, for the rest of the way it is down hill. With unrelaxed nerves, with morning vigor, sail by it, looking another way, tied to the mast like Ulysses. If the engine whistles, let it whistle till it is hoarse for its pains. If the bell rings, why should we run? We will consider what kind of music they are like. Let us settle ourselves, and work and wedge our feet downward through the mud and slush of opinion, and prejudice, and tradition, and delusion, and appearance, that alluvion which covers the globe, through Paris and London, through New York and Boston and Concord, through church and state, through poetry and philosophy and religion, till we come to a hard bottom and rocks in place, which we can call *reality*, and say, This is, and no mistake; and then begin, having a *point d'appui*. below freshet and frost and fire, a place where you might found a wall or a state, or set a lamppost safely, or perhaps a gauge, not a Nilometer, but a Realometer, that future ages might know how deep a freshet of shams and appearances had gathered from time to time. If you stand right fronting and face to face to a fact, you will see the sun glimmer on both its surfaces, as if it were cimeter, and feel its sweet edge dividing you through the heart and marrow, and so you will happily conclude your mortal career. Be it life or death, we crave only reality. If we are really dying, let us hear the rattle in our throats and feel cold in the extremities; if we are alive, let us go about our business.

Time is but the stream I go a-fishing in. I drink at it; but while I drink I see the sandy bottom and detect how shallow it is. Its thin current slides away, but eternity remains. I would drink deeper; fish in the sky, whose bottom is pebbly with stars. I cannot count one. I know not the first letter of the alphabet. I have always been regretting that I was not as wise as the day I was born. The intellect is a cleaver; it discerns and rifts its way into the secret of things. I do not wish to be any more busy with my hands than is necessary. My head is hands and feet. I feel all my best faculties concentrated in it. My instinct tells me that my head is an organ for burrowing, as some creatures use their snout and fore-paws, and with it I would mine and burrow my way through these hills. I think that the richest vein is somewhere hereabouts; so by the divining rod and thin rising vapors I judge; and here I will begin to mine.

James Thurber

University Days

I passed all the other courses that I took at my University, but I could never pass botany. This was because all botany students had to spend several hours a week in a laboratory looking through a miscroscope at plant cells, and I could never see through a microscope. I never once saw a cell through a microscope. This used to enrage my instructor. He would wander around the laboratory pleased with the progress all the students were making in drawing the involved and, so I am told, interesting structure of flower cells, until he came to me. I would just be standing there. "I can't see anything," I would say. He would begin patiently enough to explain how anybody can see through a microscope, but he would always end up in a fury, claiming that I could too see through a microscope but just pretended that I couldn't "It takes away from the beauty of flowers anyway," I used to tell him. "We are not concerned with beauty in this course," he would say. "We are concerned solely with what I may call the *mechanics* of flars." "Well," I'd say, "I can't see anything." "Try it just once again," he'd say, and I would put my eye to the microscope and see nothing at all, except now and then a nebulous milky substance — a phenomenon of maladjustment. We were supposed to see a vivid restless clockwork of sharply defined plant cells. "I see what looks like a lot of milk," I would tell him. This, he claimed, was the result of my not having adjusted the microscope properly, so he would readjust it for me, or rather, for himself. And I would look again and see milk.

I finally took a deferred pass, as they called it, and waited a year and tried again. (You had to pass one of the biological sciences or you couldn't graduate.) The professor had come back from vacation brown as a berry, bright-eyed, and eager to explain cell-structure again to his classes. "Well," he said to me cheerily, when we met in the first laboratory hour of the semester, "we're going to see cells this time, aren't we?"

"Yes, sir," I said. Students to right of me and to left of me and in front of me were seeing cells; what's more, they were quietly drawing pictures of them in their notebooks. Of course, I didn't see anything.

"We'll try it," the professor said to me, grimly, "with every adjustment of the miscroscope known to man. As God is my witness, I'll arrange this glass so that you see cells through it or I'll give up teaching. In twenty-two years of botany, I — " He cut off abruptly for he was beginning to quiver all over, like Lionel Barrymore, and he genuinely wished to hold onto his temper; his scenes with me had taken a great deal out of him.

So we tried it with every adjustment of the microscope known to man. With only one of them did I see anything but blackness or the familiar lacteal opacity, and that time I saw, to my pleasure and amazement, a variegated constellation of flecks, specks, and dots. These I hastily drew. The instructor, noting my activity, came from an adjoining desk, a smile on his lips and his eyebrows high in hope. He looked at my cell drawing. "What's that?" he demanded, with a hint of a squeal in his voice. "That's what I saw," I said. "You didn't, you didn't, you *didn't!*" he screamed, losing control of his temper instantly, and he bent over and squinted into the microscope. His head snapped up. "That's your eye!" he shouted. "You've fixed the lens so that it reflects! You've drawn your eye!"

Another course that I didn't like but somehow managed to pass, was economics. I went to that class straight from the botany class, which didn't help me any in understanding either subject. I used to get them mixed up. But not as mixed up as another student in my economics class who came there direct from a physics laboratory. He was a tackle on the football team, named Bolenciecwcz. At that time Ohio State University had one of the best football teams in the country, and Bolenciecwcz was one of its outstanding stars. In order to be eligible to play it was necessary for him to keep up in his studies, a very difficult matter, for while he was not dumber than an ox he was not any smarter. Most of his professors were lenient and helped him along. None gave him more hints, in answering questions, or asked him simpler ones than the economics professor, a thin, timid man named Bassum. One day when we were on the subject of transportation and distribution, it came Bolenciecwcz's turn to answer a question. "Name one means of transportation," the professor said to him. No light came into the big tackle's eyes. "Just any means of transportation," said the professor. Bolenciecwcz sat staring at him. "That is," pursued the professor, "any medium, agency, or method of going from one place to another." Bolenciecwcz had the look of a man who is being led into a trap. "You may choose among steam, horse-drawn, or electrically propelled vehicles," said the instructor. "I might suggest the one which we commonly take in making long journeys across land." There was a profound silence in which everybody stirred uneasily, including Bolenciecwcz and Mr. Bassum. Mr Bassum abruptly broke this silence in an amazing manner. "Choo-choo-choo," he said, in a low voice, and turned instantly scarlet. He glanced appealingly around the room. All of us, of course, shared Mr. Bassum's desire that Bolenciecwcz should stay abreast of the class in economics, for the Illinois game, one of the hardest and most important of the season, was only a week off. "Toot, tooot, too-toooooot!" some student with a deep voice moaned, and we all looked encouragingly at Bolenciecwcz. Somebody else gave a fine imitation of a locomotive letting off steam. Mr. Bassum himself rounded off the little show. "Ding, dong, ding, dong," he said hopefully. Bolenciecwcz was staring at the floor now, trying to think, his great brow furrowed, his huge hands rubbing together, his face red.

"How did you come to college this year, Mr. Bolenciecwcz?" asked the professor. "*Chuffa,* chuffa, *chuffa,* chuffa."

"M'father sent me," said the football player.

"What on?" asked Bassum.

"I git an 'lowance," said the tackle, in a low, husky voice, obviously embarrassed.

"No, no," said Bassum. "Name a means of transportation. What did you ride here on?"

"Train," said Bolenciecwcz.

"Quite right," said the professor. "Now, Mr. Nugent will you tell us ———"

If I went through anguish in botany and economics — for different reasons — gymnasium work was even worse. I don't even like to think about it. They wouldn't let you play games or join in the exercises with your glasses on and I couldn't see with mine off. I bumped into professors, horizontal bars, agricultural students, and swinging iron rings. Not being able to see, I could take it but I couldn't dish it out. Also, in order to pass gymnasium (and you had to pass it to graduate) you had to learn to swim if you didn't know how. I didn't like the swimming pool, I didn't like swimming, and I didn't like the swimming instructor, and after all these years I still don't. I never swam but I passed my gym work anyway, by having another student give my gymnasium number (978) and swim across the pool in my place. He was a quiet, amiable blonde youth, number 473, and he would have seen through a microscope for me if we could have got away with it, but we couldn't get away with it. Another thing I didn't like about gymnasium work was that they made you strip the day you registered. It is impossible for me to be happy when I am stripped and being asked a lot of questions. Still, I did better than a lanky agricultural student who was cross-examined just before I was. They asked each student what college he was in —

that is, whether Arts, Engineering, Commerce or Agriculture. "What college are you in?" the instructor snapped at the youth in front of me. "Ohio State University," he said promptly.

It wasn't that agricultural student but it was another a whole lot like him who decided to take up journalism, possibly on the ground that when farming went to hell he could fall back on newspaper work. He didn't realize, of course, that that would be very much like falling back full-length on a kit of carpenter's tools. Haskins didn't seem cut out for journalism, being too embarrassed to talk to anybody and unable to use a typewriter, but the editor of the college paper assigned him to the cow barns, the sheep house, the horse pavilion, and the animal husbandry department generally. This was a genuinely big "beat," for it took up five times as much ground and got ten times as great a legislative appropriation as the College of Liberal Arts. The agricultural student knew animals, but nevertheless his stories were dull and colorlessly written. He took all afternoon on each of them, on account of having to hunt for each letter on the typewriter. Once in a while he had to ask somebody to help him hunt. "C" and "L" in particular, were hard letters for him to find. His editor finally got pretty much annoyed at the farmer-journalist because his pieces were so uninteresting. "See here, Haskins," he snapped at him one day, "why is it we never have anything hot from you on the horse pavilion? Here we have two hundred head of horses on this campus — more than any other university in the Western Conference except Purdue — and yet you never get any real low down on them. Now shoot over to the horse barns and dig up something lively." Haskins shambled out and came back in about an hour; he said he had something. "Well, start it off snappily," said the editor. "Something people will read." Haskins set to work and in a couple of hours brought a sheet of typewritten paper to the desk; it was a two-hundred word story about some disease that had broken out among the horses. Its opening sentence was simple but arresting. I read: "Who has noticed the sores on the tops of the horses in the animal husbandry building?"

Ohio State was a land grant university and therefore two years of military drill was compulsory. We drilled with old Springfield rifles and studied the tactics of the Civil War even though the World War was going on at the time. At 11 o'clock each morning thousands of freshmen and sophomores used to deploy over the campus, moodily creeping up on the old chemistry building. It was good training for the kind of warfare that was waged at Shiloh but it had no connection with what was going on in Europe. Some people used to think there was German money behind it, but they didn't dare say so or they would have been thrown in jail as German spies. It was a period of muddy thought and marked, I believe, the decline of higher education in the Middle West.

As a soldier I was never any good at all. Most of the cadets were glumly indifferent soldiers, but I was no good at all. Once General Littlefield, who was commandant of the cadet corps, popped up in front of me during regimental drill and snapped, "You are the main trouble with this university!" I think he meant that my type was the main trouble with the university but he may have meant me individually. I was mediocre at drill, certainly — that is, until my senior year. By that time I had drilled longer than anybody else in the Western Conference, having failed at military at the end of each preceding year so that I had to do it all over again. I was the only senior still in uniform. The uniform which, when new, had made me look like an interurban railway conductor, now that it had become faded and too tight made me look like Bert Williams in his bellboy act. This had a definitely bad effect on my morale. Even so, I had become by sheer practice little short of wonderful at squad manoeuvres.

One day General Littlefield picked our company out of the whole regiment and tried to get it mixed up by putting it through one movement after another as fast as we could execute them: squads right, squads left, squads on right into line, squads right about, squads left front into line etc. In about three minutes one hundred and nine men were marching one direction and I was marching away from them at an angle of forty degrees, all alone. "Company, halt!" shouted General Littlefield. "That man is the only man who has it right!" I was made a corporal for my achievement.

The next day General Littlefield summoned me to his office. He was swatting flies when I went in. I was silent and he was silent too, for a long time. I don't think he remembered me or why he had sent for me, but he didn't want to admit it. He swatted some more flies, keeping his eyes on them narrowly before he let go with the swatter. "Button up your coat!" he snapped. Looking back on it now I can see that he meant me although he was looking at a fly, but I just stood there. Another fly came to rest on a paper in front of the general and began rubbing its hind legs together. The general lifted the swatter cautiously. I moved restlessly and the fly flew away. "You startled him!" barked General Littlefield, looking at me severely. I said I was sorry. "That won't help the situation!" snapped the General, with cold military logic. I didn't see what I could do except chase some more flies toward his desk, but I didn't say anything. He stared out the window at the faraway figures of co-eds crossing the campus toward the library. Finally, he told me I could go. So I went. He either didn't know which cadet I was or else he forgot what he wanted to see me about. It may have been that he wished to apologize for having called me the main trouble with the university; or maybe he had decided to compliment me on my brilliant drilling of the day before and then at the last minute decided not to. I don't know. I don't think about it much any more.

Mark Twain

"My Uncle John Quarles's Farm"

My uncle, John A. Quarles, was also a farmer, and his place was in the country four miles from Florida. He had eight children and fifteen or twenty negroes and was also fortunate in other ways, particularly in his character. I have not come across a better man than he was. I was his guest for two or three months every year, from the fourth year after we removed to Hannibal till I was eleven or twelve years old. I have never consciously used him or his wife in a book but his farm has come very handy to me in literature once or twice. In *Huck Finn* and in *Tom Sawyer, Detective* I moved it down to Arkansas. It was all of six hundred miles but it was no trouble; it was not a very large farm — five hundred acres, perhaps — but I could have done it if it had been twice as large. And as for the morality of it, I cared nothing for that; I would move a state if the exigencies of literature required it.

It was a heavenly place for a boy, that farm of my uncle John's. The house was a double log one, with a spacious floor (roofed in) connecting it with the kitchen. In the summer the table was set in the middle of that shady and breezy floor, and the sumptuous meals — well, it makes me cry to think of them. Fried chicken, roast pig; wild and tame turkeys, ducks and geese; venison just killed; squirrels, rabbits, pheasants, partridges, prairie-chickens; biscuits, hot batter cakes, hot buckwheat cakes, hot "wheat bread," hot rolls, hot corn pone; fresh corn boiled on the ear, succotash, butter-beans, string-beans, tomatoes, peas, Irish potatoes, sweet potatoes; buttermilk, sweet milk, "clabber"; watermelons, muskmelons, cantaloupes — all fresh from the garden; apple pie, peach pie, pumpkin pie, apple dumplings, peach cobbler — I can't remember the rest. The way that the things were cooked was perhaps the main splendor — particularly a certain few of the dishes. For instance, the corn bread, the hot biscuits and wheat bread and the fried chicken. These things have never been properly cooked in the North — in fact, no one there is able to learn the art, so far as my experience goes. The North thinks it knows how to make corn bread but this is gross superstition. Perhaps no bread in the world is quite so good as Southern corn bread and perhaps no bread in the world is quite so bad as the Northern imitation of it. The North seldom tries to fry chicken and this is well; the art cannot be learned north of the line of Mason and Dixon, nor anywhere in Europe. This is not hearsay; it is experience that is speaking. In Europe it is imagined that the custom of serving various kinds of bread blazing hot is "American," but that is too broad a spread; it is custom in the South but is much less than that in the North. In the North and in Europe hot bread is considered unhealthy. This is probably another fussy superstition, like the European superstition that ice-water is unhealthy. Europe does not need ice-water and does not drink it; and yet, notwithstanding this, its word for it is better than ours, because it describes it, whereas ours doesn't. Europe calls it "iced" water. Our word describes water made from melted ice — a drink which has a characterless taste and which we have but little acquaintance with.

It seems a pity that the world should throw away so many good things merely because they are unwholesome. I doubt if God has given us any refreshment which, taken in moderation, is unwholesome, except microbes. Yet there are people who strictly deprive themselves of each and every eatable, drinkable and smokable which has in any way acquired a shady reputation. They pay this price for health. And health is all they get for it. How strange it is! It is like paying out your whole fortune for a cow that has gone dry.

The farmhouse stood in the middle of a very large yard and the yard was fenced on three sides with rails and on the rear side with high palings; against these stood the smoke-house; beyond the palings was the orchard; beyond the orchard were the negro quarters and the tobacco fields. The front yard was entered over a stile made of sawed-off logs of graduated heights; I do not remember any gate. In a corner of the front yard were a dozen lofty hickory trees and a dozen black walnuts, and in the nutting season riches were to be gathered there.

Down a piece, abreast the house, stood a little log cabin against the rail fence; and there the woody hill fell sharply away, past the barns, the corn-crib, the stables and the tobacco-curing house, to a limpid brook which sang along over its gravelly bed and curved and frisked in and out and here and there and yonder in the deep shade of overhanging foliage and vines — a divine place for wading, and it had swimming pools, too, which were forbidden to us and therefore much frequented by us. For we were little Christian children and had early been taught the value of forbidden fruit.

In the little log cabin lived a bedridden white-headed slave woman whom we visited daily and looked upon with awe, for we believed she was upward of a thousand years old and had talked with Moses. The younger negroes credited these statistics and had furnished them to us in good faith. We accommodated all the details which came to us about her; and so we believed that she had lost her health in the long desert trip coming out of Egypt and had never been able to get it back again. She had a round bald place on the crown of her head and we used to creep around and gaze at it in reverent silence and reflect that it was caused by fright through seeing Pharaoh drowned. We called her "Aunt" Hannah, Southern fashion. She was superstitious, like the other negroes; also, like them, she was deeply religious. Like them, she had great faith in prayer and employed it in all ordinary exigencies, but not in cases where a dead certainty of result was urgent. Whenever witches were around she tied up the remnant of her wool in little tufts, with white thread, and this promptly made the witches impotent.

All the negroes were friends of ours, and with those of our own age we were in effect comrades. I say in effect, using the phrase as a modification. We were comrades and yet not comrades; color and condition interposed a subtle line which both parties were conscious of and which rendered complete fusion impossible. We had a faithful and affectionate good friend, ally and adviser in "Uncle Dan'l," a middle-aged slave whose head was the best one in the negro quarter, whose sympathies were wide and warm and whose heart was honest and simple and knew no guile. He has served me well these many, many years. I have not seen him for more than half a century and yet spiritually I have had his welcome company a good part of that time and have staged him in books under his own name and as "Jim," and carted him all around — to Hannibal, down the Mississippi on a raft and even across the Desert of Sahara in a balloon — and he has endured it all with the patience and friendliness and loyalty which were his birthright. It was on the farm that I got my strong liking for his race and my appreciation of certain of its fine qualities. This feeling and this estimate have stood the test of sixty years and more and have suffered no impairment. The black face is as welcome to me now as it was then.

In my schoolboy days I had no aversion to slavery. I was not aware that there was anything wrong about it. No one arraigned it in my hearing; the local papers said nothing against it; the local pulpit taught us that God approved it, that it was a holy thing and that the doubter need only look in the Bible if he wished to settle his mind — and then the texts were read aloud to us to make the matter sure; if the slaves themselves had an aversion to slavery they were wise and said nothing. In Hannibal we seldom saw a slave misused; on the farm never.

There was, however, one small incident of my boyhood days which touched this matter, and it must have meant a good deal to me or it would not have stayed in my memory, clear and sharp, vivid and shadowless, all these slow-drifting years. We had a little slave boy whom we had hired from some one, there in Hannibal. He was from the eastern shore of Maryland and had been brought away from his family and his friends halfway across the American continent and sold. He was a cheery spirit, innocent and gentle, and the noisiest creature that ever was, perhaps. All day long he was singing, whistling, yelling, whooping, laughing — it was maddening, devastating, unendurable. At last, one day, I lost all my temper and went raging to my mother and said Sandy had been singing for an hour without a single break and I couldn't stand it and *wouldn't* she please shut him up. The tears came into her eyes and her lip trembled and she said something like this:

"Poor thing, when he sings it shows that he is not remembering and that comforts me; but when he is still I am afraid he is thinking and I cannot bear it. He will never see his mother again; if he can sing I must not hinder it, but be thankful for it. If you were older you would understand me; then that friendless child's voice would make you glad."

It was a simple speech and made up of small words but it went home, and Sandy's noise was not a trouble to me any more. She never used large words but she had a natural gift for making small ones do effective work. She lived to reach the neighborhood of ninety years and was capable with her tongue to the last — especially when a meanness or an injustice roused her spirit. She has come handy to me several times in my books, where she figures as Tom Sawyer's Aunt Polly. I fitted her out with a dialect and tried to think up other improvements for her but did not find any. I used Sandy once, also; it was in *Tom Sawyer*. I tried to get him to whitewash the fence but it did not work. I do not remember what name I called him by in the book.

I can see the farm yet, with perfect clearness. I can see all its belongings, all its details; the family room of the house, with a "trundle" bed in one corner and a spinning-wheel in another — a wheel whose rising and falling wail, heard from a distance, was the mournfulest of all sounds to me and made me homesick and low spirited and filled my atmosphere with the wandering spirits of the dead; the vast fireplace, piled high on winter nights with flaming hickory logs from whose ends a sugary sap bubbled out but did not go to waste, for we scraped it off and ate it; the lazy cat spread out on the rough hearthstones; the drowsy dogs braced against the jambs and blinking; my aunt in one chimney corner knitting; my uncle in the other, smoking his corn-cob pipe; the slick and carpetless oak floor faintly mirroring the dancing flame tongues and freckled with black indentations where fire coals had popped out and died a leisurely death; half a dozen children romping in the background twilight; "split"-bottomed chairs here and there, some with rockers; a cradle — out of service but waiting with confidence; in the early cold morning a snuggle

of children in shirts and chemises, occupying the hearthstone and pro-
crastinating — they could not bear to leave that comfortable place and
go out on the windswept floor space between the house and kitchen
where the general tin basin stood, and wash.

Along outside of the front fence ran the country road, dusty in the
summertime and a good place for snakes — they liked to lie in it and sun
themselves; when they were rattlesnakes or puff adders we killed them;
when they were black snakes or racers or belonged to the fabled "hoop"
breed we fled without shame; when they were "house snakes" or "garters" we carried them home and put them in Aunt Patsy's work basket
for a surprise; for she was prejudiced against snakes, and always when
she took the basket in her lap and they began to climb out of it it dis-
ordered her mind. She never could seem to get used to them; her oppor-
tunites went for nothing. And she was always cold toward bats, too, and
could not bear them; and yet I think a bat is as friendly a bird as there is.
My mother was Aunt Patsy's sister and had the same wild superstitions.
A bat is beautifully soft and silky; I do not know any creature that is
pleasanter to the touch or is more grateful for caressings, if offered in the
right spirit. I know all about these coleoptera because our great cave,
three miles below Hannibal, was multitudinously stocked with them and
often I brought them home to amuse my mother with. It was easy to
manage if it was a school day because then I had ostensibly been to
school and hadn't any bats. She was not a suspicious person but full of
trust and confidence; and when I said, "There's something in my coat
pocket for you," she would put her hand in. But she always took it out
again, herself; I didn't have to tell her. It was remarkable the way she
couldn't learn to like private bats. The more experience she had the
more she could not change her views.

I think she was never in the cave in her life; but everybody else went
there. Many excursion parties came from considerable distances up and
down the river to visit the cave. It was miles in extent and was a
tangled wilderness of narrow and lofty clefts and passages. It was an
easy place to get lost in; anybody could do it — including the bats. I got
lost in it myself, along with a lady, and our last candle burned down to
almost nothing before we glimpsed the search party's lights winding
about in the distance.

"Injun Joe," the half-breed, got lost in there once and would have
starved to death, if the bats had run short. But there was no chance of
that; there were myriads of them. He told me all his story. In the book
called *Tom Sawyer* I starved him entirely to death in the cave but that
was in the interest of art; it never happened. "General" Gaines, who was
our first town drunkard before Jimmy Finn got the place, was lost there
for the space of a week and finally pushed his handkerchief out of a hole
in a hilltop near Savertown, several miles down the river from the cave's

mouth, and somebody saw it and dug him out. There is nothing the matter with his statistics except the handkerchief. I knew him for years and he hadn't any. But it could have been his nose. That would attract attention.

The cave was an uncanny place, for it contained a corpse — the corpse of a young girl of fourteen. It was in a glass cylinder inclosed in a copper one which was suspended from a rail which bridged a narrow passage. The body was preserved in alcohol and it was said that loafers and rowdies used to drag it up by the hair and look at the dead face. The girl was the daughter of a St. Louis surgeon of extraordinary ability and wide celebrity. He was an eccentric man and did many strange things. He put the poor thing in that forlorn place himself.

Beyond the road where the snakes sunned themselves was a dense young thicket and through it a dim-lighted path led a quarter of a mile; then out of the dimness one emerged abruptly upon a level great prairie which was covered with wild strawberry plants, vividly starred with prairie pinks and walled in on all sides by forests. The strawberries were fragrant and fine, and in the season we were generally there in the crisp freshness of the early morning, while the dew beads still sparkled upon the grass and the woods were ringing with the first songs of the birds.

Down the forest slopes to the left were the swings. They were made of bark stripped from hickory saplings. When they became dry they were dangerous. They usually broke when a child was forty feet in the air and this was why so many bones had to be mended every year. I had no ill luck myself but none of my cousins escaped. There were eight of them and at one time and another they broke fourteen arms among them. But it cost next to nothing, for the doctor worked by the year — twenty-five dollars for the whole family. I remember two of the Florida doctors, Chowning and Meredith. They not only tended an entire family for twenty-five dollars a year but furnished the medicines themselves. Good measure, too. Only the largest persons could hold a whole dose. Castor oil was the principal beverage. The dose was half a dipperful, with half a dipperful of New Orleans molasses added to help it down and make it taste good, which it never did. The next standby was calomel; the next rhubarb; and the next jalap. Then they bled the patient and put mustard plasters on him. It was a dreadful system and yet the death rate was not heavy. The calomel was nearly sure to salivate the patient and cost him some of his teeth. There were no dentists. When teeth became touched with decay or were otherwise ailing, the doctor knew of but one thing to do — he fetched his tongs and dragged them out. If the jaw remained, it was not his fault.

Doctors were not called in cases of ordinary illness; the family grandmother attended to those. Every old woman was a doctor and gathered her own medicines in the woods and knew how to compound doses that would stir the vitals of a cast-iron dog. And then there was the "Indian doctor"; a grave savage, remnant of his tribe, deeply read in the mysteries of nature and the secret properties of herbs; and most backwoodsmen had high faith in his powers and could tell of wonderful cures achieved by him. In Mauritius, away off yonder in the solitudes of the Indian Ocean, there is a person who answers to our Indian doctor of the old times. He is a negro and has had no teaching as a doctor, yet there is one disease which he is master of and can cure and the doctors can't. They send for him when they have a case. It is a child's disease of a strange and deadly sort and the negro cures it with a herb medicine which he makes himself from a prescription which has come down to him from his father and grandfather. He will not let anyone see it. He keeps the secret of its components to himself and it is feared that he will die without divulging it; then there will be consternation in Mauritius. I was told these things by the people there in 1896.

We had the "faith doctor," too, in those early days — a woman. Her specialty was toothache. She was a farmer's old wife and lived five miles from Hannibal. She would lay her hand on the patient's jaw and say, "Believe!" and the cure was prompt. Mrs. Utterback. I remember her very well. Twice I rode out there behind my mother, horseback, and saw the cure performed. My mother was the patient.

Doctor Meredith removed to Hannibal by and by and was our family physician there and saved my life several times. Still, he was a good man and meant well. Let it go.

I was always told that I was a sickly and precarious and tiresome and uncertain child and lived mainly on allopathic medicines during the first seven years of my life. I asked my mother about this, in her old age — she was in her eighty-eighth year — and said:

"I suppose that during all that time you were uneasy about me?"

"Yes, the whole time."

"Afraid I wouldn't live?"

After a reflective pause — ostensibly to think out the facts — "No — afraid you would."

It sounds like plagiarism but it probably wasn't.

The country schoolhouse was three miles from my uncle's farm. It stood in a clearing in the woods and would hold about twenty-five boys and girls. We attended the school with more or less regularity once or twice a week, in summer, walking to it in the cool of the morning by the forest paths and back in the gloaming at the end of the day. All the pupils brought their dinners in baskets — corn dodger, buttermilk and other good things — and sat in the shade of the trees at noon and ate them. It is the part of my education which I look back upon with the most satisfaction. My first visit to the school was when I was seven. A strapping girl of fifteen, in the customary sunbonnet and calico dress, asked me if I "used tobacco" — meaning did I chew it. I said no. It roused her scorn. She reported me to all the crowd and said:

"Here is a boy seven years old who can't chaw tobacco."

By the looks and comments which this produced I realized that I was a degraded object; I was cruelly ashamed of myself. I determined to reform. But I only made myself sick; I was not able to learn to chew tobacco. I learned to smoke fairly well but that did not conciliate anybody and I remained a poor thing and characterless. I longed to be respected but I never was able to rise. Children have but little charity for one another's defects.

As I have said, I spent some part of every year at the farm until I was twelve or thirteen years old. The life which I led there with my cousins was full of charm, and so is the memory of it yet. I can call back the solemn twilight and mystery of the deep woods, the earthy smells, the faint odors of the wild flowers, the sheen of rain-washed foliage, the rattling clatter of drops when the wind shook the trees, the far-off hammering of woodpeckers and the muffled drumming of wood pheasants in the remoteness of the forest, the snapshot glimpses of disturbed wild creatures scurrying through the grass — I can call it all back and make it as real as it ever was, and as blessed. I can call back the prairie, and its loneliness and peace, and a vast hawk hanging motionless in the sky, with his wings spread wide and the blue of the vault showing through the fringe of their end feathers. I can see the woods in their autumn dress, the oaks purple, the hickories washed with gold, the maples and the sumachs luminous with crimson fires, and I can hear the rustle made by the fallen leaves as we plowed through them. I can see the blue clusters of wild grapes hanging among the foliage of the saplings, and I remember the taste of them and the smell. I know how the wild blackberries looked, and how they tasted, and the same with the pawpaws, the hazelnuts, and the persimmons; and I can feel the thumping rain, upon my head, of hickory nuts and walnuts when we were out in the frosty dawn to scramble for them with the pigs, and the gusts of wind loosed them and sent them down. I know the stain of blackberries, and how pretty it is, and I know the stain of walnut hulls, and how little it minds soap and water, also what grudged experience it had of either of them. I know the taste of maple sap, and when to gather it, and how to arrange the troughs and the delivery tubes, and how to boil down the juice, and how to hook the sugar after it is made, also how much better hooked sugar tastes than any that is honestly come by, let bigots say what they will. I know how a prize watermelon looks when it is sunning its fat rotundity among pumpkin vines and "simblins"; I know how to tell when it is ripe without "plugging" it; I know how inviting it looks when it is cooling itself in a tub of water under the bed, waiting; I know how it looks when it lies on the table in the sheltered great floor space between house and kitchen, and the children gathered for the sacrifice and their mouths watering; I know the crackling sound it makes when the carving knife enters its end, and I can see the split fly along in front of the blade as the knife cleaves its way to the other end; I can see its halves fall apart and display the rich red meat and the black seeds, and the heart standing up, a luxury fit for the elect; I know how a boy looks behind a yard-long slice of that melon, and I know how he feels; for I have been there. I know the taste of the watermelon which has been honestly come by, and I know the taste of the watermelon which has been acquired by art. Both taste good, but the experienced know which tastes best. I know the look of green apples and peaches and pears on the trees, and I know how entertaining they are when they are inside of a person. I know how ripe ones look when they are piled in pyramids under the trees, and how pretty they are and how vivid their colors. I know how a frozen apple looks, in a barrel down cellar in the wintertime, and how hard it is to bite, and how the frost makes the teech ache, and yet how good it is, notwithstanding. I know the disposition of elderly people to select the speckled apples for the children, and I once knew ways to beat the game. I know the look of an apple that is roasting and sizzling on a hearth on a winter's evening, and I know the comfort that comes of eating it hot, along with some sugar and a drench of cream. I know the delicate art and mystery of so cracking hickory nuts and walnuts on a flatiron with a hammer that the kernels will be delivered whole, and I know how the nuts, taken in conjunction with winter apples, cider, and doughnuts, make old people's old tales and old jokes sound fresh and crisp and enchanting, and juggle an evening away before you know what went with the time. I know the look of Uncle Dan'l's kitchen as it was on the privileged nights, when I was a child, and I can see the white and black children grouped on the hearth, with the firelight playing on their faces and the shadows flickering upon the walls, clear back toward the cavernous gloom of the rear, and I can hear Uncle Dan'l telling the immortal tales which Uncle Remus Harris was to gather into his books and charm the world with, by and by; and I can feel again the creepy joy which quivered through me when the time for the ghost story of the "Golden Arm" was reached — and the sense of regret, too, which came over me, for it was always the last story of the evening and there was nothing between it and the unwelcome bed.

I can remember the bare wooden stairway in my uncle's house, and the turn to the left above the landing, and the rafters and the slanting roof over my bed, and the squares of moonlight on the floor, and the white cold of snow outside, seen through the curtainless window. I can remember the howling of the wind and the quaking of the house on stormy nights, and how snug and cozy one felt, under the blankets, listening; and how the powdery snow used to sift in, around the sashes, and lie in little ridges on the floor and make the place look chilly in the morning and curb the wild desire to get up — in case there was any. I can remember how very dark that room was, in the dark of the moon, and how packed it was with ghostly stillness when one woke up by accident away in the night, and forgotten sins came flocking out of the secret chambers of the memory and wanted a hearing; and how ill chosen the time seemed for this kind of business; and how dismal was the hoo-hooing of the owl and the wailing of the wolf, sent mourning by on the night wind.

I remember the raging of the rain on that roof, summer nights, and how pleasant it was to lie and listen to it, and enjoy the white splendor of the lightning and the majestic booming and crashing of the thunder. It was a very satisfactory room, and there was a lightning rod which was reachable from the window, an adorable and skittish thing to climb up and down, summer nights, when there were duties on hand of a sort to make privacy desirable.

I remember the 'coon and 'possum hunts, nights, with the negroes, and the long marches through the black gloom of the woods, and the excitement which fired everybody when the distant bay of an experienced dog announced that the game was treed; then the wild scramblings and stumblings through briers and bushes and over roots to get to the spot; then the lighting of a fire and the felling of the tree, the joyful frenzy of the dogs and the negroes, and the weird picture it all made in the red glare — I remember it all well, and the delight that everyone got out of it, except the 'coon.

I remember the pigeon seasons, when the birds would come in millions and cover the trees and by their weight break down the branches. They were clubbed to death with sticks; guns were not necessary and were not used. I remember the squirrel hunts, and prairie-chicken hunts, and wild-turkey hunts, and all that; and how we turned out, mornings, while it was still dark, to go on these expeditions, and how chilly and dismal it was, and how often I regretted that I was well enough to go. A toot on a tin horn brought twice as many dogs as were needed, and in their happiness they raced and scampered about, and knocked small people down, and made no end of unnecessary noise. At the word, they vanished away toward the woods, and we drifted silently after them in the melancholy gloom. But presently the gray dawn stole over the world, the birds piped up, then the sun rose and poured light and comfort all around, everything was fresh and dewy and fragrant, and life was a boon again. After three hours of tramping we arrived back wholesomely tired, overladen with game, very hungry, and just in time for breakfast.

John Updike

Excerpt from *The Dogwood Tree: A Boyhood*

CONCERNING THE THREE GREAT
SECRET THINGS: (1) SEX

In crucial matters, the town was evasive. Sex was an unlikely, though persistent rumor. My father slapped my mother's bottom and made a throaty noise and I thought it was a petty form of sadism. The major sexual experience of my boyhood was a section of a newsreel showing some women wrestling in a pit of mud. The mud covered their bathing suits so they seemed naked. Thick, interlocking, faceless bodies, they strove and fell. The sight was so disturbingly resonant that afterward, in any movie, two women pulling each other's hair or slapping each other — there was a good deal of this in movies of the early forties; Ida Lupino was usually one of the women — gave me a tense, watery, drawn-out feeling below the belt. Thenceforth my imaginings about girls moved through mud. In one recurrent scene I staged in my bed, the girl and I, dressed in our underpants and wrapped around with ropes, had been plunged from an immense cliff into a secret pond of mud, by a villain who resembled Peg-Leg Pete. I usually got my hands free and rescued her; sometimes she rescued me; in any case there hovered over our spattered, elastic-clad bodies the idea that these were the last minutes of our lives, and all our shames and reservations were put behind us. It turned out that she had loved me all along. We climbed out, into the light. The ropes had hurt our wrists; yet the sweet kernel of the fantasy lay somehow in the sensations of being tightly bound, before we rescued each other.

(2) RELIGION

Pragmatically, I have become a Congregationalist, but in the translucent and tactful church of my adoption my eyes sting, my throat goes grave, when we sing — what we rarely sang in the Lutheran church of my childhood — Luther's mighty hymn:

> *For still our ancient foe*
> *Doth seek to work us woe;*
> *His craft and power are great,*
> *And arm'd with cruel hate,*
> *On earth is not his equal.*

The immense dirge of praise for the Devil and the world, thunderous, slow, opaquely proud, nourishes a seed in me I never knew was planted. How did the patently vapid and drearily businesslike teachings to which I was lightly exposed succeed in branding me with a Cross? And a brand so specifically Lutheran, so distinctly Nordic; an obdurate insistence that at the core of the core there is a right-angled clash to which, of all verbal combinations we can invent, the Apostles' Creed offers the most adequate correspondence and response.

Of my family, only my father attended the church regularly, returning every Sunday with the Sunday Reading *Eagle* and the complaint that the minister prayed too long. My own relations with the church were unsuccessful. In Sunday school, I rarely received the perfect attendance pin, though my attendance seemed to me and my parents as perfect as anybody's. Instead, I was given a pencil stamped KINDT'S FUNERAL HOME. Once, knowing that a lot of racy social activity was going on under its aegis, I tried to join the Luther League; but I had the misfortune to arrive on the night of their Halloween party, and was refused admittance because I was not wearing a costume. And, the worst rebuff, I was once struck by a car on the way to Sunday school. I had the collection nickel in my hand, and held on to it even as I was being dragged fifteen feet on the car's bumper. For this heroic churchmanship I received no palpable credit; the Lutheran church seemed postively to dislike me.

Yet the crustiness, the inhospitality of the container enhanced the oddly lucid thing contained. I do not recall my first doubts; I doubted perhaps abnormally little. And when they came, they never roosted on the branches of the tree, but attacked the roots; if the first article of the Creed stands, the rest follows as water flows downhill. That God, at a remote place and time, took upon Himself the form of a Syrian carpenter and walked the earth willfully healing and abusing and affirming and grieving, appeared to me quite in the character of the Author of the grass. The mystery that more puzzled me as a child was the incarnation of my ego — that omnivorous and somehow preexistent "I" — in a speck so specifically situated amid the billions of history. Why was I I? The arbitrariness of it astounded me; in comparison, nothing was too marvellous.

Shillington bred a receptivity to the supernatural unrelated to orthodox religion. This is the land of the hex signs, and in the neighboring town of Grille a "witch doctor" hung out a shingle like a qualified M.D. I was struck recently, on reading Frazer's contemptuous list of superstitions in *The Golden Bough*, by how many of them seemed good sense. My grandmother was always muttering little things; she came from a country world of spilled salt and cracked mirrors and new moons and omens. She convinced me by contagion, that our house was haunted. I punished her by making her stand guard outside the bathroom when I was in it. If I found she had fallen asleep in the shadowy hallway crawling with ghosts, I would leap up on her back and pummel her with a fury that troubles me now.

Imagine my old neighborhood as an African village; under the pointed roofs tom-toms beat, premonitions prowl, and in the darkness naked superstition in all her plausibility blooms.

The Night-Blooming Cereus

It was during the war; early in the war, 1942. *Collier's* had printed a cover showing Hirohito, splendidly costumed and fanged, standing malevolently in front of a bedraggled, bewildered Hitler and an even more decrepit and craven Mussolini. Our troops in the Pacific reeled from island to island; the Japanese seemed a race of demons capable of anything. The night-blooming cereus was the property of a family who lived down the street in a stucco house that on the inside was narrow and dark in the way that houses in the middle of the country sometimes are. The parlor was crowded with obscure furniture decked out with antimacassars and porcelain doodads. At Christmas a splendiferous tree appeared in that parlor, hung with pounds of tinsel and strung popcorn and paper chains and pretzels and balls and intricate, figurative ornaments that must have been rescued from the previous century.

The blooming of the cereus was to be an event in the neighborhood; for days we had been waiting. This night — a clear warm night, in August or September — word came, somehow. My mother and grandmother and I rushed down Philadelphia Avenue in the dark. It was late; I should have been in bed. I remembered the night I was refused permission to go to the poorhouse fire. The plant stood at the side of the house, in a narrow space between the stucco wall and the hedge. A knot of neighborhood women had already gathered; heavy shoulders and hair buns were silhouetted in an indeterminate light. On its twisted, unreal stem the flower had opened its unnaturally brilliant petals. But no one was looking at it. For overhead, in the north of a black sky strewn with stars like thrown salt, the wandering fingers of an aurora borealis gestured, now lengthening and brightening so that shades of blue and green could be distinguished, now ebbing until it seemed there was nothing there at all. It was a rare sight this far south. The women muttered, sighed, and, as if involuntarily, out of the friction of their bodies, moaned. Standing among their legs and skirts, I was slapped by a sudden cold wave of fear. "Is it the end of the world?" one of the women asked. There was no answer. And then a plane went over, its red lights blinking, its motors no louder than the drone of a wasp. Japanese. The Japanese were going to bomb Shillington, the center of the nation. I waited for the bomb, and without words prayed, expecting a miracle, for the appearance of angels and Japanese in the sky was restrained by the same impossibility, an impossibility that the swollen waxy brilliant white of the flower by my knees had sucked from the night.

The plane of course passed; it was one of ours; my prayer was answered with the usual appearance of absence. We went home, and the world reconstituted its veneer of reason, but the moans of the women had rubbed something in me permanently bare.

(3) ART

Leafing through a scrapbook my mother long ago made of my childhood drawings, I was greeted by one I had titled "Mr. Sun talking to Old Man Winter in his Office." Old Man Winter, a cloud with stick legs, and his host, a radiant ball with similar legs, sit at ease, both smiling, on two chairs that are the only furniture of the solar office. That the source of all light should have, somewhere, an office, suited my conception of an artist, who was someone who lived in a small town like Shillington, and who, equipped with pencils and paper, practiced his solitary trade as methodically as the dentist practiced his. And indeed, that is how it is at present with me.

Goethe — probably among others — says to be wary of our youthful wishes, for in maturity we are apt to get them. I go back, now, to Pennsylvania, and on one of the walls of the house in which my parents now live there hangs a photograph of myself as a boy. I am smiling, and staring with clear eyes at something in the corner of the room. I stand before that photograph, and am disappointed to receive no flicker, not the shadow of a flicker, of approval, of gratitude. The boy continues to smile at the corner of the room, beyond me. That boy is not a ghost to me, he is real to me; it is I who am a ghost to him. I, in my present state, was one of the ghosts that haunted his childhood. Like some phantom conjured by this child from a glue bottle, I have executed his commands; acquired pencils, paper, and an office. Now I wait apprehensively for his next command, or at least a nod of appreciation, and he smiles through me, as if I am already transparent with failure.

He saw art — between drawing and writing he ignorantly made no distinction — as a method of riding a thin pencil line out of Shillington, out of time altogether, into an infinity of unseen and even unborn hearts.

He pictured this infinity as radiant. How innocent! But his assumption here, like his assumptions on religion and politics, is one for which I have found no certain substitute. He loved blank paper and obedience to this love led me to a difficult artistic attempt. I reasoned thus: just as the paper is the basis for the marks upon it, might not events be contingent upon a never-expressed (because featureless) ground? Is the true marvel of Sunday skaters the pattern of their pirouettes or the fact that they are silently upheld? Blankness is not emptiness; we may skate upon an intense radiance we do not see because we see nothing else. And in fact there is a color, a quiet but tireless goodness that things at rest, like a brick wall or a small stone, seem to affirm. A wordless reassurance these things are pressing to give. An hallucination? To transcribe middleness with all its grits, bumps, and anonymities, in its fullness of satisfaction and mystery: is it possible or, in view of the suffering that violently colors the periphery and that at all moments threatens to move into the center, worth doing? Possibly not; but the horsechestnut trees, the telephone poles, the porches, the green hedges recede to a calm point that in my subjective geography is still the center of the world.

A Slight Sound at Evening

In his Journal for July 10–12, 1841, Thoreau wrote: "A slight sound at evening lifts me up by the ears, and makes life seem inexpressibly serene and grand. It may be in Uranus, or it may be in the shutter." The book into which he later managed to pack both Uranus and the shutter was published in 1854, and now, a hundred years having gone by, *Walden*, its serenity and grandeur unimpaired, still lifts us up by the ears, still translates for us that language we are in danger of forgetting, "which all things and events speak without metaphor, which alone is copious and standard."

Walden is an oddity in American letters. It may very well be the oddest of our distinguished oddities. For many it is a great deal too odd, and for many it is a particular bore. I have not found it to be a well-liked book among my acquaintances, although usually spoken of with respect, and one literary critic for whom I have the highest regard can find no reason why anyone gives *Walden* a second thought. To admire the book is, in fact, something of an embarrassment, for the mass of men have an indistinct notion that its author was a sort of Nature Boy.

I think it is of some advantage to encounter the book at a period in one's life when the normal anxieties and enthusiasms and rebellions of youth closely resemble those of Thoreau in that spring of 1845 when he borrowed an axe, went out to the woods, and began to whack down some trees for timber. Received at such a juncture, the book is like an invitation to life's dance, assuring the troubled recipient that no matter what befalls him in the way of success or failure he will always be welcome at the party — that the music is played for him, too, if he will but listen and move his feet. In effect, that is what the book is — an invitation, unengraved; and it stirs one as a young girl is stirred by her first big party bid. Many think it a sermon; many set it down as an attempt to rearrange society; some think it an exercise in nature-loving; some find it a rather irritating collection of inspirational puffballs by an eccentric show-off. I think it none of these. It still seems to me the best youth's companion yet written by an American, for it carries a solemn warning against the loss of one's valuables, it advances a good argument for traveling light and trying new adventures, it rings with the power of positive adoration, it contains religious feeling without religious images, and it steadfastly refuses to record bad news. Even its pantheistic note is so pure as to be non-corrupting — pure as the flute-note blown across the pond on those faraway summer nights. If our colleges and universities were alert, they would present a cheap pocket edition of the book to every senior upon graduating, along with his sheepskin, or instead of it. Even if some senior were to take it literally and start felling trees, there could be worse mishaps: the axe is older than the Dictaphone and it is just as well for a young man to see what kind of chips he leaves before listening to the sound of his own voice. And even if some were to get no farther than the table of contents, they would learn how to name eighteen chapters by the use of only thirty-nine words and would see how sweet are the uses of brevity.

If Thoreau had merely left us an account of a man's life in the woods, or if he had simply retreated to the woods and there recorded his complaints about society, or even if he had contrived to include both records in one essay, *Walden* would probably not have lived a hundred years. As things turned out, Thoreau, very likely without knowing quite what he was up to, took man's relation to nature and man's dilemma in society and man's capacity for elevating his spirit and he beat all these matters together, in a wild free interval of self-justification and delight, and produced an original omelette from which people can draw nourishment in a hungry day. *Walden* is one of the first of the vitamin-enriched American dishes. If it were a little less good than it is, or even a little less queer, it would be an abominable book. Even as it is, it will continue to baffle and annoy the literal mind and all those who are unable to stomach its caprices and imbibe its theme. Certainly the plodding economist will continue to have rough going if he hopes to emerge from the book with a clear system of economic thought. Thoreau's assault on the Concord society of the mid-nineteenth century has the quality of a modern Western: he rides into the subject at top speed, shooting in all directions. Many of his shots ricochet and nick him on the rebound, and throughout the melee there is a horrendous cloud of inconsistencies and contradictions, and when the shooting dies down and the air clears, one is impressed chiefly by the courage of the rider and by how splendid it was that somebody should have ridden in there and raised all that ruckus.

When he went to the pond, Thoreau struck an attitude and did so deliberately, but his posturing was not to draw the attention of others to him but rather to draw his own attention more closely to himself. "I learned this at least by my experiment: that if one advances confidently in the direction of his dreams, and endeavors to live the life which he has imagined, he will meet with a success unexpected in common hours." The sentence has the power to resuscitate the youth drowning in his sea of doubt. I recall my exhilaration upon reading it, many years ago, in a time of hesitation and despair. It restored me to health. And now in 1954 when I salute Henry Thoreau on the hundredth birthday of his book, I am merely paying off an old score — or an installment on it.

In his journal for May 3–4, 1838 — Boston to Portland — he wrote: "Midnight — head over the boat's side — between sleeping and waking — with glimpses of one or more lights in the vicinity of Cape Ann. Bright moonlight — the effect heightened by seasickness." The entry illuminates the man, as the moon the sea on that night in May. In Thoreau the natural scene was heightened, not depressed, by a disturbance of the stomach, and nausea met its match at last. There was a steadiness in at least one passenger if there was none in the boat. Such steadiness (which in some would be called intoxication) is at the heart of *Walden* — confidence, faith, the discipline of looking always at what is to be seen, undeviating gratitude for the life-everlasting that he found growing in his front yard. "There is nowhere recorded a simple and irrepressible satisfaction with the gift of life, any memorable praise of God." He worked to correct that deficiency. *Walden* is his acknowledgement of the gift of life. It is the testament of a man in a high state of indignation because (it seemed to him) so few ears heard the uninterrupted poem of creation, the morning wind that forever blows. If the man sometimes wrote as though all his readers were male, unmarried, and well-connected, it is because he gave his testimony during the callow years, and, for that matter, never really grew up. To reject the book because of the immaturity of the author and the bugs in the logic is to throw away a bottle of good wine because it contains bits of the cork.

Thoreau said he required of every writer, first and last, a simple and sincere account of his own life. Having delivered himself of this chesty dictum, he proceeded to ignore it. In his books and even in his enormous journal, he withheld or disguised most of the facts from which an understanding of his life could be drawn. *Walden*, subtitled "Life in the Woods," is not a simple and sincere account of a man's life, either in or out of the woods; it is an account of a man's journey into the mind, a toot on the trumpet to alert the neighbors. Thoreau was well aware that no one can alert his neighbors who is not wide awake himself, and he went to the woods (among other reasons) to make sure that he would stay awake during his broadcast. What actually took place during the years 1845–47 is largely unrecorded, and the reader is excluded from the private life of the author, who supplies almost no gossip about himself, a great deal about his neighbors and about the universe.

As for me, I cannot in this short ramble give a simple and sincere account of my own life, but I think Thoreau might find it instructive to know that this memorial essay is being written in a house that, through no intent on my part, is the same size and shape as his own domicile on the pond — about ten by fifteen, tight, plainly finished, and at a little distance from my Concord. The house in which I sit this morning was built to accommodate a boat, not a man, but by long experience I have learned that in most respects it shelters me better than the larger dwelling where my bed is, and which, by design, is a manhouse not a boathouse. Here in the boathouse I am a wilder and, it would appear, a healthier man, by a safe margin. I have a chair, a bench, a table, and I can walk into the water if I tire of the land. My house fronts a cove. Two fishermen have just arrived to spot fish from the air — an osprey and a man in a small yellow plane who works for the fish company. The man, I have noticed, is less well equipped than the hawk, who can dive directly on his fish and carry it away, without telephoning. A mouse and a squirrel share the house with me. The building is, in fact, a multiple dwelling, a semidetached affair. It is because I am semidetached while here that I find it possible to transact this private business with the fewest obstacles.

There is also a woodchuck here, living forty feet away under the wharf. When the wind is right, he can smell my house; and when the wind is contrary, I can smell his. We both use the wharf for sunning, taking turns, each adjusting his schedule to the other's convenience. Thoreau once ate a woodchuck. I think he felt he owed it to his readers, and that it was little enough, considering the indignities they were suffering at his hands and the dressing-down they were taking. (Parts of *Walden* are pure scold.) Or perhaps he ate the woodchuck because he believed every man should acquire strict business habits, and the woodchuck was destroying his market beans. I do not know. Thoreau had a strong experimental streak in him. It is probably no harder to eat a woodchuck than to construct a sentence that lasts a hundred years. At any rate, Thoreau is the only writer I know who prepared himself for his great ordeal by eating a woodchuck; also the only one who got a hangover from drinking too much water. (He was drunk the whole time, though he seldom touched wine or coffee or tea.)

Here in this compact house where I would spend one day as deliberately as Nature if I were not being pressed by *The Yale Review*, and with a woodchuck (as yet uneaten) for neighbor, I can feel the companionship of the occupant of the pondside cabin in Walden woods, a mile from the village, near the Fitchburg right of way. Even my immediate business is no barrier between us: Thoreau occasionally batted out a magazine piece, but was always suspicious of any sort of purposeful work that cut into his time. A man, he said, should take care not to be thrown off the track by every nutshell and mosquito's wing that falls on the rails.

There has been much guessing as to why he went to the pond. To set it down to escapism is, of course, to misconstrue what happened. Henry went forth to battle when he took to the woods, and *Walden* is the report of a man torn by two powerful and opposing drives — the desire to enjoy the world (and not be derailed by a mosquito wing) and the urge to set the world straight. One cannot join these two successfully but sometimes, in rare cases, something good or even great results from the attempt of the tormented spirit to reconcile them. Henry went forth to battle, and if he set the stage himself, if he fought on his own terms and with his own weapons, it was because it was his nature to do things differently from most men, and to act in a cocky fashion. If the pond and the woods seemed a more plausible site for a house than an in-town location, it was because a cowbell made for him a sweeter sound than a churchbell. *Walden*, the book, makes the sound of the cowbell, more than a churchbell, and proves the point, although both sounds are in it, and both remarkably clear and sweet. He simply preferred his churchbell at a little distance.

I think one reason he went to the woods was a perfectly simple and commonplace one — and apparently he thought so too. "At a certain season of our life," he wrote, "we are accustomed to consider every spot as the possible site of a house." There spoke the young man, a few years out of college, who had not yet broken away from home. He hadn't married, and he had found no job that measured up to his rigid standards of employment, and like any young man, or young animal, he felt uneasy and on the defensive until he had fixed himself a den. Most young men, of course, casting about for a site, are content merely to draw apart from their kinfolks. Thoreau, convinced that the greater part of what his neighbors called good was bad, withdrew from a great deal more than family: he pulled out of everything for a while, to serve everybody right for being so stuffy, and to try his own prejudices on the dog.

The house-hunting sentence above, which starts the Chapter called "Where I Lived, and What I Lived For," is followed by another passage that is worth quoting here because it so beautifully illustrates the offbeat prose that Thoreau was master of, a prose at once strictly disciplined and wildly abandoned. "I have surveyed the country on every side within a dozen miles of where I live," continues this delirious young man. "In imagination I have bought all the farms in succession, for all were to be bought, and I knew their price. I walked over each farmer's premises, tasted his wild apples, discoursed on husbandry with him, took his farm at his price, at any price, mortgaging it to him in my mind; even put a higher price on it — took everything but a deed of it — took his word for his deed, for I dearly love to talk — cultivated it, and him too to some extent, I trust, and withdrew when I had enjoyed it long enough, leaving him to carry it on." A copydesk man would get a double hernia trying to clean up that sentence for the management, but the sentence needs no fixing for it perfectly captures the meaning of the writer and the quality of the ramble.

"Wherever I sat, there might I live, and the landscape radiated from me accordingly." Thoreau, the home-seeker, sitting on his hummock with the entire State of Massachusetts radiating from him, is to me the most humorous of the New England figures, and *Walden* the most humorous of the books, though its humor is almost continuous subsurface and there is nothing funny anywhere, except a few weak jokes and bad puns that rise to the surface like a perch in the pond that rose to the sound of the maestro's flute. Thoreau tended to write in sentences, a feat not every writer is capable of, and *Walden* is, rhetorically speaking, a collection of certified sentences, some of them, it would now appear, as indestructible as they are errant. The book is distilled from the vast journals, and this accounts for its intensity: he picked out bright particles that pleased his eye, whirled them in the kaleidoscope of his content, and produced the pattern that has endured — the color, the form, the light.

On this its hundredth birthday, Thoreau's *Walden* is pertinent and timely. In our uneasy season, when all men unconsciously seek a retreat from a world that has got almost completely out of hand, his house in the Concord woods is a haven. In our culture of gadgetry and the multiplicity of convenience, his cry "Simplicity, simplicity, simplicity!" has the insistence of a fire alarm. In the brooding atmosphere of war and the gathering radioactive storm, the innocence and serenity of his summer afternoons are enough to burst the remembering heart, and one gazes back upon that pleasing interlude — its confidence, its purity, its deliberateness — with awe and wonder, as one would look upon the face of a child asleep.

"This small lake was of most value as a neighbor in the intervals of a gentle rain-storm in August, when, both air and water being perfectly still, but the sky overcast, midafternoon had all the serenity of evening, and the wood-thrush sang around, and was heard from shore to shore." Now, in the perpetual overcast in which our days are spent, we hear with extra perception and deep gratitude that song, tying century to century.

I sometimes amuse myself by bringing Henry Thoreau back to life and showing him the sights. I escort him into a phone booth and let him dial Weather. "This is a delicious evening," the girl's voice says, "when the whole body is one sense, and imbibes delight through every pore." I show him the spot in the Pacific where an island used to be, before some magician made it vanish. "We know not where we are," I murmur. "The light which puts out our eyes is darkness to us. Only that day dawns to which we are awake." I thumb through the latest copy of *Vogue* with him. "Of two patterns which differ only by a few threads more or less of a particular color," I read, "the one will be sold readily, the other lie on the shelf, though it frequently happens that, after the lapse of a season, the latter becomes the most fashionable." Together we go outboarding on the Assabet, looking for what we've lost — a hound, a bay horse, a turtledove. I show him a distracted farmer who is trying to repair a hay baler before the thunder shower breaks. "This farmer," I remark, "is endeavoring to solve the problem of a livelihood by a formula more complicated than the problem itself. To get his shoe strings he speculates in herds of cattle."

I take the celebrated author to Twenty-One for lunch, so the waiters may study his shoes. The proprietor welcomes us. "The gross feeder," remarks the proprietor, sweeping the room with his arm, "is a man in the larva stage." After lunch we visit a classroom in one of those schools conducted by big corporations to teach their superannuated executives how to retire from business without serious injury to their health. (The shock to men's systems these days when relieved of the exacting routine of amassing wealth is very great and must be cushioned.) "It is not necessary," says the teacher to his pupils, "that a man should earn his living by the sweat of his brow, unless he sweats easier than I do. We are determined to be starved before we are hungry."

I turn on the radio and let Thoreau hear Winchell beat the red hand around the clock. "Time is but the stream I go a-fishing in," shouts Mr. Winchell, rattling his telegraph key. "Hardly a man takes a half hour's nap after dinner, but when he wakes he holds up his head and asks, 'What's the news?' If we read of one man robbed, or murdered, or killed by accident, or one house burned, or one vessel wrecked, or one steamboat blown up, or one cow run over on the Western Railroad, or one mad dog killed, or one lot of grasshoppers in the winter — we need never read of another. One is enough."

I doubt that Thoreau would be thrown off balance by the fantastic sights and sounds of the twentieth century. "The Concord nights," he once wrote, "are stranger than the Arabian nights." A four-engined air liner would merely serve to confirm his early views on travel. Everywhere he would observe, in new shapes and sizes, the old predicaments and follies of men — the desperation, the impedimenta, the meanness — along with the visible capacity for elevation of the mind and soul. "This curious world which we inhabit is more wonderful than it is convenient; more beautiful than it is useful; it is more to be admired and enjoyed than used." He would see that today ten thousand engineers are busy making sure that the world shall be convenient if they bust doing it, and others are determined to increase its usefulness even though its beauty is lost somewhere along the way.

At any rate, I'd like to stroll about the countryside in Thoreau's company for a day, observing the modern scene, inspecting today's snowstorm, pointing out the sights, and offering belated apologies for my sins. Thoreau is unique among writers in that those who admire him find him uncomfortable to live with — a regular hairshirt of a man. A little band of dedicated Thoreauvians would be a sorry sight indeed: fellows who hate compromise and have compromised, fellows who love wilderness and have lived tamely, and at their side, censuring them and chiding them, the ghostly figure of this upright man, who long ago gave corroboration to impulses they perceived were right and issued warnings against the things they instinctively knew to be their enemies. I should hate to be called a Thoreauvian, yet I wince every time I walk into the barn I'm pushing before me, seventy-five feet by forty, and the author of *Walden* has served as my conscience through the long stretches of my trivial days.

Hairshirt or no, he is a better companion than most, and I would not swap him for a soberer or more reasonable friend even if I could. I can reread his famous invitation with undiminished excitement. The sad thing is that not more acceptances have been received, that so many decline for one reason or another, pleading some previous engagement or ill health. But the invitation stands. It will beckon as long as this remarkable book stays in print — which will be as long as there are August afternoons in the intervals of a gentle rainstorm, as long as there are ears to catch the faint sounds of the orchestra. I find it agreeable to sit here this morning, in a house of correct proportions, and hear across a century of time his flute, his frogs, and his seductive summons to the wildest revels of them all.

————————

Sliding Down into the Behavioral Sink

I just spent two days with Edward T. Hall, an anthropologist, watching thousands of my fellow New Yorkers short-circuiting themselves into hot little twitching death balls with jolts of their own adrenalin. Dr. Hall says it is overcrowding that does it. Overcrowding gets the adrenalin going, and the ardenalin gets them hyped up. And here they are, hyped up, turning bilious, nephritic, queer, autistic, sadistic, barren, batty, sloppy, hot-in-the-pants, chancred-on-the-flankers, leering, puling, numb — the usual in New York, in other words, and God knows what else. Dr. Hall has the theory that overcrowding has already thrown New York into a state of behavioral sink. Behavioral sink is a term from ethology, which is the study of how animals relate to their environment. Among animals, the sink winds up with a "population collapse" or "massive die-off." O rotten Gotham.

It got to be easy to look at New Yorkers as animals, especially looking down from some place like a balcony at Grand Central at the rush hour Friday afternoon. The floor was filled with the poor white humans, running around, dodging, blinking their eyes, making a sound like a pen full of starlings or rats or something.

"Listen to them skid," says Dr. Hall.

He was right. The poor old etiolate animals were out there skidding on their rubber soles. You could hear it once he pointed it out. They stop short to keep from hitting somebody or because they are disoriented and they suddenly stop and look around, and they skid on their rubber-sole shoes, and a screech goes up. They pour out onto the floor down the escalators from the Pan-Am Building, from 42nd Street, from Lexington Avenue, up out of subways, down into subways, railroad trains, up into helicopters —

"You can also hear the helicopters all the way down here," says Dr. Hall. The sound of the helicopters using the roof of the Pan-Am Building nearly fifty stories up beats right through. "If it weren't for this ceiling" — he is referring to the very high ceiling in Grand Central — "this place would be unbearable with this kind of crowding. And yet they'll probably never 'waste' space like this again."

The screech! And the adrenal glands in all those poor white animals enlarge, micrometer by micrometer, to the size of cantaloupes. Dr. Hall pulls a Minox camera out of a holster he has on his belt and starts shooting away at the human scurry. The Sink!

Dr. Hall has the Minox up to his eye — he is a slender man, calm, 52 years old, young-looking, an anthropologist who has worked with Navajos, Hopis, Spanish-Americans, Negroes, Trukese. He was the most important anthropologist in the government during the crucial years of the foreign aid program, the 1950's. He directed both the Point Four training program and the Human Relations Area Files. He wrote *The Silent Language* and *The Hidden Dimension*, two books that are picking up the kind of "underground" following his friend Marshall McLuhan started picking up about five years ago. He teaches at the Illinois Institute of Technology, lives with his wife, Mildred, in a high-ceilinged town house on one of the last great residential streets in downtown Chicago, Astor Street; has a grown son and daughter, loves good food, good wine, the relaxed, civilized life — but comes to New York with a Minox at his eye to record — perfect! — The Sink.

We really got down in there by walking down into the Lexington Avenue line subway stop under Grand Central. We inhaled those nice big fluffy fumes of human sweat, urine, effluvia, and sebaceous secretions. One old female human was already stroked out on the upper level, on a stretcher, with two policemen standing by. The other humans barely looked at her. They rushed into line. They bellied each other, haunch to paunch, down the stairs. Human heads shone through the gratings. The species North European tried to create bubbles of space around themselves, about a foot and a half in diameter —

"See, he's reacting against the line," says Dr. Hall.

— but the species Mediterranean presses on in. The hell with bubbles of space. The species North European resents that, this male human behind him presses forward toward the booth . . . *breathing* on him, he's disgusted, he pulls out of the line entirely, the species Mediterranean resents him for resenting it, and neither of them realizes what the hell they are getting irritable about exactly. And in all of them the old adrenals grow another micrometer.

Dr. Hall whips out the Minox. Too perfect! The bottom of The Sink.

It is the sheer overcrowding, such as occurs in the business sections of Manhattan five days a week and in Harlem, Bedford-Stuyvesant, southeast Bronx every day — sheer overcrowding is converting New Yorkers into animals in a sink pen. Dr. Hall's argument runs as follows:

all animals, including birds, seem to have a built-in, inherited requirement to have a certain amount of territory, space, to lead their lives in. Even if they have all the food they need, and there are no predatory animals threatening them, they cannot tolerate crowding beyond a certain point. No more than two hundred wild Norway rats can survive on a quarter acre of ground, for example, even when they are given all the food they can eat. They just die off.

But why? To find out, ethologists have run experiments on all sorts of animals, from stickleback crabs to Sika deer. In one major experiment, an ethologist named John Calhoun put some domesticated white Norway rats in a pen with four sections to it, connected by ramps. Calhoun knew from previous experiments that the rats tend to split up into groups of ten to twelve and that the pen, therefore, would hold forty to forty-eight rats comfortably, assuming they formed four equal groups. He allowed them to reproduce until there were eighty rats, balanced between male and female, but did not let it get any more crowded. He kept them supplied with plenty of food, water, and nesting materials. In other words, all their more obvious needs were taken care of. A less obvious need — space — was not. To the human eye, the pen did not even look especially crowded. But to the rats, it was crowded beyond endurance.

The entire colony was soon plunged into a profound behavioral sink. "The sink," said Calhoun, "is the outcome of any behavioral process that collects animals in unusually great numbers. The unhealthy connotations of the term are not accidental: a behavioral sink does act to aggravate all forms of pathology that can be found within a group."

For a start, long before the rat population reached eighty, a status hierarchy had developed in the pen. Two dominant male rats took over the two end sections, acquired harems of eight to ten females each, and forced the rest of the rats into the two middle pens. All the overcrowding took place in the middle pens. That was where the "sink" hit. The aristocrat rats at the ends grew bigger, sleeker, healthier, and more secure the whole time.

In The Sink, meanwhile, nest building, courting, sex behavior, reproduction, social organization, health — all of it went to pieces. Normally, Norway rats have a mating ritual in which the male chases the female, the female ducks down into a burrow and sticks her head up to watch the male. He performs a little dance outside the burrow, then she comes out, and he mounts her, usually for a few seconds. When The Sink set in, however, no more than three males — the dominant males in the middle sections — kept up the old customs. The rest tried everything from satyrism to homosexuality or else gave up on sex altogether. Some of the subordinate males spent all their time chasing females. Three or four might chase one female at the same time, and instead of stopping at the burrow entrance for the ritual, they would charge right in. Once mounted, they would hold on for minutes instead of the usual seconds.

Homosexuality rose sharply. So did bisexuality. Some males would mount anything — males, females, babies, senescent rats, anything. Still other males dropped sexual activity altogether, wouldn't fight and, in fact, would hardly move except when the other rats slept. Occasionally a female from the aristocrat rats' harems would come over the ramps and into the middle sections to sample life in The Sink. When she had had enough, she would run back up the ramp. Sink males would give chase up to the top of the ramp, which is to say, to the very edge of the aristocratic preserve. But one glance from one of the king rats would stop them cold and they would return to The Sink.

The slumming females from the harems had their adventures and then returned to a placid, healthy life. Females in The Sink, however, were ravaged, physically and psychologically. Pregnant rats had trouble continuing pregnancy. The rate of miscarriages increased significantly, and females started dying from tumors and other disorders of the mammary glands, sex organs, uterus, ovaries, and Fallopian tubes. Typically, their kidneys, livers, and adrenals were also enlarged or diseased or showed other signs associated with stress.

Child-rearing became totally disorganized. The females lost the interest or the stamina to build nests and did not keep them up if they did build them. In the general filth and confusion, they would not put themselves out to save offspring they were momentarily separated from. Frantic, even sadistic competition among the males was going on all around them and rendering their lives chaotic. The males began unprovoked and senseless assaults upon one another, often in the form of tail-biting. Ordinarily, rats will suppress this kind of behavior when it crops up. In The Sink, male rats gave up all policing and just looked out for themselves. The "pecking order" among males in The Sink was never stable. Normally, male rats set up a three-class structure. Under the pressure of overcrowding, however, they broke up into all sorts of unstable subclasses, cliques, packs — and constantly pushed, probed, explored, tested one another's power. Anyone was fair game, except for the aristocrats in the end pens.

Calhoun kept the population down to eighty, so that the next stage, "population collapse" or "massive die-off," did not occur. But the autopsies showed that the pattern — as in the diseases among the female rats — was already there.

The classic study of die-off was John J. Christian's study of Sika deer on James Island in the Chesapeake Bay, west of Cambridge, Maryland. Four or five of the deer had been released on the island, which was 280 acres and uninhabited, in 1916. By 1955 they had bred freely into a herd of 280 to 300. The population density was only about one deer per acre at this point, but Christian knew that this was already too high for the

Sikas' inborn space requirements, and something would give before long. For two years the number of deer remained 280 to 300. But suddenly, in 1958, over half the deer died; 161 carcasses were recovered. In 1959 more deer died and the population steadied at about 80.

In two years, two-thirds of the herd had died. Why? It was not starvation. In fact, all the deer collected were in excellent condition, with well-developed muscles, shining coats, and fat deposits between the muscles. In practically all the deer, however, the adrenal glands had enlarged by 50 percent. Christian concluded that the die-off was due to "shock following severe metabolic disturbance, probably as a result of prolonged adrenocortical hyperactivity. . . . There was no evidence of infection, starvation, or other obvious cause to explain the mass mortality." In other words, the constant stress of overpopulation, plus the normal stress of the cold of the winter, had kept the adrenalin flowing so constantly in the deer that their systems were depleted of blood sugar and they died of shock.

Well, the white humans are still skidding and darting across the floor of Grand Central. Dr. Hall listens a moment longer to the skidding and darting noises, and then says, "You know, I've been on commuter trains here after everyone has been through one of these rushes, and I'll tell you, there is enough acid flowing in the stomachs in every car to dissolve the rails underneath."

Just a little invisible acid bath for the linings to round off the day. The ulcers the acids cause, of course, are the one disease people have already been taught to associate with the stress of city life. But overcrowding, as Dr. Hall sees it, raises a lot more hell with the body than just ulcers. In everyday life in New York — just the usual, getting to work, working in massively congested areas like 42nd Street between Fifth Avenue and Lexington, especially now that the Pan-Am Building is set in there, working in cubicles such as those in the editorial offices at Time-Life, Inc., which Dr. Hall cites as typical of New York's poor handling of space, working in cubicles with low ceilings and, often, no access to a window, while construction crews all over Manhattan drive everybody up the Masonite wall with air-pressure generators with noises up to the boil-a-brain decibel levels, then rushing to get home, piling into subways and trains, fighting for time and for space, the usual day in New York — the whole now-normal thing keeps shooting jolts of adrenalin into the body, breaking down the body's defenses and winding up with the work-a-daddy human animal stroked out at the breakfast table with his head apoplexed like a cauliflower out of his $6.95 semispread Pima-cotton shirt, and nosed over into a plate of No-Kloresto egg substitute, signing off with the black thrombosis, cancer, kidney, liver, or stomach failure, and the adrenals ooze to a halt, the size of eggplants in July.

One of the people whose work Dr. Hall is interested in on this score is Rene Dubos at the Rockefeller Institute. Dubos's work indicates that specific organisms, such as the tuberculosis bacillus or a pneumonia virus, can seldom be considered "the cause" of a disease. The germ or virus, apparently, has to work in combination with other things that have already broken the body down in some way — such as the old adrenal hyperactivity. Dr. Hall would like to see some autopsy studies made to record the size of adrenal glands in New York, especially of people crowded into slums and people who go through the full rush-hour-work-rush-hour cycle every day. He is afraid that until there is some clinical, statistical data on how overcrowding actually ravages the human body, no one will be willing to do anything about it. Even in so obvious a thing as air pollution, the pattern is familiar. Until people can actually see the smoke or smell the sulphur or feel the sting in their eyes, politicians will not get excited about it, even though it is well known that many of the lethal substances polluting the air are invisible and odorless. For one thing, most politicians are like the aristocrat rats. They are insulated from The Sink by practically sultanic buffers — limousines, chauffeurs, secretaries, aides-de-camp, doormen, shuttered houses, high-floor apartments. They almost never ride subways, fight rush hours, much less live in the slums or work in the Pan-Am Building.

We took a cab from Grand Central to go up to Harlem, and by 48th Street we were already socked into one of those great, total traffic jams on First Avenue on Friday afternoon. Dr. Hall motions for me to survey the scene, and there they all are, humans, male and female, behind the glass of their automobile windows, soundlessly going through the torture of their own adrenalin jolts. This male over here contracts his jaw muscles so hard that they bunch up into a great cheese Danish pattern. He twists his lips, he bleeds from the eyeballs, he shouts . . . soundlessly behind glass . . . the fat corrugates on the back of his neck, his whole body shakes as he pounds the heel of his hand into the steering wheel. The female human in the car ahead of him whips her head around, she screams . . . soundlessly behind glass . . . she throws her hands up in the air, Whaddya expect me — Yah, yuh stupid — and they all sit there, trapped in their own congestion, bleeding hate all over each other, shorting out the ganglia and — goddam it —

Dr. Hall sits back and watches it all. This is it! The Sink! And where is everybody's wandering boy?

Dr. Hall says, "We need a study in which drivers who go through these rush hours every day would wear GSR bands."

GSR?

"Galvanic skin response. It measures the electric potential of the skin, which is a function of sweating. If a person gets highly nervous, his palms begin to sweat. It is an index of tension. There are some other fairly simple devices that would record respiration and pulse. I think everybody who goes through this kind of experience all the time should take his own pulse — not literally — but just be aware of what's happening to him. You can usually tell when stress is beginning to get you physically."

In testing people crowded into New York's slums, Dr. Hall would like to take it one step further — gather information on the plasma hydrocortisone level in the blood or the corticosteroids in the urine. Both have been demonstrated to be reliable indicators of stress, and testing procedures are simple.

The slums — we finally made it up to East Harlem. We drove into 101st Street, and there was a new, avant-garde little church building, the Church of the Epiphany, which Dr. Hall liked — and, next to it, a pile of rubble where a row of buildings had been torn down, and from the back windows of the tenements beyond several people were busy "airmailing," throwing garbage out the window, into the rubble, beer cans, red shreds, the No-Money-Down Eames roller stand for a TV set, all flying through the air onto the scaggy sump. We drove around some more in Harlem, and a sequence was repeated, trash, buildings falling down, buildings torn down, rubble, scaggy sumps or, suddenly, a cluster of high-rise apartment projects, with fences around the grass.

"You know what this city looks like?" Dr. Hall said. "It looks bombed out. I used to live at Broadway and 124th Street back in 1946 when I was studying at Columbia. I can't tell you how much Harlem has changed in twenty years. It looks bombed out. It's broken down. People who live in New York get used to it and don't realize how filthy the city has become. The whole thing is typical of a behavioral sink. So is something like the Kitty Genovese case — a girl raped and murdered in the courtyard of an apartment complex and forty or fifty people look on from their apartments and nobody even calls the police. That kind of apathy and anomie is typical of the general psychological deterioration of The Sink."

He looked at the high-rise housing projects and found them mainly testimony to how little planners know about humans' basic animal requirements for space.

"Even on the simplest terms," he said, "it is pointless to build one of these blocks much over five stories high. Suppose a family lives on the fifteenth floor. The mother will be completely cut off from her children if they are playing down below, because the elevators are constantly broken in these projects, and it often takes half an hour, literally half an hour, to get the elevator if it is running. That's very common. A mother in that situation is just as much a victim of overcrowding as if she were back in the tenement block. Some Negro leaders have a bitter joke about how the white man is solving the slum problem by stacking Negroes up vertically, and there is a lot to that."

For one thing, says Dr. Hall, planners have no idea of the different space requirements of people from different cultures, such as Negroes and Puerto Ricans. They are all treated as if they were minute, compact middle-class whites. As with the Sika deer, who are overcrowded at one per acre, overcrowding is a relative thing for the human animal, as well. Each species has its own feeling for space. The feeling may be "subjective," but it is quite real.

Dr. Hall's theories on space and territory are based on the same information, gathered by biologists, ethologists, and anthropologists, chiefly, as Robert Ardrey's. Ardrey has written two well-publicized books, *African Genesis* and *The Territorial Imperative*. *Life* magazine ran big excerpts from *The Territorial Imperative*, all about how the drive to acquire territory and property and add to it and achieve status is built into all animals, including man, over thousands of centuries of genetic history, etc., and is a more powerful drive than sex. *Life's* big display prompted Marshall McLuhan to crack, "They see this as a great historic justification for free enterprise and Republicanism. If the birds do it and the stickleback crabs do it, then it's right for man." To people like Hall and McLuhan, and Ardrey, for that matter, the right or wrong of it is irrelevant. The only thing they find inexcusable is the kind of thinking, by influential people, that isn't even aware of all this. Such as the thinking of most city planners.

"The planners always show you a bird's-eye view of what they are doing," he said. "You've seen those scale models. Everyone stands around the table and looks down and says that's great. It never occurs to anyone that they are taking a bird's-eye view. In the end, these projects do turn out fine, when viewed from an airplane."

As an anthropologist, Dr. Hall has to shake his head every time he hears planners talking about fully integrated housing projects for the year 1980 or 1990, as if by then all cultural groups will have the same feeling for space and will live placidly side by side, happy as the happy burghers who plan all the good clean bird's-eye views. According to his findings, the very fact that every cultural group does have its own peculiar, unspoken feeling for space is what is responsible for much of the uneasiness one group feels around the other.

It is like the North European and the Mediterranean in the subway line. The North European, without ever realizing it, tries to keep a bubble of space around himself, and the moment a stranger invades that sphere, he feels threatened. Mediterranean peoples tend to come from cultures where everyone is much more involved physically, publicly, with one another on a day-to-day basis and feels no uneasiness about mixing it up in public, but may have very different ideas about space inside the home. Even Negroes brought up in America have a different vocabulary of space and gesture from the North European Americans who, historically, have been their models, according to Dr. Hall. The failure of Negroes and whites to communicate well often boils down to things like this: some white will be interviewing a Negro for a job; the Negro's culture has taught him to show somebody you are interested by looking right at him and listening intently to what he has to say. But the species North European requires something more. He expects his listener to nod from time to time, as if to say, "Yes, keep going." If he doesn't get this nodding, he feels anxious, for fear the listener doesn't agree with him or has switched off. The Negro may learn that the white expects this sort of thing, but he isn't used to the precise kind of nodding that is customary, and so he may start overresponding, nodding like mad, and at this point the North European is liable to think he has some kind of stupid Uncle Tom on his hands, and the guy still doesn't get the job.

The whole handling of space in New York is so chaotic, says Dr. Hall, that even middle-class housing now seems to be based on the bird's-eye models for slum project. He took a look at the big Park West Village development, set up originally to provide housing in Manhattan for families in the middle-income range, and found its handling of space very much like a slum project with slightly larger balconies. He felt the time has come to start subsidizing the middle class in New York on its own terms — namely, the kind of truly "human" spaces that still remain in brownstones.

"I think New York City should seriously consider a program of encouraging the middle-class development of an area like Chelsea, which is already starting to come up. People are beginning to renovate houses there on their own, and I think if the city would subsidize that sort of thing with tax reliefs and so forth, you would be amazed at what would result. What New York needs is a string of minor successes in the housing field, just to show everyone that it can be done, and I think the middle class can still do that for you. The alternative is to keep on doing what you're doing now, trying to lift a very large lower class up by main force almost and finding it a very slow and discouraging process."

"But before deciding how to redesign space in New York," he said, "people must first simply realize how severe the problem already is. And the handwriting is already on the wall."

"A study published in 1962," he said, "surveyed a representative sample of people living in New York slums and found only 18 percent of them free from emotional symptoms. Thirty-eight percent were in need of psychiatric help, and 23 percent were seriously disturbed or incapacitated. Now, this study was published in 1962, which means the work probably went on from 1955 to 1960. There is no telling how bad it is now. In a behavioral sink, crises can develop rapidly."

Dr. Hall would like to see a large-scale study similar to that undertaken by two sociopsychologists, Chombart de Lauwe and his wife, in a French working-class town. They found a direct relationship between crowding and general breakdown. In families where people were crowded into the apartment so that there was less than 86 to 108 square feet per person, social and physical disorders doubled. That would mean that for four people the smallest floor space they could tolerate would be an apartment, say, 12 by 30 feet.

What would one find in Harlem? "It is fairly obvious," Dr. Hall wrote in *The Hidden Dimension*, "that the American Negroes and people of Spanish culture who are flocking to our cities are being very seriously stressed. Not only are they in a setting that does not fit them, but they have passed the limits of their own tolerance of stress. The United States is faced with the fact that two of its creative and sensitive peoples are in the process of being destroyed and like Samson could bring down the structure that houses us all."

Dr. Hall goes out to the airport, to go back to Chicago, and I am coming back in a cab, along the East River Drive. It is four in the afternoon, but already the damned drive is clogging up. There is a 1959 Oldsmobile just to the right of me. There are about eight people in there, a lot of popeyed silhouettes against a leopard-skin dashboard, leopard-skin seats — and the driver is classic. He has a mustache, sideburns down to his jaw socket, and a tattoo on his forearm with a Rossetti painting of Jane Burden Morris with her hair long. All right; it is even touching, like a postcard photo of the main drag in San Pedro, California. But suddenly Sideburns guns it and cuts in front of my cab so that my driver has to hit the brakes, and then hardly 100 feet ahead Sideburns hits a wall of traffic himself and has to hit his brakes, and then it happens. A stuffed white Angora animal, a dog, no, it's a Pekingese cat, is mounted in his rear window — as soon as he hits the brakes its *eyes* light up, Nighttown pink. To keep from ramming him, my driver has to hit the brakes again, too, and so here I am, out in an insane, jammed-up expressway at four in the afternoon, shuddering to a stop while a stuffed Pekingese grows bigger and bigger and brighter in the eyeballs directly in front of me. Jolt! Nighttown pink! Hey — that's me the adrenalin is hitting, *I* am this white human sitting in a projectile heading amid a mass of clotted humans toward a white Angora stuffed goddam leopard-dash Pekingese freaking cat — kill that damned Angora — Jolt! — got me — another micrometer on the old adrenals —

Marking Chart

PARAGRAPHS

SENTENCES

PUNCTUATION

STYLE

USAGE